Here in the rapprochement subphase, we feel is the mainspring of man's eternal struggle against both fusion and isolation.

One could regard the entire life cycle as constituting a more or less successful process of distancing from and introjection of the lost symbiotic mother, an eternal longing for the actual or fantasied "ideal state of self," with the latter standing for a symbiotic fusion with the "all good" symbiotic mother, who was at one time part of the self in a blissful state of well-being.

—Margaret S. Mahler, "On the First Three Subphases of the Separation-Individuation Process"

RAPPROCHEMENT

The Critical Subphase of Separation-Individuation

edited by
RUTH F. LAX
SHELDON BACH   J. ALEXIS BURLAND

NEW YORK   •   JASON ARONSON   •   LONDON

ISBN: 0-87668-409-6

Library of Congress Catalog Number: 80-66351

Manufactured in the United States of America

Contents

Preface

The papers in this volume are a testimonial to the generativity of Margaret S. Mahler's ideas and work. Few analysts of her time have as deeply marked the thinking of a generation; such concepts as autism, symbiosis, differentiation, practicing, and rapprochement have become everyday tools in work with both children and adults. Margaret Mahler's observations, concepts, and hypotheses have fired the imagination and creativity of a generation of workers and for this we are grateful. The rapprochement conflict she has so exquisitely described is indeed the nexus of her theory, as it is of the earlier years of life. We hope that the papers collected in this book will help in the understanding of both.

The inspiration for this volume arose from scientific meetings of the New York Freudian Society, the Philadelphia Psychoanalytic Institute and Society, and the Medical College of Pennsylvania in celebration of Margaret Mahler's eightieth birthday.

The enthusiastic reception accorded these papers indicated that their collection into an available volume would be welcomed by the professional community. It soon became clear that most contributions focused on issues pertaining to the rapprochement subphase, because it is of crucial developmental and theoretical significance. The subsequent selection of papers was made with this theme in mind.

We wish to thank Dr. Margaret S. Mahler for her support and encouragement in this project, and we also extend special thanks to Dr. Selma Kramer for her many helpful and constructive suggestions.

Part I

The Original Formulation

Rapprochement Subphase of the Separation-Individuation Process

Margaret S. Mahler, M.D.

From our studies of infantile psychosis, as well as from observations in well-baby clinics, we have already learned that the human infant's physiological birth by no means coincides with his psychological birth. The former is a dramatic, readily observable, and well-defined event; the latter is a slowly unfolding intrapsychic process.

For the more or less normal adult, the experience of being both fully "in" and at the same time basically separate from the world "out there" is one of the givens of life that is taken for granted. Consciousness of self and absorption without awareness of self are the two poles between which we move with varying degrees of ease and with varying alternation or simultaneity. This, too, is the result of a slowly unfolding process. In particular, this development takes place in relation to (a) one's own body; and (b) the principal representative of the world as the infant experiences it (the primary love object). As is the case with any intrapsychic process, this one continues to reverberate throughout the life cycle. It is never finished; it can always be reactivated; new phases of the life cycle witness later derivatives of the earliest process still at work (cf. Erikson 1959). However, as we

Reprinted from *Psychoanalytic Quarterly*, 41 (1972): 487-506.

see it, the principal psychological achievements in this process take place in the period from about the fourth or fifth to the thirtieth or thirty-sixth month of age, a period that we refer to, in accordance with Annemarie Weil's helpful suggestion,[1] as the separation-individuation phase.

During the course of a rather unsystematic, naturalistic pilot study, we could not help taking note of certain clusters of variables, at certain crossroads of the individuation process, in so far as they repeated themselves at certain points of the maturational timetable. This strongly suggested to us that it would be to our advantage to subdivide the data that we were collecting on the intrapsychic separation and individuation process in accordance with the behavioral and other surface referents of that process that we had found to be repeatedly observable (Mahler 1963, 1964). Our subdivision was into four subphases: *differentiation, practicing, rapprochement*, and a fourth subphase, occurring during the third year, which, the longer we studied it, the more cautiously did we have to designate it as *the child on the way to object constancy.* And according to my definition, it should be regarded as the stage in which a unified representation of the object becomes intrapsychically available, as the love object had been available to the child in the outside world during his complete and later partial need-satisfying object relationship stage.

When inner pleasure prevails as the result of the child's being safely anchored within the symbiotic orbit (which is mainly proprioceptive and contact perceptual) and when pleasure in the maturationally widening outer sensory perception (as, for example, vision) stimulates outward-directed attention cathexis, these two forms of attention cathexis can oscillate freely (Spiegel 1959, Rose 1964). The result is an optimal symbiotic state out of which expansion beyond the symbiotic orbit and smooth differentiation from the mother's body can take place. This process, to which I gave the name "hatching out," may be looked upon as a gradual ontogenetic evolution of the sensorium—the perceptual conscious system—a "tuning in" process that leads to the infant's having a more permanently alert sensorium when he is awake (cf. Wolff 1959).

It is during the first subphase of separation-individuation that all normal infants achieve, through maturation of apparatuses, their first

1. Personal communication (1954).

tentative steps of breaking away, in a bodily sense, from their hitherto completely passive lap-babyhood—the stage of dual unity with the mother. They push themselves with arms, trunk, and legs against the holding mother, as if to have a better look at her, as well as the surroundings. One is able to see their individually different inclinations and patterns, as well as the general characteristics of the stage of differentiation itself. All five- to six-month-old infants like to venture and stay just a bit of a distance away from the enveloping arms of the mother; as soon as their motor function permits, they like to slide down from mother's lap, but they tend to remain as near as possible to her and to play at her feet.

Once the infant has become sufficiently individuated to recognize the mother, visually and tactilely, as not just part of the symbiotic dyad but as his partner in it, the fact that he is ready to take this step is indicated by his preferential, specific smiling response to and for mother. At about the same time, or perhaps within an interval of a few weeks, he then turns, with greater or less wonderment and apprehension (commonly called "stranger reaction"), to a prolonged visual and tactile exploration and study of the faces of others, from afar or at close range. He appears to be comparing and checking the features—appearance, feel, contour, and texture—of the stranger's face with his mother's face, as well as with whatever inner image he may have of her. He also seems to check back, apparently to compare all other interesting new experiences with the mother's gestalt, her face, in particular.

It should be emphasized that we view separation and individuation as intertwined developmental processes, rather than as a single process. And they may proceed divergently, as the result of a developmental lag of one or the other. We have observed that children who achieve premature locomotor development, and are therefore able and prompted to separate physically from their mothers, may become prematurely aware of their own separateness much before their individuation (reality testing, cognition, etc.) has given them the means with which to cope with this awareness. On the other hand, we have found that in infants with overprotective and infantilizing mothers, individuation may develop well ahead, and may result in a lag of boundary formation and a lag in readiness to function as a separate individual without undue anxiety.

The period of differentiation is followed or, we might better say, is overlapped by a practicing period. This takes place usually from about seven to ten months, and continues to fifteen or sixteen months of age. In the course of processing our data, we found it useful to think of the practicing period in two parts: (a) the early practicing subphase, which overlaps with differentiation and is ushered in by the infant's earliest ability to physically move away from mother through crawling, climbing, and righting himself, yet still holding on; and (b) the practicing period proper, phenomenologically characterized by free upright locomotion.

During the early practicing subphase, throughout which crawling, paddling, pivoting, climbing, and righting himself are practiced by the infant, usually with much glee, these functions widen the child's world. Not only can he take a more active role in determining closeness and distance to mother, but the perceptual modalities that had up till then been used to explore the relatively familiar environment are suddenly exposed to a wider world; the sensorimotor intelligence, in Piaget's sense, takes a big step forward.

The optimal psychological distance in this early practicing subphase would seem to be one that allows the infant, whose movements are mostly quadrupedal, freedom and opportunity for exploration at some physical distance from mother. It should be noted, however, that during the entire practicing subphase mother continues to be needed as a stable point, a "home base" to fulfill the need for refueling through physical contact. We have seen seven- to ten-month-old infants crawling or rapidly paddling to the mother, righting themselves on her leg, touching her in other ways, or just leaning against her. This phenomenon was termed by Furer[2] "emotional refueling." It is easy to observe how the wilting and fatigued infant "perks up" in the shortest time, following such contact, after which he quickly goes on with his explorations, once again absorbed in pleasure in his own functioning.

THE PRACTICING SUBPHASE PROPER

With the spurt in autonomous functions, such as cognition, but especially upright locomotion, the "love affair with the world" (Greenacre 1957) begins. The toddler takes the greatest step in human individuation. He walks freely with upright posture. Thus,

2. Personal communication (1959/1960).

the plane of his vision changes; from an entirely new vantage point he finds unexpected and changing perspectives, pleasures, and frustrations. At this new visual level there is more to see, more to hear, more to touch, and all this is experienced in the upright bipedal position. How this world is experienced seems to be subtly related to the mother, who is the center of the child's universe from which he gradually moves out into ever-widening perimeters.

During this precious six-to-eight-month period, for the junior toddler (ten-twelve to sixteen-eighteen months) the world is his oyster. Libidinal cathexis shifts substantially into the service of the rapidly growing autonomous ego and its functions, and the child seems to be intoxicated with his own faculties and with the greatness of his world. It is after the child has taken his first upright independent steps (which, by the way, more often than not he takes in a direction away from mother, or even during her absence) that one is able to mark the onset of the *practicing period par excellence* and of reality testing. Now, there begins a steadily increasing libidinal investment in practicing motor skills and in exploring the expanding environment, both human and inanimate. The chief characteristic of this practicing period is the child's great narcissistic investment in his own functions, his own body, as well as in the objects and objectives of his expanding "reality." Along with this, we see a relatively great imperviousness to knocks and falls and to other frustrations, such as a toy being grabbed away by another child. Substitute adults in the familiar setup of our nursery are easily accepted (in contrast to what occurs during the next subphase of separation-individuation).

As the child, through the maturation of his locomotor apparatus, begins to venture farther away from the mother's feet, he is often so absorbed in his own activities that for long periods of time he appears to be oblivious to the mother's presence. However, he returns periodically to the mother, seeming to need her physical proximity from time to time.

The smoothly separating and individuating toddler finds solace for the minimal threats of object loss that are probably entailed in each new stage of progressive development in his rapidly developing ego functions. The child concentrates on practicing the mastery of his own skills and autonomous capacities. He is exhilarated by his own capacities, continually delighted with the discoveries he is making in his expanding world, quasi-enamored with the world and with his own omnipotence. We might consider the possibility that the elation of this subphase has to do not only with the exercise of the ego apparatuses, but also with the infant's delighted escape from re-engulfment by the still-existing symbiotic pull from the mother.

Just as the infant's peek-a-boo games seem to turn at this juncture from passive to active, to the active losing and regaining of the need-gratifying love object, so too does the toddler's constant running off (until he is swooped up by his mother) turn from passive to active the fear of being reengulfed by, or fused with, mother. It turns into an active distancing and reuniting game with her. This behavior reassures the toddler that mother will want to catch him and take him up in her arms. We need not assume that this behavior is intended to serve such functions when it first emerges, but quite clearly it produces these effects and can then be intentionally repeated.

Most children, during the practicing subphase proper, appear to have major periods of exhilaration, or at least of relative elation. They are impervious to knocks and falls. They are low-keyed only when they become aware that mother is absent from the room, at which times their gestural and performance motility slows down, interest in their surroundings diminishes, and they appear to be preoccupied with inwardly concentrated attention and with what Rubinfine (1961) calls "imaging." During this period, the toddler's sensorimotor intelligence imperceptibly develops into representational intelligence and into concomitant emotional growth that characterizes the third subphase of the separation-individuation process—the period of rapprochement.

THE PERIOD OF RAPPROCHEMENT

The rapprochement subphase (from about fifteen to twenty-two months, and very often far beyond the second birthday) begins hypothetically with the mastery of upright locomotion and the consequent diminishing absorption in locomotion and other autonomous functioning.

By the middle of the second year of life, the infant has become a toddler. He now becomes more and more aware of and makes greater and greater use of his physical separateness. Side by side with the growth of his cognitive faculties and the increasing differentiation of his emotional life, there is also, however, a noticeable waning of his previous imperviousness to frustration, as well as of his relative obliviousness to the mother's presence. Increased separation anxiety can be observed—a fear of object loss that can be inferred from many behaviors; for example, from the fact that when the child hurts himself, he visibly discovers to his perplexity that his mother is not automatically at hand. The relative lack of concern about the mother's presence that was characteristic of the practicing subphase is now replaced by *active approach behavior,* and by a seeming constant concern with the mother's whereabouts. As the toddler's awareness of separateness grows, stimulated by his maturationally acquired ability physically to move away from his mother and by his cognitive growth, he now seems to have an increased need and wish for his mother to share with him his every new acquisition of skill and experience. These are the reasons for which I called this subphase of separation-individuation, the period of rapprochement.

Now after mastery of free walking and beginning internalization, the toddler begins to experience, more or less gradually and more or less keenly, the obstacles that lie in the way of what was, at the height of his "practicing" an omnipotent exhilaration, a quite evidently anticipated "conquest of the world." Side by side with the acquisition of primitive skills and perceptual cognitive faculties, there has been an increasingly clear differentiation, a separation, between the intrapsychic representation of the object and the self-representation. At the very height of mastery, toward the end of the practicing period, however, it has already begun to dawn on the junior toddler that the world is *not* his oyster; that he must cope with it more or less "on his own," very often as a relatively helpless, small, and separate individual, unable to command relief or assistance merely by feeling the need for them or giving voice to that need.

The quality and measure of the *wooing* behavior of the toddler toward his mother during this subphase provide important clues to the assessment of the normality of the individuation process. We believe that it is during this rapprochement subphase that the foundation for subsequent "normal neurotic" or neurosis with borderline features is set.

Incompatibilities and misunderstandings between mother and child can be observed at this period even in the case of the normal mother and her normal toddler, these being in part specific to certain seeming contradictions of this subphase. Thus, in the subphase of renewed, active wooing, the toddler's demands for his mother's constant participation seem contradictory to the mother: while the toddler is now not as dependent and helpless as he was half a year before, and seems eager to become less and less so, he even more insistently expects the mother to share every aspect of his life. During this subphase, some mothers are not able to accept the child's demanding behavior; others cannot tolerate gradual separation— they cannot face the fact that the child is becoming increasingly independent of and separate from them, and is no longer a part of them.

In this third subphase, while individuation proceeds very rapidly and the child exercises it to the limit, he is also becoming more and more aware of his separateness and is beginning to employ all kinds of partly internalized, partly still outwardly directed and acted out coping mechanisms in order to resist separation from the mother. No matter how insistently the toddler tries to coerce the mother, however, she and he no longer function effectively as a dual unit; that is to say, he can no longer get her to participate with him in his still maintained delusion of parental omnipotence. Likewise, at the other pole of the erstwhile dual unity, the mother must recognize a separate individual, her child, in his own autonomous right. Verbal communication has now become more and more necessary; gestural coercion on the part of the toddler, or mutual preverbal empathy between mother and child, will no longer suffice to attain the child's goal of satisfaction, of well-being (Joffe and Sandler 1965). Similarly, the mother can no longer make the child subservient to her own predilections and wishes.

The junior toddler gradually realizes that his love objects (his parents) are separate individuals with their own individual interests. He must gradually and painfully give up his delusion of his own grandeur, often through dramatic fights with mother—less so, it seemed to us, with father. This is a crossroad that we have termed the "rapprochement crisis."

Depending upon her own adjustment, the mother may react either by continued emotional availability and playful participation in the toddler's world or by a gamut of less desirable attitudes. From the data we have accumulated so far, we would state strongly that the mother's continued emotional availability is essential if the child's autonomous ego is to attain optimal functional capacity. If the mother is "quietly available" with a ready supply of object libido, if she shares the toddling adventurer's exploits, playfully reciprocates and thus helps his attempts at imitation, at externalization and internalization, then the relationship between mother and toddler is able to progress to the point where verbal communication takes over, even though vivid gestural behavior, that is, affectomotility, still predominates. By the end of the second or the beginning of the third year, the predictable emotional participation of the mother seems to facilitate the rich unfolding that is taking place in the toddler's thought processes, reality testing, and coping behavior.

The toddler's so-called "shadowing" of the mother at fifteen to twenty months of age (an often encountered phenomenon that is characteristic of this subphase) seems obligatory, except in the cases of those mothers who, by protracted doting and intrusiveness which spring from their own symbiotic-parasitic needs, become themselves the shadowers of the child. In normal cases, a slight shadowing by the toddler after the hatching process gives way to some degree of object constancy in the course of the third year. However, the less emotionally available the mother has become at the time of rapprochement, the more insistently and even desperately does the toddler attempt to woo her. In some cases, this process drains so much of the child's available developmental energy that, as a result, not enough may be left for the evolution of the many ascending functions of his ego. We shall illustrate the characteristics and certain typical conflicts of the rapprochement subphase with a few vignettes.

During the period of rapprochement Barney behaved with particular poignancy. He had gone through a typical, although precocious, "love affair with the world" in which he would often fall and hurt himself and always react with great imperviousness. Gradually he became perplexed to find that his mother was not on hand to rescue him, and he then began to cry when he fell. As he became aware of his separateness from his mother, his previous calm acceptance of knocks and falls began to give way to increased separation anxiety.

Early maturation of Barney's locomotor function had confronted him with the fact of physical separateness from his mother, before he was fully ready for it at nine to ten months of age. For this reason, we believe, he displayed to an exaggerated degree during his period of rapprochement the opposite of "shadowing." He would challenge mother by darting away from her, confidently and correctly expecting her to run after him and sweep him into her arms; at least momentarily he had undone the physical separateness from her. The mother's own increasingly frantic response to the dangerous darting made Barney, in turn, intensify and prolong this behavior so that his mother for a while despaired of being able to cope with Barney's "recklessness." We see this behavior as the result of the precocious maturation of the child's locomotor functions coupled with the relative lag in maturation of his emotional and intellectual functions. Hence, he could not properly evaluate, or gauge, the potential dangers of his locomotor feats.

The imbalance between the developmental line of separation and that of individuation, causing a jumbled intermeshing of factors of the second, the practicing, and the third, the rapprochement subphases, appeared to have set an overdetermined pattern of accident proneness in this child (Frankl 1963). Barney's reckless behavior had introjective qualities as well. It was, as every symptomatic behavior is, overdetermined. It no doubt also derived from identification with, or better stated, from introjection of his father's sports-loving nature. (The children were permitted to watch and admire and, at times, to participate in their father's highly risky athletic feats.)

Barney's mother, whom we observed as the ideal mother during Barney's early practicing subphase, now at his chronological age of the rapprochement subphase would alternately restrict Barney or, from sheer exhaustion, give up altogether her usual alertness to his needs and her previous high level of attunement to his cues. She would either rush to him in any situation, whether or not his need was real, or she would find herself keeping away from him at a time when she was really needed; in other words, her immediate availability became unpredictable.

The disturbance of the relationship between Barney and his mother during this period was not total, however, nor did it, we believe, inflict permanent damage on Barney's personality development. Neither hostility, splitting, nor increased and more permanent ambivalence resulted. Barney continued to bring everything within reach to his mother to share, filling her lap. He would have periods in which he sat quietly and did jigsaw puzzles or looked at picture books with his mother, while remaining full of confidence and basic trust toward the world beyond the mother.

This mother-child relationship became mutually satisfactory again with the advent of the fourth subphase, as a result of which Barney in the third year became a patient, well-functioning, and, within nor-

mal limits, more sedentary child. I believe that Barney's very satisfactory symbiotic, differentiation, and early practicing subphases, as
well as the fact that his father (with whom he roughhoused and
whom he hero-worshipped) became an important part of his world
during his second year of life, were all favorable factors in his
development.

A different manifestation of the crisis of the third subphase was
observable in Anna. Her mother's marked emotional unavailability
made Anna's practicing and exploratory period brief and subdued.
Never certain of her mother's availability, and therefore always
preoccupied with it, Anna found it difficult to invest libido in her
surroundings and in her own functioning. After a brief spurt of
practicing, she would return to her mother and try to engage her with
greater intensity by all possible means. From such relatively direct
expressions of the need for her mother as bringing her a book to read
to her, or hitting at the mother's ever-present book in which she was
engrossed, Anna turned to more desperate measures, such as falling
or spilling cookies on the floor and stamping on them, always with an
eye to gaining her mother's attention, if not involvement.

Anna's mother was observed to be greatly absorbed in her own
interests which were anything but child-centered. She emphasized
with seeming satisfaction and with some mock self-depreciation that
both her older children seemed to have preferred their father, who
had apparently shared the mother's task in diapering and bottle-
feeding the babies.

We observed in Anna, as early as the ninth and tenth month,
increased clamoring for closeness to mother, refusal to accept any
substitutes in the mother's presence let alone in her absence, and
greatly reduced pleasure in and diminution of activity. She had far
too little investment of libido in practicing the autonomous partial
functions of her individuating ego; approaching, even beseeching,
behavior toward mother far outweighed any involvement in activity
away from mother. Hence there was a complete overlapping and
intermingling of characteristics of both the practicing and rapprochement subphases.

Whereas all the landmarks of individuation—the development of
partial motor skills, of communication, of imitation and identification, and of defenses—appeared at appropriate times, there was
minimal progress toward object constancy (in Hartmann's sense).

Concomitant with Anna's inability to let mother out of sight, her activities and movements were low-keyed: they lacked the vivacity and luster that was characteristic of the behavior of her practicing contemporaries. Her happier moods and greater vivacity, which coincided with the achievement of free walking, were fleeting. On the other hand, her language development was even precocious.

Anna's chronic frustration in her attempt to win her mother's love had noticeably impaired the amalgamation of libido and aggression. Her ambivalence visibly affected her mood, which was characterized by ready smiles when her mother or a father substitute approached her, but which was quite readily switched to the opposite—moroseness, unhappiness, and even despair. This reminded us of the mood swings and fluctuations of self-esteem that we observe so conspicuously in borderline phenomena in the psychoanalytic situation.

In our study we had a fairly good setup, we feel, for gauging the junior and later the senior toddler's capacity to function in the mother's presence, and to compare it with his functioning during the brief periods of her physical absence. The latter situation varies from the mother's just being in the adjacent nursery, or in the nearby interviewing room, to being out of the building. The toddler stays within a familiar setting, with familiar adults and contemporaries.

It may be of interest for me to relate a few details of Anna's personality development in the fateful "second eighteen-month period of her life." It had already been observed by us that Anna's play had a quality of early reaction-formation. The mother reported that Anna had shown disgust when she gave her a portion of her older brother's clay to play with, and this had been at as early as eighteen or nineteen months. Anna's toilet training started at about twenty months, seemingly without pressure. Anna was already saying the word "do-do" at that age, and at first her mother was quite well attuned to cues from her concerning her toilet needs. She praised Anna whenever the latter produced either urine or feces. From her twentieth month on, Anna was repeatedly heard saying, "bye-bye, wee wee," as she pulled the chain to flush the toilet. Soon, however, many observers noted that Anna was beginning to request bathroom trips whenever she wanted her mother's attention, or whenever she wanted to prevent mother from leaving the room for an interview— in any event, more frequently than she could actually have had a bowel or urinary urge.

Anna was bowel trained by twenty-two months, and at that age she went for days without wetting. At the beginning of toilet training (particularly bowel training), we saw that Anna was willing and able to oblige her mother so that both mother and daughter found in the toileting an emotionally positively charged meeting ground. But within two months, toileting had been drawn into the conflictual sphere of this mother-child interaction. At around twenty-three months of age, Anna used wetting all across the room as a weapon. Her mother was then pregnant and, as time went on, her pregnancy caused her to become narcissistically self-absorbed. She had fewer and fewer positive reactions to Anna's demands to accompany her to the upstairs bathroom at home. In fact, she told us that she asked her then four-year-old son to substitute for her in taking Anna to the toilet. The boy, we later learned, did not miss the opportunity to provocatively and aggressively display his manly prowess, his penis, to his little sister. Anna's penis envy thus gained momentum, as did her defiance of mother.

A battle around toilet training ensued between Anna and her mother. At around two years of age (twenty-four to twenty-seven months, to be exact) Anna started to use her sphincter control to defy her mother. From twenty-two months on, severe constipation developed in the wake of Anna's deliberate withholding of her feces.

We did not see Anna for about three months (from her twenty-fifth to her twenty-eighth month) during which time a sister was born.

Anna returned at twenty-nine months of age. Her mother carried the baby sister, Susie, with Anna following close behind. The mother looked harassed and tired as she entered the room, and, with a tight smile, exclaimed, "I feel filthy dirty, and so mad, mad, mad!" She complained that Anna "is driving me crazy." Anna had indeed been very difficult, whining, and demanding, but, in addition, for the past two or three days had been withholding her feces and had not had a bowel movement. The mother mimicked Anna as she held her thighs tightly together and stamped her feet. She also said that Anna was in pain most of the time and actually very uncomfortable. The pediatrician, she reported, had assured her that this was a normal occurrence after the birth of a new baby and that she should take it calmly and pay no attention to Anna's toileting at this time. Making a hopeless gesture, she said, "But I simply can't do it; I just get so mad."

Anna was observed in the toddler's room playing with water. This, however, was not the kind of play that children her age usually enjoy, but it appeared to us to be of a compulsive nature. She began to scrub a bowl to which flour had stuck and was very determined to scrub it clean, becoming annoyed when she could not do so. She looked up at the observer and said, "Bowl not clean." All this while Anna seemed most uncomfortable. She obviously needed to defecate and was under continual bowel pressure. Beads of perspiration appeared on her forehead and the color would come and go from her face. Twice she ran to the toilet. She sat on the toilet and urinated; then she got up and became preoccupied with flushing the toilet. She went back to the toddler room and listlessly played with dough, but again, and all during her play, Anna was in discomfort and kept jiggling and jumping, with the color repeatedly draining from her face. Finally, she jumped up and ran to the toilet, sat down on it, and said to the observer, "Get me a book." Sitting and straining, she looked up at the observer with a rather painful expression on her face, and said, "Don't let Mommy in, keep Mommy out, keep Mommy out." The observer encouraged her to talk about this some more, and she said, "Mommy would hurt me." She then looked at the book, at the pictures of the baby cats and baby horses, and as the observer was showing the pictures of the baby farm animals, Anna began to look as though she was particularly uncomfortable. She looked down at her panties, which had become stained, and said she wanted clean ones. Finally, in extreme discomfort, she seemed unable to hold back the feces any longer, and called out, "Get me my Mommy, get me my Mommy." Her mother came quickly, sat down beside her, and Anna requested that she read to her.

The former participant observer watched from the booth, and noted that the mother was reading the same book about farm animals that she had previously read to Anna. Pointing to the animals, the toddler was heard to say, "My Poppy has a piggy in his tummy." Her mother looked perplexed and asked Anna, "What?" Anna repeated the sentence. The mother seemed distraught as her daughter was now talking gibberish. She felt Anna's forehead to see whether she was feverish, but the child smiled, pointed to the book again, and said, "No, it's a baby horse." At this point, with a blissful expression on her face, Anna defecated. After her bowel movement, Anna was more relaxed; she played peek-a-boo with the door, asking the observer to stand behind it.

In this episode, the sequence of behaviors and verbalizations enabled us to draw conclusions, to reconstruct, as it were, the development of Anna's early infantile neurosis *in statu nascendi*. With her deficient emotional supplies from maternal support, the development of autonomy had not been enough to gradually replace the obligatory early infantile symbiotic omnipotence. In spite of her excellent endowment, Anna was unable to ward off the onslaught of separation anxiety and the collapse of self-esteem. Her anger at mother for not having given her a penis was unmistakable in her verbal material. She coveted those gifts that mother received from father, among which was a porcelain thimble which she was allowed to keep. Anna turned in her disappointment to father, and, when mother became pregnant, in a perplexed way she obviously equated gift with baby, with feces, and with penis. She showed great confusion about the contents of the body: her own pregnancy fantasies were quite evident, but she was unclear as to who had what in his or her belly. She seemed to expect a baby in the belly of her father, as well as in her mother's. The equation of feces = baby = phallus was explicitly expressed in her behavior and verbal utterances.

The mother-toddler relationship was such that Anna had to defend the good mother against her destructive rage. This she did by splitting the object world into good and bad. The good was always the absent object representations, never the present object. To clarify this, let me describe another sequence of events and verbalizations in Anna's third year. Whenever her mother left, she had temper tantrums and would cling to her beloved and familiar play teacher, but not without verbally abusing her while still keeping her arms around her neck. When they read a book together, Anna found fault with every picture and every sentence that the playroom teacher offered; she scolded the teacher, everything was the opposite of what the teacher said, and she was "bad, bad, bad."

I watched this behavior from the observation booth and ventured quietly into the playroom where I sat at the farthest corner from Anna and her loved-and-hated teacher. Anna immediately caught sight of me and angrily ordered me out. I softly interpreted to Anna that I understood: Anna really wanted nobody else but her Mommy to come back in through that door and that was why she was very angry. She was also very angry because not Mommy but the observer was reading to her. I said that she knew that Mommy would soon come back. With my quasi interpretation, some libidinal channels seemed to have been tapped; the child put her head on the observer's shoulder and began to cry softly. Soon, the mother came back. It was most instructive to see, however, that not a flicker of radiance or happiness was noticeable in Anna at that reunion. Her very first words were "What did you bring me?" and the whining and discontent started all over again. For quite a while Anna did not succeed in attaining a unified object representation or in reconciling the synthesized good and bad qualities of the love object. At the same time, her own self-representation and self-esteem suffered.

By contrast, what we saw in Barney's case was merely a transitional developmental deviation in the form of a rapprochement crisis. In Anna we observed a truly neurotic symptom-formation, developing on the basis of a rather unsatisfactory mother-child relationship yet activated and, to a great extent, produced by accumulated traumata.

Until way beyond the fourth subphase, Anna's relationship to her mother remained full of ambivalence. Her school performance was excellent, however. Constipation continued as a symptom for several years. Her social development was good. Our follow-up study will tell us more about the fate of her infantile neurosis.[3]

SUMMARY

In our observation of two toddlers, we saw why the rapprochement crisis occurs and why in some instances it becomes and may remain an unresolved intrapsychic conflict. It may set an unfavorable fixation point interfering with later oedipal development, or at best add to the difficulty of the resolution of the oedipus complex.

The developmental task at the very height of the separation-individuation struggle in the rapprochement subphase is a tremendous one. Oral, anal, and early genital pressures and conflicts meet and accumulate at this important landmark in personality development. There is a need to renounce symbiotic omnipotence, and there is also heightened awareness of the body image and pressure in the body, especially at the points of zonal libidinization.

Three great anxieties of childhood meet at this developmental

3. The follow-up study was conducted by John B. McDevitt, M.D. with Anni Bergman, Emmagene Kamaiko, and Laura Salchow, and the author of this paper serving as consultant; it was sponsored by the Board of the Masters Children's Center.

stage. (1) While the fear of object loss and abandonment is partly relieved, it is also greatly complicated by the internalization of parental demands that indicate beginning superego development. In consequence, we observe an intensified vulnerability on the part of the rapprochement toddler. (2) Fear in terms of loss of the love of the object results in an extrasensitive reaction to approval and disapproval by the parent. (3) There is greater awareness of bodily feelings and pressures, in Greenacre's sense. This is augmented by awareness of bowel and urinary sensations during the toilet training process, even in quite normal development. There is often displayed, in some instances quite dramatically, a reaction to the discovery of the anatomical sex difference with prematurely precipitated castration anxiety.

References

Erikson, E. H. (1959). *Identity and the Life Cycle. Selected Papers.* Psychological Issues, Monograph I. New York: International Universities Press.

Frankl, L. (1963). Self-preservation and the development of accident proneness in children and adolescents. *Psychoanalytic Study of the Child* 18:464-483.

Greenacre, P. (1957). The childhood of the artist: libidinal phase development and giftedness. *Psychoanalytic Study of the Child* 12:27-72.

Joffe, W. G., and Sandler, J. (1965). Notes on pain, depression, and individuation. *Psychoanalytic Study of the Child* 20:394-424.

Mahler, M. S. (1963). Thoughts about development and individuation. *Psychoanalytic Study of the Child* 18:307-324. Reprinted in *The Selected Papers of Margaret S. Mahler,* vol. 2, ch. 1. New York: Jason Aronson (1979).

——— (1965). On the significance of the normal separation-individuation phase. In *Drives, Affects, Behavior, Vol. II,* ed. by Max Schur, pp. 161-169. New York: International Universities Press. Reprinted in *Selected Papers,* op. cit., ch. 4 (1979).

Rose, G. J. (1964). Creative imagination in terms of ego 'core' and boundaries. *International Journal of Psycho-Analysis* 45:75-84.

Rubinfine, D. L. (1961). Perception, reality testing, and symbolism. *Psychoanalytic Study of the Child* 16:73-89.

Spiegel, L. A. (1959). The self, the sense of self, and perception. *Psychoanalytic Study of the Child* 14:81-109.

Wolff, P. H. (1959): Observations on newborn infants. *Psychosomatic Medicine* 21:110-118.

Part II

Rapprochement in Psychoanalytic Thought

2

Developmental Theory, Structural Organization and Psychoanalytic Technique

OTTO F. KERNBERG, M.D.

The study of the internal relationships between descriptive symptoms, personality characteristics, transference developments, predominant instinctual conflicts, and the nature of ego and superego organization of borderline patients led me to conceptualize a framework of structural intrapsychic organization of borderline patients that might be best characterized as an ego-psychological object relations approach. The comparison of patients with borderline personality organization, narcissistic personalities, and chronic schizophrenic patients treated with intensive, psychoanalytic psychotherapy, and of patients with symptomatic neuroses and neurotic character pathologies that represent the standard psychoanalytic case seemed to require a conceptualization of psychopathology as reflecting a fixation at—or regression to—a sequence of stages of development, which, in earlier work, I called stages 1 through 5 (Kernberg 1972, 1976a, chapter 2).

These stages correspond very closely to the stages of early development described by Margaret Mahler, namely, the autistic, symbiotic, separation-individuation, and "on the road to object constancy" developmental phases. Indeed, the sequences of psychic development Mahler postulated on the basis of her work with children presenting autistic and infantile symbiotic psychosis, and her developmental studies of normal and abnormal features of separation-individuation show a remarkable correspondence with the developmental hypotheses I arrived at on the basis of the psychoanalytic and psychotherapeutic exploration of adolescent and adult patients with borderline personality organization.

This correspondence strengthens significantly, it seems to me, our respective conclusions. Mahler's findings regarding the chronology of phase sequences within her developmental framework provide fundamental evidence regarding the timetable of points of fixation and regression that were much more difficult, if not impossible, to determine on the basis of psychoanalytic work with adult patients suffering from borderline personality organization. By the same token, my findings regarding the multiple interrelationships of descriptive, dynamic, and structural features of certain transference developments in borderline patients that correspond to the main themes of the rapprochement subphase of separation-individuation provide, I think, a psychoanalytic dimension from adulthood that reinforces Mahler's assumptions about intrapsychic correlates of developmental observations in early childhood. Particularly, the predominance of splitting operations in borderline patients as well as their transferences—which reveal lack of integration of self- and object representations of "good" and "bad" kinds but no fusion of self- with object representations—reflect, structurally, the developmental stage of separation-individuation that follows symbiosis and precedes object constancy. Both Mahler and I found Jacobson's (1964, 1971) theory of the development of internalized object relations, and their integration into ego and superego structures, a crucial theoretical tool.

More recently, the application of Mahler's theoretical formulations to the psychotherapeutic treatment of borderline children and adults and to psychoanalytic technique in general (Mahler and Kaplan 1977, Furer 1977, Kramer 1979) has added another dimension to treatment technique and should permit further study of similarities and differences of our approaches to these patients.

In what follows, I spell out the principal areas of agreement between Mahler's and my conceptualizations, and those aspects of both theory and treatment technique where I see disagreements or differences in approach.

THEORETICAL ISSUES

Regarding the earliest phases of development, Mahler (Mahler and Gosliner 1955, Mahler and Furer 1968, Mahler, Pine, and Bergman 1975), Jacobson (1964), and I (Kernberg 1972, 1976a, 1979a) all agree that intrapsychic life starts out as a primary psychophysiological self within which ego and id are not yet differentiated, and within which aggression and libido are undifferentiated as well. The first intrapsychic structure is a fused representation of self and object that develops gradually under the impact of the relationship between mother and infant (Jacobson 1964). The first few weeks of life, before such a primary self-object representation is consolidated, constitute the earliest, presymbiotic, or autistic, phase of development described by Mahler (1968). Pleasurable affects, the first manifestations of the differentiating libidinal drive to emerge, are invested in a fused self-object representation, the first intrapsychic libidinal investment. Insofar as that fused structure represents the origin of both self- and object representations, libidinal investment in the self and in objects are originally one process.

The symbiotic phase of development comes to an end with a gradual differentiation of the self-representation from the object representation, which contributes importantly to the differentiation between the self and the external world. Jacobson (1964) has suggested, and I agree, that two processes make their appearance at the beginning of differentiation. The first is a defensive refusion of libidinally invested self- and object representations; this is the earliest protection against painful experiences. When excessively or pathologically maintained, this process gives rise to what will later become psychotic identifications characteristic of symbiotic psychosis of childhood and of affective psychosis and schizophrenia in adulthood (Jacobson 1954a, b, c, 1957, 1964, 1971). The second process, the differentiation of painful experiences into aggressively invested self- and object representations, is an early effort to separate and deny the frustrating interactions between self and mother and their intrapsychic representations. A fused, undifferentiated self-object representation invested with aggressive drive derivatives becomes the counterpart of the libidinally invested one, so that, at a certain point, the intrapsychic world of object relations is reflected in "good" and "bad" self-representations and, similarly, "good" and "bad" object representations.

Mahler (Mahler and Gosliner 1955, Mahler 1968, Mahler, Pine and Bergman 1975) is in general agreement with these formulations, but conveys the impression that "bad" fused self-object representations remain at the periphery of the core self and are less crucial in organizing intrapsychic experience than I have suggested. Thus, while Mahler (1971), in agreement with me, suggests that the painful "bad" quality of experience may be the first basis of later splitting mechanisms, she does not stress, as I would, the continuity of the originally fused, "bad" self-object representation of the symbiotic phase with the later splitting of "good" and "bad" mother and "good" and "bad" self of the rapprochement subphase. The difference here seems to be largely one of emphasis.

Also, while the differentiation of "good" and "bad" affects—in the context of the "good" and "bad" undifferentiated self- and object representations—constitutes, in my view, the earliest manifestation of the organization of drives into libido and aggression, and, by the same token, the simultaneous investment of these earliest drive manifestations into the earliest internalized object relations, Mahler is much less explicit regarding the relation between the earliest "good" and "bad" experiences as primitive affect states, and whether they actually represent differentiation of aggression and libido. Mahler here agrees with Jacobson (1964) in maintaining the concept of primary narcissism, that is, the investment of the primary undifferentiated self with undifferentiated drive energy, in contrast to my assumption (and Jacobson's [1954c] earlier assumption) that, insofar as the earliest manifestations of libidinal investment are into a fused self-object representation, "primary" narcissism and "secondary" narcissism (that is, narcissism related to the vicissitudes of object investments) are equivalent. If, as I think, the earliest libidinal investment is in a self and object that are not yet differentiated, the concept of primary narcissism (and, by implication, of primary masochism) is no longer warranted.

The difference in emphasis that I mentioned has relevance for the psychoanalytic psychotherapy of psychotic states. In my opinion, the analysis of intensely aggressive object relations of psychotic patients, within which self and object are not differentiated, illustrates the enormous importance of the structures governed by fused, "bad" self- and object representations.

In addition, whether the earliest affect states are representations of the beginning stage of drive differentiation or constitute in themselves the first manifestations of differentiating drives has theoretical implications. I have reached the conclusion that drives constitute overall motivational systems that stem from the hierarchical organization of affect states into a libidinal and an aggressive constellation. The linkage between biological instincts and intrapsychic drives would be represented by inborn affect dispositions that are integrated as "good" and "bad" affect states into object relations, thus determining an overall hierarchical organization of drive systems, or libido and aggression in the broadest sense.

Jacobson, Mahler, and I are in agreement that the differentiation of self- from object representations permits the consolidation of ego boundaries, reflects the end of the symbiotic stage of development, but does not yet signify an integrated ego (or, rather, an integrated self) or an integrated conception of objects. To the contrary, between the symbiotic phase and the attainment of object constancy and the related consolidation of the tripartite psychic apparatus, an intermediary developmental structure must be assumed, wherein differentiation of self from objects, and lack of integration of the self and of the conceptions of objects are key features. This is one of Mahler's crucial contributions: the enrichment of her early conception of this developmental stage into a solid body of evidence, culminating in her description of separation-individuation and its subphases.

In addition to providing the developmental and clinical evidence that was linked up with Jacobson's theoretical formulations and clinical observations of narcissistic and borderline pathology of adolescence, Mahler also provided more general clinical evidence for the ego psychology approach to structural development, as opposed to the British schools'—particularly the Kleinian's—assumption of highly sophisticated, complex intrapsychic structuring in the first year of life (which implies a full differentiation of self from object, as well as the capacity for an integration of the conception of the self and of objects in the second part of the first year of life). Mahler's evidence here prompted me to reconsider my previous, tentative, assumptions about the timetable of earliest development (Kernberg 1972, 1976a, chapter 2), alluded to earlier.

Mahler's description of the subphases of separation-individuation (differentiation, practicing, and rapprochement) allows us to examine various clinical observations regarding borderline personality organization in a new light. I fully agree with Mahler that a large majority of patients with borderline personality organization present intrapsychic structural organization and conflicts related to those of the rapprochement subphase. A small group of borderline patients, however—severely schizoid personalities for the most part—present transference developments and regression that seem more related to the differentiation subphase. In this connection, placing the degree of self-object differentiation within a developmental continuum, I have described (Kernberg 1978) the following spectrum of preobject constancy psychopathology.

First, we have the fixation at, or regression to, psychotic identifications in Jacobson's (1954a,b) terms, or the symbiotic stage of development in Mahler's terms (Mahler 1968), in which the differentiation of self from nonself is abolished and self- and object representations re-fuse: here we find only idealized, ecstatic merged states, and terrifying, aggressive merged stages. The chief emphasis in such cases has to be on gradually helping the patient to differentiate his internal life from the therapist's psychological reality, on stressing the reality of the immediate therapeutic interaction, and on being alert to the dangers in the patient's life derived from the breakdown of ego boundaries outside the therapeutic situation. It seems to me that Searles' work with schizophrenic patients (1965) speaks to this point.

Second, there are patients in whom the regression and/or fixation is primarily to a stage of differentiation preceding the typical borderline pathology (reflected in the splitting of "good" and "bad" self- and object representations) but more advanced than that of psychotic refusion. Usually, these are patients with predominant schizoid characteristics. Here, the prevailing level of regression or fixation relates to the early differentiation subphase of separation-individuation, and these patients require, as part of the treatment approach, "holding" (Winnicott 1965)—being empathized with and yet permitted to maintain their autonomy vis-à-vis the therapist—at least as an important aspect of the treatment technique in certain stages of therapeutic regression. A temporary regression to this early developmental subphase may signify a potential for new ego growth, as Balint (1968) and Winnicott (1953, 1960) have suggested.

Third, the next level of regression and/or fixation is precisely the one typical of the large majority of patients with borderline personality organization. Here, the problem is no longer the need to protect the gradually emerging autonomous self of the differentiation subphase, but rather to focus on the integration of split-off aspects of self- and object representations, which reflect pathology linked largely—as Mahler (1971, 1972a, b) found—with the rapprochement subphase. In other words, in these patients the issue is not between autonomy or merger, or between true and false self, but between nonintegrated and integrated self, nonintegrated and integrated object relations. The treatment approach I have outlined for borderline patients is consistent with this conception.

I have suggested (1975, 1976a,b) that the principal therapeutic tasks with borderline patients are to transform primitive into advanced transferences (manifest by transformation of primitive, dissociated or split object relations into integrated or total object relations) and, related to this, to transform an ego organization characterized by primitive defenses, centered around splitting, into an integrated ego characterized by defenses centering around repression. This transformation will lead to the differentiation of ego, superego, and id as integrated structures.

In this process, which is done by means of interpretation, first, the dissociated or generally fragmented aspects of the patient's intrapsychic conflicts are gradually integrated into significant units of primitive internalized object relations; second, each unit (constituted of a particular self-representation, a particular object representation, and a major affect disposition linking these) then needs to be clarified as it becomes activated in the transference, including the alternation of reciprocal self- and object reenactments in the relationship with the therapist; and third, when these units can be interpreted and integrated with other related or contradictory units—particularly when libidinally invested and aggressively invested units can be integrated—the process of working through of the transference and the resolution of primitive constellations of defensive operations characteristic of borderline conditions has begun.

As mentioned before, the principal difference between Mahler's and my approach to the pathology of the rapprochement subphase resides in the major stress, in my work, on the continuity between splitting of "good" and "bad" internalized object relations of the symbiotic and the separation-individuation stage, in contrast to Mahler's statement, referring to the rapprochement crisis (Mahler, Pine, and Bergman 1975, p. 99): "Yet splitting the object world [has] also begun." Again, these are differences in emphasis. The description, in the same book, of splitting operations in a patient during the rapprochement subphase (pp. 82-85) beautifully illustrates the patient's need to defend the good mother against the patient's own destructive rage by splitting the object world into "good" and "bad."

Mahler stresses that in the individual solutions of the rapprochement crisis there is a development of patternings and personality characteristics with which the child enters into the consolidation of individuation, an extremely important formulation, which explains the prevalence of preoedipal character constellations in borderline patients and the possibility of directly tracing character structure back to the rapprochement subphase of separation-individuation. Coercion and splitting of the object world, two mechanisms that Mahler has described as particularly characteristic of most cases of adult borderline transference, are typically exaggerated in cases of failure to overcome the rapprochement crisis. In agreeing, I would point to the splitting in borderline patients, which I have stressed, and the relation of coercion to the mechanisms of omnipotence and projective identification (with their implications of efforts to omnipotently control the object onto whom a split-off impulse has been projected.)

Regarding the next stage of development, "on the road to object constancy," I would stress my full agreement with Mahler (1975) regarding the intimate relationship between preoedipal and oedipal conflicts, an area where Mahler is still misunderstood. I am referring to the confluence of prevalent conflicts deriving from separation-individuation factors with those deriving from the following, oedipal, period. This confluence normally evolves in the context of establishing object constancy and the definite integration of the psychic structures. Jacobson, Mahler, and I agree that this stage of development consists in a gradual and more realistic integration of "good" and "bad" self-representations, and the parallel integration of "good" and "bad" object representations. In this process, partial aspects of self- and object representations become integrated or, respectively, total self- and object representations. The completion of the stage of separation-individuation and the establishment of object constancy permit the development of differentiated oedipal relations.

Differentiated oedipal relations presuppose the capacity for a differentiated conception of the parental couple, including their sexual characteristics, and differentiated relations to them which take into consideration their sexual identity. Absence of these preconditions are typical for patients with borderline personality organization, whose preoedipal conflicts, particularly around preoedipal aggression, infiltrate all object relations. In addition to reinforcing and fixating primitive defensive operations centering around splitting, excessive aggression also contaminates the later object relations characteristics of the oedipus complex. This creates characteristic distortions in the oedipal constellation, reflected in features I have described elsewhere (1977, 1979b). Here, in agreement with Mahler (1975), I am stressing that consequences of severe preoedipal conflicts derived from the pathology of development that precedes object constancy include the pathological development of oedipal conflicts, but not an absence of them. Some authors (see Masterson 1972, 1976) apply a theoretical frame of reference derived from Mahler's work to the psychotherapeutic treatment of adolescent and adult borderline patients that, in my opinion, treats these patients as if they were fixated at the conflicts of separation-individuation to the exclusion of the developments and transformations that these conflicts undergo under the influence of oedipal developments.

I believe that the controversy regarding the predominance of oedipal versus preoedipal conflicts in borderline and narcissistic conditions really obscures the significant finding that in all cases, even the nonanalyzable borderline conditions or narcissistic personalities, one consistently finds evidence of crucial oedipal pathology. The issue is not the presence or absence of oedipal conflicts, but the degree to which preoedipal features have distorted the oedipal constellation and have left important imprints on character formation (Blum 1977; chapter 6, this volume). The application of Mahler's thinking to psychoanalysis and the psychotherapeutic treatment of children as carried out by herself and her close co-workers takes these transformations and condensations of preoedipal and oedipal issues fully into consideration.

TECHNICAL ISSUES

Mahler has not so far presented a systematic approach to the treatment of borderline conditions based on her developmental and psychopathological findings, and it is my impression that she is in general agreement with the approach that I have recommended for the treatment of adolescent and adult borderline patients, namely, a

modified psychoanalytic approach or psychoanalytic psychotherapy. Basing themselves on her views, Rinsley (1977), Masterson
(1972, 1976, 1978), and Furer (1977) have proposed psychotherapeutic approaches to the treatment of borderline patients that are
essentially in harmony with the psychoanalytic psychotherapy I have
suggested for these conditions (1975, 1976a,b, 1978).

Rinsley's conclusions are based on a combination of Mahler's,
Masterson's, and my views. He states (1977, p. 67):

> Psychoanalytic therapy of borderline personalities requires con-
> frontative and interpretive exposure of the split object-relations unit
> within the therapeutic transference, which, if successful, catalyzes the
> development of the therapeutic alliance with ensuing restructuring of
> the patient's endopsychic representations ("healthy object-relations
> unit"). The resultant depressive working through enables the patient to
> achieve developmental stage 4, typified by a sense of personal sepa-
> rateness and wholeness.

His succinct statement, however, does not make clear to what extent
he is also in full agreement with Masterson and, therefore, in potential disagreement with some aspects of my approach.

Masterson (1972, 1976, 1978) proposes a psychotherapeutic approach specifically geared to the resolution of the "abandonment
depression," and the correction and repair of the ego defects that
accompany the narcissistic oral fixation of these patients by encouraging growth through the stages of separation-individuation to autonomy. He recommends that psychotherapy with borderline
patients start out as supportive and suggests that intensive reconstructive, psychoanalytically oriented psychotherapy is usually an
expansion and outgrowth of supportive psychotherapy. He stresses
the importance of the analysis of primitive transferences, and has
expanded on the description of two mutually split-off part-object
relations units (the rewarding or libidinal part-object relations unit
and the withdrawing or aggressive part-object relations unit), thus
combining an object relations viewpoint of intrapsychic structure,
following my findings, with a developmental model based upon
Mahler's work.

In that Masterson stresses the importance of the analysis of primitive transferences and the need to interpretively resolve the split-off
internalized object relations of borderline patients, his approach is
quite close to mine. However, what Masterson describes as the early

supportive stage of the treatment seems to imply a combination of supportive and interpretive techniques that I have found questionable in the treatment of borderline patients. Supportive and interpretive techniques tend to cancel each other out, and, in contrast to the possibility of combining them in patients with less severe illness, I think that the cleavage between the two approaches should be sharp and definite in the treatment of patients with borderline conditions. I have dealt with the reasons for this conclusion elsewhere (Kernberg in press).

In addition, I disagree with what I consider the relative simplification of primitive transferences in Masterson's two-part object relations units. I think one sees a wider range—both more fragmented and more integrated—of self- and object representations in borderline patients, and that primitive transferences have a more complex nature than is implied in his clinical analyses. Also, Masterson's almost exclusive emphasis, from the beginning of treatment, on interpreting primitive transferences in light of the vicissitudes of the developmental stage of separation-individuation, conveys the impression that he neglects oedipal implications of the material, and particularly the typical condensation of preoedipal and oedipal conflicts that one finds in borderline conditions—and that one could also assume to be present from his published clinical material. In short, I think Masterson may not be doing full justice to the complexity and subtlety of Mahler's theoretical and clinical approach.

Regarding similarities and differences in the application of Mahler's and my conceptions to standard psychoanalytic technique, the only paper I am aware of, so far, that has systematically applied Mahler's approach to the standard psychoanalytic technique is Kramer's (1979). Richards (1978), in jointly examining Kramer's (1979) and my own (1979b) presentations in a panel discussion, discusses both theoretical and technical agreements and disagreements of our views in succinct terms, and, given my basic agreement with his analysis, I can do no better than quote the pertinent conclusions.

> I think what both Mahler and Kernberg are implying is that their theoretical conceptions represent a special point of view which is readily integrated within the overall psychoanalytic theoretical framework that includes the tripartite model; that it is an extension and an elaboration from the angle of dyadic relationships rather than a new clinical theory or a new metapsychological point of view. I think both

Drs. Kramer and Kernberg would disagree with the theoretical pluralists who talk about different psychoanalytic models, viewed either hierarchically or in parallel, which are suitable for different kinds of psychopathology and have consequence for and result in sharply distinctive psychoanalytic and psychotherapeutic techniques.

Given, then, their basic agreement about theory, it is not surprising that Drs. Kramer and Kernberg agree on technique. They hold similar views about the relationship between preoedipal and oedipal conflicts and about the importance of preverbal communication.

Finally, they agree that ego defect or ego deficiency does not preclude conflict or require us to abandon an analytic stance.

Richards correctly stresses these areas of major agreement. He also points to a possible area of disagreement between Kramer and myself, namely, the relationship in the analytic situation between transference, genetic history, and early development. I have pointed out (1979b) that, in cases of severe psychopathology or when severe regression occurs in the transference, the road from present transference developments to the genetic or intrapsychic history of organization of the material is more indirect than in better-functioning patients, and that, the earlier the points of fixation or regression of the psychopathology, the greater is the gap between actual childhood experiences, the intrapsychic elaboration of such experiences, the structuring of these intrapsychic elaborations, and the nature of transference developments. Under these conditions, the road from current transference development to the genetic or intrapsychic history or organization of the material is more indirect, and, paradoxically, early childhood experiences can be reconstructed only in advanced stages of the treatment. Hence, there is the danger of equating primitive transferences with "early" object relations in a mechanical, direct way, and the misleading temptation to "reconstruct" the earliest intrapsychic development on the basis of primitive transference manifestations. I have also pointed out that actual regression to subphases of separation-individuation or even to symbiosis occurs rarely in the analyses of well-selected patients, requires a long time to develop, and, above all, is reflected in significant regressive changes in the total therapeutic interaction.

Therefore, I would probably be much more cautious than Kramer in attempting to reconstruct psychopathology derived from separation-individuation phases, and in subphase reconstruction. Kramer conveys the impression that she thinks our knowledge about early phases of separation-individuation can be more directly applied, from the early stages of analysis on, in contrast to my emphasis on the gradual activation and clarification of these early phases in the context of transference regression. With this proviso, I would agree fully with Kramer that the nonverbal communication of the patient (including changes of affect and mood, bodily states, anal or genital sensations, flushing, headaches, transient pain, dizziness, desires to urinate or defecate, to suck, to smoke, to keep the eyes open or closed, to struggle against remaining on the couch or in the office or against leaving the analytic session) may reflect preoedipal material expressed in the interpersonal interaction rather than in the verbal communication to the analyst.

Kramer, quoting Mahler, points out that the residues of preverbal and preoedipal conflicts may emerge in the nonverbal communicative processes of patient and analyst, and that they can be diagnosed by the analyst's empathic understanding of the total interactional process at that point. My observations on regression in the communicative process in the analytic situation (1979b) underline the importance of differentiating true regression to stages of development that predate object constancy, from fantasies about such regressive states or experiences. True regression to such early stages is usually accompanied by formal regression in the transference, which permits the analyst to differentiate these two kinds of situations.

In conclusion, I consider my theoretical formulations, stemming from the application of an object relations framework to the structural analysis of patients with borderline personality organization and the implications of this framework for psychoanalytic and psychotherapeutic technique, to be basically in harmony with Mahler's object relations approach, her developmental formulations, and their potential applications to the diagnostic evaluation and technical approach to regressive transferences. Mahler's fundamental contributions to the understanding of infantile and early childhood development and their relationship to structure formation and psychopathology have probably helped more than any other psychoanalyst's work in closing the gap between the formulation of theories of normal and pathological early development derived from adult psychopathology and psychoanalytic exploration, and the actual, psychoanalytically derived observation and exploration of the child's early development of intrapsychic experience and structure formation.

References

Balint, M. (1968). *The Basic Fault: Therapeutic Aspects of Regression.* London: Tavistock.

Blum, H. (1977). The prototype of preoedipal reconstruction. *Journal of the American Psychoanalytic Association* 25:757-785

Furer, M. (1977). Personality organization during the recovery of a severely disturbed young child. In *Borderline Personality Disorders,* ed. P. Hartocollis, pp. 457-473. New York: International Universities Press.

Jacobson, E. (1954a). Contribution to the metapsychology of psychotic identification. *Journal of the American Psychoanalytic Association* 2:239-262.

——— (1954b). On psychotic identifications. *International Journal of Psycho-Analysis* 35:102-108.

——— (1954c). The self and the object world: vicissitudes of their infantile cathexes and their influence on ideational and affective development. *Psychoanalytic Study of the Child* 9:75-127.

——— (1954d). Transference problems in the psychoanalytic treatment of severely depressive patients. *Journal of the American Psychoanalytic Association* 2:595-606.

——— (1957). Denial and repression. *Journal of the American Psychoanalytic Association* 5:61-92.

——— (1964). *The Self and the Object World.* New York: International Universities Press.

——— (1971). *Depression.* New York: International Universities Press.

Kernberg, O. (1972). Early ego integration and object relations. *Annals of the New York Academy of Sciences* 193:233-247.

——— (1975). *Borderline Conditions and Pathological Narcissism.* New York: Jason Aronson.

——— (1976a). *Object Relations Theory and Clinical Psychoanalysis.* New York: Jason Aronson.

——— (1976b). Technical considerations in the treatment of borderline personality organization. *Journal of the American Psychoanalytic Association* 24:795-829.

——— (1977). The structural diagnosis of borderline personality organization. In *Borderline Personality Disorders,* ed. P. Hartocollis, pp. 87-121. New York: International Universities Press.

——— (1978). Contrasting approaches to the treatment of borderline conditions. In *New Perspectives in Psychotherapy of the Borderline Adult,* ed. J. Masterson, pp. 77-104. New York: Brunner/Mazel.

——— (1979a). Contributions of Edith Jacobson: an overview. *Journal of the American Psychoanalytic Association* 27:793-819.

——— (1979b). Some implications of object relations theory for psychoanalytic technique. *Journal of the American Psychoanalytic Association* 27(suppl.):207-239.

——— (In press). Developments in the theory of psychoanalytic psychotherapy. In *Curative Factors in Dynamic Psychotherapy,* ed. Samuel Slipp. New York: McGraw-Hill.

Kramer, S. (1979). The technical significance and application of Mahler's separation-individuation theory. *Journal of the American Psychoanalytic Association* 27(suppl.):241-262.

Mahler, M. (1968). *On Human Symbiosis and the Vicissitudes of Individuation.* In collaboration with M. Furer. New York: International Universities Press.

——— (1971). A study of the separation-individuation process and its possible application to borderline phenomena in the psychoanalytic situation. *Psychoanalytic Study of the Child* 26:403-424. Reprinted in *The Selected Papers of Margaret S. Mahler,* vol. 2, chap. 11. New York: Jason Aronson, 1979.

——— (1972a). On the first three subphases of the separation-individuation process. *International Journal of Psychoanalysis* 53:333-338. Reprinted in *Selected Papers,* op. cit., ch. 8.

——— (1972b). Rapprochement subphase of separation-individuation processes. *Psychoanalytic Quarterly* 41:487-506. Reprinted in *Selected Papers,* op. cit., ch. 9; and this volume, ch. 1.

——— (1975). On the current status of the infantile neurosis. *Journal of the American Psychoanalytic Association* 23:327-333. Reprinted in *Selected Papers,* op. cit., ch. 12.

Mahler, M., and Gosliner, B. J. (1955). On symbiotic child psychoses: genetic, dynamic and restitutive aspects. *Psychoanalytic Study of the Child* 10:195-212. Reprinted in *The Selected Papers of Margaret S. Mahler,* vol. 1, ch. 6. New York: Jason Aronson, 1979.

Mahler, M., and Kaplan, L. (1977). Developmental aspects in the assessment of narcissistic and so-called borderline personalities. In *Borderline Personality Disorders,* ed. P. Hartocollis, pp. 71-85. New York: International Universities Press. Reprinted in *Selected Papers,* vol. 2, op. cit., ch. 13.

Mahler, M., Pine, F., and Bergman, A. (1975). *The Psychological Birth of the Human Infant.* New York: Basic Books.

Masterson, J. (1972). *Treatment of the Borderline Adolescent: A Developmental Approach.* New York: Wiley-Interscience.

——— (1976). *Psychotherapy of the Borderline Adult: A Developmental Approach.* New York: Brunner/Mazel.

——— (1978). The borderline adult: transference acting-out and working-through. In *New Perspectives on Psychotherapy of the Borderline Adult,* pp. 123-147. New York: Brunner/Mazel.

Richards, A. (1978). Discussion at the panel on "The Technical Consequences of Object Relations Theory" at the Fall Meeting of the American Psychoanalytic Association, New York, December 17, 1978.

Rinsley, D. (1977). An object-relations view of borderline personality. In *Borderline Personality Disorders,* ed. P. Hartocollis, pp. 47-70. New York: International Universities Press.

Searles, H. F. (1965). *Collected Papers on Schizophrenia and Related Subjects.* New York: International Universities Press.

Winnicott, D. W. (1953). Transitional objects and transitional phenomena. In *Collected Papers: Through Paediatrics to Psychoanalysis,* pp. 229-242. New York: Basic Books, 1958.

——— (1960). Ego distortion in terms of true and false self. In *The Maturational Process and the Facilitating Environment,* pp. 140-152. New York: International Universities Press, 1965.

——— (1965). *The Maturational Process and the Facilitating Environment.* New York: International Universities Press.

3

Rapprochement and Oedipal Organization: Effects on Borderline Phenomena

Louise J. Kaplan, Ph.D.

Over the last two decades, as the details of Mahler's discoveries of the normal symbiotic and separation-individuation subphases gradually became available to psychoanalysts and other clinicians working with borderline and narcissistic patients, the conflicts and resolutions of the rapprochement subphase have been increasingly singled out as the central dynamics of these patients. All those personality disorders not presenting a configuration of defenses, object relations, and drive development of the oedipal phase have come to be attributed to defects or inadequacies of the rapprochement subphase.

It is understandable that clinicians would have looked to the rapprochement subphase as the royal road to understanding these disorders. Within the clinical situation the persistence of certain transferential and acting-out patterns are reminiscent of the rapprochement crisis. Frequently cited are patient's expressions of panic-anxiety, rage, disappointment, disillusionment. Denials of dependency and vulnerability, grandiosity, unqualified overvaluation of self and other oscillate with clinging dependency, a sense of profound humiliation, self-denigration and devaluation of others. Nevertheless, these obvious parallels between the child's experience

of the normal rapprochement crisis and borderline personality organization have led to considerable oversimplification and premature closure regarding the precise manner in which the symbiotic and
separation-individuation subphases exert their influence on later
personality organization. In some quarters the rapprochement crisis
has eclipsed the oedipus complex as the hallmark of the psychoanalytic theory of development and the central issue for clinical
practice.

Mahler (1971), in her considerations of the applications of
separation-individuation theory to borderline phenomena, warned
against mistaking rapprochement *content* for the complex configurations within the transference. Reconstructions from unintegrated
residua are not simple or equivalent repetitions of the original
sequences of the separation-individuation process. Nor should the
clinician deduce a direct relationship between the manifestations of
borderline phenomena and the observation of normal developmental sequences in childhood (p. 415). Between the normal separation-
individuation during the first three years of life and subsequent
borderline and narcissistic disturbances of childhood, adolescence,
and adulthood lie many cumulative layers of personality organization. The principles of transformation that underly such changes in
organization have yet to be specified.

Implicit in Mahler's work is her continuing emphasis on normal
development and on the centrality of the oedipus complex as the
organizer of preoedipal development. Moreover, Mahler's findings
on *normal* subphase adequacy will eventually illuminate facets of the
oedipus complex which have remained obscure—for example, the
effects of separation-individuation on narcissism, the fate of the
libidinal and aggressive drives, and the differential outcomes of
gender identity in men and women.

Mahler and I wrote explicitly of the oedipus complex as the fourth
psychological organizer (Mahler and Kaplan 1977). The oedipus
complex is shaped by the symbiotic and separation-individuation
subphases. And in its turn, through its own resolution and mode of
dissolution, the oedipus complex restructures the outcome of these
earlier developmental events. Our paper emphasized the importance of evaluating the adequacy of the symbiotic and separation-
individuation subphases toward the shaping of the fourth organizer.
We hoped this emphasis would serve as a corrective for the increasing tendency of clinicians to perceive the dominance of one sub-

phase distortion as pathognomic for a particular category of psycho-pathology. A prevalent notion is that each subphase corresponds to a specific manifestation or form of schizophrenic, borderline, or narcissistic disorder. To focus in this manner on the dominance of one subphase manifestation in the content of treatment material, whether as transference or actual life behavior, serves to obscure that there are always corrective or pathogenic influences from other phases of separation-individuation which will also have left their imprint on oedipal organization. The simple equations: symbiosis vulnerability = schizophrenic disorder, rapprochement vulnerability = borderline disorder, and so on, are insufficient for comprehending the concept of subphase adequacy and its effects on later personality organization.

Subphase appropriate anxieties—fear of object loss, stranger wariness, and fear of the loss of the object's love—are related to the three strands of narcissism delineated by Spruiell (1975): "self-love, the regulation of self-esteem, and omnipotence" (p. 579). From the data of Mahler's original study and the follow-up studies of the subjects Sy and Cathy, we were able to illustrate some of the vicissitudes of these aspects of subphase adequacy and to suggest the principles that might regulate the transformations from rapprochement organization to personality organization during latency.

Normally, in the symbiotic and differentiation subphases, healthy narcissism is sponsored from within by a predominance of inner sensations of satisfying pleasure, and from the external world by mirroring admiration and experiences of bodily contact. During early practicing, the emotional availability of the mother as a home base for emotional refueling enhances the narcissism derived from the child's explorations of the world outside the mother-infant orbit. From the autonomous achievements of the practicing period the inner sources of narcissism are derived—self-love, the sense of mastery and valuation of accomplishments, and phase-appropriate omnipotence. Narcissism, particularly omnipotence, is subphase specifically vulnerable during rapprochement. Throughout separation-individuation, narcissistic enhancement from within must be balanced by the availability of bodily libidinal supplies from significant objects, particularly the mother.

In the case of Cathy, imbalances in the three strands of narcissism intensified the rapprochement crisis and profoundly affected her subsequent development. Cathy's developmental history also illustrates how some prototypical rapprochement behaviors might evolve into a characteristic pattern of object relations without necessarily signifying a borderline disturbance.

For example, a prominent manifestation in the transference or in the actual behavior of some individuals is the coercion of a mirroring dyadic relationship. Such coercion is believed to have as its goal the recovery of the idealized self-object and lost omnipotence of the practicing proper subphase; this behavior and goal is typical of many toddlers during the rapprochement crisis, when they become aware of their separateness from mother. Cathy, during practicing proper, was the queen bee of the nursery. Her colorless, masochistic mother would shine in the reflected glory of her precocious daughter's accomplishments. Yet, Cathy's mother was consistently unavailable when it came to supplying the bodily closeness and libidinal contact comfort that energize the other strand of narcissism in infancy— bodily self-love. The sudden collapse of Cathy's exalted omnipotence at 19 months was precipitated by her discovery of the anatomical sex difference while bathing with a neighbor's little boy. Cathy became petulant and aggressively provocative with her mother. She would no longer allow her mother to dress her or touch her. The mother, who had previously shone in her child's radiance, was now correspondingly depressed and humilated by Cathy's sullen, clinging, demanding behavior. From her third to her fifth year Cathy alternated between weakly sought triadic relations, which included both mother and father, to frantic demands for exclusive relations with *either* mother or father. Cathy's need for dyadic mirroring relationships was to become a major theme. From her third year on, she sought such relationships as a way of maintaining narcissistic well-being. The observational data and family interviews from age 3 through 13 yielded a vivid picture of shifting but inevitably disappointing relationships with the mother, the father, teachers, friends.

In Cathy's follow-up at age 13, several aspects of an advanced oedipal resolution were apparent, including a defense organization based on repression, guilt as well as shame, and signal anxiety, and the overall dominance of triadic whole-object relations. However, the effects of the imbalance in the three strands of narcissism were also evident. The outstanding clinical impression was Cathy's sense of personal inadequacy and low self-esteem. Her full scale I.Q. was 134. Yet, her school achievement was in the B-minus to C range. Other significant features were a predominance of inflexible ego-ideal and superego structures and potentials for difficulties in gender identity resolutions during adolescence.

Striking in the Rorschach protocol were Cathy's perceptions of bodies as "trapped," "slouched down," "hidden," and generally blocked in action. These responses were interpreted in part as signs of Cathy's exalted standards, her perfectionism; forms that were not "just so" were imperfect in some wáy. These body representations were also expressions of Cathy's masochistic orientation (Shafer 1954). We hypothesized, furthermore, that these "trapped" and imperfect bodies were the now distant echoes of that neglected third strand of narcissism. They represented Cathy's unsatisfied longings for bodily contact—the inadequacy of bodily love during differentiation and practicing. Perhaps the availability of such libidinal supplies during the earlier subphases might have toned down Cathy's exalted omnipotence and softened the blow of the recognition of her "anatomical shortcoming" at rapprochement.

The imbalance between exalted ego-ideals and self-experience which leads to lowered self-love, is frequently observed in adult patients; in brilliant, grandiose overachievers as well as in masochistic underachievers. The devaluation-overvaluation and sadomasochistic trends of such patients are considerably different in tone and intensity than in borderline patients. And, rapprochement characteristics, such as the coercion of mirroring dyadic relations, are expressions of a disturbance of secondary narcissism, yet within the context of a typical transference neurosis. Not surprisingly penis envy, penis awe, and castration anxiety are other outstanding features of such cases. But, here again, these features which are also prominent in borderline patients do not involve the kind of envy contaminated by overwhelming unneutralized aggression aimed at the destruction of the envied object, nor by castration reactions that are tantamount to mutilation anxiety and annihilation panic.

The *interaction* of subphase inadequacies in narcissism and quality of anxiety and its effect on the oedipal constellation were discussed extensively in the case of Sy, a child who presented the clinical picture of a borderline personality in the follow-up study conducted when he was 11 years old. Here a luxuriating symbiosis had crowded out the ego building contributions to the three strands of narcissism throughout separation-individuation and also impeded the organizing experiences of phase-appropriate anxiety.

Sy's mother's inordinate need for bodily contact with her infant, her persistent frantic efforts to turn Sy to face her or to crawl toward her when he chose instead to explore the world outside the mother-infant symbiotic orbit, deprived Sy of both the normal aggressive strivings of the practicing periods and the narcissistic enhancement provided by autonomous ego functioning. If it had not been for Sy's apparently innately powerful individuation strivings, which were so urgent that he preferred strangers to mother during the period when we typically expect stranger anxiety, he probably would not have escaped engulfment and outright psychosis.

Sy's differentiation and practicing periods were rudimentary. Subphase characteristics were confused, overlapping, and pervaded by symbiotic features. At 17 months, with the emergence of upright locomotion, Sy became suddenly and intensely aware of separation and possible object loss. In the absence of the psychological attainments of a more definitive practicing proper subphase, Sy was unable to mitigate the impact of the rapprochement crisis. He had been overwhelmed by bodily contact experiences with his mother and had been deprived throughout the earlier subphases of the phase-appropriate experiences of mastery and valuation of accomplishments and omnipotence. Thus, he was particularly vulnerable to the narcissistic deflation of rapprochement. Awareness of the separate self was contaminated by excessive castration anxiety (which later turned up as mutilation anxiety), and an overlapping of anal and phallic concerns.

Sy's excessive and premature castration anxiety was the result of inadequacies in all three strands of narcissism and *also* the result of his failure to experience the obligatory organizing fears of object loss, stranger wariness, and fear of the loss of the object's love at the phase-appropriate times. The rapprochement crisis was abortive and the entire anal phase was inundated by the precocious onset and prolonged involvement with phallic-narcissistic conflicts. Primitive symbolizations and condensations of pre-phallic and phallic conflicts during rapprochement ushered in a premature oedipal constellation. From his third to his sixth year the effects of this overlapping and premature oedipal constellation were noted in the failure of normal repression and in Sy's defective internalizations. Sometimes Sy would emulate a caricatured version of his mother. At other times he resembled an odd diminutive replica of his father.

When the projective tests were administered to Sy at age 11, the morbid nature of Sy's castration anxiety was apparent in his body mutilation fantasies and the fragmented quality of his body representations. Human body parts merged with one another and frequently were perceived as interchangeable with nonhuman objects, such as crocodile jaws, kite tails, rockets, trees. There was a striking absence of shame, social or signal anxiety, and guilt. Panic-anxiety alternated with bland passivity and sudden, unpredictable displays of clowning-exhibitionism.

Normally, during differentiation and practicing, phase-appropriate anxieties and phase-adequate contributions to narcissism prepare the infant for the subphase-specific narcissistic vulnerabilities of rapprochement with its ensuing onslaught of ambitendency and separation anxiety. When the infant is not prepared, one outcome is that premature castration anxiety overlaps with unmitigated separation anxiety ushering in a premature, distorted oedipal constellation. The orderly unfolding of the fourth organizer is prevented. Therefore, the superego structures and synthetic function associated with the "ideal" oedipal constellation also do not make their stage-appropriate contribution to the organization of the personality. The major long-term sequelae of a distorted, rudimentary, delayed, prolonged, or precocious rapprochement is the reshuffling of the organizing structures of the oedipus complex.

PRINCIPLES OF ORGANIZATION

When we examine the epigenetic principles that regulate psychological organization, the ubiquity of the rapprochement subphase in the life cycle and its specific influence on the fourth organizer is further clarified.

With the advent of ego psychology in the early 1930s, psychoanalysts began to consider the central role of the synthetic function (Nunberg 1931) within the developmental process. Development was viewed as proceeding from shifts in the patterning of already existing structures, not merely as additions of new structures. The principles of epigenesis—synthesis, progressive organization and reorganization and change of function whereby old behaviors acquire new functions—were to become the guiding principles of those analysts who went on to make explicit for theory the developmental ego psychology that had always been implicit in psychoanalytic clinical practice and conception (Silverman, Rees, and

Neubauer 1975). While the theoretical relevance of epigenetic principles was being explored, other psychoanalysts were observing developmental processes in infants and children and discovering that
their observations were consonant with these epigenetic principles.

The concept of the *organizer* was to receive its richest expression
in the writings of René Spitz where it served as a model of the
relationships among theory, observational study, and clinical work.
Independently, but paralleling Spitz's studies, were Mahler's investigations. In 1958, as Spitz was preparing his thoughts on the field
theory of ego formation, Mahler was preparing to embark on her
pilot study of the normal separation-individuation process. A few
years earlier, Spitz had already begun to formulate the characteristics of the third organizer, which he postulated would correspond in
time with the anal phase of development, and he had written about
the significance of the "No" gesture in the anal toddler and the
connection of this gesture with identification with the aggressor
(1957).

In his 1959 monograph, *A Genetic Field Theory of Ego Formation*,
Spitz would spell out in greater detail the principles for comprehending the significance of the first three organizers, their approximate
timing during the first 18 months of life and the different affective
indicators (smiling response, stranger anxiety, "No" gesture) which
would precede and therefore signal the beginnings of these emerging periods of organization.

Furthermore, Spitz went on to present his explicit formulation of
the differences between the third organizer of the anal phase and the
previous two, which he located in the oral phase. Along with this
formulation, Spitz outlined some axioms of epigenesis which will
help us to comprehend why disturbances in the first two periods of
organization might result in fixations at the anal or phallic phases and
become expressed in conflicts typical of these phases. Spitz could
not have known in 1959 that he was delineating the very propositions
which now allow us to appreciate the special significance of the
rapprochement subphase in human development.

Spitz's delineation of the maturational-developmental principles
that regulate the emergence of the first three organizers of the psyche
provide a rationale for comprehending (1) why the developmental
imbalances of the symbiotic, differentiation, and practicing periods
come to be represented in the personality through rapprochement
organization; and (2) why imbalances in rapprochement organization have the effect of distorting the oedipal constellation.

Some principles described by Spitz are relevant to all three of the first organizers. Organizers are more closely spaced and sequential development is more crucial during the first 18 months of life than at any later period. Innate maturational and growth forces (the individuation track of separation-individuation) play a large part in giving the first organizers something of a life of their own. Innate species-specific maturational patterns regulate the timing and sequence of such functions as perception, locomotion, awareness of discrepancy, attention-concentration, memory. Nevertheless, as a consequence of the long period of biological helplessness of the human infant, these first organizers are also vulnerable to environmental influences. They require an adequate soil in which to evolve—that is, they are dependent on the object relations which mobilize and stimulate progressive development.

Spitz then highlighted the difference between the third organizer of the anal phase and the first two organizers of the oral phase. The respective roles of psychological development and maturation change. Maturation plays the larger role at first and therefore the organism is relatively resistant to outside interference. By 18 months the proportions are reversed. Psychological development becomes more significant than maturation. The third organizer is more vulnerable to environmental influence and it has more enduring *psychological* significance than the first two organizers.

Spitz hypothesized that the third organizer would be the acquisition of speech. The affective indicator of the onset of this period of organization was the "No" gesture.

> In my opinion, it [the "No" gesture] represents a line of cleavage in mental and psychological development. From this point on begins a new way of being. I discussed its significance for psychic structure and object relations, into which it introduces a new mode, as the replacing of action by communication. It initiates the implementation of defense mechanisms in their enduring form, coinciding and interacting with the manifestations of the anal phase [p. 50].
>
> The third organizer opens the road for the development of object relations on the human pattern, that is the pattern of semantic communication. This makes possible both the emergence of the self and the beginnings of social relations on the human level [p. 97].

Other psychoanalysts might view drive development or developments in object relations (which are actually inseparable; there is no drive without an object) as the central impetus to the dramatic shift from the practicing to rapprochement periods. However, it is clear that Spitz regards the maturation of speech as the third organizer, an organizer that corresponds to symbolic representational thought as described by Piaget (1952). Spitz's hypothesis is also reminiscent of William James's turn of the century position vis-à-vis the significance in human life of the shift from the world of sensate flux to the world of concepts and thoughts (James 1890, 1916). Lewin (1961, p. 175) alluded to James's position and related this same shift to the necessity for the renunciation of pleasures in orality and motility (p. 174).

Although priorities regarding the major impetus for reorganization during the anal phase may differ, the similarity between Spitz's propositions on the third period of organization and Mahler's findings on the rapprochement subphase is evident. Included in both formulations are the emergence of self, the negativism and drive-object relationships of the anal phase, the transition from sensorimotor to symbolic representational intelligence and the emergence of enduring character traits and defenses, initially identification with the aggressor.

In addition, Spitz elaborated some of the principles that regulate fixation and regression. He had already considered these principles in a paper to the Vienna Psychoanalytic Society in 1936. His 1959 monograph extended these principles. Spitz distinguished between developmental arrests and developmental imbalances. The former create adaptations so deviant that they no longer resemble the ordinary course of human development. Developmental imbalances, on the other hand, are selective. Deficiencies in one sector of the personality are compensated for by combinations and alterations in other sectors. These compensatory combinations create luxuriating and abnormal ego nuclei which then come to constitute fixation points.

> By that I do not mean that when later a regression occurs, it will necessarily have to go to the very origin of these nuclei. Rather do I imagine that in the course of further development such luxuriating ego nuclei will inevitably come into conflict with the normal demands of the environment at a much later phase.
>
> *It is to this conflict that the fixation will be attached and that regression will primarily take place* [pp. 86-87, italics added].

Spitz recognized that temporal asynchronicity between maturational and developmental processes was an explanatory principle for only *one* origin of fixation. He alludes to Fenichel's theories of fixation and cites the idea that another source of fixation would be "the yearning for the satisfaction formerly enjoyed." In this connection Spitz also reminds us of Rapaport's formulation concerning those processes that "create enduring relations between drives and objects" (p. 87).

Longing for satisfaction formerly enjoyed during the oral phase may thus become attached to conflicts typical of the anal phase. Imbalances during the first two periods of organization go on to attain, during the anal phase, an enduring psychological significance along specifically human lines. During the rapprochement crisis, the leap from the world of sensate flux to the world of mental images makes possible enduring relations between drive and object, incipient character formation and gender identity, and a psychological level of defense mechanism. Our specific longings for the "all-good" mother of symbiosis come into existence in connection with our attempts to deal with the specific anxieties of separation. These longings then become associated with the narcissistic vulnerabilities of rapprochement, in particular the shattering of the omnipotence of the practicing period. Most significantly, following Spitz, it is not until the anal phase that enduring relations between drive and object become possible, along with the advent of "object relations on the human pattern, that is, in the pattern of semantic communication." The emergence of self, semantic communication and the beginning of symbolized social relations are the significant characteristics contributing to the organization of the rapprochement subphase.

Developmental imbalances during the first two periods of organization inevitably create imbalances in rapprochement organization and fixations at the anal level. And, as Spitz emphasized, distortions "of the preceding organizer must lead to a distortion of the subsequent organizing process, whether this distortion be one of delay in time or a compensatory reshuffling of the structures themselves" (p. 94). As demonstrated in the case of Sy, one outcome of the developmental imbalances of the oral period may be a premature, out-of-constellation oedipal organization, which then becomes associated with the anxieties and narcissistic issues of the rapprochement subphase.

The fourth organizer of the psyche will not immutably fix the course of later development. However, it does initiate the pattern in which future developmental events and adaptational tasks will emerge. When the oedipal constellation is premature, delayed or otherwise distorted, then it is not associated primarily with the drive-object relations, anxieties, ego functions and narcissistic issues that ideally characterize the fourth period of human organization. Up to the oedipal period, maturational forces played a major role in the patterning of personality organization. But, as previously noted, by the time of the emergence of the third organizer, the respective roles of psychological development and maturation have already been reversed. Although the emergence of the fourth organizer is stimulated by the ongoing maturation of the child, its resolution and mode of dissolution create the *psychological structures* which will go on to pattern the rest of development. Defects in oedipal organization are characterized by a paucity of those psychological structures which regulate and pattern development during latency. To put it another way, latency development tends to be underpatterned, irregular, and plastic when the psychological structures of the fourth organizer are defective. A significant aspect of such underpatterning is a weakness in the synthetic function of the ego. As Nunberg (1931) said, the earliest manifestation of the synthetic function is in the normal oedipus constellation when the superego is being formed:

> The ego's method of defending itself from the dangers of the oedipus situation is that of assimilating (ideationally) the id's objects and also the instinctual trends relating to them; this it does by identification. . . . Hence, through the process of identification certain instincts and objects which are not consonant with the ego are not merely warded off; they are also united, modified, fused, divested of their specific element of danger and transformed into a new psychic creation—the superego. . . . This process is the first and plainest of the ego's influence as an intermediary and binding force, that is, of its synthetic function [p. 121].

Out-of-constellation oedipal organization is regularly accompanied by weakness in the synthetic function of the ego. The vulnerabilities, deficits and irregular developmental patterning of children with borderline personality organization are expressions of this weakness of the synthetic function. The unevenness in developmental patterning of borderline children was described by Kut Rosenfeld and Sprince (1963), "There seems to be a faulty relationship between the drives and the ego. At no stage does the ego give direction to the drives; neither does the ego supply the component drives with the special ego characteristics and coloring. It is as if the drives and ego develop independently and as if they belonged to two different people" (p. 615). Weil (1956) has stressed that vulnerability to anxiety is the core problem in borderline children. She related this vulnerability to defects in the maturational patterning of ego and drives, and she refers to the peculiarities and unevenness in sequences in development; acceleration then regression, sudden gain then loss.

Pine (1974) expressed the idea of the defect in developmental patterning of borderline children most directly:

> A geologist may describe the shape of a stone with precision; but not so a meteorologist, a cloud. Some of the children who have been described as borderline have a quality of changing shape, a fluidity, which is far less characteristic of a neurotic child. The apparent imprecision in description may itself be a reflection of the "imprecision," i.e., the absence of clear structure, in some of these children [p. 350].

In summary, the psyche is vulnerable to primitive levels of anxiety when its organization and structures are underpatterned. Any increment in anxiety will induce the array of symptomotology that we typically find in borderline children: the primitive forms of self-esteem regulation and defense organization, primitive identifications, and, in treatment, the transference paradigms that are reminiscent of the rapprochement crisis, with its contradictory longings for merger and strivings for separateness.

The primary effect of the developmental imbalances of the separation-individuation period appears to be the compensatory reshuffling of the structures of the fourth organizer. When this occurs the identifications which would ordinarily be transformed into superego structures are not present—indicating a weakness in the synthetic function of the ego.

Mahler (1971) had said:

> In average development . . . the progressive forces of the growing ego are astonishingly successful. Often they tend to even out most of the discrepancies and minor deviations.
>
> It is precisely the deficiencies of integration and internalization which will leave residua, and thus may manifest themselves in bor-

derline mechanisms, *which indicate a degree of failure of the synthetic function of the ego* [p. 414, italics added].

Thus, the connections between borderline phenomena and the outcomes of rapprochement are not as direct as clinicians often imply. A major hypothesis of this paper is that deviant rapprochement resolutions lead to a compensatory reshuffling of the structures of the fourth organizer. The primary effect of such reshuffling would be some degree of failure of the synthetic function of the ego.

The next section of the paper will be an initial attempt to demonstrate how the typical symptoms of borderline latency-age children, particularly panic-anxiety and primitive modes of self-esteem regulation, are manifestations of this relative failure of the synthetic function. Moreover, since every subsequent developmental phase offers further opportunities for a restructuring of the rapprochement and oedipal resolutions, I will conclude with a brief consideration of how adolescent and adult modes of organization might go on to transform the infantile resolutions.

BORDERLINE PHENOMENA IN CHILDHOOD

In the introduction to his paper on the classification of borderline children, Pine (1974) presents the standard formula of the essence of neurosis: an unconscious conflict between drive and opposing force which culminates in anxiety, unsuccessful defense, and symptom formation. In Pine's presentation there is the implication of a parallel path from conflict to symptom formation in the borderline and neurotic child, the difference being merely the personality context in which the conflict arises and the more complicated path in the borderline on the way to symptom formation. While Pine's formulation often applies to adult borderline patients, my emphasis in borderline children would be on the deviation in the organization of the personality, a deviation which reflects the weakness in the synthetic function and therefore precludes the path from unconscious conflict to symptom formation set forth by Pine.

It is recognized that the borderline conditions of childhood represent a wide range of deviations ranging from mild to very severe. In the symptom picture of the milder disorders we do find distinct neurotic symptoms. However, the symptoms that we have come to identify as diagnostic of the borderline child are more directly attributable to inadequacies and imbalances in organization. These characteristic symptoms (Pine 1974, pp. 345-346) are: (1) the failure of signal affects—the absence of well-structured neurotic defenses escalating signal anxiety into panic-annihilation anxiety; (2) dependence on object contact for the maintenance of existing ego structures—a feature which leads to unpredictable shifts and regressions in levels of object relations; (3) distortions and weaknesses of superego structures and other internally structured possibilities for control and delay. Others (Mahler and Kaplan 1977, p. 77; Kut Rosenfeld and Sprince 1963, p. 622) have associated these symptoms with the prominence of primary identification, that is, the assumption of mimicked and often bizarre replications of the object rather than the introjection of the authority of the object, as represented by the superego.

These commonly identified characteristics of the borderline child are not the same as the compromise formations that are the outcomes of unconscious conflict, anxiety, and unsuccessful defense. We are, in fact, more likely to be dealing with the direct and indirect sequelae of failures of negotiation, modulation, synthesis—and the absence therefore of compromise formation. Moreover, clinical evidence demonstrates that the panic anxiety of the borderline child is *not* triggered by inner conflict but by fluidity of the primary-process displacements and primitive symbolizations which so easily convert any external object into a thing to be feared (Kut Rosenfeld and Sprince 1963, p. 624). The projection, or more precisely externalization, of an impulse does not diminish anxiety; it escalates anxiety and furnishes the world with an assortment of dreaded objects; externalization can also lead to the dread of having emptied the self of substance. The relationship between the prototypical anxiety states and other symptoms in borderline children can be further appreciated by an understanding of the significance of the term *pseudoneurotic defense.*

For example, although numerous clinicians have adopted the convention of referring to the "multiple phobias" of borderline children (and adults), these seemingly phobic reactions are not true phobias. Lacking the symbolic richness of a true phobia, they are more aptly understood as primitive fears and anxieties. As Weil (1973) has said, the borderline child has "a chronic anxiety readiness, their ever-present fears attaching themselves sometimes directly to many different and constantly changing objects. While the choice of these 'feared objects' may reflect the gradual progress in cognitive development and the acquisition of some symbolic thinking, the process by which these children's fears become attached to objects differs markedly from that of neurotic development" (p. 289). Although the borderline child, like the neurotic child, externalizes the source of danger—exchanging an internal psychic state for an imaginary external threat—in the borderline child the pathway via conflict is absent and the mechanisms of neurotic condensation and synthetic symbolization are also either absent or weak. Thus, the fears remain diffuse and they are not, as Anna Freud (1977) explained, "compressed by the child into one encompassing symbol which represents the dangers left over from preoedipal phases as well as the dominant ones due to phallic-oedipal conflicts" (pp. 87-88). The symbolizations which are involved in the formation of a true phobic symptom depend on the synthetic function. The anxiety readiness and diffuse fears of the borderline child are the result of his inability to create a neurotic symptom.

Similarly, the compulsive behaviors of borderline children, although often clearly manifest, do not represent conflicts caused by regression from the phallic-oedipal to the anal-sadistic level as they would in neurotic children. In borderline children, compulsions represent attempts to ward off disintegration. The rituals, taboos, compulsions help to maintain some semblance of stability and sameness in an environment with a high potential for threat. The anxiety readiness leads to externalization and other primitive projective mechanisms, creating a cycle of anxiety, dangerous world, escalated anxiety.

Unlike the obsessional thoughts of neurotic children the "worry words" and "worry phrases" of borderline children are so terrifying and incomprehensible that the child cannot escape them—for weeks or months on end, he may not be able to think of anything else. "Often an apparently irrelevant object becomes attached to the anxiety—anxiety is mobilized but the link to what the object stands for has been lost" (Kut Rosenfeld and Sprince 1965, p. 500). And unlike the interpretation of neurotic obsessions, "attempts to trace the worry-word to its source increase anxiety and confusion. The original anxiety may have been so unbearable that reconstruction at the height of the anxiety only serves to trigger similar disintegration, annihilation and helplessness" (p. 502).

Residues of the imbalances in the three strands of narcissism—self-love, self-esteem regulation, and omnipotence—are also reflected in the symptoms and primitive defenses of the borderline child. In contrast to neurotic children with narcissistic imbalances, borderline children manifest a heightening of primitive omnipotence in tandem with mutilation anxiety and annihilation panic. The pseudoneurotic defenses cited previously are expressions of the borderline child's defensive omnipotence in the context of insufficient libidinization of the bodily self or the self- and object representations.

Another major group of characteristics concern the borderline child's difficulties in organizing external stimuli. Frequently accompanying such difficulty is an overall deficit in figure-ground differentiation, a deficit that is too often attributed to some sort of organic defect. But figure-ground disturbance is found even in borderline children where there is no demonstrable organic defect. Moreover, a deficiency in the selective function is often present and makes it difficult for borderline children to sort out the relevant from the irrelevant. They are swamped by stimuli from within and from the external world, and many such children are therefore distractible and hyperactive. Because they lack a scale of relative importance, the borderline child's defense of omnipotence is heightened. Instead of this defense alleviating anxiety, it escalates it. If a child can knock down a chair, he feels he can knock down a building (Kut Rosenfeld and Sprince 1965, p. 500).

Summarizing thus far, the major symptom of borderline latency age children is anxiety proneness, which then leads to the other typical borderline defenses and symptoms, all of which are expressive of disturbances in the synthetic function—a function which arises in connection with a normal resolution and dissolution of the oedipus complex and the structuring of the superego.

FURTHER TRANSFORMATIONS:
ADOLESCENCE AND ADULTHOOD

Maturation during adolescence affects significant and distinctive alterations in ego organization. The panic-anxiety, pseudoneurotic defenses, failures of the selective and figure-ground functions and many of the ego deviational features which may have been part of an "organiclike" clinical picture during childhood go on to serve dif-

ferent functions, express themselves in different modes and sometimes even recede into the background of the adolescent personality.

As the epigenetic blueprint unfolds, the possibilities for progressive reorganization are as likely as the pathological regressive trends.
The maturational push of puberty often structures, organizes, and
patterns the development of ego-deviational children who had demonstrated impairments in ego functioning and drive-object relations
during latency. Artistic and intellectual talents, and athletic skills
may now flourish, bringing the adolescent into a more advantageous
position with new objects—peers, teachers, and also the parents and
siblings. On the other hand, in certain children, the maturational
spurt of puberty may bring to the surface previously unnoticed or
dormant vulnerabilities in ego development. These vulnerabilities
may be revealed by a paucity of the integrative-synthetic functions
which are characteristic of adolescent formal operational thinking.
In other cases, we observe a heightening of the abstract, formal
systems of thought in the context of gaps or deficits in sensorimotor
and concrete operational intelligence. Emphasis on the abstract, the
logical, the ideal, frequently serves as a defensive avoidance of the
temptations of the body. Bodily self-love is specifically vulnerable
during adolescence, and deficiencies in this strand of narcissism are
often compensated for by the omnipotence of the thought processes,
even in normal adolescents.

In childhood, the oedipus complex was an emotional reality only
in the form of an unconscious wish which was thwarted by the child's
realization of his physical immaturity (Blos 1972b). Sexual maturity
at puberty compels a definitive break with infantile positions. The
adolescent's sullen provocativeness and stormy mood alterations are
signs of his efforts to work out an optimal emotional distance from
the parents. In contrast to separation-individuation when each succeeding subphase made its distinctive contribution to the optimal
distance necessary for the establishment of the primary separation
between self and other, the adolescent's search for optimal distance
is in the service of individuation—the formation of the adult ego-
ideal, new identifications, and the relinquishing of the infantile
drive-object relations.

Blos (1967) said that adolescence is a "second individuation" which
offers the opportunity for a reforging of the boundaries of the self
and for discovering new modes of object relations. However, as Blos
also indicated, adolescents do not repeat the events of separation-

individuation as these were experienced in infancy. Adolescents are *not* involved in arriving at a differentiation between self and object. Furthermore, although the adolescent is dealing with object loss and the consequences of this loss for his continuing individuation, these issues are guided by the developmental potentials of adolescence with their own organizational properties and possibilities for restructuring of the psychic systems. Drive and ego maturation combine to give a new impetus to the synthetic function. Syntheses and integrations which were not accomplished earlier become possible during adolescence.

Parallels between the second individuation at adolescence and separation-individuation can be more misleading than helpful. Clinicians often compare the adolescent's defensive narcissistic omnipotence, his exaggerated valuation of accomplishments, his exalted ego-ideals with the elated mood of the practicing toddler. Or, we hear that the adolescent, like the rapprochement toddler, expresses negativism, ambitendency and splitting of the object world into "all-good" and "all-bad". The mood swings of hypomania and depression in adolescence are said to correspond to the contrast between the elation of practicing and the low-keyed and grief reactions of rapprochement. The adolescent mode of discovering his optimal distance often takes the form of moving away from "home base" and returning for emotional refueling. Though these parallels have a ring of truth to them, they are merely analogies based on overt behaviors. They do not illuminate the specific *internal* changes that are characteristic of adolescence. It is precisely the differences between the toddler and the adolescent that establishes the meaning of Blos's term "second individuation."

Adolescence presents a phase-specific transformation of the issues of separation-individuation *and* the oedipus complex. It is not a duplication or a recapitulation any more than the adult neurosis is a replica of the early infantile neurosis. Adolescence is truly a second chance, an opportunity to rectify and alter those developmental inevitabilities of narcissism and drive-object relations which were merely the tentative solutions of childhood. Only by identifying the specific rectifications of adolescence can we understand the transformations peculiar to this period of life.

As Blos has so often said, in normal development these specific rectifications involve resolutions of the negative oedipus complex and through these resolutions the formation of the adult ego-ideal:

"the ego-ideal which emerges at the termination of adolescence is the heir to the negative Oedipus complex" (1972a, p. 96). One major adaptational task of adolescence is to de-idealize the preoedipal and oedipal self- and object imagoes and to arrive thereby at a tolerance for imperfection in self and others.

Blos (1967) highlighted the idea that the second individuation is distinguished from that of the first separation-individuation process by *the opposite vicissitudes of internalization.* Whereas separation-individuation is accomplished by gaining a relative independence from external objects through internalizations of infantile parental imagoes, ideals, inhibitions, and authority, adolescents must gain independence from the very internal objects that were erected during the oedipal and preoedipal periods of childhood. They must give up these internal objects by transforming them into the adult ego-ideal, a structure which allows them to establish a new level of actual relationship with husband or wife, child, parents, and adult peers (p. 163).

In a 1978 paper, Blos stated that at adolescence preoedipal issues will rival oedipal issues or blend with them in deceptive guises. However, when ego development has been distorted during latency, the passions of adolescence are weakened. What will then demand our clinical attention will be the ego deficits which have been carried over into adolescence, rather than the reawakening of preoedipal and oedipal drive manifestations. Again, with the borderline adolescent, we find ourselves confronted with imbalances between ego development and drive development; developmental lines which, under normal circumstances, are mutually potentiating.

The developmental imbalances and fixations of separation-individuation produce their effects by distorting oedipal organization during childhood. These distortions then carry over into adolescence by hindering the regressions which would allow for the resolution of the negative oedipus complex and the emergence of the adult ego-ideal. In contrast to the relatively normal-neurotic adolescent, who can yield temporarily to the frightening regressive pulls of the preoedipal period, the borderline adolescent must defensively exaggerate the positive oedipus complex, often in the form of hypermasculine or hyperfeminine caricatures of gender. As Kut Rosenfeld and Sprince (1963) have noted: "The borderline adolescent's attempt to maintain himself on the phallic and oedipal level as a defense against a strong regressive pull must therefore be differentiated not only from that of the neurotic patient who regresses *from* the phallic phase due to conflict but also from that of the psychotic patient who loses the positive oedipus complex entirely" (p. 618).

As the adolescent period draws to a close, the opportunity to achieve phase-appropriate resolutions within the phase-appropriate time within the context of mutually facilitating ego and drive development, also closes down. Nevertheless, unresolved issues (of which there are several even in relatively normal development) continue to serve as incentives and potentials for further development.

The epigenetic blueprint continues to unfold, exerting its influence on personality organization and bringing new forms of biological and psychological organization with new potentials for the restructuring of the past. By the time one reaches adulthood, developmental imbalances and fixations that are residues of the separation-individuation process have been filtered through many layers of cumulative revision—the adult personality inevitably will bear the stamp of adult psychobiological organization—albeit an adult organization bearing the imprints of deficits in the synthesizing and integrative functions of childhood and adolescence.

With the adult borderline, one is faced with the more or less finished product of the developmental failures, arrests, and interferences with organization and structuralization that clinicians who work with children and adolescents are observing in the process of unfolding and organizing, failing to ripen in the appropriate constellation or sequence, disorganizing and fragmenting, reorganizing and reintegrating. Even though we are undoubtedly dealing in the borderline adult with various problems of early inadequacies in the positive contributions of the separation-individuation process, we must always remind ourselves of our perspective on these developmental imbalances. The imbalances must be evaluated in the context of the organization of an already matured organism with a character structure that is the product of both the transformations of the earliest biopsychological organizations of infancy and childhood and the organizational features of adolescence and adulthood.

Although they have not experienced the full advantages of adolescent reorganization, borderline adults will usually evidence some degree of adult organization, an organization which includes an increased potential for conflict. And, as a result of maturational changes in intellectual organization, there is usually a more advanced level of synthetic functioning in the adult than that observed in borderline children and young adolescents. However far a borderline adult may regress to earlier levels of personality organization, the path of the regression will be determined by the quality of the adolescent reorganization, the degree of distortion of the oedipal constellation, *and* the specific resolutions of the rapprochement crisis.

In summary, there are, to be sure, continuities of symptomotology and of developmental issues in borderline children, adolescents, and adults. However, it is from the discontinuities and from our increasing appreciation of the differences among the organization, structures, and synthetic functions of children, adolescents, and adults that we can better delineate the manner in which the genetic viewpoint of psychoanalytic metapsychology might be reconciled with our developmental perspectives.

The genetic and developmental positions could be mutually enhancing, but the difficulty in achieving this advantage has been that the pathways between the two are not as direct or simple as customarily presented. For example, reflections of the normal rapprochement subphase will be found in every nosological disorder and in relatively normal conditions as well. When confronted with life's inevitable trials, we all doubtless try to revive some version of the experiences associated with "the erstwhile 'good' symbiotic mother, whom we long for from the cradle to the grave" (Mahler 1971, p. 415). These longings usually occur in some context typical of the conflicts and anxieties of rapprochement, but such longings may also be activated by developmentally later conflicts.

In describing the major advantage of the developmental perspective for the understanding of borderline phenomena Meissner (1978) said, "The developmental focus adds a specific and important dimension to other theoretical accounts, namely progression through time. This allows for the emergence of certain deficits in phase-specific sequence which may undergo a variety of developmental vicissitudes in subsequent phases" (p. 579).

One way of bringing the psychoanalytic metapsychology into harmony with clinical theory would be further investigation of the epigenetic principles governing the transformations which are responsible for "the variety of developmental vicissitudes in subsequent phases." Currently in the arts and physical sciences (Piaget

1968, 1971, Chomsky 1957, Levi-Strauss 1962, 1964), the search for the principles that regulate transformations has long been under way. Challenged by the discrepancy between the genetic and developmental viewpoints (which corresponds somewhat to the discrepancy between the possible and the actual in mathematics and physics), psychoanalysts might begin to address this more general, fundamental issue. However, in response to the challenge some psychoanalysts defensively maintain that classical formulations with regard to the central role of the oedipus complex and neurotic conflict are sufficient for an understanding of borderline and narcissistic disorders. Others, perhaps in reaction to the rigidity of the classical stance, have begun to focus exclusively on the preoedipal period; on the symbiotic phase in the schizophrenic disorders, on the rapprochement subphase in the borderline and narcissistic disorders. In either instance, such premature closure can only lead to theoretical oversimplifications and to blind spots in the clinical situation. The time seems ripe for appreciating that the complicated discrepancies between the genetic and developmental viewpoints can be an advantage to theory-building and clinical practice rather than a hindrance. The unresolved questions and ambiguities would then serve as the incentives and potentials for a new phase of psychoanalytic inquiry.

References

Blos, P. (1967). The second individuation process of adolescence. *Psychoanalytic Study of the Child* 22:162-186.

——— (1972a). The function of the ego ideal in late adolescence. *Psychoanalytic Study of the Child* 27:93-97.

——— (1972b). The epigenesis of the adult neurosis. *Psychoanalytic Study of the Child* 27:106-135.

——— (1978). Modification in the classical psychoanalytic model of adolescence. Paper presented at the New York Psychoanalytic Society, October 31, 1978 (unpublished).

Chomsky, N. (1966). *Cartesian Linguistics*. New York: Harper and Row.

Coleman, R. W., Kris, E. and Provence, S. (1953). A study of variations of early parental attitudes: a preliminary report. *Psychoanalytic Study of the Child* 8:20-47.

Freud, A. (1977). Fears, anxieties and phobic phenomena. *Psychoanalytic Study of the Child* 32:85-90.

James, W. (1890). *The Principles of Psychology*. New York: Henry Holt.

———— (1916). *A Pluralistic Universe*. New York: Longmans, Green.

Kut Rosenfeld, S. and Sprince, M. P. (1963). An attempt to formulate the meaning of the concept "borderline." *Psychoanalytic Study of the Child* 18:605-635.

———— (1965). Some thoughts on the technical handling of borderline children. *Psychoanalytic Study of the Child* 20:495-517.

Levi-Strauss, C. (1962). *The Savage Mind*. Chicago: University of Chicago Press, 1966.

———— (1964). *The Raw and the Cooked*. New York: Harper and Row, 1969.

Lewin, B. D. (1950). *The Psychoanalysis of Elation*. New York: W. W. Norton, 1961.

Mahler, M. S. (1971). A study of the separation-individuation process: and its possible application to borderline phenomena in the psychoanalytic situation. *Psychoanalytic Study of the Child* 26:91-128. Reprinted in *The Selected Papers of Margaret S. Mahler*, vol. 2, ch. 11. New York: Jason Aronson, 1979.

Mahler, M. S. and Kaplan, L. (1977). Developmental aspects in the assessment of narcissistic and so-called borderline personalities. In *Borderline Personality Disorders*, ed. P. Hartocollis. New York: International Universities Press. Reprinted in *Selected Papers*, op. cit., ch. 13.

Meissner, W. W. (1978). Theoretical assumptions of concepts of the borderline personality. *Journal of the American Psychoanalytic Association* 26:559-598.

Nunberg, H. (1931). The synthetic function of the ego. In H. Nunberg, *Practice and Theory of Psychoanalysis*, vol. I. New York: International Universities Press, 1955.

Piaget, J. (1936). *The Origins of Intelligence in Children*. New York: International Universities Press, 1952.

———— (1967). *Biology and Knowledge*. Chicago: University of Chicago Press, 1971.

———— (1968). *Structuralism*. New York: Basic Books, 1970.

Pine, F. (1974). On the concept "borderline" in children. *Psychoanalytic Study of the Child* 29:341-368.

Schafer, R. (1954). *Psychoanalytic Interpretation in Rorschach Testing*. New York: Grune & Stratton.

Silverman, M. A., Rees, K., and Neubauer, P. B. (1975). On a central psychic constellation. *Psychoanalytic Study of the Child* 30:127-157.

Spitz, R. A. (1957). *No and Yes*. New York: International Universities Press.

———— (1959). *A Genetic Field Theory of Ego Formation*. New York: International Universities Press.

Spruiell, V. (1975). Three strands of narcissism. *Psychoanalytic Quarterly* 44:577-595

Weil, A. P. (1956). Some evidence of deviational development in infancy and early childhood. *Psychoanalytic Study of the Child* 11:292-299.

——— (1973). Ego strengthening prior to analysis. *Psychoanalytic Study of the Child* 28:287-301.

4

Instinct Theory, Object Relations and Psychic-Structure Formation

Hans W. Loewald, M.D.

I can best pay tribute to Margaret Mahler's outstanding contributions to psychoanalysis by presenting some facets of my own work in psychoanalytic theory and its conceptualization. I trust that in the course of this paper, necessarily quite brief and condensed, it will become apparent how much I owe to her observations and concepts, although my conceptual language in a number of ways differs from hers. I know how much I have learned from her ways of perceiving psychological material with the eyes, ears, and other perceptual organs of a psychoanalyst, while I often organize such data in a somewhat different, but I believe congenial, manner. In part this is the case because my psychoanalytic experience is based exclusively on therapeutic work with adults, however regressed or infantile they may have been in aspects of their personalities. In part the differences, not in approach but in conceptualization, derive from my abiding special preoccupation with certain issues of psychoanalytic theory and concept formation, issues that have not been in the forefront of her work.

Reprinted from *Journal of the American Psychoanalytic Association* 26 (3):463-506 by permission of International Universities Press, Inc. Copyright © 1978 by the American Psychoanalytic Association. This paper was presented at the Margaret Mahler Symposium on "Symbiosis and Separation-Individuation Theory and Instinct Theory," Philadelphia, May 21, 1977.

I shall define, provisionally, individuation as that group of psychic processes or activities by which the separateness of subject and object as distinct psychic organizations becomes increasingly established. Since the formulation of the structural theory, the organization of the mind or personality has progressively been conceived of as a more or less orderly sequence, and synthesis, of differentiating-integrative processes by which id, ego, and superego become constituted as the three substructures of the individual psyche.

These processes begin with the differentiating activities taking place within the "dual unity" of the infant-mother psychic matrix, equivalent to Mahler's early symbiotic phase. In terms of the structural theory, individuation can be described as the total of the activities culminating in psychic-structure formation. Individuation or intrapsychic-structure formation is brought about, not by unilateral activities on the part of the infant organism, but by interactions taking place at first within the infant-mother unitary field, and progressively between elements that become more autonomous as differentiating activities within that field progress. The mother's various ministrations to the infant, although prompted by biological necessities and interactions of infant and mother, are organized on a far more advanced level of mentation than that of the infant's incipient mentation. They begin to organize his vital processes in such a way that one can more and more speak of the infant's *instinctual* life in contrast to a purely biological life with its physiological prerequisites. Following a formulation of Freud's—to which he himself and other analytic theorists have not consistently adhered—I define instinct (or instinctual drive) here as a *psychic representative* of biological stimuli or processes, and not as these biological stimuli themselves. In contradistinction to Freud's thought in "Instincts and Their Vicissitudes" (1915, pp. 121-122), however, I do not speak of biological stimuli impinging on a ready-made "psychic apparatus" in which their psychic representatives are thus created, but of interactional biological processes that find higher organization on levels which we have come to call psychic life. Understood as psychic phenomena or representatives, instincts come into being in the early organizing mother-infant interactions. They form the most primitive level of human mentation and motivation. In their totality, and as mental life progresses toward more complex organization of different levels of mentation and interplay between them, instincts constitute the id as distinguishable from ego and superego. Thus I conceive instincts (considered in the framework of psychoanalytic psychology), and the id as a psychic structure, as originating in interactions of the infantile organism and its human environment (mother), that is, in what Mahler calls the dual unity of the infant-mother symbiosis.

As for ego as a psychic substructure, and superego, they too, although on already more complexly organized levels of interaction, come into being resultant of interactions of the individuating child and its human environment. Internalization of such interactions leads to their formation. Perhaps this was more readily acknowledged in respect to the superego, because Freud began his investigations into the process we now call internalization by studying the phenomena of identification as they came to light in the area of ideal-formation and superego development. But it is equally true of the ego as a coherent organization that it is formed in those primary identifications taking place during preoedipal stages.

Several implications of this view of things should be briefly indicated. (1) If individuation is defined as that group of processes by which increasing separateness of subject and object comes about, it means that, in and by these processes, both subject and object (in early stages, mother as object) become organized in the child's mental experience as more or less distinct entities. As I have expressed it elsewhere (Loewald 1962, pp. 492-493), in regard to early differentiating activities internalization and externalization are processes by which internality and externality first become constituted. I shall return to this point.

(2) I do not agree with the view that memory, perception, reality testing, etc., are ego functions pure and simple that do not have their origin and their equivalents in instinctual life. In this sense I do not see that there are ego apparatuses with primary autonomy. Perception and memory in their primitive conformations, which remain basic ingredients of their later transformations—more familiar to us—are, I believe, unconscious instinctual activities, aspects of libidinal processes that only later gain a comparatively autonomous status. Expressed differently: in assuming an undifferentiated phase, instinctual in nature, from which id and ego differentiate, we assume undifferentiated libidinal-aggressive processes that bifurcate into what we can eventually distinguish as instinctual-affective life and cognitive functions. In such bifurcation the original global functioning, although dominated and overshadowed by specialized modes

of functioning, remains preserved: libidinal-aggressive elements remain ingredients of perception and memory, considered as ego functions, and constitute the unconscious motivational aspect of the latter. On the other hand, cognitive aspects remain implicit in affective life, being from the beginning undifferentiated aspects of instinctual processes.

(3) I think that the now commonly accepted definition of psychic structures as simply different groups of mental functions is not tenable. Take the ego as example: the ego is not defined as a structure by having functions such as memory, perception, reality testing, etc., but by its being a coherent organization on a certain level of mental functioning. It is its *mode of functioning,* which is due to its particular differentiation and integration of mental activities and "percepts," that makes us speak of it as a psychic structure distinct from the other structures. In general, the character of being a structure is not determined by the fact that certain components are simply grouped together, whether these components are functions or material parts, but by the interrelations of the components as dominated by the organization of the whole, by the particular principles of arrangement and mutual relatedness of its component elements. We approach a psychoanalytic understanding of the structuredness or organization of a structure such as the ego or superego by understanding how it has come about, that is, in terms of its genesis— granted that later factors may, and normally do, greatly modify and make more complex its organization and functioning. This is surely one of the reasons why we concern ourselves so much with early development—not only in order to understand children, but adults as well. I am not speaking in favor of reductionism. There is a vast difference between, on the one hand, deriving something from its origins and antecedents, thus reconstructing its structure and functioning, and, on the other hand, reducing some extant structure to its original rudiments, as though no development had taken place. Without focusing on such reconstruction, we will never understand the unconscious organization and aspects of the human mind, or how where id was, ego may come into being.

It is quite likely that the notion of psychic structures being defined by their functions is due, at least in part, to confusion between the concepts of functioning, function, and process. We speak of a psychic structure as a functioning unit that can be said to be extant only inasmuch as it functions, unlike a material structure such as a building, which, if abandoned, has no function while remaining that material structure. It is one thing to say that psychic structures can be perceived or conceived as structures only insofar as they function, that they each are differently organized modalities of psychic activity or functioning. It is quite another thing to maintain that they each are clusters of specified mental functions.

Regarding process: it is true that we recognize immediately, in contrast to material structures, the process-nature of psychic structures. Their structuredness consists in particularly organized activity-patterns, and not in arrangements of component elements that would have the nature of material particles of some kind. Apparently the definition of psychic structures as groups of *functions* has to do with our direct awareness of the process-character of psychic structures. However, while functions spell activity and process, function and process are concepts with different meanings. That functions manifest themselves in activities, have process-character, and that psychic structures are process-structures *par excellence*, does not mean that psychic structures are groups of mental functions. Different psychic structures are characterized by different ways of *functioning;* they perform mental functions in differently organized process-patterns and configurations, rather than different mental functions. Sphincter morality (Ferenczi), for example, shows how what we tend to single out as superego function operates (functions) on a primitive level of mentation, that is, on a level of mentation earlier than and different from superego organization and its particular mental process-structure.

If id, ego, and superego have their origins in interactions with environment that are internalized, interactions transposed to a new arena, thus becoming intrapsychic interactions, then psychic-structure formation and individuation are dependent on *object relations.* The separateness of subject and object—I am not speaking of the objective separateness of two biological organisms—becomes established by way of internalization and externalization processes in which both infant and mother participate, and, later, the child and its broadening human environment. Disturbances of internalizing and externalizing processes, caused by deficiencies—for whatever reasons—in the vicissitudes of attunement between child and human environment, spell disturbance of individuation, of psychic-structure formation. Mahler's clinical research work furnishes many examples of such disturbances due to disharmonies between child and mother both in the early symbiotic phase and in the separation-individuation subphases.

Individuation, the organization of instincts, of id, ego, and super-ego, I have said, is dependent on object relations. The term *object relations* is by tradition used in a loose and rather imprecise way in psychoanalysis. It comprises the relations between child and adult— and the human environment, regardless of the level of psychic development on which these relations occur. Psychoanalytic theory makes the important distinctions between object choice and identi-fication and between object cathexis and narcissistic cathexis. If we keep these distinctions in mind, and if we consider more closely the concepts ego (self, subject) and object, it becomes apparent that not all relations between child or adult and human environment are relations between a subject and an object. We have learned from psychoanalytic child observation and from the so-called narcissistic personality disorders that what for an observer is an object related to a subject, may be, for the infant or narcissistic patient, an aspect or part of himself or unspecified as to inside or outside, subject or object.

Let me give a brief clinical illustration. Some years ago I had a patient in his middle twenties in analysis who suffered from a narcissistic character disorder with depressive and hysterical fea-tures. We had established a fragile rapport consisting mainly in a volatile, easily disrupted empathic bond, with subtle indications of a powerfully demanding attitude on the patient's part, reminiscent of the nonverbal demanding quality of a small child's ties to his mother. Some of the patient's precarious object relations in current life had begun to come under our scrutiny. Over one weekend I had a slight accident which made it necessary to wear my left arm in a sling, but which did not interfere, as far as I was aware, with attending to my work and my patients; I was not in pain. On the following Monday I saw all my patients. With the patient under discussion there imme-diately occurred a palpable disruption of our rapport. I briefly explained to him the reason for the sling. He was able to tell me, in vague language, that he experienced me as not being there and that he himself felt lifeless, without feelings or thoughts. Then he lapsed into silence. After some reflection I told the patient that I thought what he experienced must be like the experience of a small boy when his mother, of whom he is in need, is sick and appears unavailable; for him she then no longer exists, and together with this the boy then no longer feels alive, or dissolves. This interpretation led to gradual reestablishment of contact and of his functioning again.

In her book *On Human Symbiosis and the Vicissitudes of Individuation* Mahler writes (1968, p. 220): "The danger situation in the symbiotic phase is loss of the symbiotic object, which amounts, at that stage, to loss of an integral part of the ego itself, and thus constitutes a threat of self-annihilation." Assuming the essential correctness of my interpretation, one may formulate the state of affairs, using Mahler's terms, as follows: the therapist, in this context a symbiotic object for the patient, is suddenly lost, having become a strange, unattached figure; and this coincides with, or is the same as, loss of self or annihilation. With the loss of the symbiotic object "an integral part of the ego itself" is lost. To put it in somewhat different terms, ego and object are not sufficiently differentiated, on the then dominant level of the patient's mentation, for him to experience a difference between ego and object. The patient seemed not to be bereft or anxious, but deadened. I should prefer to conceptualize this, not as a loss of symbiotic object and integral ego-part, but as a disintegration of nondifferentiated ego-object. As nondifferentiated, ego or self (I use these terms here interchangeably) and object are, so to speak, consubstantial. Disintegration of the meaningful organization of the object *is* disintegration of the ego and vice versa, insofar as they are identical in experience. This unitary organization or structure (the so-called self-object, Kohut 1971), in the developmental phase Mahler calls the symbiotic phase, is brought about and maintained by the conjoint organizing activities of mother and infant. The more this conjoint activity is dependent on the mother's contribution, that is, the more the infant is still at the mercy of his mother's organizing psychic activity for his own to be viable, the less is there differentiation of ego from object as different structures. If for some reason, as in the case of my patient, the object falls apart as a meaning-giving and meaningful agent, then the patient's ego disintegrates because the symbiotic object and the ego are not experienced as separate or separable. My interpretation, my organizing meaning-giving activity, presumably reactivated the patient's organizing potential so that we could reconstitute the self-object as a live psychic structure. Such an organization, undifferentiated as to id-ego and ego-object, could not be called an intrapsychic structure; internality and externality are disestablished as distinguishable worlds. On the higher level of superego formation we

observe similar unitary structures where internal and external authority and constraints are not yet or no longer differentiated sufficiently to speak of superego as an internal structure. Such
intermediate constraints, as we can see in children as well as in many
adults, are not truly intrapsychic, but are experienced by the persons
involved as taking shape and having force *between* them. They are
neither internal nor external; and this is so despite the fact that an
internal world, an intrapsychic id and ego of significant consolidation is established.

In psychoanalytic research on early child development and during
therapeutic analysis, especially with patients suffering from narcissistic disorders, we are able to observe the organization and
dedifferentiation of psychic structure and object relations as ongoing
processes. We can see that object relations and intrapsychic structure
formation and their maintenance are intimately interrelated. And
further, that there are psychic process-structures which are not
intrapsychic but in an intermediate region, as it were, analogous to
Winnicott's transitional phenomena.

As mentioned before, in using the terms "object relations," "ego,"
"object," as applied to interactional processes within the infant-
mother matrix and to identificatory interactions at later stages, we
speak from a standpoint that is incongruous with the level of mental
organization we wish to understand and describe. The word, object,
categorizes the human environment in terms of the adult's advanced
and dominant "objective" level of mentation, a level different from
that form of mentation we attempt to comprehend in psychoanalysis
when we investigate archaic mental processes. It may be permissible
to speak of object relations in reference to preobjective and identificatory interactions if we keep this incongruity in mind, if we
remember that we deal here with phases of mental development in
which subject and object are not, or not sufficiently, differentiated.
Thus we are dealing with something other than two different organizations that could be said to be in a relationship to each other.
Relationship, in contrast to sameness, identity, or "symbiotic fusion,"
implies difference, presupposes differentiation.

I provisionally defined individuation as that group of processes by
which the separateness of subject and object becomes established.
Obviously, this does not mean that prior to these processes ego and
object were not separate but together like two entities in one con-
tainer or two ideas in the same mind; or that they were so close

together that we were not aware of their separateness. It means, instead, that in beginning stages there was, as far as the mentation of the infant is concerned—and it is that mentation we want to understand—only one global structure, one fleeting and very perishable mental entity that was neither ego nor object, neither a self nor another. My patient, at the time of the episode I described, because of the intensity of the transference, at least momentarily functioned on a comparable level of mentation. For the archaic layers of the mind there is no separation experience leading to differentiation, separateness, or "separation anxiety"; but, as Mahler expresses it, there is danger of annihilation, of disruption of functioning, when there is disruption of the symbiotic unity. On the other hand, during periods of physical separation of infant and mother, if they are not unduly prolonged (if the infant is in a state of satisfaction), the global organization, which is neither ego nor object, is preserved. I venture to suggest that the "good enough" mother, during certain periods or moments in early motherhood, functions on a similar level of mentation. I believe that Winnicott's understanding of early development, in which he includes the mother's archaic experience-level—activated by pregnancy and early motherhood—as an integral component, is in essential agreement with such a view. We also begin to realize that the therapist, in order to work analytically with patients with narcissistic disorders, must rely on his ability to reactivate such archaic levels of mental functioning within himself, at given moments during treatment. In other words, he needs the flexibility or mental agility to suspend, when required, his ego boundaries for a long enough period if he is to understand the patient's experience and then interpret it to him. His interpretation, if adequately attuned, raises the experience to a higher level of mental organization, a level where we can more properly speak of object relations.

If we use the term "object relations" for any and all psychic interactions of objectively distinguishable human beings, regardless of whether or not instincts and ego are differentiated from object, then the primary datum for a genetic, psychoanalytic psychology would be object relations. This relatedness is the psychic matrix out of which intrapsychic instincts and ego, and extrapsychic object, differentiate.

I shall conclude my remarks with some comments on the "widening scope of psychoanalysis." The scope of psychoanalytic investigation and treatment was, during the earlier phase of its development, determined by those aspects of the mental life of patients that could in essence be derived from the oedipal stage at which ego and (libidinal) object are sufficiently differentiated. Already with the tracing of libido development in terms of oral, anal, phallic, and genital stages the picture began to change. But it was the investigation of psychosis, of the archaic mentality of young children, of "savages," and of group psychology (where individuation regresses) that initiated an understanding of instinctual-cognitive processes on different levels of mentation. The comprehensive title for such investigations became: analysis of the ego, that is, of the graded levels of more or less coherent organization. Ego, at that point, was the title for the totality of these levels *considered as a comprehensive organization.* Freud at times spoke, in reference to this ego, as the *Gesamt-Ich,* "the ego as a whole" (1921, p. 130), when he wanted to distinguish it from the ego considered as counterpart to id and superego. Organization here means organizing activity as much as the totality resulting from such activity.

Analysis of the ego in this sense means: to investigate how such an encompassing and increasingly coherent organization comes into being; what are its antecedents and ingredients? What are the processes that bring about and determine this organization? It became apparent (1) that a coherent organization of some solidity was already present by the time the object relations forming the oedipus complex and, with that, the starting point for neurotic conflict could be discerned. (2) What became known as ego defects or deficiencies and may lead to borderline and psychotic phenomena could not be understood *on the basis* of the oedipal conflict. They antedate and are apt to distort *the very development* of the oedipal stage and its object relations. The organizing activities leading up to the oedipal stage, themselves, and their disturbances, became the subject of analytic investigation and, if feasible, of therapeutic repetition and reconstruction in the transference.

One can speak, following Kohut (1971), of narcissistic *transference*—or self-object transference (Kohut 1977)—insofar as there is a relatedness, a rapport between patient and analyst which is mainly based on an archaic form of relatedness, close to or reproducing "symbiosis," and which is repeated in or transferred to the analytic situation. There is transfer of the archaic relatedness, with its blurring or lack of ego boundaries, from the preoedipal prototypes to given current figures and specifically to the analyst. By virtue of the

undifferentiated nature of this transference such patients have difficulty not only in distinguishing between themselves and the analyst
but also between infantile and current figures, between infantile or
archaic and current, more advanced levels of relatedness: not only
the differentiation of internal and external, but also that of past and
present is deficient. For patients with predominantly oedipal unresolved conflicts, ego and object as well as temporal modes are
sufficiently distinguishable.

I fail to see that the attempts at therapeutic reconstruction and
interpretation of these far more archaic phases and levels of mental
life, when working with more deeply disturbed patients, is any less
psychoanalytic than work with the classical neuroses. It only seems
that way because levels of relatedness, involving both patient and
analyst, come into play that are far less familiar to most of us than
oedipal and postoedipal levels. And furthermore, verbal interpretation itself, the mainstay of psychoanalytic intervention, takes on
connotations and aspects of meaningfulness—of which we as analysts need to be aware—that derive from or hark back more directly
to that "magical" power and significance of words which plays a
predominant role in the preverbal and early verbal period of life and
the resonance and responses of the young child to parental verbal
material.[1]

No one who has tried such work can doubt that a great deal about
early and archaic mentation can be learned from it. Only further
work with patients can help us answer the question of its therapeutic
value in terms of lasting change. Temporary changes undoubtedly
occur with adult patients of the type under discussion. But it is not
clear to me whether, given the early onset of the disturbances, and in
view of the primitive nature of their object relations, sufficient true
internal structure formation is likely, or whether such patients periodically will require equivalents of that "refueling" Mahler, Pine,
and Bergman (1975), following Furer, describe in the practicing
subphase of individuation.

References

Freud, S. (1915). Instincts and their vicissitudes. *Standard Edition* 14:117-140.
——— (1921). Group psychology and the analysis of the ego. *Standard Edition* 18:69-143.

1. Some of the preceding formulations grew out of personal communications
between Calvin Settlage and myself.

Kohut, H. (1971). *The Analysis of the Self*. New York: International Universities Press.

——— (1977). *The Restoration of the Self*. New York: International Universities Press.

Loewald, H. W. (1962). Internalization, separation, mourning, and the superego. *Psychoanalytic Quarterly* 31:483-504.

Mahler, M., (1968). *On Human Symbiosis and the Vicissitudes of Individuation*. In collaboration with M. Furer. New York: International Universities Press.

Mahler, M. S., Pine, F., and Bergman, A. (1975). *The Psychological Birth of the Human Infant*. New York: Basic Books.

5

The Psychoanalytic Understanding of Narcissistic and Borderline Personality Disorders: Advances in Developmental Theory

Calvin F. Settlage, M.D.

Psychoanalyst theoreticians—notably Greenacre (1960, 1967, 1971), Jacobson (1964), Kernberg (1966, 1974, 1975), Kohut (1971), and Mahler (1968) Mahler, Pine, and Bergman (1975)—have over the past decade provided us with a still expanding theory of earliest psychic development which is enabling an understanding of the psychopathology of the more severe psychologic disorders hitherto not possible. Witness Blum's (1974) reexamination and reformulation of Freud's case of the Wolf Man as being, in today's terms, not an infantile neurosis but a borderline condition with episodes of infantile psychosis. Drawing on Mahler's separation-individuation theory (Mahler 1971), Blum emphasizes the possibly greater impact of a serious and extended malaria on the patient at eighteen months of age than of the primal scene experience, as it was reconstructed during his analysis with Freud as an adult. Blum postulates that, in addition to parental psychopathology, the malarial infection, because of its disruption of the separation-individuation process during the rapprochement subphase, would have led to disturbance in the then rapidly developing ego functions having to do with the estab-

Reprinted from *Journal of the American Psychoanalytic Association* 25 (4):805-833 by permission of International Universities Press, Inc. Copyright © 1977 by the American Psychoanalytic Association.

lishment of the basic mood and the related capacity for trust or distrust, and with language and secondary process (pp. 733-734). Blum relates the Wolf Man's ego disturbance, narcissistic disorder, and vulnerability to severe regression to the infantile developmental disruption.

Analysts are thus engaged in a new effort at defining the pathogenesis, the pathologic formations, and the means of treatment of narcissistic, borderline, and psychotic disorders. The potential for such definition rests upon the precise correlation of traumatic experience during the first years of life with the newly delineated phases of *primary psychic development* and the specific emerging developmental attainments these comprehend: self-object differentiation; core identity and the sense of self; autonomous and experientially shaped basic ego functions; early defensive and adaptive mechanisms and modes; initial control and modulation of drive and affect expressions; libidinal object constancy; initial capacity for one-to-one relationship.

Recent advances in psychoanalytic knowledge have been derived, in the main, from work by psychoanalysts in three areas. The widening scope of psychoanalysis in its clinical application accounts for two of these, namely, an ever-increasing experience in the analytic treatment of narcissistic and borderline personality disorders in adults and children, and a similarly expanding experience in the analytic treatment of very young children, under the age of 3 years. In both instances, the resulting theoretical formulations about early psychic development are based primarily upon the process of reconstruction. Even the psychologically disturbed 2- or 3-year-old has a psychogenetic past. In the analytic treatment of a young child, however, one has a much closer view of the beginnings of formation of psychic structure and function, of the innate and experiential developmental factors and influences, normative and traumatic, that shape personality in healthy or pathologic directions. The third area of work is that of direct observational studies of the development of children during the first three years of life, work such as Mahler's, which I shall be citing in the body of this paper.

THE RECONSTRUCTIVE AND THE DIRECT
OBSERVATIONAL APPROACHES

Each of the mentioned approaches, the reconstructive and the direct observational, has its merits and its limitations. The reconstructive or retrospective view from the analytic situation provides an understanding of the vicissitudes of development over time and of the eventual outcome of the impact of traumatic experience. This understanding cannot be equalled through attempting to predict the future results of currently known trauma in the developing child. On the other hand, the reconstructive formulation of the precise nature and timing of trauma and of the details of the normal developmental progression is, although impressive, unable to approximate these delineations as gained *in statu nascendi* from direct observation. It seems evident that the approaches are complementary to rather than in conflict with each other, and that both of them are valuable and essential to a full psychoanalytic understanding. Indeed, Freud observed as much in 1905: "Psychoanalytic investigation, reaching back into childhood from a later time, and contemporary observation of children combine to indicate to us still other regularly active sources of sexual excitation. The direct observation of children has the disadvantage of working upon data which are easily misunderstandable; psycho-analysis is made difficult by the fact that it can only reach its data, as well as its conclusions, after long detours. But by co-operation the two methods can attain a satisfactory degree of certainty in their findings" (p. 201). And Ernst Kris (1950) stated that the data furnished by direct observation have attained the dignity of an analytic study proper and become increasingly capable of integration with material derived from reconstruction in the analysis of adults and children.

Yet, the psychoanalytic legitimacy of direct observational studies of development has, in contradiction of these views, been held in question. Although later in agreement with Kris, Anna Freud (1958) at first felt that such work would be useful merely in proving or disproving the correctness of analytic reconstructions, but would not break new ground. Currently, and bearing on the topic under consideration, Kohut (1971) has expressed himself on this issue in a comparison of his and Mahler's conceptual frameworks. He characterizes his formulations as being in conformance with psychoanalytic metapsychology, requiring the empathic reconstruction of childhood experiences through their revival in the transference. He sees Mahler's formulations as belonging to the realm of "psychoanalytic interactionalism," having their basis in the sociobiologic framework of the child in interaction with the environment. "Mahler observes the behavior of small children; I reconstruct their inner life on the basis of transference reactivations" (p. 219).

Central to Kohut's comparison is the premise that child observation cannot lead to the formulation of metapsychological theory
because it does not involve empathy with the introspection of the
child and it does not give access to the psychic organization of the
child. Kohut's delineation of direct observational studies of young
children as being in the realm of sociobiologic psychoanalytic interactionalism and the resulting premise do not, though, do justice to
such studies as they are conducted by analysts. Although the position
of the analyst observer in the developmental observational situation
is not the same as in the analytic situation and the data are also in
some ways different, the observing instrument (analyzing instrument), the conceptual frames of reference regarding the nature of
the human psyche, and the modes of thought and understanding—in
short, the knowledge, orientation, and skills of the analyst, including
the capacity of the psychoanalyst researcher for introspective empathy with the observed child and parent—remain the same. On these
grounds, Mahler's conceptualization of the intrapsychic *process of
separation-individuation,* as distinguished from her description of
overtly observable *separation-individuation behavior,* is both psychoanalytic and metapsychological.

A statement by Kernberg comparing his and Kohut's conceptualizations provides the basis for a further comment on the issue of
reconstruction versus direct observation. Kernberg stresses that the
concept *quality of object relations* should be used to refer to the
quality of intrapsychic object relations, that is, to the depth of the
patient's internal relations with others, rather than to the extent of his
involvement in social interactions. He suggests that this clarification
may be particularly relevant in discussing Kohut's work because
Kohut tends to use the term *object relations* in its behavioral rather
than intrapsychic sense (Kernberg 1975, p. 308). Kernberg thus
perceives Kohut to be using the term *object relations* in an interactional behavioral sense and, by implication, to be in this instance
outside the traditional observing position of the analyst—the very
position in which Kohut places himself vis-à-vis Mahler. Perhaps the
seeming inconsistency is due to the fact that the analyst, figuratively,
occupies both of the described positions, both inside and outside the
psychic organization of the observed individual.

I cite Kernberg's definition because it seems to reflect the commonly held view that thinking in behavioral terms is antithetical to
and mutually exclusive with thinking in intrapsychic terms and is

therefore inimical to psychoanalysis. Because the findings of direct observational studies rest in part on behavioral data, they tend to be bracketed by the same, I believe, erroneous view. It is evident that intrapsychic object relations develop and become internalized as a result of experience with external objects, whether during childhood development or during the course of analytic treatment. To be interested in the nature of the infantile relationship and interaction with the external love object, and to study the developmental process of internalization is not to be disinterested in or fail to appreciate the importance of the psychoanalytic focus on the intrapsychic end result.

Invaluable as it is, the genetic, reconstructive approach has limitations with regard to those aspects of development, particularly infantile development, that are subsequently condensed, telescoped, integrated, synthesized, or transformed so as to be difficult to perceive in the analysis of the older child or adult. The lack of capacity during the preverbal and preoedipal phases for conscious memory and full verbal symbolization tends to preclude the clear representation of earliest psychic experience in the analytic situation, thus seriously handicapping reconstruction of those phases. Psychoanalytically based empathic observation of interpersonal behavior during this developmental period, along with a study of its determinants, is thus essential to a complete and accurate psychoanalytic understanding of the initial development of object relations and of psychic structure, and to the process of reconstruction in the treatment of disorders whose psychopathology involves these areas of development.

THEORETICAL CONSIDERATIONS

The distinction between narcissistic and borderline disorders in terms of differences in their specific determinants and psychopathologies has not yet been adequately drawn. As one possibility, these differences may prove to be due to a difference in the timing of traumatic experience in the developmental sequence. The generally held clinical impression that borderline disorders are more severe than narcissistic disorders may be accounted for by a developmentally earlier, and therefore more devastating, trauma in the borderline disorder. A second possibility is that the difference between these two conditions will be explained by the degree of traumatic impact and the extremity of defensive response. And thirdly, the difference may come to be understood in terms of the area of personality involved in developmental arrest and pathologic formation, for example, involvement of the sense of self and identity as these can be distinguished from ego capacities and functions per se.

In any case, the potential for defining the psychopathology of these severe disorders would appear to rest, as was expressed earlier, upon the precise correlation of psychic trauma with the newly delineated phases and emerging developmental attainments of primary psychic development. My own evolving understanding of the genesis of narcissistic and borderline disorders stems from the experience of concurrently analyzing adults, adolescents, and young children. I have found that the comparison of psychopathology as fully formed in the adult, as temporarily "exploded" apart in the adolescent, and as in the process of formation in the preoedipal and oedipal child becomes much more meaningful when viewed from the perspective of emerging developmental theory.

I have found Mahler's separation-individuation theory to be especially helpful in understanding the disorders under consideration. I will therefore set forth the developmental issues and attainments of the rapprochement subphase preparatory to demonstrating their clinical pertinence. I choose to focus on but one contribution from among the many that constitute the psychoanalytic view of early psychic development because Mahler's formulations, in addition to their explanatory power, offer a detailed conceptualization of the early developmental progression. They are also, in support of my earlier arguments, derived largely from direct observational studies of normal, preoedipal children.

The Rapprochement Subphase[1]

The rapprochement subphase, which spans the period from about 14-16 to 22-24 months of age, is the third of four subphases in the separation-individuation process. It is preceded by the differentiation and practicing phases, and followed by the phase termed *on the way to object constancy*.

1. Some of the material presented here is excerpted and adapted from an earlier paper on separation-individuation theory (Settlage 1974a).

The relative lack of separation anxiety and obliviousness to the mother's presence characteristic of the practicing phase is, in the rapprochement phase, replaced by an acutely heightened separation anxiety and active approaches to the mother, along with a seemingly constant concern with her whereabouts. Advancing cognitive development has made the toddler acutely aware of his physical separateness from his mother. This awareness, when combined with his now practiced ability to move away from his mother, introduces the double-edged threat of losing the mother or being lost from her.

In addition, as the excitement attendant to locomotion and the assumption of upright posture wanes, the toddler's collisions with the unyielding and hurtful world of physical reality and with the demands of socialization in the form of parental discipline have made him uncomfortably aware both of his vulnerability and relative helplessness and his dependency on the big and powerful adult. Metaphorically speaking, he begins to realize that it is not he, the fly on the side of the chariot wheel, that so powerfully raises the huge following cloud of dust, but the chariot wheel itself. His developmentally normal sense of omnipotence, implicit in the dual oneness of the symbiotic phase, is thus threatened and necessarily deflated.

The toddler's situation is complicated further by his anger and rage toward the parent who, as he experiences it, fails to protect him from physical hurt, frustrates his hitherto mostly unfrustrated wants, and makes new demands on him, as in saying "No" and in toilet training. The anger of the child toward the very object he loves, whom he now realizes he desperately needs, only enhances separation concerns and the threat of loss.

The described plight of the child accounts, then, for a heightened separation anxiety and constitutes, when highly charged, what Mahler (1972; see chapter 1, this volume.) has termed the *rapprochement crisis*. "The junior toddler gradually realizes that his love objects (his parents) are separate individuals with their own individual interests. He must gradually and painfully give up his delusion of his own grandeur, often through dramatic fights with mother, less so it seemed to us, with father. This is a crossroad that we have termed the 'rapprochement crisis'" (p. 495).

In Mahler's view, adequate resolution of the issues of this subphase enables the child to move firmly toward the attainment of object constancy. Failure to resolve these issues can, depending upon the degree of failure, lead either to the establishment of a nidus of

intrapsychic conflict predisposing to neurosis, or to faulty or incomplete structural development predisposing to narcissistic or
borderline disorders (1972, pp. 494, 504).

Crucial to the healthy resolution of the developmental issues of the
rapprochement subphase is the continued libidinal availability of the
mother. The child's sense of omnipotence and control associated
with the symbiotic phase, rather than being deflated precipitously
and overwhelmingly, needs to be gradually replaced by belief in and
enjoyment of his own rapidly developing ego capacities, by a
developing sense of autonomy. Hence, the child's great emotional
investment in eliciting the mother's interest, in sharing things with
her, and in her power. He needs her affirmation of him in his
changing and expanding sense of self and identity, her validation of
his continuing importance to her, of his developing skills and abilities, of his urges and feelings and their acceptability and man-
ageability, and of the continuity of his old and new self in her eyes. A
too sudden deflation of his sense of omnipotence and control tends to
evoke the grandiose view of the self and idealization of the omnipotent parent, the narcissistic defenses described by both Kohut (1971)
and Mahler (1971).

It is especially important that the mother continue to be empathically tolerant of the child's behavior and libidinally available to
him in the face of apparent regression from the independent behavior of the practicing subphase to the clinging behavior of the
rapprochement subphase, as well as in the face of the often intense
ambivalence and stubborn defiance that result from the anger and
rage mobilized by disciplinary frustration and its intrusion on autonomy. A supportive maternal response affirms the previously developed sense of trust and helps the child amalgamate libidinal and
aggressive urges toward the love object in the attainment of libidinal
object constancy. At the same time, it is essential that the mother
recognize and accept the child's developmental need to become
increasingly separate and independent. Despite his clinging behavior and wish for reassurance, the child can no longer be a part of
the mother, subservient to her wishes and predilections. The mother
must let the child individuate. In this connection, Mahler (1972)
makes the important observation that the father, as a familiar but
different love object, serves to help the child resist the powerful
attraction to the symbiotic partner in the move toward increasing
autonomy.

Focusing more pointedly on the intrapsychic processes, the rapprochement subphase is concerned largely with initial internalization and beginning structure formation, these under the circumstance of awareness of separateness and its implications and in the face of the anxiety it engenders. The first need is reaffirmation, through interaction with the mother, of the precognitive or preverbal sense of core identity. Also, as the child proceeds through this subphase, an increasing differentiation of self- and object representations normally takes place. The originally comingled, primary narcissistic cathexes of the "self" and the mother in the symbiotic dual unity is sorted out and transformed into secondary narcissistic self- and object cathexis. As these differentiations take place, the sense of well-being characteristic of the preverbal period becomes, in effect, the nucleus for the sense of self-esteem. As is true of his sense of identity, the child's self-esteem is also tied to his mother's continued acceptance and approval of him. As anger and aggression come to the fore, the mother's tolerance and appropriately dosed assistance in managing the child's impulses and hostility is essential to the cathexis of self- and object representations with neutralized energy.

The successful transition of the rapprochement subphase is crucial to the ultimate attainment of libidinal object constancy. In defining object constancy, it is necessary to distinguish object constancy as a psychoanalytic concept from Piaget's concept of object permanency. According to Piaget (1954), the child acquires the concept that an object is permanent, even when out of sight, through four successive stages spanning from about 9 to 20 months of age (pp. 13-96). Piaget's concept of object permanence is derived from study of the child's relationship to inanimate objects and is framed in purely intellectual cognitive terms. The psychoanalytic concept of object constancy includes, in addition to the permanence of cognitive representation, the permanence of the intrapsychic representation of the human love object in libidinal and affective terms. The internalized representation of the love object, initially the mother, continues to be libidinally cathected in the face of both absence of the object and anger toward the object. The intrapsychic representation of the love object includes images of the object as both loving and disapproving and as both loved and hated, as good and bad. Although ambivalently regarded, the object representation persists.

Mahler, Pine, and Bergman (1975, p. 111) postulate, therefore, that object constancy has its libidinal and affective beginnings in infancy in the myriad of experiences with the mother that lead to the establishment of the precognitive sense of basic trust. On the other hand, it is not attained until about 36 months of age or later, more than a year after the establishment of object permanence in Piaget's sense. As a matter of fact, Mahler, in agreement with Hartmann, feels that the attainment of object constancy is not absolute but relative—a degree of vulnerability and a need for reaffirmation, albeit by new love objects, continuing throughout the life cycle (Mahler, Pine, and Bergman 1975, p. 112).

It is during the rapprochement subphase that the earlier and developmentally normal tendency to avoid anxiety by separating the good from the bad representations of the love object—the prototype of the defense of splitting—is replaced by repression. In Mahler's view, which is in agreement with that of Kernberg (1966, pp. 247-249; 1975, pp. 25-30), splitting as a means of dealing with the conflicted and incompatible affects of love and anger toward the love object, is a transitory defense which yields later to the defense of repression. Mahler postulates that the defense of splitting drops out toward the end of the second year of life when the bulk of the infantile hostility toward the parent is submerged by repression, with only a normal degree of ambivalence remaining operative thereafter (Mahler, Pine, and Bergman 1975, p. 211).

Mahler (1966) places another important developmental issue within the rapprochement subphase. She believes that the described predicament of the child results in the establishment of a basic depressive response or mood as a normal part of the human condition: "the collapse of the child's belief in his own omnipotence, with his uncertainty about the emotional availability of the parents, creates the so-called 'hostile dependency' upon and ambivalence toward the parents. This ambivalence seems to call for the early pathological defense mechanisms of splitting the good and bad mother images and of turning aggression against the self; these result in a feeling of helplessness, which, as Bibring (1953) has emphasized, creates the basic depressive affect" (p. 162). Mahler understands the most favorable resolution of this depressive response as probably entailing grief and sadness as part of a mourning of the loss of the "good," need-satisfying symbiotic mother (p. 163).

In summary, the main intrapsychic, phase-specific developmental tasks of the rapprochement subphase, which also constitute the areas of vulnerability in the rapprochement crisis, are: (1) mastery of the cognitively intensified separation anxiety; (2) affirmation of the sense of basic trust; (3) gradual deflation and relinquishment of the sense of omnipotence experienced in the symbiotic dual unity with the mother; (4) gradual compensation for the deflated sense of omnipotence through development of the child's burgeoning ego capacities and sense of autonomy; (5) a firming up of the core sense of self; (6) establishment of a sense of capability for ego control and modulation of strong libidinal and aggressive urges and affects (e.g., infantile rage); (7) healing the developmentally normal tendency to maintain the relation with the love object by splitting it into a "good" and a "bad" object, thus also healing the corresponding intrapsychic split; and (8) supplanting the splitting defense with repression as the later defensive means of curbing unacceptable affects and impulses toward the love objects.

CLINICAL CONSIDERATIONS

My focus here is narrowed to questions and issues encountered in the treatment of narcissistic personality disorders. I shall attempt to demonstrate the mainly rapprochement-subphase origin of clinical phenomena extrapolated from the analytic treatments of a preoedipal child and an adolescent. Narcissistic disorders are, in my clinical experience, more severe than neurotic but less severe than borderline disorders. Individuals with narcissistic disorders do not generally suffer from severe ego defects in thought processes, in reality testing and reality judgment, or in delineation of body-ego boundaries and of self from other. And they are usually capable of functioning quite well in the area of work responsibilities. Yet they have major difficulty in regulating affects and self-esteem, in maintaining a cohesive sense of self, and in their capacity for intimacy in full object relations. What might account for this in psychogenetic terms?

The lack of ego deficit and the generally good functional capacity suggest that the mother-infant relation had a favorable beginning. The first year of life—in Mahler's terms, the normal autistic and symbiotic phases and the subphases of differentiation and practicing—would therefore have been reasonably satisfactory, allowing for adequate primary ego development and adequate self-object differentiation. Difficulty arising thereafter during the rapproche-

ment subphase could account, though, for the later clinically observable deficit in self-esteem and sense of self, and the longing for but
fear of intimacy in object relations. It has been noted, both clinically
and in direct observational studies, that some mothers can quite
capably minister to the needs of the infant when he is totally
dependent and appreciatively responsive, but have difficulty in
meeting the developmental needs of the toddler with his now
individuating assertive personality and his resistance to control and
discipline. A mother with this kind of problem can, defensively,
temporarily withdraw emotional support from the discipline-
protesting child, abandoning him effectively to his already intense
impulses and affects. Or she can respond, because of her own poorly
modulated anxiety, with abrupt, unempathic, and excessively strong
and frighteningly overwhelming expressions of anger and assertions
of control over the child's behavior. In either case, the mother's not
being libidinally and helpfully available to the child poses the threat
of intrapsychic loss (Mahler 1968, pp. 225-226), potentially engender-
ing a severe rapprochement crisis.

Two Case Illustrations

An excerpt from the treatment of a 3-year-old girl offers a speculative illustration of this possible genetic situation. In addition to her
primary presenting symptom of severe chronic constipation, this
child suffered from intense separation anxiety, a morbid fear of
being injured, and an associated lack of normal initiative and aggressiveness. Her mother had a long-standing severe separation
problem of her own and a very low tolerance for angry or aggressive
displays.

A major transference issue in the analysis represented failure in the
separation-individuation process, with resulting tenuous libidinal
object constancy and vulnerability to severe separation anxiety. The
related theme in my little patient's play was concerned with a stuffed
dog who was repeatedly being lost and found because the owner
carelessly dropped the leash, the transference role assigned to the
analyst. In one particular session, well into the treatment, the child
became increasingly excited as she played out her story. Suddenly
and impulsively, she had the dog, which here represented her angry
urges, bite an obnoxiously bossy figure in the play. She abruptly
dropped the evolving story and began a new story, which ended

shortly in the death and burial under a pile of wooden blocks of the play figure that had, from the beginning of the treatment, represented the child patient. At the end of this session, as the mother was speaking to the analyst affirming the next appointment, the patient made a gesture of biting herself on the wrist. In a subsequent exploration with the mother of the child's biting behavior, she recalled a hitherto unreported but significant fact. Between 9 and 24 months of age, the child had quite regularly resorted to biting herself on the wrist in response to the mother's slapping her lightly but angrily on the bottom to get her to hold still during diapering.

This child had thus begun at that early age to curb the expression of her angry urges and affects by directing them toward herself rather than her mother because she was afraid of jeopardizing her relation with her mother. Her self-imposed restraint was by age 3 well supported defensively and on the way to becoming part of personality structure. In the therapeutic atmosphere of the analytic situation, she allowed her excitement and her aggressive feelings to get out of hand, and the biting occurred. Her 3-year-old view of the consequence is revealed in the immediately ensuing death of her symbolically represented self. Were such a failure in modulated self-regulation of urges and affects to persist, it would, to my mind, make for an excessive and eventually characterologic continued dependence on the environment for regulation. This would in turn interfere with the development of the child's capacity for regulation of self-esteem and for one-to-one relations as an increasingly psychologically independent being. The intrapsychically blocked aggression would furthermore make for problems in establishing and monitoring close and intimate relationships. This little patient might thus have been on the way to a narcissistic personality disorder.

A genetic-dynamic configuration similar to that of the 3-year-old patient was discernible in an 18-year-old college dropout. This late adolescent girl was totally and intensely but unsuccessfully preoccupied with her wish to establish and maintain friendships with male and female peers, a preoccupation that precluded the effective use of her very good intelligence in academic studies. She was also engaged in intermittent angry conflict with her parents, protesting their infringement on her autonomy and independence while being psychologically still very dependent upon and therefore tied to them.

An apparently comfortable, satisfactory infancy was disrupted when the mother became pregnant with the brother to be born when the patient was 18 months old. With this second pregnancy, the mother became seriously depressed, but continued to function as housekeeper and caretaker of her child. Although the depression was overtly the consequence of repressed anger in reaction to her husband's frequent absences on business trips, it had its roots in the mother's unresolved loss experiences in her own separation-individuation phase of development.

Beginning at about 10 months of age, the patient became terribly distressed whenever the mother left her, even if only to go to an adjacent room. With the advent of crawling, and later with toddling, the patient, still upset and crying in protest, would, to the mother's great frustration, pursue her everywhere. In consequence, the play-pen was employed for physical restraint. The still distressed child was, as a result, left to cope with her strong and thereby intensified affects without external help. After several months, the distressed behavior subsided. When the brother was born, the mother's depression deepened, and the patient, now in the anal and rapprochement phases, manifested angry, demanding, obstreperous behavior, again for a few months. The mother, through her own treatment which began at that time, recognized that she had, in her depressed withdrawn state, been emotionally quite unavailable to her child, even though adequately meeting her physical needs.

The patient's development proceeded well during the oedipal and latency stages. She became in fact a model child, tractable, cooperative, seemingly social, and an excellent student in the elementary grades, fully engaged in developing her emerging skills and capacities. With the advent of puberty, however, this model child became angry, rebellious, provocative, and demanding of her parents and her teachers. Her formerly excellent school performance dropped substantially, and she maintained a marginal college entrance grade point level, not from ambition and work but because of her truly superior intelligence. Her social relationships also fell apart, and it was at this time that the described preoccupation with peer relationships had its beginning.

As could later be formulated from the data gained in treatment, the patient had, during the period between 10 and about 24 months of age, twice "solved" the problem of her helplessness and her angry feelings toward her mother by curbing her anger, as did my 3-year-old patient. She, too, had sacrificed autonomy and self-regulation to the priority need of maintaining the relation with the mother. As a result, though, she remained, through the oedipal and latency years, unduly psychologically dependent on her parents as external regulatory egos. Puberty forecast and thrust upon the patient the adolescent tasks of experiencing and managing the normally heightened sexual and aggressive urges and feelings, and of attaining true independence and autonomy for the pending move into adulthood. The development and resolution of these phase-specific issues was complicated and aggravated, however, by the unresolved rapprochement crisis and the dyadically distorted and also unresolved oedipal conflict, which were reawakened and readdressed, again unsuccessfully. The move away from home to college deprived the patient of the resented and rejected, but in fact still needed, external supportive regulation, and her intrapsychic equilibrium was sufficiently disturbed to cause a collapse in her ability to function.

In the treatment begun at age 18, it was learned that the patient initiated relationships from a position of intense inner need for emotional exchange, but with her feelings paradoxically kept out of the relationship. The position was one of vulnerable dependence on the sought object, wherein her need for love and her wishful fantasies of involvement were in conflict with her fear of her rage should her wishes be disappointed. Her attempted solution was to turn off her anger and aggression, thus counting naively on the object's being totally trustworthy. But because her aggressive affects were not available to her, her ability to monitor and judge the safety of the relationship was impaired—aggressive affects being essential to the function of signal anxiety—and also prevented her from making the kind of healthy aggressive confrontation that might straighten out the relationship. She was therefore doubly vulnerable to exploitation and hurt. When she finally allowed herself to perceive that the object was not trustworthy, she would break off the relationship in a fit of rage at the now totally bad and hated object. Then would ensue a hurtful sense of having been abandoned, a plummeting sense of self-esteem, and a state of withdrawal and depression characterized by feelings of emptiness, loneliness, and despair. She epitomized this state as one in which she had lost her sense of "center."

The described pattern, which reflects a defensive splitting, was of course expressed in and understood through the transference. The patient's anticipation of being again woefully hurt and suffering feelings of loss made her extremely cautious in the treatment, and the transference developed only slowly. Her caution and the delicacy of the treatment process were exemplified by the communicative mode evolved during the introductory, face-to-face phase of the treatment. Although not simply resistant and clearly wanting involvement, as evidence by her alert, even penetrating, observation of the analyst, she did not initiate the sessions, but remained silent and refused to speak until I spoke. Once I had spoken, she then participated verbally in the treatment.

The first step toward understanding this behavior was my later realization that I had, in meeting the patient's requirement, resorted to observing her facial and postural expressions and gestures, commenting then on her apparent state or mood. It also became evident that her nonverbal behavior, except at times of conscious or unconscious resistance, communicated how she felt. Still later, as a result of the analytic work, we understood the purpose of this way of beginning the sessions. If my opening comment was empathically correct, she then felt assured that I was still interested in helping her and that I had not changed and become a different person—that I was, in short, constant. It was then safe for her to proceed.

Although the transference ultimately developed fully and with all of the intensity of primitive, inadequately modulated affects, its doing so required the parallel development of a real, as opposed to idealized, sense of trust, this arising out of the analytic relationship and experience. Throughout the analysis, the developing trust was, however, very fragile and vulnerable to the slightest failures of empathy on the part of the analyst. In the final phases of the treatment, an unwitting lapse on my part into a defensive reaction to an aspect of the now intensely demanding transference triggered rageful homicidal and suicidal fantasies. By then, such fantasies could be both experienced and communicated because of a sufficient sense of the relationship being sustained—of object constancy—despite the hurt and anger.

The patient's fully developed transference plight in the analytic relationship, which sought to reproduce the same struggle she was currently having with her parents, revealed itself as that of an adolescent harboring, in addition to the usual adolescent conflicts, a child in the rapprochement crisis. She felt that I had omniscient powers and that she could not survive without me; and she resented her relative helplessness and rebelled against the dependency. She wanted desperately to be on her own and do for herself, but feared the consequent sense of emptiness and loneliness and vacillation between the polar states of being either feelingless or overwhelmed by feelings. A major objective of the therapeutic process was the alleviation of the rapprochement-crisis feelings of vulnerability and helplessness, experienced in relation to both the object and the power of her own untamed impulses and affects.

This objective was gradually achieved though the patient's insistence on what amounted to being in control of the situation and thus the focus and pace of the process. Once she began her verbal participation, she objected most vigorously to questions or comments from me, particularly so in the beginning phase of treatment, experiencing them as intrusions on her autonomy. If I then assumed a lower profile, she demanded with equal vigor that I speak up and help out. She monitored the time in the treatment sessions literally to the second, insisting that whatever time was lost, due, for example, to a late start, be made up as proof of my good motives and my concern for her. She repeatedly checked the remaining time in the session so that she, not I, could declare that the ending was at hand. She also regularly ended her work on the couch a minute or two before the close of the session, this to get herself together emotionally and in a state of control suitable to leave and reenter the outside world. When her associations to a dream enabled me to make an interpretation that she had not seen coming, which was seldom the case, she became terribly upset, feeling that I had willfully and with malice intruded on her autonomy and emotional equilibrium. Depending upon her mood, I either should or should not ask her about how she was feeling, and she would or would not respond, stating that feelings were just not available to her or complaining, alternatively, that my office was insufficiently isolated and soundproofed for her to voice her feelings in their full intensity. In all of this there was the constant concern that I was either withdrawing my interest from her in my silent presence behind the couch or straining with impatience to take over and force my egocentric, self-serving, and inaccurate understanding upon her.

Control and autonomy in the treatment situation were similarly important to the 3-year-old patient. She announced the play activity of the day and began issuing instructions as she entered the office, doing so in a "bossy" way that brooked no deviation or lack of compliance on my part, at least early in the treatment. When I, out of my adult reserve and preference for economy of effort, suggested eminently sensible ways of containing the play within closer bounds than she chose, she rejected my proposals out of hand, sulked, and threatened to leave if I persisted. She also, as is not uncommon with children in analysis, drowned me out or covered her ears so as not to hear me. This was, as I see it, done in anticipation of the intrusion on her control, not only over me, but over her inner self, that might result from my comment or interpretation. Her play was in fact replete with episodes designed to reexperience and master life's intrusions upon the autonomy of the child. She repeatedly played that she was an infant closing her eyes against bright lights, or a child trying to cope with loud noises such as sirens, or with being made to go to sleep, or being forced to eat, to take medicine, to receive an injection, to go to the toilet, etc. Given her symptomatic concerns about control and autonomy, it was a clear sign of her readiness for termination when she one day ambled aimlessly into the office, slouched against my couch, said she had nothing in mind to do today, and asked me for suggestions.

Discussion

Psychoanalytic understanding derived from and illuminated by direct observational studies of developing children—here, Mahler's separation-individuation theory—can be further conveyed through discussion of the issue of control and autonomy as a part of the analytic process. The control which these patients exercised over the analyst in his analytic functioning can be understood as serving the developing task of self-regulation, a first level of which is attained during the rapprochement subphase of the separation-individuation process. Control over the analyst serves the dual purpose of avoiding external traumatic intrusion over the patient's psychic functioning and, therefore, of maintaining control over the internal emotional equilibrium. The maintenance of internal equilibrium keeps the ego from being overwhelmed from within and thus furthers the development of ego autonomy. Because the analyst is experienced by the patient as respecting the need for autonomy and not as overly powerful or overwhelming, independence is similarly furthered. It is noteworthy that respect for the patient's need for ego autonomy has from the very beginning been embodied in the analytic method, as is exemplified by Freud's abandonment of hypnosis in favor of free association. Although designed to diminish repressive control over unconscious mental content, the technique of free association also clearly places the control over the associative process in the hands of the patient. This same respect is demonstrated in the technique of defense analysis, developed later (see, for example, Settlage 1974b).

The psychoanalytic treatment of neurosis modifies psychic structure by resolution of intrapsychic conflict among the id, ego, and superego elements of psychic structure. Although the same is also accomplished in the treatment of narcissistic and borderline disorders, psychoanalysis is currently addressing the controversial question of whether the analytic method and process can, in these disorders (and perhaps in the neuroses as well), promote the development of psychic structure. (See, for example, Kohut 1971, pp. 100-108 and 165-168.) To my mind, the understanding and concepts presented in the herein described treatment favor the process of internalization and formation of psychic structure through identification with the analytic functions of the analyst—e.g., empathy, observation and introspection, understanding and insight, abstinence from gratification in favor of delay, ego control, and modulation of urges and impulses—as these functions contribute to expansion of the patient's capacity for psychic regulation. Such temporarily provided external auxiliary ego functions of the analyst (Loewenstein 1967, p. 800) are, in analogy to the child-parent developmental relationship (Loewald 1960), relinquished as self-regulation is gradually achieved through their internalization.

Internalization was similarly involved in the furtherance of the development of libidinal object constancy in these patients. The 3-year-old patient reenacted in the transference her anxiety that her aggressive acts could turn an affectionate, loving mother into an angry, hating mother. Early on, a suddenly injected warning from me to prevent her from unwittingly bumping her head on an open desk drawer caused an immediate shift from comfortable, although aggressively active, fantasy play to a panicky flight across the playroom with an anxious cry for her mother. As a result of numerous subsequent testings of my anger and their interpretation, she could, toward the end of the analysis, engage in forthrightly provocative acts of messiness in further reliving her transference past, but now with little anxiety and a sly smile that conveyed her trust that I would not hurt or overwhelm her in my limit-setting response. An important parallel aspect of the analytic process involved not only the acceptance of the patient's feelings toward me, but their being verbally identified and labeled (Katan 1961).

The adolescent patient dealt similarly with her feelings, also through the transference. With regard to both her positive libidinal feelings and her angry, rageful feelings, it was necessary that I convey my empathy, not only as it is normally reflected in an accurate interpretation, but also by directly acknowledging and characterizing her feelings. Short of this, she was not sure that her feelings were real, or acceptable, or even usual human feelings, let alone useful and manageable in relationships. Here, too, repeated and increasingly intense transference episodes, wherein her feelings were thus empathically acknowledged, led to a gradual building of trust in the analyst and a correlated internal sense of self-acceptance and self-control, a sense of self with a more stable "center." At the same time, her relations with parents and peers also improved.

In theoretical terms, it appears that the analyst's overall constancy and analytic participation in the process of ego mastery over impulses and affects helped these patients achieve a better amalgamation of their libidinal and aggressive strivings, which, along with relinquishment of the tendency toward splitting, enabled a greater sense of object and self-constancy. This was accomplished despite the fact that the intensity and primitivity of the transference demands of such patients severly test analytic neutrality, objectivity, and empathy, sometimes evoking temporarily undiscerned countertransference responses inimical to constancy.

The presented developmentally-derived formulation of trust being, in these cases, the result of analytic process suggests reconsideration of the concept of therapeutic alliance. With neurotic patients, the capacity for trust is regarded as a *sine qua non* for such alliance, basic trust having been reinforced during the separation-individuation process (see, for example, Zetzel 1965). In narcissistic and borderline patients, such trust is lacking, and the capacity for trust appears to be more an outcome than a precondition of treatment. The long-term motivated involvement of such patients in analytic treatment must rest, therefore, on other bases: perhaps on residual basic trust, or on basic or primordial transference (from a satisfactory symbiotic relationship), or on the still obscure determinants of attitudes of hope and perseverance.

Psychoanalysis is also addressing another controversial question, namely, whether psychoanalytic process is at one and the same time therapeutic process and developmental process (Loewald 1960, Zetzel 1965, Fleming 1975, Greenacre 1975). Here, too, the presented

concepts and clinical material support the affirmative view, suggesting that the undoing of psychopathology and the furtherance of
development proceed hand in hand. As Loewald (1960) observes, the
developmental aspect has always been a part of analytic process,
although not well discerned or defined in the treatment of neuroses.
It takes on a new importance, however, and demands definition
when the analytic method addresses not only the problem of resolution of conflict within psychic structure, but that of development of
structure. It is thus necessary to continue to study and understand
development and developmental process, and to define and determine the limits of the presented analogy between the analytic
situation and the developmental situation. In my own attempts to
contribute to such an undertaking (Settlage 1976), this paper included, I have found it essential to distinguish between the basic
concepts and precepts of the analytic method and the techniques for
their implementation, as was proposed in the 1974 Position Paper of
the Preparatory Commission on Child Analysis (Goodman 1977, p.
84). The analyst can thus function technically as a temporary auxiliary ego while adhering, at the same time, to the precept of abstention
from gratification of the patient's libidinal, as opposed to ego, needs
(Settlage and Spielman, in prep.). Through the combination of the
expression of needs and anticipations in the transference and the
analyst's neutrality toward them, the patient can have an experience
different from the one he had with the parent in the original developmental situation. This is not, however, because the analyst has
abandoned the analytic posture and actively assumed a parental role
or parental rather than analytic attitudes. The transference is, as
usual, interpreted to provide insight into its genetic origins and is not
manipulated or allowed to remain unconscious. These conditions
assure analytic change and answer the expected objection that the
developmental aspect of the analytic process, as I have called it, is
not an analytic but a corrective emotional experience in the pejorative meaning of that term.

SUMMARY

I have reviewed and supported the proposition that theory-
building in psychoanalysis requires the careful correlation and meaningful interpenetration of the data and hypotheses from both the

reconstructive and direct observational approaches. In illustration of this premise, I postulated that failure to achieve age-adequate self-regulation and ego autonomy during the rapprochement subphase of the separation-individuation process contributes crucially to the pathogenesis of narcissistic and borderline disorders. I have also described the rapprochement subphase of the separation-individuation process and attempted to draw some correlations between it and the psychological formations characteristic of narcissistic personality disorders. Clinical material from the analyses of a 3-year-old girl and an 18-year-old girl was employed to demonstrate the genetic origin of such pathology and to illustrate some facets of analytic process in the treatment of a narcissistic personality disorder. Lastly, I noted and supported the controversial concepts of structure formation as a result of psychoanalytic treatment, and of analytic process as being both therapeutic and developmental. In these attempts, I have been viewing mostly familiar concepts and clinical experience mainly from the perspective provided by advances in the psychoanalytic theory of early psychic development.

References

Bibring, E. (1953). The mechanism of depression. In *Affective Disorders*, ed. P. Greenacre, pp. 13-48. New York: International Universities Press.

Blum, H. P. (1974). The borderline childhood of the Wolf Man. *Journal of the American Psychoanalytic Association*, 23:721-742.

Fleming, J. (1975). Some observations on object constancy in the psycho-analysis of adults. *Journal of the American Psychoanalytic Association* 23:743-759.

Freud, A. (1958). Child observation and prediction of development: a memorial lecture in honor of Ernst Kris. *The Writings of Anna Freud*, vol. 5, pp. 102-135. New York: International Universities Press, 1969.

Freud, S. (1905). Three essays on the theory of sexuality. *Standard Edition* 7:135-243.

Goodman, S. (1977). *Psychoanalytic Education and Research: The Current Situation and Future Possibilites*. New York: International Universities Press.

Greenacre, P. (1960). Considerations regarding the parent-infant relation-ship. In *Emotional Growth*, pp. 199-224. New York: International Universities Press, 1971.

——— (1967). The influence of infantile trauma on genetic patterns. In *Emotional Growth*, pp. 260-299. New York: International Universities Press, 1971.

—— (1971). Notes on the influence and contribution of ego psychology to the practice of psychoanalysis. In *Separation-Individuation: Essays in Honor of Margaret S. Mahler*, ed. J. B. McDevitt and C. F. Settlage, pp. 171-200. New York: International Universities Press.

—— (1975). On reconstruction. *Journal of the American Psychoanalytic Association* 23:693-712.

Jacobson, E. (1964). *The Self and the Object World*. New York: International Universities Press.

Katan, A. (1961). Some thoughts about the role of verbalization in early childhood. *Psychoanalytic Study of the Child* 16:184-188.

Kernberg, O. F. (1966). Structural derivatives of object relationships. *International Journal of Psycho-Analysis* 47:236-253.

—— (1974). Contrasting viewpoints regarding the nature and psychoanalytic treatment of narcissistic personalities. *Journal of the American Psychoanalytic Association* 22:255-267.

—— (1975). *Borderline Conditions and Pathological Narcissism*. New York: Jason Aronson.

Kohut, H. (1971). *The Analysis of the Self*. New York: International Universities Press.

Kris, E. (1950). Notes on the development and on some current problems of psychoanalytic child psychology. In *Selected Papers*, pp. 54-79. New Haven: Yale University Press, 1975.

Loewald, H. (1960). On the therapeutic action of psychoanalysis. *International Journal of Psycho-Analysis* 41:16-33.

Loewenstein, R. M. (1967). Defensive organization and autonomous ego function. *Journal of the American Psychoanalytic Association* 15:795-809.

Mahler, M. S. (1966). Notes on the development of basic moods: the depressive affect. In *Psychoanalysis, a General Psychology*, ed. R. M. Loewenstein, et al., pp. 152-168. New York: International Universities Press.

—— (1968). *On Human Symbiosis and the Vicissitudes of Individuation: Volume 1, Infantile Psychosis*. New York: International Universities Press.

—— (1971). A study of the separation-individuation process: and its possible application to borderline phenomena in the psychoanalytic situation. *Psychoanalytic Study of the Child* 26:403-424. Reprinted in *Selected Papers*, op. cit., ch. 11.

—— (1972). The rapprochement subphase of the separation-individuation process. *Psychoanalytic Quarterly* 41:487-506. Reprinted in *Selected Papers*, op. cit., ch. 9, and this volume, ch. 1.

Mahler, M. S., Pine, F., and Bergman, A. (1975). *The Psychological Birth of the Human Infant: Symbiosis and Individuation*. New York: Basic Books.

Piaget, J. (1954). *The Construction of Reality in the Child*. New York: Basic Books.

Settlage, C. F. (1974a). Danger signals in the separation-individuation process; the observations and formulations of Margaret S. Mahler. In *The Infant at Risk*. New York: Intercontinental Medical Books Corporation.

――― (1974b). The technique of defense analysis in the psychoanalysis of an early adolescent. In *The Analyst and the Adolescent at Work*, ed. M. Harley, pp. 3-39. New York: Quadrangle.

――― (1976). The contribution of child analysis to the training in adult analysis: A commentary on the 6th Pre-Congress Conference on Training of the International Psycho-Analytical Association. *International Journal of Psycho-Analysis* 57:205-210.

Settlage, C. F. and Spielman, P. M. (in prep.), On the psychogenesis and psychoanalytic treatment of faulty structural development. Presented at the Meetings of the Association for Child Psychoanalysis, Bal Harbor, Fla. (Under revision prior to submission for publication).

Zetzel, E. R. (1965). A developmental model and the theory of therapy. In *The Capacity for Emotional Growth*, pp. 246-270. New York: International Universities Press, 1973.

6

Separation-Individuation: An Organizing Principle

Gertrude and Rubin Blanck

Periodically, in the history of psychoanalytic theory construction, there appear new organizing principles that bring theory to a point of culmination and, simultaneously, provide a new point of departure for future theory construction. These organizing principles are analogous to the organizers of the psyche as described by Spitz (1959)—a period of extensive ego building culminates in a new level of organization, which in turn leads to a greater degree of integration and to a next higher level of organization.

Freud himself reached several such historical milestones in theory construction: in *The Interpretation of Dreams* (1900), in the *Three Essays* (1905), in *The Ego and the Id* (1923), among others.

It was the structural theory that paved the way for Hartmann's far-ranging conceptualizations regarding the ego (1939). Hartmann is in turn to be regarded as a major theorist—one who provides a new organizing principle as a point of culmination of theory and, at the same time, a new point of departure. Hartmann's work paved the way for the discoveries of ego psychologists who used his concepts as the basis for new theory construction.

This paper was presented at the Margaret Mahler Symposium on "Symbiosis and Separation-Individuation Theory and Instinct Theory," Philadelphia, May 21, 1977.

It remained for Mahler, however, to provide yet another organizing principle, embodied in her statement, "a major organization of intrapsychic and behavioral life develops around issues of separation-individuation . . . " (Mahler, Pine, and Bergmann 1975, p. 4). Mahler's organizing principle paves the way for elaboration of theory in many directions and contains important implications for technique as well.

Here we shall present two interrelated themes deriving from Mahler's organizing principle:

1. That the *ego* is now to be regarded not as an entity, nor even as a construct, but as the very process of organization per se, encompassing even drive organization in that process.

2. That this makes it possible to understand how normal narcissism and its pathological deviations develop in the subphases as organization encompasses the interaction of drive components with self- and object images.

EGO AS ORGANIZATION

The history of the evolution of the concept ego into the form in which we understand it today has been reviewed by Hartmann (1950, 1956) and Rapaport (1959). Yet it bears another review now in the light of accretions in knowledge which illuminate and emphasize those aspects of ego which have not yet been appreciated fully. Before Freud arrived at the clarity of his 1923 definition of ego, he struggled with it repeatedly, while its meaning remained ambiguous. In his early writings it was conceived variously as censorship; an obstruction to uncovering the unconscious; the self; and other intermediate meanings.

Freud altered his views as clinical observation dictated, for he held to the firm conviction that observation is the true foundation of science. That methodology is of particular pertinence today, as we consider Mahler's findings, derived from the most minute observations of mother-child pairs.

As we know, it was not until 1923 that Freud arrived at his final definition of ego: "We have formed the idea that in each individual there is a coherent organization of mental processes, and we call this his ego" (p. 17).

Not long after publication of *The Ego and the Id*, Glover (1924) proposed that the ego is not born full-blown. His was a theory of ego development. The early experiences of infantile life form separate clusters, consisting of nuclear-like islands of memory traces. They are affective reactions. Loosely arranged at first, these islands gradually coalesce, and it is only then that one may speak of coherence in the organization of mental processes. Glover's theory of ego nuclei reverberates especially in the works of the developmentalists.

In 1939, Hartmann broke new ground with his revision of ego theory. We list those of his contributions most pertinent to the theme we wish to develop:

1. The ego does not, as Freud had thought, grow out of friction or contact of the id with reality but, rather, both ego and id develop out of a common matrix. By this proposal Hartmann opened the door to elaborations of differentiation processes—psyche from soma, self from object, inside from outside, drive differentiation, affect differentiation, and the like.

2. Part of the ego does not derive from conflict, but exists in a conflict-free sphere that is the locus of apparatuses of primary autonomy.

3. Most important to our immediate purpose, there is an *organizing function of the ego*. This relieves us from regarding the ego as an entity of some sort rather than as organizing process.

It is of significance to note that long before *The Ego and the Id*, Freud (1912) had already said: "It must further be borne in mind that many people fall ill precisely from an attempt to sublimate their instincts beyond the degree permitted by their organization" (p. 119).

Defining the ego by its very functions, Hartmann selected the organizing function as one of special significance, thereby enlarging upon Nunberg's (1931) description of the synthetic function: "the term *organizing function* may fit the facts better than *synthetic function* because in the concept of organization we include elements of differentiation as well as of integration"(Hartmann 1947, p. 62).

Differentiation and integration are, of course, hallmarks of ego development. Hartmann also referred to the "centralization of functional control" (1950, p. 117) and to "that special functional control and integration that we know under the name of synthetic, or better, organizing function" (1951, p. 145). He emphasized the special position of the organizing function as follows:

> But many misunderstandings and unclarities are traceable to the fact that we have not yet trained ourselves to consider the ego from an

intrasystemic point of view. One speaks of "the ego" as being rational, or realistic, or an integrator, while actually these are characteristics only of one or the other of its functions [1950, p. 139].

And:

An equilibrium between the various adaptive trends will finally, more or less successfully, be established by experience and by the integrative, or synthetic, or organizing function of the ego, which works on several levels and correlates aspects of mental functioning with each other and with outer reality [1956a, p. 254].

Hartmann's views correlate exquisitely with Mahler's organizing principle. Hartmann's preferred term *organizing function*, because it includes elements of differentiation and integration, can be transposed directly to processes of separation-individuation. Indeed, individuation refers precisely to the integration of the effects of separation processes, namely, that capacity for internalization organizes drive elements, affective reactions, and autonomous functioning to deal with transient feelings of object loss. This locates the process squarely in the intrasystemic realm. Achievement of adaptive equilibrium, established by the interaction of experience with the organizing function, working upon many levels to correlate mental functioning with reality, is now described in specific detail by Mahler's delineation of the various subphases of separation-individuation, the tasks involved in them, and the problems encountered.

While Mahler's description of development as encompassing symbiosis and the subphases of separation-individuation has been available for many years, a significant addition is provided in her new formulation (Mahler, Pine, and Bergman 1975) that ego structure per se evolves out of these processes as they encompass the simultaneous impact of reality and the instinctual drives. Mahler's elaboration and refinement of the experiences in the phases and subphases show how these constitute the bottom layer, influencing later levels of organization. She also stresses the infant's part in the dyad, the necessity for employment of his adaptive capacities, as she demonstrates that the lion's share of adaptation rests with the infant and represents the very tasks of organization that devolve upon him. Spitz's concept of organizers of the psyche (1959) had begun to approach the extension of theory that we propose—namely, that the ego *is* organizing process. And he affirmed that this process is continuous by demonstrating how the appearance of the indicators proves that organization has been proceeding.

It is with these considerations that we trust that we do no violence to Hartmann's definition of ego if we amend it to state that the ego is defined, not by its functions, but by the way it functions. The apparatuses, the drives, affective reactions, object relations, and external reality all become represented in what Hartmann called the inner world, as development proceeds. It is these myriad representations that organize experience into structure, a process in which the ego will use the facilities at its command to attain coherence. Lichtenberg (1975) distinguishes self-images from self-representations, reserving the former to denote the impact of immediate experience—following Sandler and Joffe's description (1969) of an experiential realm—and the latter to denote internalization leading to structure formation. What is it that changes image at the experiential level into a structured representation? Rapaport's (1959) definition of structure as consisting of configurations, abiding patterns with a slow rate of change, is useful here. May we not say that, when structuralization reaches such point, the organizing process has attained not only coherence, but constancy as well?

Our proposal that ego is organizing process dovetails with Hartmann's basic proposition of an undifferentiated matrix within which are contained the apparatuses of primary autonomy. It accords, also, with Glover's view of nuclear ego development.

The organizing process can be seen at work as postuterine physical maturation results in the rooting reflex, visual tracking, and the one-month maturational crisis. These are indicative of organizing processes which take place in nuclear islands, not yet interconnected but nevertheless unmistakable as forms of organizing activity. The postulate of autonomously developing islands of ego nuclei accords also with Spitz's (1965) view that residuals from the coenesthetic state persist in later periods of life; it adds emphasis to Mahler's concept (Mahler, Pine, and Bergman 1975) that pathology arises out of precocious development of nuclear ego fragments, and to her description of the infinite variety and complexity of individual growth.

From this, we suggest that a number of hypotheses can now usefully be combined into a single statement: There is an innate capacity to organize mental processes into coherent form; such organization takes place at the outset in islands of experience, employing whatever apparatuses are available at the time. With organization, cumulation of experience makes for qualitative change which becomes observable at points in development where certain peaks in organization are attained. Organizing processes continue throughout the life cycle as completion of various tasks peak, according to the level reached.

We believe that the technical advantages of regarding ego as an organizing process abound. By focusing on process rather than effect, evenly suspended attention is enhanced. It avoids emphasis upon nomenclature or categories or rigidly established stages of development, thereby drawing attention to the person as a whole; it also avoids one-sided concentration on ego, superego, or id. It recognizes the importance of the patient's endowment and behavior (activity); it is not limited to a theory of object relations in the narrow sense, but encompasses the broader one of psychoanalytic developmental psychology as a whole. It also clarifies what is meant by the term *weak ego*, which describes, really, that latent apparatuses have not been quickened, or that they are used maladaptively. In other words, we imply that ego exists when it functions.

NARCISSISM

Narcissism, we believe, is best understood within the broad framework of psychoanalytic developmental psychology. It does not yield its secret readily, as Freud's struggles with it testify. His repeated attempts at understanding led him to think of narcissism in many ways—to link narcissism with libido theory, to separate sexual libido from ego libido, to see narcissism as reflected in the narcissistic neuroses (psychoses), in megalomania, in homosexuality. Libido theory alone shed a very dim light indeed. Nor did it help matters greatly when the dual drive theory was introduced. The mystery of narcissism is broader than drive theory alone. It reflects vicissitudes of drive maturation, of affect development, structuralization and internalization, and development as a whole.

One reason why narcissism has remained so baffling these many years is that it has been approached, theoretically, mainly as a pathology. As such, the very nature of the narcissistic arrangement is relatively impervious to clinical intervention. Another reason is that it has its beginnings in early, preverbal life and therefore yields its secrets in language which we were, until Mahler's work, unable to comprehend. With Mahler's illumination of subphase development, we now understand the early vicissitudes of narcissism and are in a better position, clinically, to tune in to reflections of preverbal experience as they appear in the therapeutic situation.

It seems now that features familiarly designated as grandiosity, magical omnipotence and like aspects of narcissism are more precisely regarded as behavioral manifestations of unfulfilled or distorted developmental tasks—as clinical evidences of phase and subphase inadequacies for, in whichever phase or subphase that development is first affronted, the seat of the damage is in the organizing process itself, in the organizational forms that the individual has been able to elaborate. Thus, narcissism is an intimate and inseparable aspect of organization.

In a developmental scheme, no single phase or subphase can be designated as the seat of narcissistic pathogenicity. We (1979), following Mahler and Kaplan's introduction of this theme (1977), correlate specific forms of narcissistic and borderline vulnerability with inadequate development within the several subphases of separation-individuation. Mahler regards each subphase as making its particular contribution to normal or pathological narcissism. Bodily libidinal supplies are especially necessary during the symbiotic, differentiation, and practicing subphases. At the practicing subphase, self-love, primitive valuation of accomplishment and omnipotence contribute to narcissistic formation and are normal and necessary to further development and vulnerable to subphase inadequacy. The rapprochement subphase has been described as even more delicate. There is continuing reliance upon subphase adequate mothering if narcissism is to develop normally.

When Freud struggled to understand narcissism, he was working with the only developmental theory available to him at the time—libido theory. Therefore, he saw narcissism as normal when the progression of libido was from autoerotism to primary narcissism to object love, and pathological when libido was withdrawn from the object world and reinvested in the ego (or as we would now say, the self). Thus, so-called secondary narcissism has long been thought of as the pathological core of the "narcissistic neuroses."

Development was at first conceptualized in polar form, with object cathexis at one extreme and narcissism at the other. Indeed, Loewald (1960) interprets Freud's concept of transference as synonymous with the capacity to cathect objects with libido. It took Freud many years to revise and restate his position. His new thought was no longer in polarities, but, rather, in dynamic and economic terms: in love (libidinal cathexis of the object), narcissism is at a low ebb. He said (1914):

> We must recognize that self-regard has a specially intimate depen-
> dence on narcissistic libido. Further, it is easy to observe that libidinal
> object-cathexis does not raise self-regard. The effect of dependence
> upon the loved object is to lower that feeling: A person in love is
> humble. A person who loves has, so to speak, forfeited a part of his
> narcissism [p. 98].

By 1917 we find Freud working once again with the concepts ego and narcissism as he began to see that the theoretical problems inherent in both are interrelated and pertain to the very beginnings of extrauterine life. With foresight that extends to the present day and predictably beyond, he said, "We are bound to suppose that a unity comparable to the ego cannot exist in the individual from the start; the ego has to be developed" (pp. 56-77).

As he continued his work (1917) he began to distinguish sexual libido from ego libido (the energy of the ego instincts) but still expressed continuing bewilderment about the ego. "But the ego, its composition out of various organizations and their construction and mode of functioning, remain hidden from us" (p. 415).

His definition of secondary narcissism as the recathexis of the ego with narcissistic libido because of disappointment in the object world compounded the puzzle of the so-called "narcissistic neu-roses." Belief in their intractability rested on the assumption that libido is immobile; once withdrawn from the object world it could not find its way back to it. This was explained by differences in innate dispositions and by fixations which are irreversible because they originated at early phases of development. Freud (1917) was, nevertheless, quite optimistic about future conquest of the narcissis-tic neuroses by coming to understand the ego, its disturbances and disruptions. He regarded this task as greater than that of understand-ing libidinal development, expressing "a low opinion of our present knowledge of the vicissitudes of the libido, which we have gained from a study of the transference neuroses." (pp. 422-423).

To accomplish the greater task, he said, "Our technical methods must accordingly be replaced by others" (p. 423). Here Freud clearly turned from libido theory, demonstrating his readiness to relinquish older conceptualizations in favor of bringing about order and coherence as observation provided new data. For a short while, he continued to use the term ego instincts, but abandoned it as he turned to a theory of ego development. He foresaw that libido theory might not serve the purpose and announced the shift in his thinking: "Nor can I think that it would be a disaster to the trend of our researches, if what lies before us is the discovery that in severe psychoses the ego-instincts themselves have gone astray as a primary fact" (p. 430).

The term narcissism has come to acquire a variety of meanings. In pathology it is a form of personality disturbance; in developmental theory it is a normal developmental line and an essential prerequisite for mental well-being. Freud attributed the term to Nacke and to Havelock Ellis, both of whom used it to denote the taking of one's own body as a sexual object, therefore, a form of perversion in which external objects play an insignificant role. By defining secondary narcissism as he did, Freud moved narcissism one small step away from a perversion. Nevertheless, serious theoretical problems were left. If we continue to define libido as sexual energy, then narcissism remains a perversion. If we used Freud's last definition of libido as the force that seeks to connect and to establish ever greater unities (1940) what is being connected and to what?

There is an inherent fallacy in a theory of narcissism that involves polarization of self- and object cathexis. The developmental position is that narcissism and object relatedness are two separate lines of development, not polar but interlocking, as suggested by Hartmann and Loewenstein (1962) in their reference to the process of absorption of grandiose self-images and idealized object images into the normal ego-ideal. We propose that it might be useful to take this line of thought another step. Following Freud's final statement on drive theory—that libido is the force that connects, and aggression the force that serves to undo connections—we (1977) have suggested that affects are to be regarded as separate from the drives. Libidinal cathexis, then, results from innate need for union—first, symbiosis and later, identification. Aggression powers the processes of separation-individuation. This states in terms of drive theory the means by which the adult attains the state of normalcy that Mahler describes as being fully in the world and yet fully separate from it. It suggests that both drives tend to operate in concert, exerting forces toward the object (libido) and away from it (aggression). These movements, which Mahler has termed *ambitendency,* are to be seen in each subphase as the child distances himself from mother and, at the same time, seeks reunion with her. In the differentiation subphase, the upper part of the torso thrusts away from the mother's body while the child retains contact with the lower part; in the practicing subphase, the child is first a crawler and then a toddler, and so he now moves his entire body away, retaining contact by seeking out the mother visually from time to time; in the rapprochement subphase, he has the locomotive power to reverse the aggressive thrust away from and can return to mother at will.

Desirably, aggression should remain relatively latent in the symbiotic phase while libido should dominate. As symbiosis wanes, aggression tends to come into ascendancy, impelling the individual toward separation-individuation. This view of the drives makes it possible to refer to cathexes with positive or negative value but without confusing drive with affect—libido with love or aggression with hostility. It shakes narcissism loose from the restricting confines of libido theory and shifts it to the status of a developmental line.

Mahler believes that the innate capacity to extract what is necessary from the environment is essential for the infant to be able to enter the dyad. Such innate endowment requires libidinal energy to power it. If, by some unfavorable distribution of drive energy, aggression should differentiate prematurely and become dominant, then harmonious symbiotic unity is precluded by the obstacle of the aggressive drive serving separation, when the phase-specific requirement is for union. If the libidinal drive is phase-appropriately dominant, however, symbiotic union is facilitated. Here is the point where we think normal narcissism has its inception. The self-object unit is cathected with positive affective value.

As we discuss normal narcissism, we are obliged to think of it differently at different grades of self-object differentiation. Just as in the symbiotic phase it is the unit that is valued with entry into the subphases one thinks more in terms of degree of differentiation as well as of balance of positive and negative valence.

As development proceeds, further distinctions are made. Of particular importance to normalcy is that experiences of "good" self- and object images predominate over "bad." In effect, there are, at this stage, four sets of images determined by the affective qualities of the experiences—"good" and "bad" self and "good" and "bad" object. It is conceivable that, just as the self-object unit at the symbiotic stage was valued, now the two sets of "good" images are valued. The separation-serving feature of the aggressive drive is used to exclude the set of "bad" images splitting them from the "good," while the infant still needs a preponderance of "goodness" with which to linger before becoming capable of tolerating the realization that the "good" and "bad" must be combined into representations of self and object as whole persons. Structure begins here (Sandler and Joffe 1969, Lichtenberg 1975).

Pathological narcissism reflects deficits in the simultaneous and mutually enhancing elaboration of self- and object esteem. The specific form of the pathology is the outcome of the manner in which the organizing process proceeds as it is forced now to include within it the consequences of affront to development at particular levels.

Already in the symbiotic phase, there is pathogenic potential if symbiosis is not sufficiently gratifying to generate a surplus of positive cathexis. Imbalance may be the consequence of mismatching because of discordant rhythm between the partners in the dyad. Mahler has described these vicissitudes in the incapacity of some infants to enter the symbiotic phase, in imbalance in the differentiating drive configuration, in inadequacy stemming from the maternal contribution to the dyad, or from combinations of all of these. Such deficits make for failure in the fitting-together that Hartmann (validated by Mahler) regarded as an essential aspect of the process of adaptation. Cathexis of the self-object unit with value is essential at all phases and subphases if development is to proceed normally. Affront from either side of the dyad at such early levels results in psychosis.

With adequate symbiosis, development proceeds; cathexis of the differentiating self- and object images will lead ultimately to self- and object esteem—to the evenly distributed cathexis that Jacobson (1964) describes.

With entry into the subphases, there are myriad opportunities for enhancement (or impairment) of self-esteem. Optimal fulfillment of the central developmental purpose of each subphase propels the child into the next subphase. But the affective experiences that are accompaniments of the main subphase purpose are significant for normal narcissistic development. Self-esteem remains exceedingly vulnerable in the subphases because it still relies on magical omnipotence and is readily lost if not supported from without.

For development to proceed to next higher levels, balance of libido and aggression is necessary to maintain continuous libidinal connection, while aggressive thrusts toward separation propel the individual ever forward toward psychological birth. The capacity to deal with normal separation anxiety is best developed when there is this even balance between the drives. Then "bite-sized" movement toward independence and mastery becomes tolerable. We wish to convey that as development is continuous, so is pathogenicity.

By the rapprochement subphase, a reversal begins to take place propelled in large measure by better reality testing and by separation anxiety, that is, by the realization that the primary object can no longer be used to reestablish omnipotent dual unity. The rapprochement toddler is forced to more realistic discovery of the self and its capabilities and of the object world and what can be expected from it. The delicacy of this subphase comes into focus as we understand the necessity for favorably balanced cathexis of self- and object images.

It occurs to us here that the tendency to use the adjective, narcissistic, in a pejorative way arises from the counterreaction we experience when we see the effect in an adult of disappointment in the subphases. Such an individual suffers from failure to have integrated realistic, object related requirements with realistically evaluated self-esteem. There is a regressive trend toward the comfort of the magical omnipotence of the practicing subphase. As adults, such persons remain tyrants of the nursery. But with optimal completion of the subphase tasks, the rapprochement subphase becomes the crucible for melding of the two poles as Freud saw them—narcissism and object relations. Then the elation of independent mastery in the practicing subphase can be laid aside as the "senior toddler" discovers the truth that he and mother no longer fit together, as before, and he now has to begin to rely on his own still-embryonic self-esteem and also on his increasing autonomy for narcissistic supplies. It is this radical shift from reliance upon the external world and upon magical omnipotence that makes the rapprochement subphase so delicate and vulnerable. Although it will be a short while yet before full psychological birth, the rapprochement subphase represents a transition from the adaptedness of mother and infant fitting-together (in Hartmann's sense) for the physical and psychological survival of the infant, to the adaptedness that is attained as the result of structuralization and internalization culminating in the oedipus complex and its resolution.

Adequate completion of the requirements of the rapprochement subphase accelerates processes of internalization. With the discovery that the former omnipotent dual unit is no longer recoverable because neither partner can now find a comfortable fit in it, the child is forced ever more strongly in the direction of object constancy. The dramatic fights with mother which Mahler noted represent the toddler's defense against the depressive realization that the object world, including the primary object, is no longer his oyster.

With rapprochement adequacy, there is an accretion in self-esteem, which Mahler designates as sound secondary narcissism. We suppose that she is referring to the shift, at this subphase, from the state of dependence upon the outside for narcissistic supplies, to greater reliance upon realistic and ever more securely internalized self-valuation propelled by ever-increasing autonomous functioning of the apparatuses. This becomes possible as admired qualities of the object images are incorporated into the self-images. Interpersonal transactions, while continuing in importance for a long time to come, begin to be replaced by structural transactions.

Narcissism takes pathological forms *not* only when there is affront to its phase-specific developmental formations, but also if it fails to proceed, as it should, in equal balance with its partner, object love. If one track of this parallel of ongoing development should outpace the other, the organizing process will henceforth proceed in pathological directions. Self-esteem, if sacrificed in favor of excessive valuation of the object, will remain fixated in primitive form. Development will proceed nonetheless, but in distorted form toward disturbances in identity formation. If the outpacing occurs on the other track of the parallel, narcissism will luxuriate at the expense of capacity to love and will reflect, in adulthood, infantile distortions and object conflictual dependency.

The central organizational failure in pathological narcissism is impairment in the developing capacity for reality testing in the circumscribed area of self-object relations because, with affront to that capacity at whatever level of development, there is relative cessation of object negotiation. That pathogenicity may exist at any level explains why narcissism cannot be regarded as a distinct entity. Rather, it is a feature of development.

It becomes clear, then, that narcissistic pathology cannot be regarded as a stable configuration but must be seen, rather, as a deficit that can ensue anywhere along the growth continuum, having its inception wherever developmental affronts produce distorted ego organization. This position has the advantage of leaving open the possibility that distortion may accompany other developmental failures, may be overshadowed by them, or may be pulled into a state of remission and progression by later developmental successes. To state that normal or pathological forms of narcissism are results of organizational successes or failures reasserts that stability is a consequence of the organizing process.

We return full circle to Freud's definition of secondary narcissism. In a sense, he was correct. Libido is indeed turned upon the ego, if we understand this to mean upon the self-images. This comes about, not out of disappointment in the object world, but because, as Freud (1917) said, "A person in love has, so to speak, forfeited a part of his narcissism" (p. 98). As we now understand that phrase, what has been forfeited is the infantile narcissism that preceeds the rapprochement crisis. We have elaborated upon Mahler's description of the special vulnerability of the rapprochement subphase and her suggestion that it is the fulcrum around which early magical narcissistic formations shift toward more realistic self-evaluation. With this shift, *narcissism approaches the healthy state where it exists side by side with object love.* This arises when there has been developmental opportunity to endow the self-images with positive value. It underscores the status of narcissism as a development within the concept of ego as organizing process, and it follows the direction that Freud indicated in 1917:

> I have now led you into the region in which the next advances in the work of analysis are to be expected. Since we have ventured to operate with the concept of ego libido (the energy of the ego interests) the narcissistic neuroses have become accessible to us: The task before us is to arrive at a dynamic elucidation of these disorders and at the same time to complete our knowledge of mental life by coming to understand the ego. The ego psychology after which we are seeking must be based . . . on the analysis of disturbances and disruptions in the ego [p. 422].

It also fulfills Freud's hope that, by studying the narcissistic disorders, we would gain insight into the way in which the ego is put together. We are left with no doubt that narcissism must be studied within a developmental frame of reference, within the ego psychology that Freud was seeking.

CONCLUSION

Beginning with her study of infantile psychosis several decades ago, Mahler has systematically extended her conceptualizations to a theory of normal development—to a psychoanalytic developmental psychology. Many have found her work useful in delineating the problems of children. We ourselves have used it as the basis for understanding the severe adult pathologies and for elaborating techniques for their treatment. Mahler has made a profound contribution, also, to more precise understanding of neurosis. Her distinction between normal and pathological neurosis was made in Paris in 1973 and was elaborated upon at the Philadelphia Mahler Symposium of 1974. The impact of that contribution upon the psychoanalytic theory of neurosis is yet to be felt.

It is Mahler's organizing principle, however, that will bring about far-reaching knowledge of development, pathology, and elaboration of technique as yet unpredictable in nature. It brings us to the threshold of understanding "the ego, its composition out of various organizations and their construction and mode of functioning" (Freud 1917, p. 415).

References

Blanck, G., and Blanck, R. (1977). The real object and the transference object. *International Journal of Psycho-Analysis* 58:85-97.
Freud, S. (1900). The interpretation of dreams. *Standard Edition* 4/5:1-622.
——— (1905). Three essays on the theory of sexuality. *Standard Edition* 7:135-243.
——— (1912). Recommendations to physicians practicing psycho-analysis. *Standard Edition* 12:111-120.
——— (1914). On narcissism; an introduction. *Standard Edition* 14:73-102.
——— (1917). The libido theory and narcissism. *Standard Edition* 16:412-430.
——— (1923). The ego and the id. *Standard Edition* 19:6-63.
Glover, E. (1924). The significance of the mouth in psycho-analysis. In *On the Early Development of the Mind*, pp. 1-24. New York: International Universities Press, 1956.
Hartmann, H. (1939). *Ego Psychology and the Problem of Adaptation*. New York: International Universities Press, 1958.
——— (1947). On rational and irrational action. In *Essays on Ego Psychology*, 37-68. New York: International Universities Press, 1964.
——— (1950). Comments on the psychoanalytic theory of ego. In *Essays on Ego Psychology*, op. cit., pp. 113-141.

—— (1951). Technical implications of ego psychology. In *Essays on Ego Psychology*, op. cit., pp. 142-154.

—— (1956a). The development of the ego concept in Freud's work. In *Essays on Ego Psychology*, op. cit., pp. 268-296.

—— (1956b). Notes on the reality principle. *Essays on Ego Psychology*, op. cit., pp. 241-267.

Hartmann, H., and Loewenstein, R. M. (1962). Notes on the superego. *Psychoanalytic Study of the Child* 17:42-81.

Jacobson, E. (1964). *The Self and the Object World*. New York: International Universities Press.

Lichtenberg, J. D. (1975). The development of the sense of self. *Journal of the American Psychoanalytic Association* 23:453-484.

Loewald, H. W. (1960). On the therapeutic action of psycho-analysis. *International Journal of Psycho-Analysis* 41:16-33.

Mahler, M. S., Kaplan, L. (1977). Developmental aspects in the assessment of narcissistic and so-called borderline personalities. In *Borderline Personality Disorders: The Concept, the Syndromes, the Patient*, ed. P. Hartocollis, pp. 71-85. N. Y.: International Universities Press.

Mahler, M. S., Pine, F., and Bergman, A. (1975). *The Psychological Birth of the Human Infant: Symbiosis and Individuation*. New York: Basic Books.

Nunberg, H. (1931). The synthetic function of the ego. *International Journal of Psycho-Analysis* 12:123-140.

Rapaport, D. (1959). A historical survey of psychoanalytic ego psychology. Introduction to *Identity and the Life Cycle*, Part I, ed. E. H. Erikson, pp. 5-17. New York: International Universities Press.

Rapaport, D. and Gill, M. M. (1959). The point of view and assumptions of metapsychology. *The Collected Papers of David Rapaport*, pp. 795-811. New York: Basic Books, 1967.

Sandler, J., and Joffe, W. (1969). Towards a basic psycho-analytic model. *International Journal of Psycho-Analysis* 50:79-90.

Spitz, R. A. (1959). *A Genetic Field Theory of Ego Formation: Its Implications for Pathology*. New York: International Universities Press.

—— (1965). *The First Year of Life*. New York: International Universities Press.

Tolpin, M. (1972). On the beginnings of a cohesive self: an application of the concept of transmuting internalization to the study of the transitional object and signal anxiety. *Psychoanalytic Study of the Child* 26:316-352.

7

The Primal Matrix Configuration

BERNARD L. PACELLA, M.D.

The pursuit of and search for a union with the primal need-satisfying (symbiotic) love object remains throughout life a major motif for existence, for instinctual gratification, for narcissistic replenishment, and for "ego security positioning." This longing (urge) for a union with the symbiotic love object continually alternates however. It is in conflict with the fear of reengulfment which threatens the personal identity and entity of the individual (fear of loss of individuality). This basic conflict of human existence, that is, the longing for union and the fear of reengulfment, necessitates those psychic operations which serve as defense against this bipolar anxiety and sets in motion various maneuvers of the ego which have as their aim to hold and to keep the object at an optimal distance from the self.

It has been suggested by the observations of Mahler (1968), Spitz (1965), Bowlby (1969), and Winnicott (1971) that the representation of the primal love object of the first few years of life acts as a quasi-anchor[1] from which the genetic-dynamic extensions of further object representations proceed throughout life. This anchor, comprised of

---

1. Although these authors do not employ the term *quasi-anchor* in this connection.

the totality of sensory, affective, motor and cognitive experiences of the infant in relationship to the parents in the first thirty months of life (symbiotic and separation-individuation phases), constitutes that anchor which I shall name *matrix configuration.* It is this totality of experiences which becomes the fabric to which all later experiences must accommodate.

Very early in life the infant begins to discriminate the mother from the nonmother by a scanning action which forms the functional basis of the primitive matrix configuration which I call the *waking screen.*[2] This scanning action serves the familiarizing need and thus the safety principle (Sandler 1960) from early infancy on throughout life. I assume the existence of a waking screen (scanning screen) which has both a passive (receptive) and an active characteristic and which is concerned with relating the experiences to the anchor, that is, the early matrix configuration.

The familiarizing need and the safety principle serve to establish the anchor as a basic dynamic structure of the psyche which constantly interacts with subsequent experiences and perceptions, and automatically exerts a gravitational pull to itself in times of stress or crisis situations.

In a previous paper (Pacella 1972), I referred to the tendency of the infant's visual and tactile "comparative scanning" and screening action during the latter part of the first year of life. This consists of the infant examining the mother's features, particularly her face, carefully, and comparing them with that of the stranger. Brody and Axelrad (1966) have referred to this early scanning action as "customs inspection." In my 1972 paper I made the following comment:

> It might be useful to conceive of the "customs inspection" as representing two kinds of tactile and visual examination by the infant, one consisting merely of sensory scanning for the purpose of developing the sensual mold of an object and deriving gratification from this sensual exploration; the other consisting of comparative scanning action, driven by a measure of stranger anxiety and always motivated by the need for familiarization, i.e., for fitting the new object mold into the familiar configuration. This latter procedure represents a defensive and adaptive operation.

2. This term was originally introduced by me in an earlier version of this paper, entitled "The Waking Screen" at the Mid-Winter meeting of the American Psychoanalytic Association, December 1972, and is distinctly different in meaning from the "waking screen" described by Joseph Slap in a later publication.

It was further noted (Pacella 1972) that the "comparative scanning" activities, in addition to being triggered by a certain amount of anxiety when confronted by a "strange other-than-mother object," also involves the matter of object permanency in Piaget's sense.

A familiarizing drive or need was suggested by Sandler (1960) according to which the "ego makes every effort to maintain a minimum level of safety feeling"; this effort Sandler calls ego-tonic. Through the development and control of these ego-tonic integrative processes within the ego, perception is foremost. In other words, perception can be said to be in the service of the safety principle. If the child's environment appears to carry a distinctive positive value then it serves the safety principle.

The dream screen was conceptualized by Lewin (1946) as a projection of the primitive visual representation of the mother: her breast, her face, and the complex sensory experiences, particularly the feeding experiences associated with her during sleep. I am suggesting that the waking screen during waking life has a similar background consisting of the primitive matrix or mold constantly operating within the psychic structure to project the primitive parental representations internally towards the unconscious and externally to conscious representations of the external objects and situations *during waking life*. I propose that comparative scanning (Pacella 1972), that is comparing the familiar with that of the non-familiar, is an unceasing action representing an automatic and obligatory function of the ego.

Early cognition, memory, and language development are related to and influenced by the above described action of the early *matrix configuration*. If there is no adequate or stable prototype within the matrix configuration for accommodation or adjustment to certain types of later experiences in life, or if the function of autonomous comparative scanning becomes inhibited or defective for various reasons, anxiety in varying degrees or its derivative manifestations will occur. Such anxieties may occur, for instance, when rapid and sudden awakening from sleep takes place so that there is not enough time for proper scanning and for recognition of the surroundings; for example, in confused patients awakening rapidly from the deep coma of a convulsive shock treatment, or in cases of cerebral atrophy with confusion where relatives are not recognized or misidentified.

Of interest in connection with cases of cerebral impairment caused by chronic atrophic processes is the observation that events and experiences of the past, especially the very distant past, are more readily recalled than current or recent experiences (close to the "anchor"). There may be a variety of reasons to account for this phenomenon but in the context of this paper the importance of the anchoring action of the early matrix configuration and the action of the waking screen, and its continuing reflection later on in life upon subsequent object experiences,[3] has partial relevance. The more distant memories which are more closely connected with the waking screen have a more protective value to the confused patient than more recent experiences, since the gravitational or magnetic pull of the maternal anchor exerts the greater effect upon the earlier reminiscences (closer proximity in time). Thus they lend more basic security to individual existence. Although late and intermediate experiences are also subject to the gravitational pull of the anchor, in crisis situations it is the very early maternal or parental representations, called matrix configurations, which are crucial for safety and self-preservation (Pacella 1972, Mahler 1968, Greenson 1971).

In the expanding life of the infant, succeeding objects and part objects which he or she meets are automatically compared with and unconsciously fitted into the matrix configuration; this screening serves to reinforce or modify aspects of the primal matrix. The extent to which a new object molds into or engages the matrix configuration affects the quality and intensity of the reactions and the relationship to the new object. During the life cycle, accretions drawn from the described object interactions with new objects in addition to modifications caused by the instinctual vicissitudes will be integrated into the primitive matrix. In this way a fabric is woven which is subject to and represents a continuum of alterations of the original symbiotic and early object representations within the psyche without the core of the original matrix being significantly altered. New object representations are automatically compared and filtered through the waking screen to influence the feeling states and cognitive processes directed to the new object. This screen can be conceived of as having both active and passive elements. It is not only passively subjected to the input of new objects, but actively (though unconsciously) seeks (extracts as it were) from the environment suitable elements for attachment. In this process, the person even attempts to remodel the

---

3. Perhaps similar to the reverberations referred to by Mahler (1972) or the "later derivatives" of Erikson (1959).

new objects to make them fit for attachment. Of interest in this connection is a comment by Freud in an unpublished letter written in 1911 to an anthropologist, wherein he states that the individual in the course of his development rhythmically seeks out from the environment what he needs for his purposes (Pacella 1956). On a number of occasions Freud referred to the ego as *actively* searching for the specific object, the mother or the earliest symbolic representation of the mother: the breast of the symbiotic mother. In *The Interpretation of Dreams* (1900), and in the *Project* (1895), Freud mentioned that the object to be refound is the mother's breast; in the *Three Essays* (1905), he stated: "The finding of an object is in fact a *refinding* of it." But it was only much later (1925) that Freud referred again to the concept of the ego's search for the primal object in discussing perception and reality testing:

> . . . perception is not a purely passive process. The ego periodically sends out small amounts of cathexes into the perceptual system, by means of which it samples the external stimuli, and then after every such tentative advance it draws back again.

In the same article, Freud also writes:

> The first and immediate aim therefore of reality testing is not to find an object in real perception which corresponds to the one presented but to refind such an object, to convince one's self that it is still there.

Although the later stages of development, rapprochement in particular, add new features or modifications to the totality of psychic representation of the original matrix configuration, it seems reasonable to assume that the primal love object of the symbiotic period of life and the early subphases of the separation-individuation process remain indelibly imprinted within the psyche as the core or nucleus of the parental matrix, capable throughout life of manifesting itself through the translucence of numerous layers of additional memory traces.

In the practicing period, there is more active interchange of feelings, sensations and experiences involving the child-mother dyad with a gradually developing "intermolding," the "mutual cueing" of Mahler and Furer (1963). By this intermolding, I mean that the infant partially molds the mother to its demands, needs, and wishes, and that the mother in turn exercises a similar impact upon the child. This interchange assists in the formation of the primitive matrix, and in the succeeding, rapprochement, subphase, in particular, the "mother of separation" with more or less conspicuous struggle is forced to fit into this matrix and to become part of it. In short, the historical progression of the individual's object relations may add new cloaks and garments to the core, so that the original matrix will appear at varying times to be "dressed up" in keeping with current phase-specific developments, yet the core substance remains essentially unaltered.

During the rapprochement subphase (beginning roughly at 16 to 18 months of age), the toddler's dyadic relationship with the mother becomes increasingly ambitendent and hence the bipolar struggle seeking the optimal distance is increasingly evident. The infant wishes more for union with mother as he becomes increasingly aware of his separateness from the love object, and vice versa, while at the same time the developmental and maturational spurt towards individuation causes an equally increased need for motor and cognitive independence. The original longing for unity as well as fear of reengulfment become now quite evident in the child's behavior.

The importance of the waking screen is of particular interest since it was brought to my attention by a patient because of her specific pathology and family relationships which permitted a clear study of the waking screen and the matrix configuration. A clinical vignette is presented to illustrate the function of the matrix configuration (waking screen), in which the bipolar nature of the screening function was particularly instructive because of its diametrically opposite emotional valence (fusion panic versus separation anxiety).

CLINICAL EXAMPLE

Carolyn was 18 years old when she came to me for consultation and therapy. She was a very attractive, dark complexioned, dark haired, a well-built, athletic type. She appeared very pleasant, cooperative, friendly and anxious to begin treatment. A modified analysis was begun extending over a period of four years. This had to be interrupted in the second year of analysis for approximately three months because of a recurrence of a profound depressive episode of which the patient had episodically suffered in early adolescence. It became necessary to place her in a residential treatment center where she remained for three months, subsequently resuming therapy with me. It is of interest to mention that during her hospital stay, she desperately insisted that she be allowed to be at home with her mother. On the other hand, as soon as she was home she demanded to be allowed to move away from home, particularly from mother, to get her own apartment. When her wish was finally granted and she moved into her own apartment, she felt so lonely that she could not help but spend most of her time in her parents' home. We can see how Carolyn searched desperately and unsuccessfully to find the optimal distance from her love object. Although we know of the prevalence of this adolescent struggle with the problem of wanting and not wanting to be at home in less disturbed and even normally developing adolescents, with Carolyn it was especially acute.

Carolyn had actually started analytic therapy at about 13½ years of age with another analyst, because of severe depression, anxiety, and deterioration in her academic work. Her grades in school had slumped terribly at that time; she wanted particularly her mother's presence, especially at night, and she finally made a suicidal attempt by ingesting a large quantity of alcohol. Immediate treatment was required. Carolyn gradually improved during the course of this treatment, became "alive," active, almost elated, and functioned very well both socially and academically in high school until her senior year. However the improvement seemed to be largely due to a very intense positive transference to the therapist. The patient herself repeatedly asserted that she functioned well only "because of him."

She described mother as being cold, reserved, unaffectionate, too logical, and distant; on the other hand, at times the mother could be pleasant, supportive, and helpful. The mother actually was a highly intelligent, well-organized person, closely attached to the husband, active in various community projects. The father was described as warm, occasionally affectionate but readily punitive, and given to sudden outbursts of temper associated with yelling and self-pity because of heavy financial burdens and business worries. He was considered brilliant in his field with a significant national reputation. Carolyn accused the father of always being too busy to spend time with her, and of always siding with the mother against her. At 17, after more than three and a half years of treatment, without the working through of the problems, the analyst seemed to have felt that she was ready to stop therapy and go away to college, and finally told her so. Carolyn experienced this pronouncement from the doctor as a sudden terrible blow; she felt that he did not care whether he ever saw her again. She rapidly grew depressed and again her work at school fell down substantially. She refused to attend classes, or to be graduated by taking exams, became confused and began to experience delusions and illusions. All of these developments occurred quite rapidly. She again attempted suicide by ingesting a large quantity of barbiturates. Carolyn was hospitalized in a psychiatric unit for a period of approximately six months and improved considerably. Treatment with me began shortly after she left the institution. However, during the early course of her treatment with me, relatively short episodic periods of depression occurred associated with visual illusions which induced panic and rage. During interval periods, when she was relatively symptom-free, she would seem quite normal, and at times even elated.

In the childhood material certain distinct feelings and experiences represented recurrent themes. She continually complained of her mother's unaffectionate and reserved attitudes towards her, letting the maid care for and do everything for the patient. She felt that the mother always wanted to distance herself from her daughter. The mother always showed a strong preference and attentiveness to the patient's 18-month-older brother. Her earliest vivid memory, apparently a significant traumatic episode, could be placed in her second year of life. This consisted of her standing up in her crib peering through its bars and seeing mother and brother standing side by side holding hands. Both were looking at her, saying and doing nothing, though it must have been obvious to them, according to the patient, while she desperately attempted to get out of the crib to reach mother. The patient described her intense helplessness, frustration, and abandonment. This memory represents one of her most important screen memories.

Carolyn recalled another vivid memory, probably also a screen memory: when she was about 8 years old and the brother 9½ years of age, they were walking in a forest. At a certain point, the brother was reluctant to go any farther for fear they might get lost. Carolyn insisted they continue further in order to find "signs of a mythical witch" in the woods. The brother was the one who had been leading the way up to now, Carolyn trying desperately to keep up with him. Now Carolyn took the lead, telling him he could either follow her or return alone to the house. He resigned himself to let her take command of the expedition. She raced through the woods in a feeling of elation, abandon, and great excitement, with her brother desperately trying to keep up with her, until she reached a "distorted, gnarled tree." This represented for Carolyn the witch; finding the gnarled tree was the culmination of the expedition. She was exultant. Carolyn was magnetically drawn and impelled to find the tree-witch much in the same manner as she was impelled to seek out mother during her panics and depressions, already in her early teens when she could not sleep without the mother being incessantly at her bedside at night. We see here the basic problem of human existence as mentioned earlier in this paper.

This gnarled tree-witch seemed to represent a basic fantasy dominating the life of the patient. Carolyn depicted herself and her mother as deformed and witchlike when either of them were depressed or in a rage. It is important to note that the mother had a shortened and deformed left arm as the result of a birth injury. Also, the mother, like Carolyn herself, had depressive periods. During her depressions, Carolyn would perceive in her own mind "distorted and mechanical" people who kept staring at her. She would frequently say of these images that they stood by coldly watching her, saying nothing, just as in her early screen memory the mother and the brother were looking coldly on, "saying nothing." She would frequently draw them as robotlike, lifeless heads without limbs or trunks. In the analytic material the distorted people could be very dangerous, could displace her into another world of a "living death" occupying a different spatial dimension. At the same time the distorted people could be protective by guarding her with their intense gaze. Thus, the tree-witch of childhood is symbolic not only of both the symbiotic mother and the bad "mother of separation" but also a symbolic representation of the distorted "bad-good" people. The elation in discovering the tree seems to be related to a rediscovering or "fusion" with the symbiotic mother without brother. In the race with the brother, she was the first to reach the tree and to lean on it before brother caught up. She was victorious in the pursuit of mother.

The deformed tree-witch of her childhood seemed to be both a self-representation and a representation of mother, suggesting the bad "mother of separation" (Mahler 1972) during the separation-individuation phase of development, whence in the rapprochement subphase, the obligatory cognitive stage of development results in the child's having to recognize the mother as separate from the self with her own individuality and interests in whose omnipotence she herself is unable to partake. Carolyn's entire history from the rapprochement crisis onwards bears out her incessant struggle to reach the tree-witch, the bad mother of separation (Mahler 1972).

The symptom manifested by the patient and referred to earlier, was a tendency to animate inanimate objects, certain photographs of mother and friends, and wallpaper designs. She would have the illusion of wallpaper depicting the heads of live tigers ready to jump at her and devour her; in her own words, she would disappear and merge with them. In the same way, she felt an extremely strong pull from the photographs which she felt powerless to resist, as though she would be forced to fuse with them and be completely dissolved. At these times she desperately attempted to restrain herself from destroying them, and in fact, on one occasion she smashed a framed photograph of her mother and some other objects in the room. At this point she was in both an unbearable rage and a paralyzing panic which immobilized her. The result of the double action of this rage and panic which the distorted people exercised upon her was felt at the same time as an important protecting action which she craved and needed as a defense against her destructive rage. In this immobile state of paralytic pain, the ceiling seemed to be closing down upon her, while the walls of the room took on bizarre shapes as if they were moving towards her to ultimately crush her. In panic, she would scream for mother, rush out of the room, or lie immobile awaiting the ultimate end of her existence. The "final crush" would consist in actual fusion with the wall, combined with the frightening feeling that she would be entering into an existence "of suspended animation" in a different spatial dimension, permanently.

Let us see what we can reconstruct of Carolyn's earliest life: approximately two to three months after her birth, Carolyn's mother fell into a severe postpartum depression and paid very little attention to the patient. As a consequence of the mother's later guilt feelings over her neglect of Carolyn, she attempted, in her own words, to overcompensate in her actions after Carolyn was over 18 months old, showering her with much attention while resenting her need to overcome her own guilt. The mother of the patient once confided to Carolyn herself that the patient rarely accepted the mother's offers of affection and acted coldly and distantly to her. We may assume that Carolyn sensed the mother's ambivalence. In other words, the mutual intermolding between mother and child described above in detail had already gelled the pattern and quality of the early psychic maternal matrix which Carolyn had to cope with all her life. During treatment the external manifestations in search for optimal distance (as was manifest in the transference) are significant for evaluating the progress of therapy.

Carolyn projected these ambivalent affects and experiences onto the illusory bizarre walls and wallpaper designs, as well as onto the photographs, as if they were all a kind of screen.

It is the constant dynamic action of this waking screen which causes the regression pull to the primal love object, which our patient experienced in her visual illusions as both destructive with loss of identity by fusion or complete reassurance by the strange immobilization described above which, in an idiosyncratic way, guaranteed safety of oneness in reunion (fusion). Reunion with the original love object is the ultimate or final pathway for complete safety, albeit in a highly pathological way in the case of Carolyn. In this connection, it is of interest to refer to an experience occasionally related by patients who had been subject to extremely dangerous situations where life hung momentarily in the balance consisting of a sudden fleeting, yet vivid review of their past life. This rapid historical regression of mental content often reflects at its very end peaceful reunions with mother directly, or symbolically. In one such instance a 16-year-old girl felt that she was drowning while swimming and experienced a flash of reminiscences which terminated in a feeling of peaceful ecstasy as if she were "as one with water, being rocked to and fro." In another instance, an adult male, who was a passenger in an airplane which was being tossed about by unusually strong turbulence, experienced panic and a psychic historical regression, rapidly reviewing certain incidents relating to both parents and finally recalling play activity with mother which he believed occurred when he was about 3. The feeling attached to this play activity was that of an unusually "intense peacefulness." Nothing could happen to him in this state of omnipotent safety. A somewhat parallel instance of a case described by Greenson (1971) refers to a regressive reunion with mother in a case of near drowning.

Why the regression to the symbiotic love object should occur rather than to the representations of the post-rapprochement or oedipal object, or to later object representations is an important question. One partial answer (in addition to the feelings of reunion, total safety, and omnipotence) is that the primal object representations are conflict-free and economically require the least expenditure of energy for recathexis. My thesis is that the waking screen exerts its influence constantly in terms of anchoring new perceptual experiences internally and externally. In acute crises, through an autonomous comparative scanning process, it is readily available to the perceptual ego.

If we consider the question concerning the reason or reasons for the regressive use of visual imagery to reflect primitive representations of mother and the intense ambivalence directed towards her, one answer could be that the visual imagery, as the major sensory adaptive mode, recaptures or attempts to recapture the primal love object of the symbiotic phase of infant development (3 to 6 months) when all incorporation and all fusion with mother represents the total life of the infant, with complete gratification of its needs and a conflict-free existence (oceanic feeling of unity).

During the succeeding phases of development (Mahler's separation-individuation process, 5 months to 3 years), the infant gradually recognizes the mother as a separate and specific object and its libidinal investment of the mother increases with time as he undergoes a parallel increase in separateness from its primal love object. Thus two major developments almost antithetical in nature occur during the separation-individuation process: (a) the increasing perception that mother is a separate object, that he or she cannot participate in her omnipotence; and (b) the increasing object libidinal investment of the mother.

During the rapprochement phase there is a maturational pressure which forces the infant to the awareness of separateness. The clinical evidence which lends support to these statements have been amply noted in the observations of infant behavior by Mahler (1968). During the practicing subphase, when the infant begins to walk, he practices moving away from mother only to return again for "emotional refueling" (Furer 1959), and reacts to strangers with anxiety while attempting to familiarize their features by comparing them visually and tactiley with mother's. During the rapprochement subphase (15 to 25 months), the toddler in addition has attained representational intelligence and symbolic thinking. He is desirous to share with mother every one of his new experiences and skills on a much higher intellectual level. He is resistive to being separated from her, yet he insists upon functioning autonomously as a separate individual. He wants to be autonomous, yet cannot be autonomous. He wants to fuse yet is fearful of reengulfment.

The symbiotic mother, who up to the rapprochement subphase was felt more or less as part of the self, is now in the second half of the second year in the rapprochement subphase—through the maturation of the ego and the coming of age of representative instead of psychomotor intelligence—perceived as separate from the self. As Mahler and her co-workers found, the now separate maternal representation in the rapprochement subphase quasi-automatically becomes the ambivalent, decathected "bad mother of separation."

No matter how good a mother may be through the rapprochement subphase she is always felt as unsatisfactory because she does not let the toddler partake of her own omnipotence in which the child still believes; on the other hand, she is always felt as potentially dangerous because the longing for fusion and thus the loss of identity persists.

A lack of proper development during the separation-individuation process, and especially the lack of resolution of the rapprochement crisis with the concomitant failure of object constancy, did not at the same time allow the subsequent perceptual experiences to be properly integrated into the waking screen to permit the "anchor" (matrix configuration) to stabilize and organize the ego sufficiently in its object relations development to move into the oedipal period of life without excessive handicaps.

SUMMARY

It is hypothesized that a waking screen exists as a function of the primal matrix configuration corresponding with Lewin's concept of the dream screen. It consists of a primitive parental configuration referable to the symbiotic and the separation-individuation periods of life as a kind of basic memory complex acting as an organizing function of the ego. It exerts its influence in varying degrees upon the dynamic-economic aspects of psychic activity. The earliest sensory experiences with the symbiotic mother and the later experiences with the parents during the separation-individuation process form the early matrix which continues to act as a "waking screen." The matrix memory complex represents the anchor upon which new objects and new experiences impinge. It plays an active role in scanning, integrating, rejecting, or modifying all the newer percepts of object representations throughout life. It is a specifically woven fabric derived from the primitive ego representing a basic core from which further object relations develop, and towards which regressive or return paths allow for rapid retreat to the safety of reunion with the primal love object.

References

Bowlby, J. (1969). *Attachment and Loss. Volume 1: Attachment.* New York: Basic Books.

Brody, S., and Axelrad, S. (1966). Anxiety, socialization and ego-formation in infancy. *International Journal of Psychoanalysis* 47:218-229.

Erikson, E. H. (1959). *Identity and the Life Cycle.* Psychological Issues Monograph 1. New York: International Universities Press.

Freud, S. (1895). Project for a scientific psychology. *Standard Edition* 1:281-397.

——— (1900). The interpretation of dreams. *Standard Edition* 4/5:1-622.

——— (1905). Three essays on the theory of sexuality. *Standard Edition* 7:135-243.

——— (1925). On negation. *Standard Edition* 19:235-239.

Furer, M. (1959). Personal communication.

Greenacre, P. (1952). Pregenital patterning. *International Journal of Psycho-Analysis* 33:410-415.

Greenson, R. R. (1971). A dream while drowning. In *Separation-Individuation: Essays in Honor of Margaret S. Mahler,* ed. J. B. McDevitt and C. F. Settlage, pp. 377-384. New York: International Universities Press.

Lewin, B. D. (1946). Sleep, the mouth and the dream screen. *Psychoanalytic Quarterly* 15:419-434.

Mahler, M. S. (1968). *On Human Symbiosis and the Vicissitudes of Individuation, Volume 1: Infantile Psychosis.* New York: International Universities Press.

——— (1972). On the first three subphases of the separation-individuation process. *International Journal of Psychoanalysis* 53:333-338. Reprinted in *The Selected Papers of Margaret S. Mahler,* vol. 2, ch. 8 New York: Jason Aronson, 1979.

——— (1975). Discussion of Dr. Pacella's paper, "Early ego development and the déjà vu." *Journal of the American Psychoanalytic Association* 23:322-326.

Mahler, M. S., and Furer, M. (1963). Certain aspects of the separation-individuation phase. *Psychoanalytic Quarterly* 32:1-14.

Pacella, B. L. (1956). Paper presented at the Freud Centenary Meeting of the New York Psychoanalytic Institute, May 6, 1956; and at the Mid-Winter Meeting, American Psychoanalytic Association, December 1956.

——— (1972). The waking screen. Paper presented at the Mid-Winter Meeting of the American Psychoanalytic Association, December 1972.

——— (1975). Early ego development and the déjà vu. *Journal of the American Psychoanalytic Association* 23:300-318.

Sandler, J. (1960). The background of safety. *International Journal of Psycho-Analysis* 41:352-360.

Spitz, R. A. (1965). *The First Year of Life.* New York: International Universities Press.

Winnicott, D. W. (1971). *Playing and Reality.* New York: Basic Books.

Part III

Rapprochement and Developmental Issues

8

The Role of Internalization in the Development of Object Relations During the Separation-Individuation Phase

John B. McDevitt, M.D.

Many authors—Jacobson (1964), Mahler (1968), Mahler, Pine, and Bergman (1975), Spitz (1957, 1965)—as well as the members of today's panel (Gedo and Goldberg 1973, Kanzer 1957, Lichtenberg 1975, Meissner 1971, Spruiell 1974) have pointed out that incorporation, imitation and identification, and introjection play a significant role in the development of object relations.

In this paper I intend first to examine a few aspects of the subphase-specific development of internalization in terms of its role in beginning the establishment of object relations. This development is inferred from the behavior of children observed during a research study of the separation-individuation process (Mahler, Pine, and Bergman 1975, McDevitt 1975, Pine and Furer 1963). I then illustrate identification and introjection in one child, Donna, both at the time of the research study in the first three years of life and at the time of a follow-up study when she was 8½ years old. These internalizations

Reprinted from *Journal of the American Psychoanalytic Association* 27 (2):327-343 by permission of International Universities Press, Inc. Copyright © 1979 by the American Psychoanalytic Association. Presented in a shortened version at the Panel on Current Concepts of Object Relations Theory, Fall Meeting of The American Psychoanalytic Association, December 1977.

and their outcome are unique, of course, for Donna's particular development.

Prior to the differentiation subphase, the mother organizes her baby's activities and experiences according to her own conscious and unconscious needs and fantasies. Through mutual mirroring, cueing, and scanning, the infant incorporates the mother's attributes, traits, or expectations (see Jacobson 1964, Lichtenstein 1961, Loewald 1978, Meissner 1979, Schafer 1968). The infant presents to the mother a large variety of cues—to indicate needs, tension, and pleasure (Mahler and Furer 1963). In a complex manner, the mother responds selectively to only certain of these cues. The infant gradually alters his behaviors in relation to this selective response and does so in a characteristic way—"the result of his own endowment and the mother-child relationship" (Mahler 1968, p. 18). From this circular interaction emerge patterns of behavior that contribute to the infant's first inner regulations; for example, the states of sleep-wake patterns (Sander et al. 1970, Sander 1974); the gradual establishment of basic trust; the beginning attainment of such ego qualities as anxiety and frustration tolerance (Meissner 1973, Tolpin 1971); and eventually, "hatching," self-object differentiation, and the beginnings of object relations (Mahler 1967, Mahler, Pine, and Bergman 1975).

Even when the differentiation subphase is well under way, we may see a regression to a type of merging, incorporative relationship with the mother under situations of stress. In our research study we noticed that soon after the beginning of the differentiation subphase (5 to 9 months), the infant shows behaviors from which it may be inferred that he misses and longs for the mother during her brief absences—for example, when the mother was out of the room for an interview (McDevitt 1975). As early as 7 to 8 months, Donna cried bitterly and helplessly during her mother's brief absences, at the same time looking repeatedly at the door through which her mother had departed. Slowly, over a period of several months, Donna, as well as other children, developed a narcissistic regressive defense as a way of managing this painful situation.

We have termed this defensive and adaptive phenomenon "low-keyedness" (Mahler and McDevitt 1968). The children often withdrew into themselves and lost interest in their surroundings when the mother was absent. They seemed to become preoccupied with an inner feeling of a previous state of closeness or "oneness" with the mother, apparently in an attempt to maintain their emotional equilibrium in the mother's absence. In order to do so, the children would shut out affective and perceptual claims from external sources (especially human) in order to cope with the pain of physical separation. They regressed to the earlier symbiotic union with the mother as described by Mahler (1966) and merged with the mother in a manner described by Jacobson (1964) as representing the foundations on which all future object relations as well as all future identifications are built. We assume that in the phenomenon of "low-keyedness" a sensorimotor and affective memory of the mother in interaction with the baby is consolidated at times of need, promoting the earliest internalizations and emotional ties to the mother.

During the differentiation and practicing subphases (from 5 to 15 months), we infer that the child imitates his love objects—their gestures, tone of voice, affects, behavior, and actions—in his more intimate relationships and in playing such games as peekaboo, pat-a-cake, bye-bye, and rolling a ball. These imitations are founded on the close emotional tie between the mother and her baby. They occur at first only in the presence of the parent who serves as a model for the baby to imitate.

An exception to this occurs in the use of a protosymbolic object (Werner and Kaplan 1964) during the mother's absence. By her tenth month, although Donna could be comforted by observers during the time her mother was out of the room, she could not snuggle up to them, nor could she rest her head upon their shoulders as she did with her mother. On one occasion while her mother was absent, Donna did find comfort in hugging and resting her head on a Teddy Bear, much as she rested her head on her mother's shoulder. The Teddy Bear represented her mother and was a protosymbolic object. Again, we see how the mother's brief absence may promote internalization.

At the end of the practicing subphase and the beginning of the rapprochement subphase (between 12 and 18 months) we see a more active type of imitation in which the child takes more initiative. Imitations of the adult's behaviors are observed in the child's spontaneous activities and games, even in the absence of the adult. The child may go to the door and say "Bye-bye" or "Mama" in anticipation of or during his mother's absence; the junior toddler—especially the little girl—may mother her doll in symbolic play, using this play to comfort herself while her mother is away. She may murmur "Mama" and "Baba" while cradling and rocking her doll. It is striking how often such play is an exact replication of the significant qualities of the actual mother-child relationship. Donna, for example, was an active, loving "little mother" to her dolls, just as her mother was to her.

The model now used by the junior toddler for his imitations and beginning identifications consists of mental representations of the behavior patterns of the love object. As Piaget (Piaget and Inhelder 1969) has pointed out, deferred imitations and symbolic play, as well as the verbal evocation of the mother in her absence, indicate that behavior has become detached from its previous motoric context and now rests on representation in thought.

Such play based on deferred imitation serves as an intermediate step in the child's inner world between the actual mother-child relationship and the transfer of this relationship to the child's internal world. It also permits a continuing relationship with the love object during the latter's absence (Pine 1975, Schafer 1968). Furthermore, by actively showing care and concern for the doll, the child repeats the same behaviors and emotions that the mother has shown toward him and begins to develop the *capacity* and means of *actively expressing* comforting and loving *feelings* toward others. Donna, over the next two and a half years, frequently demonstrated the same care and concern toward younger children and a favorite playmate that she had shown toward her doll.

The ability to identify with and repeat previously enjoyed activities with the mother in games and symbolic play enables the junior toddler to function with greater ease during his mother's brief absences toward the end of the practicing period and in the early part of the rapprochement subphase. Ball play, sitting in mother's chair, and a variety of games with observers are favorite activities.

In the first part of the rapprochement subphase (from 15 to 18 months), the junior toddler begins to turn his attention away from practicing his motor skills and his "love affair with the world" to a greater interest in social interactions. He frequently offers gifts and shares objects with his mother and, on occasion, even feeds her as he has been fed by her. In these activities the junior toddler identifies with his mother's previous giving and sharing and with her accompanying pleasurable affect. By identifying with her he has found additional ways of *expressing his positive feelings.* The mother's availability and readiness to accept her toddler's gifts and to share with him are extremely important for the development of his object relations. At this same time we also see temporary imitations of other children and the beginnings of empathy.

In the expression of his negative, aggressive feelings the toddler may also identify with his mother who often has had to prohibit his activities. A well-known example of this, described in detail by Spitz (1957, 1965), is the toddler's identification with his mother's prohibitions by the use of the word "no." This identification with the aggressor leads to an increasing objectivation of the mother. A little later, the child's repetition of the word "no" to himself leads to a greater objectivation of the self. Both enhance self-object differentiation and *self-awareness*.

Between 18 and 24 months of age a crisis, the rapprochement crisis, occurs in the child's development (Mahler 1972, McDevitt 1975). This is a critical period during which the child becomes much more acutely aware of his mental self. Profound changes occur in his mental and emotional development: independent walking, the capacity for evocative memory, the beginnings of representational thought, the more precise demarcation of the self- and object representation, and the shift to the anal-sadistic and early genital phases of psychosexual development (Roiphe 1968, Galenson and Roiphe 1971). On the one hand, the toddler wants to fully exercise his new-found autonomy and independence; on the other hand, he painfully feels the loss of his former sense of omnipotence and is distressed by his relative helplessness (Mahler 1966, 1972). Although he wants to share toys and activities with his mother, the toddler also shows an increasing possessiveness and jealousy of both his mother and inanimate objects, competing for and defending both, as demonstrated by his frequent use of the word "mine."

The toddler cannot always have his mother's attention, the toys he desires, or the space he would like to occupy; he may become jealous of the interest mother pays to siblings or other children. Forced to limit the toddler's activities, the mother cannot restore his former sense of omnipotence, nor is she always able to relieve his sense of aloneness and helplessness. The junior toddler comes to feel hurt, frustrated, and angry with his mother, whom he still considers to be omnipotent. As a result, a struggle ensues in which the child either fights with or clings to his mother. Ambivalence becomes marked. Even if the mother is understanding, it is still difficult for her to relieve the child of his conflicts. It is especially important at this developmental stage that the mother understand her child's ambivalence; it is equally important that she encourage her toddler's autonomy and identifications, particularly those that promote such ego functions as frustration tolerance.

If the toddler is fortunate in having a reasonably good relationship with his mother and other favorable conditions for development, he will proceed to higher levels of object and self-constancy during the slow course of resolution of the rapprochement crisis during the third and fourth subphases. Identification with the parents is an essential element in this developmental advance. Just as the infant resolved his distress over mother's leaving the room when he was younger by imitating her, he now resolves his actual and intrapsychic conflicts between his own wishes and his parents' prohibitions, as well as his feelings of helplessness and his wish to please his parents, by selectively identifying with them. If he is successful in these efforts, individuation, sound secondary narcissism, and the development of psychic structure progress rapidly.

In addition, partial resolution of the ambivalence characteristic of the rapprochement crisis by means of identification makes possible the beginning attainment of object constancy in the fourth subphase (from 24 to 36 months). It brings about a primarily libidinal cathexis of the maternal representation, which is one of the essential determinants of object constancy (Mahler 1966, Mahler, Pine, and Bergman 1975, McDevitt 1975). The toddler is now able to integrate the "good" and "bad" aspects of the mother into one unified representation and no longer needs to use the defense mechanism of "splitting the object representation."

Another essential determinant of object constancy is the quality of the maternal representation—one that produces in the child a sense of security and comfort, just as the actual mother had in the past. As Mahler (1968) has stated, "By object constancy we mean that the maternal image has become intrapsychically available to the child in the same way that the actual mother had been libidinally available— for sustenance, comfort, and love" (p. 222). A similar point of view has been expressed by Joffe and Sandler (1965), Kohut (1971), Tolpin (1971), and Spitz (1965).

In the fourth subphase the senior toddler's more complex fantasy play, more friendly and cooperative behavior, more mature ego-determined object relations, and increased regard for others, all suggest that his identifications have moved from the previous primitive imitations to more selective ego identifications (Jacobson 1964).

So far we have discussed one type of internalization, namely, imitation and identification within the context of a reasonably good mother-child relationship and favorable conditions for development. Had the situation been otherwise, identifications might not have had a beneficial influence on object relations.

Let us now retrace our steps and turn our attention to a negative outcome of the rapprochement crisis. If this crisis leads to intense ambivalence and splitting of the object world into "good" and "bad," the maternal representation may be internalized as an unassimilated, dissociated foreign body, as a hostile, "bad" introject (Mahler 1971). The relationship with the actual mother is preserved, that is, protected from the child's hostility, by introjection of the representation of the "bad" mother (McDevitt 1967, 1971). This is most likely to occur under certain conditions: (1) when the love object is emotionally unavailable or excessively unreliable and intrusive; (2) when the child experiences the realization of his helplessness too abruptly and too painfully, resulting in a too sudden deflation of his sense of omnipotence; and (3) when there has been an excess of cumulative or shock trauma (Mahler, Pine, and Bergman 1975). In such cases, the behaviors characteristic of the rapprochement subphase more or less persist and there is a concomitant delay in the development of object relations. These behaviors include excessive separation anxiety, helplessness, passivity, and inhibitions, on the one hand, and demandingness, coerciveness, possessiveness, envy, and temper outbursts, on the other.

When ambivalence is marked during the rapprochement crisis, the child's ability to identify with the mother is hampered (McDevitt 1975). A similar disruption of identifications has been observed in slightly older children separated from their parents for longer periods of time (Heinicke and Westheimer 1965). Although introjects may exert a favorable influence on the development of object relations at other times, they cannot do so when the rapprochement crisis is severe since they are brought on by intense conflict, ambivalence, and anxiety.

An unfavorable outcome of the rapprochement crisis was seen with particular clarity in the case of Donna. Although she had been too closely tied to her mother, her development until the age of 18 months seemed fairly normal. In addition, her mother seemed to be the perfect mother, one who appeared to offer "optimal mothering." By 18 months of age, however, Donna developed a severe rap-

prochement crisis. This reaction continued in varying degrees
throughout the remainder of the second and third year. Donna had
experienced a too sudden deflation of her omnipotence. By now we
recognized that the mother's guilt over her own aggression, as well as
her need to infantilize Donna, did not allow her to firmly encourage
autonomy, frustration and ambivalence tolerance, and realistic
achievement. Further, Donna had suffered an unusual number of
shock trauma and showed a beginning castration reaction (Roiphe
1968, Galenson and Roiphe 1971). On the one hand, Donna's ambivalent feelings toward her mother became marked; on the other
hand, her mother was intolerant of aggressive impulses in herself or
in anyone else, including Donna. The result was that Donna, who had
previously been overly aggressive, projected her hostile impulses
onto the maternal representation which then became internalized as
a hostile, "bad" introject. Donna began to see herself and the world
around her according to the effect this hostile introject had on her
self- and object representations instead of in accordance with the
actual reality of her relationship with her mother. As a consequence,
Donna became a quiet, shy, overly cautious, inhibited little girl who
was quite possessive of her mother and who suffered more than the
usual amount of separation distress. She needed to maintain a more
than usual distance between herself and the other-than-mother object world. When particularly upset, she turned aggression on herself, chewing and biting her fingers, leaving distinct teeth marks.

Donna's inability to resolve satisfactorily the rapprochement crisis
contributed to the onset of a marked castration reaction in her third
year. This brought on renewed ambivalence and a regression to the
need to be close to and cling to her mother that had been present in
the rapprochement subphase.

Despite these difficulties, Donna did manage on a number of
occasions to resolve temporarily her rapprochement crisis and her
castration reaction by identifying with maternal aspects of the
mother. She would once again become a loving "little mother" of her
dolls and of younger children, taking over many of her mother's
attitudes, expressions, and functions.

During her fourth year when she was in nursery school, Donna
assisted the teacher in a motherly manner and often mothered other
children. She was the homemaker and the mother—bathing, feeding, and dressing her dolls. In play sessions her continued castration
reaction led to additional shifting identifications: with a boy doll;

with a baby doll who would be cared for by mother and who would grow a penis; and with a girl doll who tentatively replaced mother in father's affections.

At the time of a follow-up study[1] when she was 8½ years old, Donna still liked to mother her dolls and stuffed animals and to help her mother about the house. The identification with the caretaking-domestic functions of the mother had persisted almost unchanged, although it had gained considerable autonomy. Psychological tests indicated that Donna was capable of caring for others and of affection, warmth, and empathy. We concluded that the early imitations and identifications with the mother's maternal aspect had become an essential part of Donna's psychic structure and no longer required external reinforcement. They contributed in a positive, ego-syntonic, nonconflictual manner to her object relations.

This was not the case, however, with the main findings of the follow-up study. In her interviews Donna was shy, quiet, reticent, and controlled. She did not speak spontaneously and answered questions in a soft, plaintive, almost inaudible voice. She preferred that her mother remain in the room with her during the first few sessions. When she finally did let her mother leave the room she was only slightly less inhibited. We inferred from other material that Donna's inability to assert herself was the result of the use of the mechanisms of repression and reaction formation.

Passive-dependent trends were pronounced in the psychological tests and were inseparable from Donna's anxiety about any display of initiative or assertiveness. The tests revealed that the preservation of the dependent relationship to the mother (the maternal introject) took precedence over more advanced developmental tasks. Even the oedipal relationship with the father was expressed in passive-oral terms. It was as though Donna felt that, if she were to be more assertive, she would lose or damage her mother. In many ways she seemed to fit Anna Freud's description of altruistic surrender (1936).

At the age of 8½ Donna had not successfully resolved the conflicts of the rapprochement crisis and in many respects remained fixated in the rapprochement subphase. As a result, her object relations suffered.

The follow-up study of Donna as well as those of other children

1. Seventeen of the thirty-eight children originally studied were followed up by means of interviews with the children, the parents, school and home visits, and psychological testing.

indicates that the consequences for personality development of the resolution of the rapprochement crisis are extensive and enduring. Jacobson (1964) speaks of a compromise achieved by selective identification between the child's need to retain the symbiotic relationship and opposing tendencies to loosen the symbiotic ties by aggressive, narcissistic expansion and independent ego functioning. She adds that, under the influence of oedipal rivalry, this *conflict* reaches its *first climax* toward the end of the oedipal period and is then resolved by superego formation (p. 50).

I am suggesting that this same conflict reaches an earlier climax at the time of the rapprochement subphase and is resolved by the formation of psychic structure in the ego and superego precursors (see also Mahler, Pine, and Bergman 1975). The identifications employed to resolve the rapprochement crisis are probably forerunners of those employed to resolve oedipal conflicts.

As we have seen, the formation of psychic structure at this time may be expressed by neurotic symptoms and defenses, and may persist more or less unchanged into latency. As we would expect, external circumstances had remained essentially unchanged during the phallic-oedipal phase of Donna's development.

The formation of sufficient psychic structure following the resolution of the rapprochement crisis also makes analysis possible by the fourth subphase; probably makes prediction more reliable by this time; and partly explains why reconstruction based on analytic (primarily verbal) data cannot, as a rule, go further back than the rapprochement subphase.

The development of object relations and object love is a gradual and complex process. Its beginnings are determined by the child's evolving biological and psychological needs and drives, by his ego development, and his interactions with his love objects. Following the specific attachment to the mother at approximately 5 months of age and following a period of ambivalence in the second year, in the third year the senior toddler becomes capable of beginning object constancy and a more give-and-take relationship in which he shows affection for his mother or father as a real (true) object.

In this presentation I have examined only one aspect of the young child's developing object relations, that of internalization. Internalization is an active, repetitive principle stemming from within the child. Its outcome will depend both on the child's endowment and the nature of the parent-child interaction.

Object relations and internalizations develop hand in hand, and internalizations play a significant role in the development of object relations. Due to the infant's immaturity, the first internalizations or incorporations are in the form of merging or primitive global imitations. Later, as his developing nature permits, the child takes over from his parents those selective identifications that are essential elements in the development of his object relations. Identifications contribute to the development of the self and of psychic structure. They also modify and enrich object relations. Identifications with a mother's loving care foster the very beginnings of love and concern for others. I am suggesting a developmental progression in which the human bond, trust and confidence, mutual love, and altruism have their roots in the preoedipal mother-child interaction and the internalizations that result from this interaction.

Most important, I have emphasized the crucial role of the rapprochement crisis in the development of object relations. If the child is fortunate, identifications will help him to resolve the ambivalence and conflicts of the rapprochement crisis and to begin to attain object and self-constancy. On the other hand, if he is not so fortunate in coping with the rapprochement crisis, even though his earlier development may have been reasonably successful, he may remain more or less fixated at the rapprochement subphase, and, as a result, the resolution of his oedipal conflicts and the development of his object relations will suffer.

SEPARATION-INDIVIDUATION THEORY AND OBJECT RELATIONS THEORY

Mahler (personal communication, 1977) does not consider her theory solely or exclusively an object relations theory. She regards her work as a general psychoanalytic theory of early development, with special emphasis on the mother-child dyad. Her theory deals as much with the differentiation of the self and identity formation as with the differentiation of the object. I would add that her work delineates invariant, albeit overlapping, stages in development that are determined as much by innate maturation of the drives and the ego as they are by the child's object relations. Nature and nurture mutually influence each other in determining the autistic and symbiotic phases and the subphases of the separation-individuation process. This interaction probably occurs in a manner similar to that described by Escalona (1965) who places an intervening variable, the child's concrete subjective experiences, between nature and nurture, on the one side, and current behavior and personality outcome, on the other. From a more psychoanalytically oriented perspective, this interaction of nature and nurture is probably similar to Loewald's (1971) view that the id and the ego, conceived as psychic structures, gradually come into being through the intricate interchanges in the psychic field of the mother-child dyad. The infant's innate potentialities both shape and are shaped by the relationship with the mother. The well-endowed child can extract to a remarkable degree the necessary ingredients for satisfactory object relations from the most meager environmental circumstances; conversely, the poorly endowed child finds it difficult to develop satisfactorily even in the best of circumstances.

Although it is too early to compare the terms used in object relations theory which have been extrapolated from work with adults (for example, Kohut 1971) with the terms used in separation-individuation theory based on naturalistic, observational research studies, a beginning can be made, as long as we realize that much more work needs to be done both on the clinical-observational and the theoretical level.

It seems likely that in normal development the exhibitionistic grandiose self and the idealized self-object exist prior to the profound sense of separateness and helplessness and loss of omnipotence that occur at the time of the rapprochement crisis. In normal development the senior toddler's realistic abilities and achievements, improved reality testing, and secondary-process functioning, along with selective ego identifications, enable him to overcome his sense of separateness, helplessness, and hostility. Successful self-assertion in the world of reality and the beginnings of true object relations (Jacobson 1964, p. 51), as opposed to magical solutions of closeness, merging, or sameness, contribute significantly to a more realistic and satisfactory appraisal of the self and the object in the fourth subphase and, therefore, to sound secondary narcissism, and to self- and object constancy.

References

Escalona, S. K. (1965). Some determinants of individual differences. *Transactions N.Y. Acad. Sci.*, Ser. II, Vol. 27, No. 7, pp. 802-816.

Freud, A. (1936). *The Ego and the Mechanisms of Defense*. New York: International Universities Press, 1966.

Galenson, E., and Roiphe, H. (1971). The impact of early sexual discovery on mood, defensive organization, and symbolization. *Psychoanalytic Study of the Child* 26:195-216.

Gedo, J. E., and Goldberg, A. (1973). *Models of the Mind: A Psychoanalytic Theory*. Chicago: University of Chicago Press.

Heinicke, C. M., and Westheimer, I. J. (1965). *Brief Separations*. New York: International Universities Press.

Jacobson, E. (1964). *The Self and the Object World*. New York: International Universities Press.

Joffe, W. G., and Sandler, J. (1965). Notes on pain, depression, and individuation. *Psychoanalytic Study of the Child* 20:394-424. New York: International Universities Press.

Kanzer, M. (1957). Acting out, sublimation, and reality testing. *Journal of the American Psychoanalytic Association* 5:663-684.

Kohut, H. (1971). *The Analysis of the Self*. New York: International Universities Press.

Lichtenberg, J. D. (1975). The development of the sense of self. *Journal of the American Psychoanalytic Association* 23:453-484.

Lichtenstein, H. (1961). Identity and sexuality: A study of their interrelationship in man. *Journal of the American Psychoanalytic Association* 9:179-260.

Loewald, H. (1971). On motivation and instinct theory. *Psychoanalytic Study of the Child* 26:91-128.

——— (1978). *Psychoanalysis and the History of the Individual*. New Haven: Yale University Press.

Mahler, M. S. (1966). Notes on the development of basic moods: the depressive affect. In *Psychoanalysis—A General Psychology: Essays in Honor of Heinz Hartmann*, ed. R. M. Loewenstein et. al, pp. 152-168. New York: International Universities Press. Reprinted in *The Selected Papers of Margaret S. Mahler*, vol. 2, ch. 5. New York: Jason Aronson, 1979.

——— (1967). On human symbiosis and the vicissitudes of individuation. *Journal of the American Psychoanalytic Association* 15:740-763. Reprinted in *Selected Papers*, op. cit., ch. 6.

——— (1968). *On Human Symbiosis and the Vicissitudes of Individuation*. In collaboration with M. Furer. New York: International Universities Press.

——— (1971). A study of the separation-individuation process and its possible application to borderline phenomena in the psychoanalytic situation. *Psychoanalytic Study of the Child* 26:403-424. Reprinted in *Selected Papers*, op. cit., ch. 11.

——— (1972). Rapprochement subphase of the separation-individuation process. *Psychoanalytic Quarterly* 41:487-506. Reprinted in *Selected Papers*, op. cit., ch. 9; and as ch. 1, this volume.

Mahler, M. S., and Furer, M. (1963). Certain aspects of the separation-individuation phase. *Psychoanalytic Quarterly* 32:1-14. Reprinted in *Selected Papers*, op. cit., ch. 2.

Mahler, M. S., and McDevitt, J. B. (1968). Observations on adaptation and defense *in statu nascendi:* Developmental precursors in the first two years of life. *Psychoanalytic Quarterly* 37:1-21. Reprinted in *Selected Papers*, op. cit., ch. 7.

Mahler, M. S., Pine, F., and Bergman, A. (1975). *The Psychological Birth of the Human Infant.* New York: Basic Books.

McDevitt, J. B. (1967). A separation problem in a three-year-old girl. In *The Child Analyst at Work*, ed. E. R. Geleerd, pp. 24-58. New York: International Universities Press.

——— (1971). Preoedipal determinants of an infantile neurosis. In *Separation-Individuation: Essays in Honor of Margaret S. Mahler*, ed. J. B. McDevitt and C. F. Settlage, pp. 201-226. New York: International Universities Press.

——— (1975). Separation-individuation and object constancy. *Journal of the American Psychoanalytic Association* 23:713-742.

Meissner, W. W. (1971). Notes on identification. II. Clarification of related concepts. *Psychoanalytic Quarterly* 40:277-302.

——— (1973). Identification and learning. *Journal of the American Psychoanalytic Association* 21:788-816.

——— (1979). Internalization and object relations. *Journal of the American Psychoanalytic Association* 27:345-360.

Piaget, J. and Inhelder, B. (1969). *The Psychology of the Child.* New York: Basic Books.

Pine, F. (1975). Libidinal object constancy: A theoretical note. In *Psychoanalysis and Contemporary Science*, vol. 3, pp. 307-313. New York: International Universities Press.

Pine, F., and Furer, M. (1963). Studies of the separation-individuation phase: A methodological overview. *Psychoanalytic Study of the Child* 18:325-342.

Roiphe, H. (1968). On an early genital phase: with an addendum on Genesis. *Psychoanalytic Study of the Child* 23:345-365.

Sander, L. W. (1974). Primary prevention and some aspects of temporal organization in early infant-caretaker interaction. In *Infant Psychiatry— A New Synthesis*, ed. E. Rexford, L. W. Sander, and T. Shapiro, pp. 187-206. New Haven: Yale University Press.

Sander, L. W., Stechler, G., Julia, H., and Burns, P. (1970). Early mother-infant interaction and twenty-four hour patterns of activity and sleep. *Journal of the American Academy of Child Psychiatry* 9:103-123.

Schafer, R. (1968). *Aspects of Internalization*. New York: International Universities Press.

Spitz, R. A. (1957). *No and Yes: On the Genesis of Human Communication*. New York: International Universities Press.

Spitz, R. A., and Cobliner, W. G. (1965). *The First Year of Life* New York: International Universities Press.

Spruiell, V. (1974). Theories of the treatment of narcissistic personalities. *Journal of the American Psychoanalytic Association* 22:268-278.

Tolpin, M. (1971). On the beginnings of a cohesive self: an application of the concept of transmuting internalization to the study of the transitional object and signal anxiety. *Psychoanalytic Study of the Child* 26:316-352.

Werner, H., and Kaplan, B. (1964). *Symbol Formation: An Organismic-Developmental Approach to Language and the Expression of Thought*. New York: Wiley.

9

Triangulation, the Role of the Father and the Origins of Core Gender Identity During the Rapprochement Subphase

Ernest L. Abelin, M.D.

INTRODUCTION: THE EVOLUTION OF THE "EARLY TRIANGULATION" MODEL

In this paper, I will summarize the current, fourth phase of my investigation of the earliest role of the father, dealing with gender differences in "early triangulation." Unfortunately, within the format of a paper, I can give no more than the most schematic overview of a complex new theoretical model. For any details or elaborations, I must refer to my forthcoming book on the subject.

For over twenty years, Mahler has insisted on the early importance of the father: "beyond the eighteen-months mark and even earlier,

This paper is an expanded version of a paper read at a special scientific meeting of the New York Society of Freudian Psychologists on the occasion of Dr. Margaret S. Mahler's 80th birthday, April 24, 1977 in New York City. Different versions were read at the Fall Symposium of the San Francisco Psychoanalytic Institute, Extension Division, on October 24, 1976 (Abelin 1977); and for the Panel on the Role of the Father in the Preoedipal Years at the 66th Annual Meeting of the American Psychoanalytic Association in Quebec, on April 29, 1977 (Prall 1978).

I wish gratefully to acknowledge the critical suggestions from Drs. Margaret S. Mahler, Otto F. Kernberg, and William I. Grossman, as well as Ms. Elsa First's invaluable editorial help [the stable image of a father] . . . is perhaps . . . necessary to . . . and Gosliner 1955, p. 209). "The inner image of the father has never drawn to itself so much of the unneutralized drive cathexis as has the mother's" (p. 200); the father is an "uncontaminated" mother substitute (p. 210). In 1966 she explained the "comparative immunity against contamination of the father image" by the fact that "the mother image evolves by being first differentiated within the symbiotic dual unity complex and then separated out from it; . . . the father image comes towards the child . . . from outer space as it were . . . as something gloriously new and exciting, at just the time when the toddler is experiencing a feverish quest for expansion" (pp. 8-9). He thus becomes the "knight in shining armor" during the practicing subphase.

In the process of writing my dissertation on families of schizophrenic children, while still in Switzerland, I developed my "early triangulation" model. This model led me independently to predict a similar early role of the father (Abelin 1971a).

What is "early triangulation?" I hypothesized the existence of this process as part of normal development to integrate all the scattered data on the origin and nature of the schizophrenias. This construct also served to unify the developmental models of Spitz and Piaget. The reasoning ran something like this: In the last analysis, schizophrenia consists of a breakdown of symbolic functioning and of the mental image of the self. In normal development, these two achievements appear jointly around 18 months (Piaget 1937, Piaget and Inhelder 1966). What is the mechanism of their appearance? They presuppose a satisfactory relationship not only with each parent but also *between* father and mother, to judge from the family dynamics of schizophrenia. This suggests that in normal development, some kind of internalization of the relationship between the parents takes place around the age of 18 months (Abelin 1971a, p. 125, quoting Bateson). This internalization somehow leads to the formation of the self-image and of symbolic mental representations in general.

To understand why this should be so and how it comes about, we must try to recreate the experience of Piaget's sensorimotor world, which he described as "egocentric without an ego." While being at the center of his own world, the child before 18 months knows only about the world and not about himself. Indeed, before the child is able to construct symbolic mental images of absent objects, he experiences only a succession of scenes ("tableaux") in front of him. He has no concept of himself as a subject like others. His world has only one focus at any one time—prototypically his libidinal attachment object. Even his own motivation is perceived as a quality of the outside object: the child does not desire the object; he sees the object as desirable.

According to Piaget, a Copernican revolution of the mind is achieved around 18 months (1937, my translation): "In order to situate himself within space—which is the only way to construct a homogeneous and relative space—the child must . . . imagine himself as though he saw himself from the outside" (p. 177); "because imitation has been internalized and transmuted into symbolic mental images, the child is now able to picture in his mind his very own body. . . . This will enable him to view himself as just one cause and one effect among many others" (p. 76). In this quotation, Piaget refers to his rather convincing theory that a mental image of an object derives from imitation of that object. As a first step, the child learns to defer imitation. A few weeks later, action is dispensed with altogether; imitation of the object has been internalized into the image of that object (Piaget and Inhelder 1966, p. 56). However, what brings about this crucial step—this transmutation from an action in time into an image in space? How could this theory apply to the child's image of himself, since he cannot possibly see and imitate that self? And most of all, how does the toddler learn "to view himself as just one cause . . . among . . . others?"

It is my contention that the toddler cannot construct a true image of the self as long as he does not realize that *he* is the origin of the "desirability" of the object. Selfhood is the acknowledgment of one's core wish. But this core wish is always a wish for the libidinal object. It can only be seen and imitated, and therefore represented, in a triangular constellation such that the toddler perceives his one object desiring his other object. Faced with this excruciating experience of ultimate exclusion, the toddler recognizes for the first time in the rival's wish for the object his own frustrated wish for the same object. His action being suspended (because all his familiar attachment schemata are blocked), what he can do is actively to *imagine* himself as being like his rival—indeed, as *a* being like his rival: "There must be an I, like him, wanting her." Early triangulation is this identification with the rival.

By the same token, the first mental representation of the self is also the first symbolic image; it is the bridge between sensorimotor and symbolic functioning. After this, objects can be evoked in their absence; the signifier is now distinguished from the signified. However, the model implies that the first symbolic representation is at once a total wish-constellation, including the object and the separate self, desperately yearning for that object: "I want mommy." This, I believe, is the origin of the rapprochement wish. The first self-and-object image constellation is the intrapsychic structure (in the contemporary structuralist sense of that term) underlying the rapprochement crisis. Because of the schizophrenia data mentioned above, I assumed during that first phase of my research that the prototypical object of early triangulation was the mother and that the prototypical rival was the father—an assumption I was later to question. Early triangulation, then, would be triggered when the toddler perceives his father loving his mother—perhaps holding her in his arms or any related gesture. I will call this the *primal constellation.*

The first mental image constellation also constitutes the foundation of the mental representation of space. Piaget has shown that although the toddler has already constructed a well-organized sensorimotor or practical space, he must then reconstruct space from scratch on the level of internal representations. This will take several years. More generally, development of symbolic images recapitulates sensorimotor development, step by step, with a type of lag that Piaget has termed "vertical decalage."

The first core self-and-object image constellation is a very rudimentary representation. In particular, it does not include the image of the rival; indeed, the memory of the rival is obliterated in this symbolic representation. It has fused into the self-image, energizing it, as it were. It will take two to three years before the complete father/mother/self triangle can be represented on the level of the mental images. Thus, oedipal triangulation recapitulates early triangulation on the level of symbolic representations, in "vertical decalage." I will try to demonstrate elsewhere that the earlier stages of mental image constellations coincide with the oral, anal, and phallic stages of psychosexual development. As we know, instinctual drives comprise an origin, an aim, and an object. Their structure *presupposes* the first image constellation, consisting of the self, the wish, and the object. Thus, instinctual drives, too, are symbolic representations.

Now it is also more evident why my model predicted an early role for the father: he must be cathected as a second specific attachment object before early triangulation can take place, that is, before the rapprochement crisis around 18 months of age.

For the second phase of my investigations, I had the good fortune to work under the guidance of Dr. Margaret Mahler and to observe these processes directly at Masters Children's Center. In a substudy, I confirmed the early salience of the father as a second attachment object (Abelin 1971b).[1] Indeed, the father is never a stranger to the infant in average expectable circumstances. He soon becomes a second specific attachment object. However, the father is a different *kind* of parent, particularly tuned into the wild exuberance of the toddler during the practicing subphase. In times of distress or fatigue, the toddler will more likely turn to the mother for comfort. This seems to be due to the unique symbiotic roots of the mother relationship (Mahler 1966). During the rapprochement subphase, the father continues to represent a stable island of practicing reality, whereas the mother becomes contaminated by feelings of intense longing and frustration. The father may thus play an indispensable role in the resolution of that ambivalence.

In that study, I also began to gather indirect evidence for my hypothesis that "early triangulation" is the mechanism underlying the phenomena of rapprochement. In this respect, however, I found more than I had bargained for. Although the father emerged so clearly as an object of deep and specific attachment during the first two years of life, so did siblings and other children, grandparents, and various other familiar adults. Moreover, I observed that during the weeks preceding rapprochement and my hypothetical early triangulation, toddlers became sensitive to situations of triangular rivalry with other children more than with their fathers. Was early triangulation perhaps normally not an identification with the rival father but rather with the rival baby? Did it take place not in the primal constellation, but in what we might call the *Madonna constellation*—the toddler faced with another baby in his mother's arms? Come to think of it, this constellation (or its derivatives) might well represent an even more universal experience than the primal constellation.

I could not answer this question during the third phase of my investigation, which centered on the longitudinal study of a little boy whom I had had the chance to observe within his family (Abelin 1975). In that particular case, the full "identification with the rival

1. I wish to acknowledge again Dr. Mahler's invaluable and inspiring mentorship; in addition, that study was indebted to the observations and ideas of all the other members of the staff of the Masters Children's Center. The research was supported by N.I.M.H. Grant MH-08238. My particular substudy was made possible by my research training fellowship grant from the Medizinisch-Biologische Stipendienstiftung, Basel, Switzerland.

father" seemed to be barely observable, but could be inferred from various derivatives.

In the current phase of my research, I have begun investigating the differences between boys and girls in regard to early triangulation (Abelin 1977, Prall 1978). In the present paper, I will postulate that in actual development the early triangulation process involves three separate steps. The last step differs in girls and boys. I will call this more developed model the *tripartite model of early triangulation* to distinguish it from the earlier *general early triangulation model*. The former does not invalidate the latter, however; it only gives it a more specific content, related to gender differences.

Again, Mahler has adumbrated such gender differences when she commented on "the different flavor of the girl's reinvolvement with mother as compared to the boy's" during the rapprochement subphase (Mahler, Pine and Bergman 1975, p. 214). Along with this greater reinvolvement with mother, the little girl shows a heightened ambivalence to her, and her basic mood takes on a depressive tinge. By contrast, "identification with the father . . . facilitates a rather early beginning of the boy's gender identity". By the same token, "the boy seems better able to cope with 'symbiosis anxiety,' and to disidentify from mother (Greenson 1968)" (p. 215). "Identificatory and disidentificatory mechanisms . . . must be . . . different in boys and girls" during the rapprochement subphase (p. 216). Similarly, Stoller (1975, p. 294) now feels that "the process of the development of core gender identity is not the same in males as in females." He too thinks that masculine core gender identity must be preceded by "disidentification" from mother. To quote Greenson (1968): "The boy must renounce the . . . closeness that identification with the mothering person affords, and he must form an identification with the less accessible father" (p. 372).

My original data consist of a comparison of the development of a little boy with that of his younger sister, within the family setting. Of course, a single comparison can only be paradigmatic; however, in my conclusions, I also draw on innumerable observations at Masters Children's Center, as well as on a growing research literature.

THE OBSERVATIONAL COMPARISON

Like Michael, Kathy developed an affectionate attachment to her father during the first months of life. Unlike Michael, however, she always remained clearly more attached to her mother than to her father during the subphases of differentiation and practicing. At 9 months, her "flirtatiousness" with her father was noted for the first time. Later, when she was able to toddle, she would excitedly run away from her father so that he would chase her. Like Kleeman (1967, 1973), I feel that such patterns reveal an early erotization of stranger anxiety. By the same token, all through the practicing subphase Kathy experienced her father as a "knight in shining armor" (Mahler 1966), beckoning from outside the symbiotic orbit. Typically, she would be in her mother's arms, making coy overtures to her father. By contrast, Michael seemed to be as close to his father as to his mother during the practicing subphase, and, in his father's absence, he would playfully begin to imitate some of his father's patterns. He had disidentified from his mother (Greenson 1968). Kathy, after imitating Michael's more masculine games for a few weeks, began to play more and more at imitating her mother at about 17½ months.

My observations of Kathy and Michael also confirmed the emergence of masturbation and of the awareness of genital differences in the late practicing subphase. Both children began to integrate genital sensations into the mother-and-father relationships. For example, Kathy loved to ride horseback on father's lap. She also showed some evidence of early penis envy. However, this did not seem to be a crucial issue at the onset of the rapprochement crisis, around age 18 months.

Both children went through a clear-cut rapprochement crisis, just on schedule. Kathy developed a brief but passionate love affair with her father. Eventually, however, these feelings were drowned in the overwhelming separation struggle with mother. For both children, there were many times when the father, too, became "contaminated" with rapprochement ambivalence; but he was no match for mother in this respect.

During the months following the rapprochement crisis, both children seemed to experiment with various solutions to the basic rapprochement conflicts. But most consistently, Michael would seek out his father; he also preferred to play with boys, especially older boys. He seemed very conscious and proud of being a boy. He was keenly aware of gender differences among family members. During the corresponding age span, Kathy was almost exclusively involved with her mother. This attachment now had an ambivalent, clinging tinge. Kathy seemed to have traded off her father to Michael in order to have mother to herself. She saw herself most consistently as "mommy's baby," and there was evidence that this self-image was neutral in regard to gender. As an extension, Kathy saw family members mostly on a generational or power scale throughout her third year of life. Only around age 3 did an *oedipal* triangulation gradually emerge, and only then could she begin to accept seeing herself as having two sexually differentiated love objects, and as being herself different in gender from boys.

THE TRIPARTITE MODEL OF EARLY TRIANGULATION

A comparison of Kathy and Michael tends to confirm my previous hunch that around 18 months, *gender identity* emerges more readily in boys, *generational identity* in girls (Abelin 1975, p. 295). Generational identity establishes the self "between" two objects, along one linear dimension. "I am smaller than mother, but bigger than baby," or, rather, in terms of wishes: "I wish to be taken care of by mother and I wish to take care of baby." By contrast, gender identity classifies the self in relation to the dichotomy male/female (or perhaps at first only to the dichotomy male/nonmale). Thus in the girls' first self-and-object image constellation, the self would not be explicitly represented as being different in gender from her object(s). We may thus derive the following tentative generalization from the comparison of Michael and Kathy.

Before rapprochement, the father remains a peripheral, if exciting, object for the girl, tinged with eroticized stranger anxiety. By contrast, he has become the primary attachment object for the boy. The rapprochement wish—the first longing of the separate self—is the same in boys as in girls: "I want mommy." However, the underlying core self-image constellation may be gender-specific for boys only: "I (male) want mommy (female)." In girls, the corresponding core self-image constellation would be "I (a child) want mommy (big)," alternating with "I (a child) want baby (small.)"

How can we account for these gender differences? To organize the following review of data, I will anticipate here the postulates of the new *tripartite model of early triangulation.*

In boys as well as in girls, early triangulation occurs around 18 months of age and leads to the formation of the first core self-image, separate from and desperately longing for mother. However, only boys approach "early triangulation" after a change of primary attachment object: only boys have "disidentified" from mother during the practicing subphase. Consequently, the core self-image is the result of a full-blown identification with the rival father only in boys; and this is why core gender self-classification is achieved only by boys at that age. Psychoanalytic evidence suggests that this early triangular identification with the father confers an irreversible *phallic* attribute to the boy's core self-image. His longing is for a *different kind* of object, no longer mirroring his body. By contrast, in the girl, the father is not yet metabolized into the mental image system around 18 months of age. Her *generational* self-image derives from two identifications within the mother/baby/self triangle, the "Madonna constellation:" the girl identifies with the wishes of both the passive rival baby and of the active mother.[2]

In girls as well as in boys, core gender self-classification must derive from an identification within the mother/father/self triangle, the "primal constellation." I will call this a *sexual triangulation*. But in the girl, this sexual triangulation will take place later, on the classical oedipal level. Only in the boy is there an *early sexual triangulation*, which is then replicated by the oedipal triangulation on the higher level of symbolic images. On the other hand, boys are exposed to the tensions of the "Madonna constellation" just as girls are. But they touch base only briefly at the levels of "identification with the rival baby" and of "identification with the active mother"; by age 18 months, these levels have been superseded in boys by "identification with the rival father."

Incidentally, it is not clear to me at this point to what degree the girl's generational identification and her disregard for sexual differences represent a defensive retreat, because of early penis envy. There can be no doubt about the existence of such penis envy (e.g., Mahler, Pine, and Bergman 1975, p. 214; Galenson and Roiphe 1976). This penis envy is based on a sensorimotor, here-and-now perception, like all the other situations of envy that herald the rapprochement subphase. As such, the discovery of the genital difference may well contribute to preventing early core identification with the rival

---

2. In this "pregenital" triangle, the opposition of active versus passive takes precedence over the wish-vector. This will be expanded on elsewhere.

father in the girl. At any rate, this early penis envy must be distinguished from that of the phallic phase, which corresponds to the later symbolic representation of the phallus.

There is another, cognitive dimension to this new model, which can only be mentioned here in passing. Indeed, a lot of data would fall into place if we assume that sexual self-classification, which implies the highest degree of spatial organization of the mental image, is also the best foundation for the development of spatial ability. But this is only achieved by a triangulation within the primal constellation; it presupposes a triangular metabolization of the father, as it were. By contrast, generational identification, which has a greater affinity with the linear dimension of time, would constitute the foundation of grammatical language. Therefore, language would be enhanced by a triangular identification within the Madonna constellation. In either case, the establishment of a symbolic function (Piaget and Inhelder 1966), that is, of mental representations, would be contingent on a triangulation. This theory would explain, among other things, why girls are more advanced in language skills, whereas most boys will eventually be superior in mechanical and spatial abilities. The tripartite model of early triangulation would even allow for the considerable overlap in these abilities, and for their ultimate convergence on the adult level—Piaget's formal level.

A word on narcissism. Mahler has, of course, described the loss of the illusion of narcissistic omnipotence in the rapprochement subphase (Mahler, Pine, and Bergman 1975). In my model, narcissism is a quality derived from the mirroring one-to-one nature of all relationships before rapprochement. Narcissism can only be reduced through the formation of symbolic mental images of the self and its objects by way of early triangular identifications. But the comparison between Michael and Kathy suggests that in addition there are gender differences in this process. In Michael, identification with the rival father led to an image of himself and of his mother in which the generational or power gradient between himself and his father was obliterated. Indeed, he arrogated to himself some rather incredible capabilities, as if he shared implicitly in his father's powers. His smallness and helplessness did not seem to be included as yet in his newly formed self-image. By contrast, a generational gradient did differentiate Kathy's earliest self-image from its first two represented objects; but she behaved as if she was of the only kind there is. Her first self-image was neutral in regard to gender; it was feminine only implicitly, because of the persistence of the mirroring with mother. Thus, it was as if a different part of the illusory prerapprochement narcissism had been preserved in each sex: the illusion of uniqueness in the girl, and the illusion of omnipotence in the boy. And these were also the aspects of narcissism that were yet to be transmuted onto the level of symbolic representation by way of the subsequent oedipal triangulations.

REVIEW OF DATA

There are large clusters of data that tend to buttress various aspects of this model; they also contributed to its construction. They pertain to such disparate fields as biological and psychological gender differences and their origins, ethology, social affinities of infants, the corticalization of the extrapyramidal system, the early genital stage, early language development, self-recognition in the mirror, Piaget's findings, psychoanalytic reconstruction, family dynamics, or systems theory. Even in the book that I am preparing, some of these areas will only be covered cursorily; and here, I can give no more than a few essential references.

The early role of the father as a second attachment object has been abundantly confirmed (Lamb 1976a). Moreover, during the second year of life, boys tend to become as comfortable with their fathers as with their mothers, or even to prefer their fathers (Lamb 1977); for girls, fathers remain literally more peripheral, that is, they tend to relate to their fathers through distal sensory modalities, to their mothers through proximal modalities (Ban and Lewis 1974). Generally, babies are attracted by similarities and are afraid of differences; thus, they are attracted by other babies and by persons of the same sex, but are most wary of male adult strangers. However, this preference for redundancy would seem to be more pronounced in girls than in boys (Lewis and Brooks 1974, 1975). Such factors may prime the boy toward identification with the rival father at 18 months of age, and may derive in turn from the priming of the male brain with androgen hormones at an early critical stage of intrauterine development. The self-image has been shown to appear rather suddenly, anytime between 18 and 22 months of age (Piaget 1937, Amsterdam 1972, Lewis and Brooks 1974). Studies of transsexualism (Stoller 1968) or of hermaphroditism and other sexual disorders

(Money and Ehrhardt 1972) have shown that core gender identity becomes almost irreversible after 18 months; its major determinants are the conscious and unconscious attitudes of the parents. Statistics confirm that preschool boys tend to make sex-typed discriminations much more often than little girls do; on the other hand, girls tend to identify more often with the mother's adult characteristics and to learn more age-graded aspects of social role (Emmerich 1959).

Finally, *absence* of a father during the first two years of life has been found to be much more detrimental to boys than to girls (Biller 1974); it irreversibly leaves boys with a feminine core gender identity, although from latency on, this is covered up in most cases by masculine overcompensation (Burton 1972). In addition, these boys are less aggressive, less competitive and more dependent than boys who lost their father after the age of 2 to 4 years (Hetherington 1966, Santrock 1970, 1972, Biller 1974). These boys resemble girls even in that they stress parent-child rather than sexual differences (Sears 1951)! At the same time their mechanical interests are affected. They develop field-dependent perceptions and a cognitive profile resembling that of girls, with verbal abilities higher than spatial abilities (Barclay and Cusumano 1967, Carlsmith 1964). A well-structured mother-child relationship has been shown to promote verbal ability (Levy 1943); in this case, fatherless boys may compensate linguistically for their handicap in spatial skills.

Although father-absent girls do develop a feminine core gender identity, and although their ego development is less seriously affected, they will have difficulties in their social and sexual relationships with males (Hetherington 1972, Jacobson and Ryder 1969). Their nonverbal intellectual abilities will be affected as in father-absent boys, but mostly when the loss of the father occurs at a later age, between 3 to 7 years (Landy, Rosenberg, and Sutton-Smith 1969; see Biller 1974, p. 129). Similarly, there is some evidence that the father does contribute to the girl's core femininity, but at a later age, namely, around 5 to 6 years (Lynn 1974, p. 162).

Most of these data, however, could be accounted for by any kind of early internalization of the father, and not specifically by a triangular one. On the other hand, there does exist a growing set of data suggesting that the effects of early father absence are duplicated or even surpassed by the effects of maternal dominance in the parental couple. This must be understood in the light of a large set of data suggesting that children tend to imitate that parent who dominates in the parental couple (Lynn 1974, pp. 122-130). Obviously, then, early triangulation in the boy consists of an identification with the father's *actively* loving mother. Maternal dominance prevents this process and therefore has the same effects as father-absence. Only an early triangulation model can account for these data.

Moreover, some research suggests that early mother-absent boys raised by their fathers also develop a feminine cognitive profile (Gregory 1965, Nelsen and Maccoby 1966). These data, too, can be explained only if the early core identification of boys with their father is a triangular one.

CONCLUSIONS

More generally, I suggest that an early triangulation model may account for all of the data just reviewed. In particular, we may safely assume that the first core self-and-object image constellation in the boy contains a higher degree of simultaneous information in space than the corresponding core images in the girl, namely, the information that people come in two shapes, with or without a phallus. This would explain the parallelism between the cognitive and the psychosexual effects of father absence. In my model, the core wishes and fantasies described by psychoanalysis coincide with the deep structures discovered by cognitive psychology and by linguistics although their surface effects may secondarily become distorted and dissociated in some cases.

The model may also help to clarify certain points of psychoanalytic theory. I can mention here only a few of its implications. For example, there can be no doubt that there is a specific early attachment not only to mother but also typically to father, and perhaps to other familiar adults, too. Therefore, as Lamb (1976b) or Kotelchuck (1976) have pointed out, Bowlby (1958) was certainly wrong in postulating the monotropy of early human attachment. But is this what Freud was talking about when he inferred by the psychoanalytic method that the earliest libidinal tie of an infant is to his mother? On close scrutiny, what analysts have reconstructed as exclusive attachment to "mother" or to the "breast" could refer quite correctly to one of three different things: (1) It could refer to the dyadic structure of the sensorimotor world itself, which allows only for one-to-one relationships *at any one time*. Incidentally, this mode of functioning may persist and take on the defensive function that we call splitting. (2) It could refer to the symbiotic mother, who is indeed the infant's first and (for a while) foremost mirroring object within that world, although by no means an exclusive one. (3) Finally, "mother" refers most often to the earliest *mental image*, namely, the image of the longed-for rapprochement mother. In this case, the psychoanalytic reconstruction of an exclusive object cathexis is valid, but only as far back as there was a *symbolic level*.

By contrast, because it is presymbolic, the *father's role before the rapprochement subphase* and in early triangulation *cannot be reconstructed* by the psychoanalytic method. The memory of the primordial rival is obliterated after early triangulation. This is probably why our science has not discovered early father attachment, although it is readily observable, and indeed "known" to everyone. Within the symbolic level, it is quite true that the core image of the father does enter the scene as late as during the phallic-oedipal stage. This is the level on which Freud reconstructed, for example, the prolonged involvement of the girl with her mother, and her turning to father because of a sense of castration. Freud's reconstructions always pertained to the level of unconscious wish-vectors.

Thus, the following two levels must be clearly distinguished: on one hand, the *level* of interactional, *mirroring relationships* within the family, which is rooted in the sensorimotor mode of functioning; and, on the other hand, the *symbolic level*, on which these relationships become represented with more or less distortion. Confusion between these two levels pervades the psychoanalytic literature. This confusion is all the easier to make as the symbolic level represents an isomorphic recapitulation of the mirror level. From behind the couch—and through the smokescreen of language—these two levels of the Unconscious are bound to be telescoped. Whatever we may think of his technical innovations and of his one-sided exaltation of linguistic structure, Lacan's great merit has been to introduce the distinction between the mirror stage (1949) and the symbolic level; he also adumbrated the role of the father ("name of the father") in the transition from one level to the other (1959), and the symbolic nature of the self *(sujet)* and the core wish *(désir;* Lacan 1958).

Another implication of my model relates to the controversy about *determinants of gender identity*. According to Kohlberg's (1966) "cognitive-developmental" theory, "sex-role development" depends on the child's discovery of being a boy or a girl. Incidentally, Freud has attributed a similar role to the "discovery" of the anatomical difference between the sexes. According to my model, however, girls are feminine and boys are masculine much before they could possibly make such a discovery. The early triangulations are the foundation of gender identity precisely because they represent an acknowledgment and a transmutation of already existing feminine or masculine mirror object choices. Later, when the implications of these early triangulations have unfolded so as to constitute the phallic stage of development, the ensuing representation of the anatomical difference is attributed to some fortuitous external discovery. But the latter only serves to rationalize instinctual premonition, as it were. The core "discoveries" are always recognitions.

More generally, it should be obvious that my model represents a radical departure from any naive empiricism. In this, I believe, I am true to the spirit of Freud. I believe that there is an inner blueprint for epigenetic development. For example, there are maturational factors and laws of integration and equilibration that constitute, in effect, a "mother attachment system" and a "father attachment system." In the average expectable "primal constellation," these two systems, in turn, will combine around 18 months of age to constitute a preordained "early triangulation system."

In conclusion, I wish to mention briefly some evolutionary vistas opened up by the new model. Early triangulation is a "critical period" par excellence. I think that Spitz (1957) was literally right in comparing his critical periods to the "organizers" of fetal development: they represent a recapitulation on the psychological level of the intrauterine sexual differentiation of the brain. This differentiation depends on the presence or absence of androgen hormones at an early critical period in utero. In all other mammal species, however, this recapitulation is incomplete; it is arrested prematurely, perhaps by the hormonal flooding of sexual maturity. By the same token, the developmental potential of the central nervous system is never actualized in animals (cf. Hutt 1972, p. 22-25 and p. 41-44). Their hereditary instinctual behaviors can be viewed as premature closures of sensorimotor development. Only in man is maturational timing such that even the initial priming of the brain with androgens is recapitulated on the experiential level. Indeed, on the level of early sexual triangulation, it is the psychological internalization of the father that adds masculinity to an otherwise feminine core gender identity—just as at a critical period in fetal development, androgens had irreversibly primed an otherwise feminine brain into a masculine track; and this, in turn, must be a recapitulation of the fundamental asymmetry of the Y chromosome, which adds the message "male" to an otherwise feminine chromosomal blueprint. Each level replicates that one additional bit of information that makes all the difference between male and female. On the symbolic level, of course, this difference is represented by the phallus. Thus, the different timing and mode of sexual triangulation in boys and in girls ultimately reflects the difference of the chromosomal messages. As postulated earlier in this paper, this difference might be mediated by the greater responsiveness of the male brain to discrepancy, and the greater responsiveness of the female brain to redundancy.

Intrapsychic triangulation thus represents a specifically human achievement. In this process, all the mirroring, instinctual, energic currents and all the sensorimotor resources are funneled to master one "primal constellation," which lies just beyond the reach of any of the sensorimotor schemata. Only in man does this Copernican revolution of the mind take place. In other words, only in man is the father internalized into psychic structure. To be more precise, it is the truth of the father-mother relationship that is internalized, the truth about one's origin—the forbidden fruit of knowledge. In sexual triangulation, the Self is engendered by father and mother—and with it the explosion of symbolic thought. This indeed is an important step toward the psychological birth of the human infant.

Thus, in addition to providing an explanatory framework for the phenomena of the rapprochement subphase, the early triangulation model, which was partly based on Piaget, may serve as a conceptual bridge to span the gap between psychology and psychoanalysis.

References

Abelin, E. L. (1971a). *Esquisse d'une Théorie Etiopathogénique Unifiée des Schizophrénies*. Bern: Hans Huber.

——— (1971b). The role of the father in the separation-individuation process. In *Separation-Individuation*, ed. J. B. McDevitt and C. F. Settlage, pp. 229-252. New York: International Universities Press.

——— (1975). Some further observations and comments on the earliest role of the father. *International Journal of Psycho-Analysis* 56:293-302.

——— (1977). The role of the father in personality development. In *Fall 1976 Symposium of the San Francisco Psychoanalytic Institute, Extension Division*. New York: Psychotherapy Tape Library, Jason Aronson.

Amsterdam, B. (1972). Mirror self-image reactions before age two. *Developmental Psychobiology* 5:297-305.

Ban, P. L., and Lewis, M. (1974). Mothers and fathers, girls and boys: attachment behaviors in the one-year-old. *Merrill-Palmer Quarterly* 20:195-204.

Barclay, A. G., and Cusumano, D. (1967). Father-absence, cross-sex identity, and field-dependent behavior in male adolescents. *Child Development* 38:243-250.

Biller, H. B. (1974). *Paternal Deprivation.* Lexington, Mass.: D. C. Heath.

Bowlby, J. (1958). The nature of the child's tie to his mother. *International Journal of Psycho-Analysis* 39:350-373.

Burton, R. V. (1972). Cross-sex identity in Barbados. *Developmental Psychology* 6:365-374.

Carlsmith, L. (1964). Effect of early father-absence on scholastic aptitude. *Harvard Education Review* 34:3-21.

Emmerich, W. (1959). Parental identification in young children. *Genetic Psychology Monograph* 60:257-308.

Galenson, E., and Roiphe, H. (1976). Some suggested revisions concerning early female development. *Journal of the American Psychoanalytic Association* 24:29-57.

Greenson, R. R. (1968). Dis-identifying from mother: its special importance for the boy. *International Journal of Psycho-Analysis* 49:370-374.

Gregory, I. (1965). Anterospective data following childhood loss of a parent. II. Pathology, performance, and potential among college students. *Archives of General Psychiatry* 13:110-120.

Hetherington, E. M. (1966). Effects of paternal absence on sex-typed behaviors in Negro and white preadolescent males. *Journal of Personality and Social Psychology* 4:87-91.

——— (1972). Effects of father-absence on personality development of adolescent daughters. *Developmental Psychology* 7:313-326.

Hutt, C. (1972). *Males and Females.* Middlesex, England: Penguin Books.

Jacobson, G., and Ryder, R. G. (1969). Parental loss and some characteristics of the early marriage relationship. *American Journal of Orthopsychiatry* 39:799-887.

Kleeman, J. A. (1967). The peek-a-boo game. Part I: Its origins, meanings and related phenomena in the first year. *Psychoanalytic Study of the Child* 22:239-273. New York: International Universities Press.

——— (1973). The peek-a-boo game. Its evolution and associated behavior, especially bye-bye and shame expression, during the second year. *Journal of the American Academy of Child Psychiatry* 12:1-23.

Kohlberg, L. (1966). A cognitive-developmental analysis of children's sex-role concepts and attitudes. In *The Development of Sex Differences,* ed. E. E. Maccoby, pp. 82-173. Standford, Calif.: Stanford University Press.

Kotelchuck, M. (1976). The infant's relationship to the father: Experimental evidence. In *The Role of the Father in Child Development*, ed. M. E. Lamb, pp. 329-344. New York: John Wiley and Sons.

Lacan, J. (1949). The mirror stage as formative of the function of the I as revealed in psychoanalytic experience. In *Écrits: A Selection*, pp. 1-7. New York: W. W. Norton, 1977.

——— (1958). The signification of the phallus. In *Écrits: A Selection*, op. cit., pp. 281-291.

——— (1959). On a question preliminary to any possible treatment of psychosis. In *Écrits: A Selection*, op. cit., pp. 179-221.

Lamb, M. E. (1976a). The role of the father: An overview. In *The Role of the Father in Child Development*, ed. M. E. Lamb, pp. 1-63. New York: John Wiley and Sons.

——— (1976b). Proximity-seeking attachment behaviors: A critical review of the literature. *Genetic Psychology Monograph* 93:63-89.

——— (1977). The development of parental preferences in the first two years of life. *Sex Roles* 3:495-497.

Landy, F., Rosenberg, B. G., and Sutton-Smith, B. (1969). The effect of limited father-absence on cognitive development. *Child Development* 40:941-944.

Levy, D. M. (1943). *Maternal Overprotection*. New York: Columbia University Press.

Lewis, M. and Brooks, J. (1974). Self, other and fear: reactions to people. In *The Origins of Fear*, ed. M. Lewis and L. Rosenblum, pp. 195-227. New York: John Wiley and Sons.

——— (1975). Infant's social perception: A constructivist view. In *Infant Perception: From Sensation to Cognition*, vol. II., ed. L. B. Cohen and P. Salapatek, pp. 120-148. New York: Academic Press.

Lynn, D. B. (1974). *The Father: His Role in Child Development*. Belmont, California: Brooks/Cole.

Mahler, M. S. (1966). Discussion of Dr. Greenacre's: Problems of overidealization of the analyst and of analysis. *Unpublished manuscript*. (Abstracted in: *Psychoanalytic Quarterly* 36:637, 1967.)

Mahler, M. S., and Gosliner, B. J. (1955). On symbiotic child psychosis: genetic, dynamic and restitutive aspects. *Psychoanalytic Study of the Child* 10:195-212. Reprinted in *The Selected Papers of Margaret S. Mahler*, vol. 1, ch. 6. New York: Jason Aronson, 1979.

Mahler, M. S., Pine, F. and Bergman, A. (1975). *The Psychological Birth of the Human Infant*. New York: Basic Books.

Money, J., and Ehrhardt, A. A. (1972). *Man and Woman, Boy and Girl*. Baltimore: Johns Hopkins Press.

Nelsen, E. A., and Maccoby, E. E. (1966). The relationship between social development and differential abilities on the scholastic aptitude test. *Merrill-Palmer Quarterly* 12:269-284.

Piaget, J. (1937). *La construction du réel chez l'enfant.* Neuchâtel: Delachaux and Niestlé, 3d ed., 1963. (*The Construction of Reality in the Child.* New York: Basic Books, 1954.)

Piaget, J., and Inhelder, B. (1966). *The Psychology of the Child.* New York: Basic Books, 1969.

Prall, R. C. [rep.] (1978). The role of the father in the preoedipal years. *Journal of the American Psychoanalytic Association* 26:143-161.

Santrock, J. W. (1970). Paternal absence, sex typing, and identification. *Developmental Psychology* 2:264-272.

—— (1972). The relation of type and onset of father absence to cognitive development. *Child Development* 43:455-469.

Sears, P. S. (1951). Doll-play aggression in normal young children: Influence of sex, age, sibling status, father's absence. *Psychological Monograph* 65, No. 6.

Spitz, R. A. (1957). *No and Yes.* New York: International Universities Press.

Stoller, R. J. (1968). *Sex and Gender.* New York: Jason Aronson.

—— (1975). *Sex and Gender,* vol. 2. New York: Jason Aronson.

10

Self-Love and Object-Love: Some Problems of Self and Object Constancy, Differentiation and Integration

> Sin of self-love possesseth all mine eye
> And all my soul and all my every part;
> And for this sin there is no remedy,
> It is so grounded inward in my heart.
> Methinks no face so gracious is as mine,
> No shape so true, no truth of such account,
> And for myself mine own worth do define
> As I all other in all worths surmount.
> But when my glass shows me myself indeed,
> Beated and chopped with tanned antiquity,
> Mine own self-love quite contrary I read;
> Self so self-loving were iniquity:
> 　'Tis thee (myself) that for myself I praise,
> 　Painting my age with beauty of thy days.
> 　　　　　—Shakespeare, Sonnet 62

The relationship between self-love and object-love has puzzled and intrigued philosophers, poets, and psychoanalysts down to our day; the myth of Narcissus illustrates the dangers of self-love, whereas the myth of Helen illustrates the dangers of object-love. Freud more than once tackled the apparent paradox involved, without ever being entirely satisfied with his answer. The history of the problem and Freud's view have been beautifully summarized by Bergmann (1971, 1978), who cites two landmarks: the original discovery that the finding of love is the re-finding of the mother (Freud 1905) with its complication of the split between tender love and sensuality, and the second discovery of narcissistic love versus anaclitic love (1914), with its complication that the beloved narcissistic self-object is essentially unstable and leads to disillusionment, whereas the beloved anaclitic object is often surrendered to and thus endangers narcissism and self-esteem. Freud's resolution of these paradoxes is most concisely stated as follows:

> Loving in itself, in so far as it involves longing and deprivation, lowers self-regard; whereas being loved, having one's love returned, and possessing the loved object, raises it once more. When libido is repressed, the erotic cathexis is felt as a severe depletion of the ego, the satisfaction of love is impossible, and the re-enrichment of the ego can be effected only by a withdrawal of libido from its objects. The return of the object-libido to the ego and its transformation into narcissism represents, as it were, a happy love once more; and, on the other hand, it is also true that a real happy love corresponds to the primal condition in which object-libido and ego-libido cannot be distinguished [Freud 1914, pp. 99-100].

As every analyst knows, the problem is immensely complicated and begins with confusing definitions of the word; how do we distinguish the love of the pervert for his fetish, of the mother for her unborn child, of husband for wife and of patient for analyst? Here I shall only attempt to illustrate some of the problems encountered in the analysis of patients with prominent narcissistic difficulties who present dilemmas of both self-love and object-love, which they tend to resolve either by loving themselves uniquely (the classical ego-centric type), or by submitting themselves to some anaclitic or narcissistic love object (the classical love addicts, extremely submissive women, "as if" types, etc.). To anticipate a conclusion, I might add that these dichotomies are rarely found in pure type, because analysis generally reveals that the person immersed in self-love always yearns for submission to an object and has acted this out in some way, whereas the object-submissive type always yearns for liberation from bondage and the restoration of self-love, and acts this out in some other way. Frequently, as I hope to demonstrate, these issues of self-love and object-love relate to fundamental problems of self-constancy and object-constancy. Let me begin with the highest level at which one sees this problem, namely, those patients who consciously oscillate between the extremes of self-love and object-love.

A successful professional woman in her forties came for consultation with the complaint that she had never been able to achieve mutual orgasm with her lovers. Having been in a previous analysis, which had been quite helpful, she was able to discuss the problem with unusual frankness and lucidity. Remarking on the difference between herself and her current lover, she said:

"Tony seems to live in the real world all of the time . . . whether we're at his apartment or my apartment, whether it's the morning or the evening, whether he's just been reading a book or telling me about work, he can start to make love and he doesn't seem to need any special conditions. . . . Sex is just another part of his life, and I don't mean that he doesn't care or isn't involved. . . .

But I have to prepare things, and it's not a question of foreplay . . . it's like I have to create a special world, centered around myself . . . a sexual Shangri-la in which I'm the queen, and then I can allow him to enter *my* world and then I can have pleasure. . . .

I can't make the smooth transition . . . I'm either *me*, totally me and so excited that nothing else exists, or else I'm Tony's lover and I can give him pleasure but then I don't have it myself. . . ."

We know that normal sexuality requires the capacity to simultaneously enjoy oneself as subject and as object by identifying with the object; it requires the capacity to accept objects that differ from oneself. In the perversions this is attempted through denial of the difference between the sexes, through fantasies of bisexuality, etc. Here the act seems normal, but the significance is narcissistic: the patient can make the separation from the object and also can own her own body and accept the difference between the sexes, on the condition that they don't come together or occur simultaneously. One person can *serve* the other, but mutuality is excluded. Here questions of reality testing are not at issue. Whereas psychotic and borderline patients in principle try to change reality to conform with their inner life, narcissistic patients have generally made peace with reality on condition that they don't always have to live in it. They inhabit the world without being embedded in it. The interpenetration and mutual enrichment of inner life and reality are a problem for them; a problem concretely exemplified by their difficulty in coordinating self-love and object-love.

From the phenomenological point of view, the dilemma is beautifully expressed in the words: "I can't make the smooth transition . . . I'm either *me*, totally me and so excited that nothing else exists, or else I'm Tony's lover and I can give him pleasure but then I don't have it myself. . . ."

This state of being "totally me" I shall call *subjective awareness* and the state of being "Tony's lover" will be called *objective self-awareness*. These states have a long history of discussion in philosophy and psychology, and the development of objective self-awareness has been extensively studied by Piaget (1954) who demonstrated the slow and laborious acquisition of the ability to put oneself in the place of another and to view oneself from this external perspective. In a paper on the rapprochement phase, Mahler noted:

> For the more or less normal adult, the experience of being both fully 'in' and at the same time basically separate from the world 'out there' is one of the givens of life that is taken for granted. Consciousness of self and absorption without awareness of self are the two poles between which we move with varying degrees of ease and with varying alternations or simultaneity. This, too, is the result of a slowly unfolding process. In particular, this development takes place in relation to (a) one's own body; and (b) the principal representative of the world as the infant experiences it (the primary love object) [Mahler 1972, p. 487].

Thus it appears that in certain states we are totally immersed in our own thoughts or actions and unaware of ourselves, or aware of ourselves only as the agent or subject of thought and action (subjective awareness); whereas in other states our self becomes the object of our thought or action (objective self-awareness). It was in part to this peculiarity that Bohr (1948) referred when he frequently noted that we are both actors and spectators in the drama of our existence.

Let me clarify this distinction with two clinical vignettes.

A disturbed young man with homosexual predilections and difficulties in object-constancy, in the course of his treatment development the conviction that he would only be "cured" if he could give vent to some shattering "primal" scream that would somehow change his existence. My efforts to understand this were largely unsuccessful, in part because the patient himself was less interested in reflecting on the meaning of his conviction than in the action of screaming itslef. Cursorily dismissing my misguided attempts at understanding, he would begin the hour with a preparatory silence, slowly gathering his strength, and eventually emitting one or two blood-curdling shrieks which, unfortunately, never seemed to bring him the relief he sought. For about a week he pursued this strange ritual at home as well as on the couch, but it was only some time later that we began to understand its significance. It seemed that he experienced the activity of his mind as a painful process of constant self-scrutiny or awareness of scrutiny by others; rarely was he able to lose himself completely in any activity, and then only for short periods of time.

The torments of this condition are difficult to imagine and can only be likened to the inability to forget. In truth, he could forget himself only at a moments of orgasm and this explained his constant quests for bigger and better orgasms with anonymous objects, a quest analogous to his search for the "primal" scream that would annihilate objective self-awareness. I would add that it took me some time to understand this condition because the patient was not clinically depressed, nor was guilt a major factor in the treatment which eventually brought him some relief.

This patient suffered from constant self-observation and could not lose himself in his actions; others complain of a persistent inability to observe themselves objectively. A young woman who had been treated as her mother's self-extension and even dressed in her mother's clothes was unable to visualize what she looked like and constantly reiterated: "If only I could get outside of myself, just once, and see what I really look like and know, once and for all. . . ."

Thus, one might say that the child is confronted with the double or complementary task of establishing a sense of self as a center for action and thought, and of viewing this self in the context of other selves as a thing amongst things. What is required is both a subjectification and an objectification; two different perspectives on the same self. Further consideration suggests that there may indeed be a multiplicity of such perspectives in that, since the self is both subject observed may be drawn at an infinite number of positions and may shift from one moment to the next. We are all familiar with the adolescent who at one moment may be so totally absorbed that he forgets where he is and, at the next, may feel compelled to specify his exact location in the city, planet, and galaxy.

I have made this brief digression on subjective and objective self-awareness because the issue so typically arises whenever certain patients attempt to characterize their difficulties in loving; they can be either "all themselves" or "all somebody's lover," but seem to find it difficult or impossible to integrate or articulate these two apparently complementary views on the self. And the problem is not just confined to love but typically exists in the area of work as well. A young woman with difficulties in writing made the following observation about her work:

"When I'm doing the writing for *myself*, then I'm enthused, it becomes meaningful and I work on it, but I seem to lose sight of the goal and then it may take forever because I want to make it so perfect; I'm just totally absorbed in myself. . . . But if I'm doing the writing for *someone else*, I begin to feel coerced, it becomes boring, repetitious, and monotonous, I lose pleasure in the actual doing of it and sometimes stop working . . . ."

Speaking of a life-long difficulty in reading, she said:

"When I'm having trouble reading I'm jumping out of my own head into the head of some transcendental other watching myself read, and then I can't. . . . When I'm troubled reading there's a part of me, still me, not outside of me—already at that point I'm not only reading but *trying* to read and with that division I begin to feel self-conscious. . . . Then not only am I trying but then watching myself trying and then there's a field of anonymous others watching and criticizing and by that point I'm outside with them and by then I can't read. . . ."

At another point in the analysis she reflected:

"I seem to need some combination of inner reality and outer reality, or inner and outer life, or talking with myself and talking with someone else to balance out the day. . . . The more conjectural or theoretical or abstract my thoughts, the more I feel a loss of contact with things that are substantial or real or tangible. . . . If I'm involved in hours of reading or studying, then I feel a great need to say it to someone and to validate it as something real, to rebound the idea off someone and have them respond to it. . . . The other extreme is when I spend several hours talking with someone. . . . Then I feel a great desire to be alone. . . . It's very wearing to be so many hours with people. . . ."

This patient is saying that when she is centered on herself in subjective awareness she is enthusiastic and works well, but gradually begins to lose some perspective on reality, some sense of contact with others and of where she fits in as a person among other people. Conversely, when she is centered on objective self-awareness, herself as seen through the eyes of others, her self-orientation improves, but she loses her pleasure and enthusiasm along with her ability to work. While different levels of defensive operations are commonly involved, what I am pointing to here is a basic difficulty in the maintenance of self-constancy and object-constancy, and their mutual reinforcement, differentiation and articulation.

In his classic paper on multiple function, Waelder (1930) demonstrates that each psychic act is an attempt to resolve multiple conflicts and therefore has multiple meanings, depending on the perspective from which it is viewed. He notes that although it is quite impossible for any one act to be equally successful in resolving all the ego's tasks, "the incomparable significance of the act of love in the household of the psyche is to be understood in the circumstance that it comes closest to being a complete and equable solution of the ego's contradictory tasks" (p. 73).

But a solution which can be so supremely satisfying must, by its very complexity, also be extremely difficult. From the perspective of varieties of awareness, we may note that the act of love demands an extraordinary interplay, synthesis, and flexibility of both subjective and objective self-awareness. Hence the complaint: "I can't make the smooth transition. . . . I'm either *me*, totally me and so excited that nothing else exists, or else I'm Tony's lover and I can give him pleasure but then I don't have it myself. . . ."

Certain patients with this problem may resort to fantasy or even to concrete operations to help them make the transition. A young woman with a similar difficulty, whenever she felt herself slipping too much into objective self-awareness as her husband's wife, would interrupt the intercourse to smoke a cigarette or take a drink, after which she could resume, having redressed the balance in favor of her narcissism.

An actor with an unusual gift for self-observation recounted an evening at the theatre: "I was sitting way back, at the top of the theatre, and watching the players from on high they seemed like utter perfection, faultless, as if *they* were acting and what I did was something else entirely. I felt small, worthless and despondent about myself. At intermission a friend offered me a seat in the front row. From there I could see the makeup, the actors straining and sweating, the cues, the errors in footwork. Now it was clearly the same thing that I did, I could identify with the actors which I hadn't been able to do before, and I even began to learn from what I was seeing. . . ."

This remarkable change in attitude, correlated at least in part with a simple change in perspective, illustrates the paradigmatic dichotomy between objective self-awareness, with its emphasis on observation, separation, and lowered self-esteem, and subjective awareness with the emphasis on participation, merger and heightened self-esteem.

In this instance the patient, unable to make the transition from objective to subjective awareness, was helped to do so by a change in physical distance and perspective. Other patients report similar experiences of being helped to switch from one mode of awareness to another by a change of physical position, by a change from passivity to activity, by a change from the distal senses to the proximal ones, by a change from the symbolic to the concrete, etc. It seems worth mentioning that this patient, as well as the others quoted, was not simply unable to switch to an experiential modality because he feared competitive or aggressive impulses, which indeed he did; he experienced equal difficulty in switching to objective self-awareness when *that* was appropriate.

As I have noted elsewhere (Bach 1977), one of the major problems in dealing with narcissistic patients is the characteristic difficulty they have in holding both themselves and the analyst in consciousness at the same time. Presumably Lacan was referring to this in his aphorism (1966) that when they are talking about themselves they are not talking to you, and when they are talking to you they are not talking about themselves. Other formulations have been made in terms of lack of differentiation between self- and object representations, in terms of narcissistic cathexes and object cathexes, or in terms of (object) idealizing transferences and (self) mirroring transferences. Without attempting to deal with the theoretical issues that these various perspectives raise, I would prefer to emphasize the general agreement at least on the nature of the problem. Here I am concerned with one concomitant of this issue, the dichotomy between subjective awareness, rooted in predominantly proprioceptive sources and the internalization of the mother of dual-unity, and objective self-awareness, rooted in predominantly exteroceptive sources and the internalized appraisals of the mother of separation.

Unfortunately, we know too little about the development of subjective awareness and the firm establishment of a sense of self, although the work of Mahler, Winnicott, Kohut and others has begun to delineate this area. The development of objective self-awareness includes issues of separation, reality testing, identification and ego and superego formation. From the cognitive point of view, Piaget has done the most extensive work on this ability and has traced its development into early adolescence.

The patients I am describing possess varieties of subjective and objective self-awareness in varying degrees, but their common difficulty seems to be in the flexible and appropriate articulation of these capacities. I was first led to understand this by a patient who alternated between exultant moods when he was full of himself, needed no one and told tales of grandiose accomplishments, and depressed moods when he felt "unreal," idealized the accomplishments of others and would sometimes fall asleep on the couch. When he was 7 years old, his mother had recorded the following remarks, made within a few days of each other: (a) "This world terrifies me sometimes. It seems to be all me!" corresponding to an increase in subjective awareness, and (b) "Is this world a *dreaming,* or is it real?" corresponding to a decrease in subjective awareness and an increase in objective self-awareness. The context of this last remark made it clear that all figures, including the subject, were seen objectively, from a great distance, and that cathexis had been withdrawn in defense against rage, loss, and annihilation.

Thus, the decrease of objective self-awareness and increase of subjective awareness led to feelings of terror (the world is all me), whereas the decrease of subjective awareness and increase of objective self-awareness led to feelings of unreality (I am insignificant and the world is a dream). It would seem that there is some "normal" homeostasis in which the self- and object world both seem real, intermingled, and relatively stable. As the homeostasis becomes unbalanced in the direction of overcathexis of the self, one sees growing self-esteem, elation, grandiosity; fears of object loss, isolation and loss of reality, and fears of overstimulation (i.e., loss of control, exploding, flying off into space, etc.). Finally, the world is all me—a dedifferentiation has occurred in which subject and object are one; the patient has eaten up reality (Lewin 1950).

Contrariwise, as the homeostasis becomes unbalanced in the direction of overcathexis of the object world, one sees growing loss of self-esteem, feelings of depersonalization, depression, fears of understimulation (which may be countered by masturbation, sexual acting-out, psychosomatic responses, head-banging, scarification, etc.) and fears of loss and disintegration of the self. Finally, the self is absorbed by the world—a dedifferentiation has occurred in which subject and object are one; reality has eaten up the patient. Thus, the deviations from normal homeostasis start in opposite directions but join in a circle, and join at that point of dedifferentiation where dual unity is recreated, and to eat, to be eaten, and to sleep are once more the same (Lewin 1950).

In one sense, of course, the extremes of subjective awareness, as in (a) above, are related to Kohut's (1971) "grandiose" mirroring transferences, while decreases of subjective awareness as in (b) may be related to the idealizing transferences. Developmental analogues seem to be found in Mahler's practicing and rapprochement subphases where the child alternates between periods of great narcissistic investment in his own functions, almost oblivious of the mother, and intermittent returns for emotional refueling (Mahler, Pine, and Bergman 1975). Normally, these oscillations between "shadowing" and "darting away" start to become integrated and synthesized in the rapprochement phase.

Let me conclude with an example of a temporary catastrophic loss of perspective from a patient who was experiencing a reversal because her husband had left on a trip:

"I feel very disoriented today because Paul went away. . . . It's not so great to feel confused when somebody leaves . . . to be alone is confusing . . . but no wonder, we're moving the day after he gets back, there's all kinds of details he's taking care of, the painter, the floor scraper. . . . I'm disoriented because he left. . . . I feel morbid about what will happen to him . . . we're moving, the baby's coming, the painter's acting weird, it's a jumble, confused, I don't know how to get from A to B, the ground isn't stable under me. . . . If something happened to Paul, would I be able to go on without him?

"Presumably we're going to be moving, but I can't seem to grasp what it would be like, to imagine it. . . . Presumably we're going to have a baby, but I can't seem to grasp that either, to imagine it or understand it. . . . I wish I could talk to Paul about these things, that's what I miss, it's the feedback. . . . Although sometimes I think that if I didn't have to worry about Paul I could do everything my own way, but sometimes I don't know how I think. . . . I miss him very much. . . ."

I have discussed elsewhere the altered concepts of self, body, space, time, and causality which reappear in such a regression, and their implications for clinical practice (Bach 1977). Here I would emphasize the concomitant shifts in perspective in that the patient is temporarily unable to stabilize and integrate appropriate subjective and objective perspectives on herself, having lost this function which her husband subserved and which at this point had not been adequately internalized. This temporary loss was temporarily remedied when she was able to understand her reaction and to see herself through the analyst's eyes in a way that she could accept and assimilate. In fact, within a day or two she was functioning more than adequately, having taken one small step towards internalizing and cathecting a more stable set of perspectives on herself.

In this sense, of course, I am using perception as a paradigm for all other modalities of experience as well. One might equally speak of the inner life when it enters into transactions with the outer life, and the mutual enrichment which normally takes place. This patient employs her husband or analyst as a function to stabilize outer reality and objective self-awareness, and also to help her cathect portions of her inner life and subjective awareness; others employ the analyst as a function to help coordinate sharply alternating perspectives on the self and the object.

With these patients, the analyst essentially finds himself in the position of a transitional object. He must provide the transitional perspectives and the tolerance for ambiguity, and permit the transitional experiences which are essential for learning to differentiate, articulate, and integrate multiple perspectives on the self. In the following sections I shall discuss some developmental and therapeutic implications.

DEVELOPMENTAL CONSIDERATIONS

In an early note Ferenczi (1914) drew attention to sensations of giddiness at the end of the analytic session and related them to the patient's disillusionment at his return to "reality" and the sudden loss of the analyst's psychic support which this entailed. Hermann, a student of Ferenczi, later postulated (1936) an instinctual pair of "clinging" and "going-in-search" and related these to sadomasochism. Balint (1959), continuing this line of interest in archaic object relationships, described two extreme manifestations met with in the transference, the ocnophil and the philobat:

> Accordingly, the ocnophilic world consists of objects, separated by horrid empty spaces. The ocnophil lives from object to object, cutting his sojourns in the empty spaces as short as possible. Fear is provoked by leaving the objects, and allayed by rejoining them. . . . The whole world is different for the *philobat*. . . . The philobatic world consists of friendly expanses dotted more or less densely with dangerous and unpredictable objects. One lives in the friendly expanses, carefully avoiding hazardous contacts with potentially dangerous objects. Whereas the ocnophilic world is structured by physical proximity and touch, the philobatic world is structured by safe distance and sight. . . . The ocnophil is confident that *his chosen object will "click in"* with him and protect him against the empty, unfamiliar, and possibly dangerous world; the philobat feels that using his equipment he can certainly cope with any situation; *the world as a whole will "click in"* and he will be able to avoid treacherous objects. While the ocnophil has to presume that he can win the favour and partiality of the object, the philobat feels that it is within his power to conquer the "world" without relying on the favours of untrustworthy individual objects [pp. 32-35].

More recently, from a very different perspective, Kohut (1971) has described these archaic transferences and shown in detail how they are related to specific defects in the facilitating environment. He has emphasized the developmental necessity of these primitive "world views" and shown how the analyst may be used as a "self-object" to sustain them and overcome the developmental arrest. Thus the philobatic position, with its grandiosity and narcissistic overinvestment, is related to the "mirroring" transference by the patient's need for a confirming "world as a whole" which "clicks in" without any effort on his part; likewise the ocnophilic position is related to the "idealizing" transference by the patient's feeling that only a perfect object can protect him from the empty, unfamiliar, and dangerous world.

Much earlier, of course, Melanie Klein (1934) had described a grandiose "manic" transference position and its relationship to the "depressive" and "paranoid" positions. This work stemmed from Freud's earlier investigation of melancholia and the swing to mania (1917), as well as Abraham's (1924) study of the manic-depressive states. Although these papers all emphasize the complexity of the interactions and their relation to normal developmental phenomena, one has the impression that by an unfortunate historical oversimplification the grandiose transference positions came to be viewed largely in their defensive aspects as denial and acting-out, with rather less emphasis on the constructive aspects of self-love, creativity and going-in-search. It was partially to this that Balint was referring when he spoke of "*the ocnophilic bias of our modern technique* and its consequences" (1968, p. 169).

Clearly, many investigators, starting from diverse theoretical presumptions, have described a group of archaic transferences which are omnipotent, moving-away-from, and require a mirroring object, and another group which are dependent, clinging, and require an idealized object. But many problems arise in trying to compare and conceptualize these data. For one, the transference data are to a considerable extent an artifact of the analytic technique which may or may not be comparable. And secondly, it is unclear how these transference data are to be understood genetically, and even less clear how they are to be correlated with normal developmental data and especially with observational data.

It is nevertheless intriguing and important that in studying the development of children, Mahler has also observed two groups of behaviors: a seemingly grandiose, elated, adventurous and mirroring behavior in the practicing period, alternating with emotional refueling and modulating to the characteristic "shadowing" and "darting away" of the rapprochement subphase. Although the archaic transferences described may relate genetically to many levels, it is tempting to speculate that the process of maturation, whether developmental or therapeutic, involves oscillations between positions of dependence and independence, experienced on each maturational level as being less and less absolute. At different points either position may be seen as a defense against the other and also as a further developmental step in relation to the other. These oscillations, whether observed in normal development or experienced in the archaic transferences, seem to reduce most primitively to dependence upon one's own body/mind or dependence upon the object's body/mind.

I have mentioned that the child is confronted with the double or complementary task of establishing a sense of self as a center for action and thought, and of viewing this self in the context of other selves as a thing amongst things. Paradoxically, it is when we subjectively *experience* ourselves the most that we objectively *know* ourselves the least, a dilemma related to the cultural and generational shifts between the imperatives "know thyself" and "experience thyself." As one young man remarked: "Your generation feels that the unexamined life is not worth living, but *we* feel that the unlived life is not worth examining!" It was still not quite clear to him that this might be an unnecessary dichotomy.

When the normal child or the regressed child is most narcissistically invested he is least conscious of himself as a thing amongst things, that is, his perspective is limited to his own absorption in whatever he is doing, and he is least "aware of himself" from an objective point of view, although he may feel most *alive* and *himself* at the same time. Conversely, when he is least narcissistically invested and more absorbed in the other, he is most aware of himself from an objective point of view as seen through the eyes of another, although he may feel less *himself* and more dependent and helpless. Of course, in the archaic transferences, the empathic object becomes a self-object, narcissistically invested, thus helping to bridge the gap not only between self and object, but also between "subjective" self and "objective" self.

What is required, then, is both a subjectification and an objectification of the same self, two different yet coordinated perspectives on the self. Part of the pathology of the archaic transferences is precisely that these different perspectives are distorted, used defensively and not yet articulated into a "same self," although the integration presumably takes place in the course of treatment.

In this connection it is interesting to note that Zazzo (1975), who has extensively investigated the development of self-recognition in the mirror, has observed a phase of indecision, usually between 24 and 30 months, when the normal child can recognize himself in the mirror but apparently has not yet integrated this "objective" percept of himself with the "subjective" sense of himself. It was observed that for a period of about three months after recognition had been established, children called the mirror image by their own name, "Johnny," while referring to themselves as "me."

> Long after the child has learned the use of the personal pronoun, he continues to designate himself in the mirror by his first name. . . . For example, Barbara, who has used *I* and *me* since the age of 2 years 4 months, at 2 years 7 months always designates herself in the mirror by her name. She even resists the suggestion: *It's you! Say: it's me!* She responds with hesitation: *It's . . . it's me*, but immediately continues: *It's Barbara!* [Zazzo 1975, p. 176fn].

We should note that this "premature interpretation": *It's you!* does not immediately heal the "split" any more than when we call the attention of narcissistic patients to the fact that they often think of themselves in the third person: *Watch out, Ruthie!* or *You've done it again, Bill!*

When the child who unknowingly has had his nose reddened with lipstick, first perceives the red-nosed image in the mirror and touches his own nose, we are witnessing an experience of insight: he knows it's himself! But the three-month period before he can say: *It's me!* presents a paradox, for how can one use a self-reference to refer to something that's out there? Do we in our sophistication know something the child has yet to learn or, like the emperor's new clothes, has he caught sight of a truth we have long denied?

I am suggesting that at this point our little subject is caught in the epistemological problem of the "world knot"—that split between mind and body, subject and object, and intrinsic and extrinsic perspectives which is related to the ambiguity of the developing symbolic process. He has recognized that for others "Johnny" and "me" have the same referent, but he has not yet succeeded in creating that psychic space we call the "self," within which our multiple subjective and objective perspectives are paradoxically conceived of as transformations of the same invariant ongoing person. This is one important aspect in the continuing development of self-constancy.

This fundamental difficulty is further complicated by the pathological vicissitudes of projection, introjection, and splitting of self- and object representations which are, in some way, attempts to solve a basic epistemic problem. In any case, the question of how one relates a "what" out there to a "who" in here, or how one integrates multiple perspectives on the self, remains a thorny issue for theoreticians as well as children. In reflecting on the gap between the self-world and the object world, Winnicott developed the immensely rich concept of transitional phenomena and frankly proclaimed a paradox:

> I am proposing that there is a stage in the development of human beings that comes before objectivity and perceptibility. At the theoretical beginning a baby can be said to live in a subjective or conceptual world. The change from the primary state to one in which objective perception is possible is not only a matter of inherent or inherited growth process; it needs in addition an environmental mini-

mum. It belongs to the whole vast theme of the individual traveling from dependence to independence.

This conception-perception gap provides rich material for study. I postulate an essential paradox, one that we must accept and that is not for resolution. This paradox, which is central to the concept, needs to be allowed and allowed for over a period of time in the care of each baby [Winnicott 1971, p. 151].

In a similar context, I am here emphasizing the gap between the subjective self and the objective self and the importance, especially in therapy, of allowing for transitional experiences along the way to the development of self-constancy. While the good-enough environment or therapist can facilitate this, the construction of the self lies essentially within the creative omnipotence of each individual. As a friend who should know once remarked to me: Creating an imaginary twin was a narcissistic support, but having a real live twin was a narcissistic disaster!

Thus it appears that every person must learn to accept the paradox between his experience of himself as a "who" based on the processing of primarily subjective, intrinsic data, and his knowledge of himself as a "what" based on the processing of primarily objective, extrinsic data. He must, in other words, arrive at some personal resolution of an epistemic problem and come to believe that these two kinds of experiences and their infinite mixtures are transformations of some invariant supraordinate meaning or symbolic creation which we call the "self."

Classical structural or ego psychology takes essentially a functional or external perspective on the person; certain object relations or "self" theories such as Balint's, Winnicott's, or Kohut's take an essentially phenomenological or internal perspective on the person. The integration or articulation of these two kinds of theorizing seems in many ways to present problems parallel to those which the individual seeks to resolve by integrating intrinsic and extrinsic perspectives on himself. This problem may be epitomized by the difficulties that some patients have in integrating subjective and objective self-awareness. Indeed, the achievement of this integration is in itself so astonishing that we may well wonder how it ever succeeds, rather than why it sometimes fails.

I am in agreement with Winnicott that from a certain perspective what is required is the acceptance of paradox. And it appears that this acceptance can only take place in a context of basic trust, that is, an expectation that the facilitating environment and its feedback bear some trustworthy, invariant relationship to our phenomenal world, so that the construction of a reliable, continuous, and meaningful "self" is possible.

Mahler's research suggests that the rapprochement subphase is a crucial period for working through both the self/object differentiation and reintegration, and the subjective self/objective self differentiation and reintegration. It would appear that identifications at many levels are involved. A primary identification with the mother of symbiosis seems necessary for the cathexis of inner reality, for subjective awareness and self-absorption, and for experiences of merger and bliss. A later identification with the mother of separation seems necessary for the capacity to be alone, for objective self-awareness, and for the ability to love as two autonomous objects rather than as part-objects of a dual unity. Defects in the functioning or integration of these identifications lead to defects in self-constancy and are reflected in defects of object constancy. One of the prominent clinical manifestations of such problems are defects in the functioning or articulation of subjective awareness and objective self-awareness, paralleled by difficulties in the articulation of self-love and object love.

In the archaic transferences which have been described, a satisfactory equilibrium between this differentiation and integration has not been achieved, with the result that the patient is fixated primarily on one perspective or the other, or oscillates inappropriately between the extremes. In the next section I return to some clinical material to illustrate how these issues present themselves in the course of analysis.

SOME CLINICAL EXAMPLES

> . . . *Ach, wen vermögen wir denn zu brauchen? Engel nicht, Menschen nicht, und die findigen Tiere merken es schon, dass wir nicht sehr verlässlich zu Haus sind in der gedeuteten Welt.*

> . . . Alas, who is there for us to make use of? Neither angels nor men, and even the beasts can sense that we scarcely feel at home within our world of interpreted meanings.

> (Rilke, *Duino Elegies*, 1939)

A patient who made a serious suicide attempt shortly after the completion of an apparently successful analysis, came for consultation and after a period of testing decided to begin treatment again. It appeared that in some respects this young woman had presented a "false self" in her previous analysis. After working through a near-suicidal crisis with me, she related how incredulous her former analyst had seemed when he learned of her post-analytic suicide attempt, and she stated that although scarcely a day of her life had passed without suicidal thoughts, this had hardly come up in the previous analysis. Her subjective experience was *not* that she had deliberately suppressed this material but, rather, that it had rarely occurred to her during the hours that she was actually with her analyst; it was not, one might say, in the nature of their relationship.

Another patient, betrayed by a former therapist, demonstrated not only a justified mistrust of treatment, but also the same splitting of experience as the previous patient. Although reality testing was never at issue, the *sense* of reality *was,* and both constantly wondered whether the suicide attempt or betrayal had happened the way they *knew* it to have happened; whether the relationship with the therapist, which seemed so real, had been only illusory; whether they themselves were really good or really bad, really victim or really victimizer? Post-traumatically, both patients tended to become anxious and panicky the more comfortable a situation appeared. They suffered from a kind of "signal contentment" which warned them that some important aspect of subjective or objective reality was being omitted and that sooner or later some catastrophic reversal would ensue in which black would become white, happiness become misfortune and the world be turned inside-out again. Like Alice, they felt they had stepped through the looking-glass and could never be quite certain again.

While the splitting of affect and of self- and object representations were obvious and the genetic determinants rather clear, both aspects of the split were alternately available to consciousness, and the therapeutic problem was how to facilitate some synthesis that could feel consistently real and believable to the patient. Constantly uncertain whether to trust their subjective experiences or their objective knowledge of what had occurred, they reminded me of little Barbara in front of the mirror, hesitant or unable to put together her sense of herself with the image of herself in the mirror.

It seemed to me significant that transitional modes of thinking and

experiencing were very problematic for these patients. I am referring to Winnicott's area of "playing" and its necessary prerequisite,
the capacity to be alone. Such patients typically have difficulty with
relaxation and unplanned interludes, such as driving home from
work, moving from the couch to the "real world," entering and
leaving the office or beginning and ending the hour; in short, all
transitions between the subjective self-world and the objective object world. They are confused by a multiplicity of perspectives and
seem unable to feel both "in" the world and separate from it at the
same time; they feel forced to choose between one "reality" or the
other, or to live in a horrifying "gap." Thus, the creation of a
transitional "medium," life-supporting and nourishing, trustworthy
and reliably reversible or bi-directional, becomes one of the major
goals of the work together.

Another patient, a lawyer who had barely gotten through school,
presented a classic narcissistic type: apparently cold, uncaring, and
totally fixated on his own drive for power. In the course of our work
together, he became quite successful and, by his own report, was
able to love someone for the first time in his life. But he was still
dissatisfied with the treatment because he "couldn't learn to play
tennis." Considering the previous therapies, the original poor prog-
nosis and the admitted gains, I was at first inclined to view this
complaint as evidence of pathological envy, an inability to be
grateful, a striving for perfection, etc. Only slowly did I realize that
the complaint was valid and referred to his inability to become
absorbed or lose himself in something. At first his success in the law,
to which he devoted much time, seemed like a major counter-
example, but we eventually realized that it had been accomplished
by using other people who *were* able to "lose themselves" in pieces of
the work. The patient remained outside of it all, manipulating others
but frequently unable himself to understand the technical details of
the brief or contract, although these details were well within his
grasp. He couldn't concentrate long enough or immerse himself
thoroughly enough to understand, although he was gifted at listening
to his subordinates' reports and making correct decisions without
knowing why. He dejectedly referred to himself as "some kind of
idiot savant!"

One day he began with a typical complaint of driving home from
the office, watching someone jogging by, and realizing with despair
that he would never be able to engage in a sport, have a hobby, or

otherwise relax. I suggested that to jog mindlessly one would have to be certain that the rest of the world was taking care of itself. He responded by telling of a dinner party last night where he had arrived early and been seated next to the hostess, but she was distracted by the arrival of each new guest. He reported a dream: *The actual host that evening turns to him as the party is breaking up and asks him to pay the bar bill and his own share of the dinner.*

Although he realized that objectively he hadn't been seriously slighted by either host or hostess, his associations were to feelings of not being taken care of, having to remain alert, suspicious, and maintain a social facade. He recalled a period in analysis when he had made a supreme effort to free associate, but would become hopeless if he couldn't remember the thread from session to session and couldn't get me to supply it. He felt now that the major difficulty had been his despair that if *he* hadn't observed and remembered his associations and *I* hadn't preserved and taken care of them, he would be lost—who would be minding him? He remembered reading about some baby monkeys who had been forcibly separated from their mothers—there was a picture of one little monkey with his arms wrapped around himself. At that moment the patient realized he was holding himself like the monkey and he began to cry.

This man's rapprochement phase had been affected by his mother's extreme narcissism and further disturbed by the birth of a sister, reflected in his sensitivity to the distracted hostess. The mother, an aging actress, had for a long time refused to acknowledge in public that he was her son. He had early displaced his affections onto his father, who was enormously attentive and concerned, provided only that the little boy remained within his orbit. At boarding school, a feeble attempt to disagree with father about a minor issue had led to massive rejection—the father was prepared never to speak to him again until an abject apology was made. This material, although consciously available, was so traumatic that the patient could not deal with it until a repetition in the transference and a threatened termination on his part brought it to light. This patient felt like a puppet on a string: whenever he would begin to "lose himself" either in work or in love, he would be pulled back to "reality" and painful self-awareness by the threat of engulfment in a dependency which could end only in loss and longing or in catastrophic self-surrender.

This analysis was interesting in demonstrating how the same rapprochement issue had remained unresolved with mother, unresolved when displaced onto father, and unresolved yet again in subsequent transference paradigms. While the previour therapies had been helpful in working through some version of the oedipal conflicts and promoting behavioral change, the chronic intrapsychic dissatisfaction, depression, and rage were modified only when we could understand the particular shape that rapprochement had given to the oedipus conflict and slowly work this through in the transference.

Finally, let me present some typical fantasies and dreams of a patient who came with complaints that he was living behind a screen, that he was constantly playing roles, observing himself critically, and that he never felt real or alive or successful. He fantasied himself a man from Mars, watching the earthlings swarming like ants on the globe below. He dreamed he was seated on a pillar fifty feet high, like St. Simeon stylites, wondering how he had gotten there and if he could get down. After a while it became clear that he could scarcely relax or cease self-observation except occasionally with the aid of drugs or sex.

In the first year of therapy, self-object fantasies of a sadomasochistic nature began to emerge: he would keep some woman like a miniature doll in his pocket, to take out when needed, or chain her to the wall and gag her so that she was always available but never intrusive. With the help of these fantasies he could study, concentrate, and feel alive. This material first began to take meaning in terms of his fear of isolation and loneliness, his need for a protective presence, his concern that this needed figure would take over and dominate him, and his inability to feel sufficiently autonomous and real so that he could affirm his own needs and boundaries. Coincident with the establishment of a narcissistic transference, I was able to point out to him that he seemed to need someone around in order to work or to love, but that apparently he could not trust that someone to willingly fit in with his needs. Considerable historical come and I would hurriedly have to replace it in the brain case, but anxious and depressed in his second year following a death in her family. From the time he could walk he would often get lost; at other times he was kept in the backyard, attached to a pole by a sort of expandable baby harness which limited him to a ten-foot perimeter.

In the second year of treatment he began to fall asleep on the couch, fought this impulse because it was "too expensive," learned that it was too dangerous, and became aware of his fear and desire to lose himself in others. He fantasied that he was floating in warm water with his brain detached and floating nearby, connected only by the cranial nerves. "At first I was frightened that someone would come and I would hurriedly have to replace it in the brain case, but then I felt safe and peaceful. . . . There's no desire to touch it or manipulate it or to interfere with it. . . . just to watch it. . . .

"And yet I want to know what it's doing there, want to see into it, to see it closer, but it's not paying attention to anything at all . . . just quietly . . . humming is too busy a sound . . . it's resting. . . .

"It's so hard to let myself lie there for even a minute not doing something. . . . But what I really want to do is float, just let my brain float there and not be bothered. . . ."

And so I did not bother him, although clearly there was much to be said about this fantasy both dynamically, genetically, and in the transference. Dreams of being nestled amidst protective mountains or parked in a nearby garage gave way to fearful dreams of loss of support and falling, recalling a similar recurrent dream from childhood. This was eventually connected with the emergence of a reliable maternal substitute, an aunt who lived nearby and with whom I was identified in the transference. Little by little we were able to relate the wishes and fears of engulfment to the wishes and fears of separation, and connect these with the sadomasochistic impulses.

Derivatives were now constantly becoming more obvious. For example, he obsessed about designing a work bench in which all his tools would be available to hand but instantly storable under a sort of smooth rolltop cover. The connection with his object relationships and the doll fantasy was now easy for him to make; friendly smooth expanses were bought at the price of objects, which were becoming less dangerous for him to use and be with.

Concurrent with the working through of these merger and separation issues, an individuation seemed to be taking place, a recathexis of his private self which seemed, as it were, to have been shelved for the duration. He dreamed of discovering an ancient stone tablet with hieroglyphics he began to decipher; of soaring over landscapes, of finding a hidden road. He was sometimes excited, exuberant, and exultant; he began a variety of projects and was either anxious and overexcited by their success or enraged, depressed, and withdrawn at their slightest failure.

This period coincided with a change in emphasis from a generally idealizing to a generally mirroring transference in which specific omnipotent fantasies and defenses were repeatedly worked through. There were mood swings between elation and depression, each of which was carefully traced back to its current origin, with the occasional recovery of early memories. As he began to view his mother with some objectivity and to recognize the depression into which he had followed her as a child, her critical influence on his every endeavor began to fade. He dreamed that she was dead, but then almost immediately had to restore the equilibrium with an array of restitutive and self-stimulative fantasies.

His need for a regulatory presence was still great, however, and in the period of consolidation that followed, this could now be consistently interpreted in the transference. The oscillations between subjective and objective awareness became not only less extreme but also more appropriate and integrated. And there was now a notable increase in emotional range, including not only rage and emptiness, but longing; not only exultation and despair, but quiet relaxation.

It should be clear that the material from the first year or two was handled largely in terms of separation-individuation problems, with the transference at first serving as a transitional bridge between self and object and then, increasingly, as an exemplar of the conflicts and defenses around these issues. I was enormously impressed, however, with the condensation of oedipal and preoedipal material even in the early phases, although the patient's associations and the archaic nature of the transference itself consistently led us back to early issues of self- and object differentiation and regulation. When, in the third year, a clearer sense of self, purpose, and engagement in the world, and a growing resistance, heralded a clear object transference, very similar themes could now be reworked in the context of birth, rescue, and other oedipal fantasies. On balance, I have consistently underemphasized this later phase of the treatment because it is so similar to the analysis of the classical neuroses, and I have concentrated on the events occurring before the engagement of an oedipal paradigm. Here I would merely emphasize the following points:

1. There is a group of patients who present dilemmas of self versus object in both the areas of loving and working. In the latter case the work is treated as being done *for* the self or *for* the object. This dilemma tends to be presented in terms of self-love or object-love, of isolation or merger, of sadism or masochism, and it is accompanied

by a mirroring (controlling) transference or by an idealizing (submissive) transference. The sadomasochism, of course, reflects the fact that the object line of rapprochement overlaps the instinctual line of anality, and the coercion of the object serves to reduce or deny the awareness of separation.

Even when sadomasochistic fantasies are not conscious, the phenomenal experience is of a choice between two alternatives: either one submits totally to the object or the object must be totally submissive to oneself. Both sides of this dilemma are invariably present, although one side may be unconscious, or displaced to another object or arena, or otherwise split off. In its simplest form the patient's phenomenal experience is that he can either love himself or love an object, but not both simultaneously.

2. This dilemma tends to be associated with oscillations between subjective and objective self-awareness, such that the patient can either be lost in an absorbed state without being aware of himself or is constantly aware of himself without being able to lose himself. By analogy one might say that he can either experience himself subjectively, from the side of the self, or objectively, from the side of the object, but not both simultaneously, appropriately or in some integrated fashion. The articulation of the subjective and objective views on the self is part of the developmental line of object constancy and separation. Both lines are inextricably intertwined; different perspectives on the same process.

3. The clinical hallmark of these problems of self- and object love and constancy is the formation of an archaic or narcissistic transference; whether of the clinging, ocnophilic, idealizing or object variety, or of the grandiose, philobatic, mirroring or self variety. These transferences are pathological analogues of phases of separation-individuation relating to oneness and separateness. They are basically *complementary* relationships, where the one supplies what the other feels lacking, rather than *symmetrical* relationships between independent people or, as one engineer was fond of saying, between stand-alone units.

In normal development, the rapprochement phase is crucial for learning to live with and negotiate between oneself and one's object as separate autonomous beings; that is, for the establishment of both self-constancy and object constancy. Just as thing constancy and object constancy imply the integration of multiple perspectives upon the thing and the object, self-constancy requires the integration of multiple perspectives upon the self.

4. For patients who develop these archaic transferences, individuation is just as problematic as is separation. Consequently the vicissitudes of these transferences may be viewed not only as a struggle of love and hate between the self and the merged or separated transference object, but also as a struggle within the self to differentiate and integrate multiple perspectives on the self, thereby articulating both the subjective and the objective worlds.

In the early phases of treatment, the analyst will be required as a kind of transitional object to bridge the gap not only between the self and the other, but also between the subjective and objective worlds. By tolerating a wide variety of experiences between self-love and object love, subjectivity and objectivity, the analyst promotes the possibility of integration rather than dichotomization or oscillation. Put otherwise, it is the good-enough analyst who can be used both subjectively and objectively, as the object of symbiosis and of separation, lending himself to experiences of merger and self-object love as well as experiences of separation, hate, and object-longing. It is worth noting that some of these experiences, such as the "floating brain fantasy," occur in relatively drive-free states which are akin to Winnicott's transitional area and the concept of "playing." While drive material is always available for interpretation, in the beginning of these treatments it seems crucial to allow for an area in which questions of conflict, reality, decisions, and *doing* may be temporarily put aside in favor of moments of just *being*—of being alone with someone near.

For the developing self is also developing a healthy immune reaction—it rejects a foreign body with narcissistic rage—and although this must necessarily be worked through at a later stage, it must first be allowed for and, in compliant patients, even encouraged. The value of the archaic transferences is that they allow us to operate without prematurely provoking this reaction, since in his transitional mode, the analyst is neither subjective nor objective, neither self nor other, but rather the medium which makes this transition and articulation possible.

When Mahler writes that "the experience of being both fully 'in' and at the same time basically separate from the world 'out there' is one of the givens of life that is taken for granted," she is pointing to a paradox which the child begins to confront during rapprochement, and which is never to be finally resolved in his lifetime. Logically, the paradox seems to involve the disparate sets of data from which we construct our multiple perspectives on the world. Since philosophers have apparently not yet succeeded in resolving this paradox, the child-as-philosopher must make do with partial, temporary, and phase-appropriate solutions. Although I believe that many issues in contemporary theory are essentially attempts to grapple with this dilemma, I have tried in this paper to explore some of the more clinical implications of the problem.

References

Abraham, K. (1924). A short study of the development of the libido, viewed in the light of mental disorders. In *Selected Papers of Karl Abraham*, pp. 418-501. New York: Basic Books, 1960.

Bach, S. (1977). On the narcissistic state of consciousness. *International Journal of Psycho-Analysis* 58:209-233.

Balint, M. (1959). *Thrills and Regression*. New York: International Universities Press.

——— (1968). *The Basic Fault*. London: Tavistock.

Bergmann, M. (1971). Psychoanalytic observations on the capacity to love. In *Separation-Individuation: Essays in Honor of Margaret S. Mahler*, eds. J. McDevitt and C. Settlage, pp. 15-40. New York: International Universities Press.

——— (1978). On the intrapsychic function of falling in love. Paper presented to the New York Psychoanalytic Society.

Bohr, M. (1948). On the notions of causality and complementarity. *Dialectica* 2:312-319.

Ferenczi, S. (1914). Sensations of giddiness at the end of the psycho-analytic session. In *Further Contributions to the Theory and Technique of Psycho-Analysis*. New York: Basic Books, 1952.

Freud, S. (1905). Three essays on the theory of sexuality. *Standard Edition* 7:128-243.

——— (1914). On narcissism: an introduction. *Standard Edition* 14:73-102.

——— (1917). Mourning and melancholia. *Standard Edition* 14:243-298. London: Hogarth Press, 1957.

Hermann, I. (1936). Clinging-going-in-search: a contrasting pair of instincts and their relation to sadism and masochism. *Psychoanalytic Quarterly* 45:5-36, 1976.

Klein, M. (1934). A contribution to the psychogenesis of manic-depressive states. In *Contributions to Psycho-analysis, 1921-1945*, pp. 282-310. New York: McGraw-Hill, 1964.

Kohut, H. (1971). *The Analysis of the Self*. New York: International Universities Press.

Lacan, J. (1966). *Écrits*. Paris: Editions du Seuil.

Lewin, B. D. (1950). *The Psychoanalysis of Elation*. New York: W. W. Norton.

Mahler, M. S. (1972). Rapprochement subphase of the separation-individuation phase. *Psychoanalytic Quarterly* 41:487-506. Reprinted in *The Selected Papers of Margaret S. Mahler*, vol. 2, ch. 9. New York: Jason Aronson, 1979. Also, this volume, ch. 1.

Mahler, M. S., Pine, F., and Bergman, A. (1975). *The Psychological Birth of the Human Infant: Symbiosis and Individuation*. New York: Basic Books.

Piaget, J. (1954). *The Construction of Reality in the Child*. New York: Basic Books.

Rilke, R. M. (1939). *Duino Elegies*. New York: W. W. Norton.

Shakespeare, W. (n.d.). *Shakespeare's Sonnets*, ed. S. Booth. New Haven: Yale University Press, 1977.

Waelder, R. (1930). The principle of multiple function: observations on over-determination. In *Psychoanalysis: Observation, Theory, Application*, ed. S. Guttman, pp. 68-83. New York: International Universities Press, 1976.

Winnicott, D. W. (1971). *Playing and Reality*. New York: Basic Books.

Zazzo, R. (1975). La genese de la conscience de soi (La reconnaissance de soi dans l'image du miroir). In *Psychologie de la Connaissance de Soi: Symposium de l'Association de psychologie scientifique de langue francaise (Paris, 1973)*, by R. Angelergues, D. Anzieu, E. E. Boesch, Y. Bres, J.-B. Pontalis, and R. Zazzo, pp. 145-188. Paris: Presses Universitaires de France.

11

Ours, Yours, Mine

ANNI BERGMAN

Fights over possessions—often fought with a fierceness that in no
way seems warranted by the possessions themselves—are all too
familiar to those in close contact with young children.

But this attachment to "things" does not end with the end of
childhood; it is an important and often plaguing part of adult life as
well. There are those who hold onto all the bits and pieces that they
have accumulated, whether they are of objective value or not; and
there are those who like to live with the bare minimum of possessions. There are those who can give away their possessions but
cannot share them; and there are those to whom possessions become
most valuable when shared with another person. There are those
who know how to take care of their possessions, and who always
know where they are, and those who forever lose or misplace them.
We could go on and on describing attitudes toward possessions, and
it is quite clear that these are deeply ingrained and hard to modify.
This paper will describe uses of inanimate objects as they unfold in
the course of the separation-individuation process, with special
emphasis on rapprochement, as well as developing feelings of possessiveness toward those objects. It is our thesis that attitudes toward
objects reflect the beginning sense of one's own self as separate,
emerging from the former state of dual unity with mother.

Psychoanalysis traditionally has connected the attitude toward possessions and such character traits as stinginess or generosity to the anal phase of development (Fenichel 1945). The stool part of the self is eventually relinquished—the first true gift to mother. The anal phase coincides with that subphase of the separation-individuation process designated as rapprochement, that crucial time from 15 to 24 months when the toddler becomes aware of his separateness, a time during which the intrapsychic self- and object representations become well established. I will attempt to show how the developing sense of self, unfolding through the separation-individuation process, is worked out not only with mother and others but also with inanimate objects in the outside world, and how in turn it influences attitudes toward such objects, beginning with holding on and letting go of them, and eventually possessing or sharing them. Holding on or letting go does not require the recognition of a separate human object; giving and taking does. I will trace some of the developmental steps that lead to the realization of "mine," "yours," and "ours" by examining how these concepts arise in the course of the separation-individuation process from 5 months, the height of symbiosis, to somewhere in the third year when an intrapsychic differentiation between the self and object has been attained.

A study of the concepts of "mine" and "yours" emphasizes that aspect of the separation-individuation process which propels an individual to take possession of his life and enjoy it, which in turn helps him tolerate the losses that are entailed in becoming a separate individual, and thereby renouncing a symbiotic oneness with mother.

The sense of "mine" and "yours," according to our observations and the symbiosis theory of human development (Mahler, Pine, and Bergman 1975), seems to develop out of an earlier sense of "ours" that starts with the symbiotic union between mother and child, widens with the expanding space between them, and finally expands toward interactions with the other-than-mother world—a world which is "other," but onto which some of the mother attributes are displaced as well so that the investment in it becomes libidinal.

In the discussion which follows, I will consider the importance of the space between mother and child, the function of transitional and shared objects within that space, and the gradual development of the concepts of "mine" and "yours."

In our observations of psychotic children we noted that certain aspects of development—which in normal children seem "fleeting"—happen so slowly and laboriously that they can be observed as if with a magnifying glass. Simply for the purposes of contrast and comparison, and to highlight the normal development of a sense of "mine" and "yours," I have included clinical vignettes from our study of infantile psychosis (Mahler 1968).

THE SPACE BETWEEN MOTHER AND CHILD

Mahler's theory of human symbiosis postulates that at the beginning of life and for the first five months or so mother and baby constitute a dual unity, and for the baby an omnipotent system. At this time, there is no outside world for the child; the outer world, as it develops, happens in the space between mother and child. This space at first is created by mother's comings and goings. On the baby's side, the space between self and object begins to be created by the baby in the beginning of the differentiation subphase, when he begins to look around and pushes away from mother's enveloping arms. Thus begins a process of distancing from mother and exploration of the world outside. But as the baby creates this distance, he also gets a different view of mother. The differentiation subphase begins at the height of symbiosis at around 5 months of age. We found that those children who had an unusually close symbiotic relationship in which the mother experienced special pleasure started to differentiate and seek distance most actively; in one case, where the mother acted out her own symbiotic need, the child sought distance almost vehemently. Sammy,[1] whose mother was symbiotically enveloping, for a while actually preferred to be held by adults other than his mother, adults who would provide him with greater opportunity to visually explore the environment while being held. The seeking of distance during the differentiation subphase coincided with greater awareness of mother as a special person, even if this awareness, as in Sammy's case, was a negative one.

Winnicott (1971) says that play and creative activity take place in the space between mother and child. In the study of the separation-individuation process in average mother-child pairs it was literally that space which was observed, a space very small at first, slowly expanding with the growing capacities of the baby, and traveled

1. Some of the children mentioned here are also described by Mahler, Pine, and Bergman (1975).

over and over again, first with the reaching arms, the searching and finding look, the listening and hearing ear, and finally, with the growing capacity for independent locomotion, the entire body.

During the earliest beginnings of the study on separation-individuation conducted in a playroom-like setting, the mothers and babies were free to create the space that was optimal for each of them as individuals, as well as for each particular age. How this space was used and traversed eventually led to the formulation of the subphase theory of separation-individuation (Mahler 1961). For instance, there was a little girl, one year old, preciously and precariously performing daring feats of climbing and balancing at a distance from mother. Her courage seemed to be for the benefit of her mother, who felt that girls had to be tough and could not be taught independence early enough. This mother-child pair seemed then separated from each other to an exaggerated degree, and both mother and child gave some signs that they entertained longings for greater closeness. Martha was the first child of this family in the study. Subsequently, we saw the same mother with three more children—all boys—and were impressed with her ability to fulfill their needs as lap babies. When we had first seen her with Martha we did not as yet have any conception of subphases, and we were therefore not aware of two important points. One, what seemed like premature separateness on the child's part was only partly that—it was also to an extent the child's desire and need during that time to explore the environment even at the expense of the former closeness to mother. We were also unaware of the fact that this mother, who seemed to us not to be providing enough mothering to her separating one-year-old, was more at ease with her children during the symbiotic stage and was able to give them a solid start in life during that period of dual unity. In addition, being fledgling observers, perhaps, we were not fully aware of the importance of the actual space between the mother and child, that is, of the fact that the space between mother and child is created by both in the course of the separation-individuation process. At the beginning there is no space as there is yet no consciousness of self and other, but as the space is created it becomes the common orbit. While the symbiotic unity is an illusory "we" experience that cannot last, the space between mother and child is a true "we-ours" experience, as it evolves with the differentiation in the child's psyche of the object and the self-representations as separate entities from the self-object representation of the symbiosis.

Another mother-child pair observed early in the study was Tommy and his mother, who showed the opposite of what we saw in Martha and her mother. Tommy was a quiet little boy, slightly anxious and restricted in his movements, and with a tendency to stay quite close to his mother. The mother was very eager to talk about her feelings toward Tommy when he was first born and said she had then found his demands quite intolerable. When he first woke her up at night, she remembered crying and feeling that she no longer had a life of her own. During the first weeks and months of Tommy's life, she would frequently feel compelled to rush out of the house to go shopping, since staying home with him made her feel dreadfully confined. At around one year of age, when Martha had seemed so prematurely separate, Tommy seemed overly close. And later, during his second year, he became very anxious about his mother's whereabouts, and would need to be close to her at all costs. If she would leave him, he would respond quite often with severe temper tantrums. This mother-child pair was observed long before characteristics of subphases had been delineated, and what we did not know at the time was that the shadowing behavior seen in Tommy was only in part a function of this particular mother-child relationship; it was also a phenomenon characteristic of the age later designated as the rapprochement subphase. Tommy's mother, for whom motherhood had been such an enormous struggle as long as the baby was totally dependent on her, functioned much more comfortably with a growing, individuating child who allowed her more separateness and *Lebensraum*. Tommy, who had seemed so troubled earlier, developed very well during his third year.

Once the child is able to move away independently, he seems to rediscover mother as he returns to her. Once he is able to move away, albeit only the tiniest distance at the beginning, he experiences not only a new view of the world but a new view of the mother as well. As the baby's locomotor functioning matures, he is able to move away further, his world begins to widen, there is more to see, more to hear, and more to touch, and each time he returns to mother he brings with him some of the new experience. In other words, each time he returns he is ever so slightly changed. The mother is the center of his universe to whom he returns as the circles of his explorations widen.

How much pleasure there is in the actual finding and refinding of mother perhaps partly depends on how much the mother permits the child the illusion that by finding her he has just created her (Winnicott 1971). If she is too intrusive, it is as if he were being deprived of this process of creating her as he refinds her. If, on the other hand, she is too elusive, the process of creating and finding becomes too much of a strain. One little girl we saw gave up on her efforts to some extent, and instead of finding and creating mother, turned to herself. Her favorite activity was rocking in front of a mirror.

For the psychotic child the adaptive and creative use of space between himself and mother becomes impossible; indeed, this space does not seem to exist. Instead of space, there is only the dread of abandonment or engulfment—in either case, annihilation of the developing self (Mahler 1968). In treatment of psychotic children, this space, the shared reality, may slowly be created by the therapist who acts as a bridge between mother and child, and who slowly and patiently teaches both mother and child that a space can be created which is not too dangerous. The mother must learn that the total rejection she has experienced is only the reverse side of desperate need, and the child must learn that his needs can be fulfilled and that interaction with an "other" can be comforting and pleasurable (Mahler 1968).

OBJECTS AND THEIR TRANSFORMATION INTO POSSESSIONS

According to Mahler's theory of human symbiosis, for the first five or six months of life mother and baby constitute a dual unity. The transitional object (Winnicott 1953) of the early months is an object found by the baby which stands between the self- and the object world and provides a safe intermediary area of experience which allows both separateness and fusion.

We have observed a related phenomenon in babies during the differentiation subphase, that is, from 5 to 8 months, when they develop a special interest in objects that seem to be a part of the mother and yet are not, namely such objects as the mother's jewelry or her glasses. Why do these detachable objects hold such special fascination, and why are they especially suitable as comforting objects? I believe that these objects represent both mother and the outside world. Thus they may serve both as a confirmation of the early "we"[2] and "ours" experience—one moment part of the mother, the next moment part of the self, a self not yet fully experienced as separate—and at the same time are experienced as not-mother, that is, part of the world outside. Thus, while confirming the symbiotic experience, they also serve as vehicles in the process of differentiation. Winnicott makes the point that the transitional object, though it already exists, is created by the baby. The prototype for this is the way in which the mother gives the breast to the infant, allowing him to create it as he finds it, that is, allowing him the illusion that he has created it. Carrying this concept a bit further, one might apply it to a cherished activity in young children, then they find things in the outside world and act as if they had just created them. We can observe children creating the outside world anew as they find it, and invest it with their own unique way of seeing it. This is intimately bound up with the libidinal investment in mother. The shiny pebble found at the beach by the older child may be like the shiny bit of jewelry found on the mother by the baby.

Thus, during differentiation, the baby's interest in mother's possessions may be seen as a function of his wanting to own and incorporate her while at the same time be separate from her. The differentiating child makes mother, or parts of her, part of himself. He does this by investigating and manipulating parts of her, especially those he can take off, like jewelry or eyeglasses. These inanimate objects are invested with libido which stems directly from mother, but in contrast to the transitional object they cannot be totally possessed— only borrowed. They may be used but they cannot be used up.

Thus, already during the first few months of life there are two kinds of inanimate objects that take on a special importance and serve the infant in the process of becoming separate. First, the transitional object, described by Winnicott, that is given by the mother and created by the baby; second, the borrowed object which is discovered and thus created by the baby but is ultimately kept by the mother. Thus, it would seem that the transitional object serves the illusion of oneness while the borrowed object serves separateness in a shared place.

2. "We" as used here is a primitive feeling state which does not require self-object differentiation. The feeling of "we" referred to is psychically experienced as the "me" of primary narcissism which still dominates the symbiosis. Only gradually does this archaic "we" experience develop to include differentiated "me" and "we" experience. However, it is the author's contention that even in adulthood intense "we" experiences retain an element of the archaic "we."

During the practicing subphase (10-15 months) the child actually begins to move away from mother as he learns to move on his own. His relative obliviousness of her is determined in part by the pleasures in his own functioning and the widening of his world. But it also seems that, even though separated in space, he still acts as if mother were somehow part of him, with him. In other words, symbolically he takes her along. He greatly enjoys the world of inanimate objects. He picks them up, examines them and drops them. The world is there to be explored. He usually will easily accept one object or toy as a substitute for another. He might cry briefly when something is taken away, but on the whole, the world seems too big and too interesting to be bothered by small frustrations. Objects or activities that seem to be most comforting during the practicing stage are those that seem to confirm the toddler's sense of his omnipotence, which is still shared with mother. For example, we found that an unhappy child of that age could be comforted by being allowed to play with a light switch, turning lights on and off, preferably while being held up by an adult, or else by working a toy such as a jack-in-the-box or top, whose movements he can actively control and which contain some element of surprise and magic.

Mahler's theory states that during the differentiation and practicing subphases of the separation-individuation process, the child gradually comes to a dawning awareness of his separateness. While in the first months of a baby's life the mother comes and goes, towards the end of the first year the baby himself begins to go and come back. During the subphase of rapprochement, beginning at about 15 months, an important change takes place. Mother is now seen as a separate person out there, with whom one might share one's possessions and one's experiences. She can no longer be experienced as part of the self and thus the relationship has to be reestablished and reaffirmed over and over. Moveable objects at this point seem to serve the purpose of affirming over and over the connection between toddler and mother. Toddlers at this age are indefatigable in depositing objects in mother's lap.

During the rapprochement subphase, the toddler has achieved a first real awareness of separateness. The bringing of objects to mother, just as the earlier act of removing objects from her, seems to serve two different functions: one, to bridge the gap by giving *her* what he now begins to experience as *his;* the other, to put into mother's lap for safekeeping what he wants to return to but at the moment does not want to use. Earlier, what isn't used is simply discarded, no longer exists. In many instances, in the same action one can see elements of opposing tendencies—to affirm separateness, and to maintain oneness. At one level the mother is an extension of the self; her lap is part of the infant. At the other, separateness is recognized and dealt with.

When we compare these stages in the normal child's attitude toward possessions to those observed in the psychotic child, we observe marked distortions. Psychotic children have not developed to the point of separateness experienced by average normal children during the rapprochement subphase. This can be seen by the way in which they relate to the inanimate world. The transitional object of the normal baby becomes the psychotic fetish (Furer 1964)—the total absorption with an object or activity that represents the mother, that is clung to with desperate feeling, and that seems to represent the merged identity without which the child would be totaly lost or destroyed. A psychotic child whose fetish object is removed from him will break into desperate tantrums. Whereas the transitional object of the normal child is needed mostly at times of fatigue or unhappiness or at bedtime, the psychotic fetish object is held onto almost constantly. It is most characteristic in the observations of such children that while they may hold on frantically to their psychotic fetish (Furer), objects in general are cathected only during the moment of the immediate usefulness. It is difficult to describe satisfactorily how a psychotic child during the phase of denial of separateness will dispose of a toy. It is not put away, it is not thrown away, it is not handed to another person. Rather, it is treated as if suddenly it no longer existed. That part of relating to objects that serves separateness is strenuously rejected.

Rachel, whose separation-individuation process during her first two years of treatment has been described elsewhere (Bergman 1971), at first would not touch objects or toys at all. Later, she discarded them as if they had never existed, and still later, after she had developed a rudimentary sense of self, demanded that her mother or the therapist find any object that she could not find. Mother's refusal or inability to do this would send Rachel into a rage. The child absolutely refused to look for anything herself. Thus, like the toddler during the rapprochement subphase but typically for the psychotic child in highly exaggerated form, Rachel, increasingly aware of separateness, attempted to undo it by insisting that mother act as if still part of her. Like the toddler during rapprochement, she created an impossible situation between herself and mother, acting this out with inanimate objects which she could not truly possess. To Rachel, during this period of beginning separateness, her whole world had to be mother's lap; or rather, mother's lap had to be powerful enough to extend into all of Rachel's world. For years afterwards Rachel was unable to take care of any of her possessions. To her mother's great exasperation, she would lose and forget everything; she never knew where anything was.

Returning to the normal child in the rapprochement subphase of separation-individuation, and his growing sense that objects in the outside world can be part of him, belong to him, but can also be part of someone else, that such possessions can be used, manipulated, held onto or given up, lost or destroyed, we found that at around 15 or 16 months a clustering of several phenomena occurs: (1) resistance to being dressed or undressed; (2) increasing desire to have or do whatever the child saw others having or doing; (3) nonacceptance of substitutions for wished-for possession; (4) conflict over holding on or giving up of a possession that another child wanted; and (5) object-directed aggression in defense of one's own property or interest.

During the following month (16-17 months) we found an increase in possessiveness, but we also found the most frequent source of anger involved having one's autonomy interfered with, not being allowed to do as one wished, to do things by oneself, etc. In other words, we found a stronger push toward individuation.

Another month later, 18 to 19 months, constitutes the height of the rapprochement crisis. This is a time when some degree of disturbance in the area of object relations is a universal phenomenon (Mahler 1966, 1971). The bipolar, ambivalent pull—"to be separate" and to be "fused with the object"—creates what we have called this "crisis." The rapprochement crisis is complicated by the fact that for the child this is not only a time of painful awareness of separateness and vulnerability, but also of defense against this awareness. The child may thus swing back and forth between an exaggerated independence and an exaggerated dependence, with attempts to coerce the mother to be ever-present and powerful. From these opposite poles, the child seems to say to mother: "I am me. You cannot touch me or tell me what to do." Or, "You must be a part of me, fulfill my wishes, and be ever-present." As part and parcel of this crisis, the child experiences on the one hand the fear of being abandoned, alone, unloved, and on the other hand the fear of being reengulfed, overwhelmed, swallowed up. Around the rapprochement crisis we found an interesting cluster of phenomena: (1) increased independent functioning; (2) greater self-assertiveness; (3) increased use of the word "mine"; (4) increased ability and wish to play at some distance from mother; (5) increased awareness of body sensations (for instance, making faces in front of a mirror, water play, riding on the rocking horse, etc.); and (6) competitiveness over possession being the most frequent source of anger.

Thus, what we seem to find is that the rapprochement subphase was ushered in by a great pleasure in sharing possessions, in give-and-take, in using mother as an extended part of the self but also as a separate person with whom to share. But along with greater awareness of separateness seemed to go a greater need to assert the budding self, a greater need to compare it with others, and a greater resistance to intrusion and interference with one's wishes. It seems that in the midst of all this we find a moment of conflict about whether to hold on or give up, and then an increased need to defend one's possessions with one's growing awareness of self, which is frequently expressed by insistance on what is "mine."

THE IMPORTANCE OF CLOTHES

During the second half of the second year, when the toddler begins to insist on his autonomy by saying "no" (Spitz 1957), dressing, undressing, and diapering generally become a battlefield between mother and child. Clothes and wraps during that period seem to have a very special meaning, or rather at this age we seem to see the beginnings of the importance of clothes.

Clothes are not-me possessions that are most closely connected to the "me." They are part of the body, and yet they are taken off and put on. They have color, texture, they can be alluring and soft or hampering and hard or rough. They circumscribe individuality or identity. This function of clothes can be observed later in childhood when boys and girls play dress-up by putting on someone else's clothes and become that person. Hats and shoes often seem to have an especially symbolic meaning, perhaps because they are most easily put on and taken off. The special significance of these articles of clothing is indicated by such common sayings as, "I would not like to be in his shoes," or "I'll put on another hat."

In normal development, clothes seem at first to be experienced as part of the self, and quite early in life it seems that pride in the self can be expressed through pride in one's clothes—again, often shoes and hats. During the rapprochement subphase clothes begin to have special significance.

Peter was a little boy in our study of normal children whose mother had a particularly difficult struggle over dressing and undressing him. When he first started to play in our toddler room, that is, the room where two to three-year-olds could play together at some distance from the mother, he went through a ritual where he would stop at the threshold, wait to be greeted there by his toddler room teacher, and would then show her his pants. She would admire them, and finally he would enter the activities of the playroom. Charlie, on the other hand, would come in wearing his jacket and hat. He would stand on the sidelines and observe. If urged to take his jacket off, he would leave the room, sulk, or cry. If left to his own devices, he would eventually take it off on his own and then slowly enter into play.

Donna, a little girl who had difficulty in separating from her mother, but who could play well and happily once she had made the separation, developed a pattern of pulling at her clothes while she was in the throes of a conflict over leaving mother.

It seems that clothes begin to have symbolic meaning as a result of the rapprochement conflict—and it may be at a particular moment of the conflict. This could be the point when the toddler not only becomes increasingly aware of his own separateness and vulnerability, but in addition becomes aware of sexual differences as well as of the loss of his feces. At this time the taking off and putting on of clothes by the mother becomes a threat to developing body integrity, while on the other hand it also becomes possible to displace some of the conflicts about separateness as well as castration onto the use and possession of clothes.

In later development, of course, clothes take on many other meanings, but it is interesting that they again become so very important during adolescence, the second period of individuation (Blos 1967), and can express both belonging (group fashion) and individuality (separation from parental demands).

Psychotic children often experience clothes as an extreme source of discomfort. For Rachel, for instance, buying new shoes was an ordeal. She would often get blisters from shoes, and her mother would only find this out accidentally, as Rachel would never let her know. Very early in life she was said to have pulled off all her wraps and later she went through a long period of feeling simply miserable in her clothes, taking them all off as soon as she came home and complaining endlessly that a hat wouldn't cover her ears, that a belt was not tight enough, too tight, etc.

Violet (Mahler 1968), a severely autistic girl who had been in treatment for nine years, since the age of three, displaced her conflicts onto clothes in extreme ways. She was about eight years old when she began to emerge as a separate little girl with a growing sense of self-awareness. At the age of nine she went to camp with normal children. She was relatively happy there, but began the painful journey of recognizing that she was different from the others. Though she was speaking by then, her speech remained peculiar and her ability to play in adequate ways was very rudimentary. When she returned from camp she drew pictures of her camp experience, and especially concentrated on remembering and drawing the clothes of the other children. From then on, clothes became an obsession, as she hoped that by wearing the right clothes she could undo the differences between herself and others. She would not allow her mother to choose any of her clothes, and buying trips to Macy's became long looked forward to treats and also ordeals of disappointment. Finally, two years later, at the age of 11, Violet could come to a more satisfactory solution in which true sublimation could replace the earlier displacement. She now began to design and sew her own clothes, an activity in which she was able to excel and elicit the genuine admiration of others.

Another example of conflict displaced onto clothes was displayed by a severely deprived adolescent boy in therapy. This boy denied any need for help. Although he came to his once- or twice-a-week treatment hours with fair regularity, he consistently belittled the therapist and insisted that nothing was wrong in his life and that, if there were, nobody could help him anyway. Following a joint session with his guardian, during which the therapist was able to act as a bridge between them, interpreting some of the mutual wishes and disappointments, this boy brought to his therapy session a pair of badly worn jeans that he wished the therapist to patch with hand-crocheted patches which he had occasionally seen her make. From then on he periodically returned with the same pair of jeans in need of patching, and along with this his resistance to admitting his own needs gradually diminished. It seemed that he could use his torn jeans as a symbol through which he could begin to admit some need for patching of his own self.

PLAY WITH TOYS AND THE ACCEPTANCE OF SEPARATENESS

To accept fully one's separateness is a lifelong task and one way in which this task is continually worked on by children as well as by adults is through the use of objects.

By the second half of the second year, children become capable of enjoying the world of objects in a new way, namely, through beginning symbolic play (Galenson 1971, Eckstein 1966), mostly still on a nonverbal level. What are some of the most favored toys of this period? Which ones seem to help the toddler master some of the conflicts and anxieties he experiences, such as mother or parts of the self (feces) disappearing, about being in control, that is, being omnipotent, strong and powerful, and being a helpless baby and cared and provided for? Puzzles, blocks for building towers, balls for throwing, nesting cubes and other toys that make things appear and disappear, as well as dolls and Teddy bears, are toys with universal appeal for the toddler during this period. They are used in ever so slightly different ways by each child, indicating not only the extent of his skill and ego mastery, but also the particular way in which the conflicts over separation-individuation as well as psycho-sexual conflicts are experienced at the time.

All of these early games are played at first in the space between mother and child, and it is one of the characteristics of the child in acute conflict over separation that he is unable to play. When this acute conflict is settled, either by the child's allowing mother to leave or accepting a substitute, or by mother's remaining close enough to satisfy him, the child is usually able to return to play. In a state of acute longing, most children are not able to turn to play, but will, rather, turn to direct instinctual gratification, such as food, autoerotic activity or, in other circumstances, sleep. Sometime in the third year, along with the ability for verbal communication, the child can use toys at a higher symbolic level to play out experiences of the past or anticipated in the future. This type of play no longer uses the space between mother and child in as direct a way as before, but already depends on the ability to internalize and identify.

Looking at books and being read to is an activity that is of particular importance and interest to toddlers beginning at the time of rapprochement. Going back to the concept of finding and creating, here we may have an activity that allows the toddler to create the story of his activities and life, his budding self as he relates to the world around him by finding it in stories. Sometimes these stories can be directly concerned with the child's life—"When Susie goes to sleep . . . " or "When Daddy comes home. . . . " Sometimes the stories can be about animals, animal mothers and babies, by which the process of being cared for as a baby can be enjoyed in a doubly removed way, first, by way of a story; second, displaced on animals.

The following examples of children around two years old show how play can help the child deal with developmental tasks and conflicts.

Here is a description of Teddy, two years old, reported by a play session observer: "Teddy asked for a puzzle. He chose the puzzle with the vegetables. He worked on the puzzle very seriously, taking each piece out, looking at it, and carefully putting it back again. He identified some of the vegetables in an original way. So, for instance, he called a bunch of celery, flowers. He recognized the carrot and the potato, pretended to eat them, and said 'tough.' Then he said, 'my puzzle.'"

Teddy at this time was very concerned with toilet training, and when he had a bowel movement in his pants he would say "me BM." Here individualistic ego activity—fitting together pieces of a puzzle—goes hand in hand with working out anal conflicts.

Peter, at the same age, loved to build high towers and knock them down and build them up again. Also, Peter, a child who very early seemed to have turned away from showing direct concern over his mother's whereabouts, was particularly interested in building tunnels with blocks, making the train go in and out of the tunnels. He seemed delighted to see the train reappear through the tunnel—his way of coping, we thought, with his mother's comings and goings.

Three girls during the rapprochement subphase used ball play in slightly different ways. Wendy, who always needed to relate rather exclusively to one adult, used the ball play as a way of interacting with an adult. Donna, who was very concerned with separation, used the ball play more in an active, coping way, throwing the ball away, then running after it, scooping it up, sometimes saying, "Mommy, Mommy," as she did so. Harriet, who had a very disturbed relationship to her mother, would lose balls and then want the observer to retrieve the ball for her.

Thus, the rapprochement period is ushered in by a growing wish to share with mother. The space between mother and child now takes on more and more meaning in terms of being a space that bridges a gap between the now more separate self, alone out there in the big world, and mother, whose presence and availability take on renewed importance as the awareness of separateness increases. As the awareness of separateness becomes more threatening, the mother becomes both the restorer of well-being and the person who threatens or interferes with separate functioning. It seems to be at that point that possessions become important and are recognized as "mine" and eventually reluctantly renounced as "yours." It may be that at that point the old comfortable sense of "ours" becomes impossible, and has to be replaced by an eventual ability to share on a higher level. But it may also be that all sharing, shared experiences, shared possessions, when they give a feeling of pleasure and fulfillment, retain some of the flavor of the early "ours" experience.

SUMMARY

I have attempted in this paper to show how a sense of "mine" and "yours" seems to develop out of an earlier sense of "ours" that starts with the symbiotic union between mother and child and widens with the expanding space between them to include shared possessions as well as shared space. The realization of "mine" and "yours" emerges at the height of the rapprochement subphase of the separation-individuation process, confirmation of and insistence on separate experience and possession. Along with that emerges a possibility to use these possessions to reenact and master the conflicts connected with separateness.

I have tried further to show that perhaps creative experience in Winnicott's sense can be applied not only to the creation of the transitional object but also to the creating of the mother as a separate person. The expanding space between mother and child which belongs to both, is bridged at first by what happens in that space and later by activities displaced onto objects in the outside world, such as clothes, and eventually toys.

Finally, I have considered the first experiences of "mine" as an important step in individuation that may have repercussions in later attitudes toward possessions which form an important part of each person's life style.

References

Bergman, A. (1971). "I and You": the separation-individuation process in the treatment of a symbiotic psychotic child. In *Separation-Individuation: Essays in Honor of Margaret S. Mahler,* ed. J. B. McDevitt and C. F. Settlage, pp. 325-355. New York: International Universities Press.

Blos, P. (1967). The second individuation process of adolescence. *Psychoanalytic Study of the Child* 22:162-186.

Eckstein, R. (1966). *Children of Time and Space of Action and Impulse.* New York: Appleton.

Erikson, E. H. (1959). *Identity and the Life Cycle* (Psychological Issues Monograph 1). New York: International Universities Press.

Fenichel, O. (1945). *The Psychoanalytic Theory of Neuroses.* New York: Norton.

Furer, M. (1964). The development of a preschool symbiotic boy. *Psychoanalytic Study of the Child* 16:332-351.

Galenson, E. (1971). A consideration of the nature of thought in childhood play. In *Separation-Individuation: Essays in Honor of Margaret S. Mahler,* ed. J. B. McDevitt and C. F. Settlage, pp. 41-59. New York International Universities Press.

Mahler, M. S. (1965a). Thoughts about development and individuation. *Psychoanalytic Study of the Child* 18:307-324. Reprinted in *The Selected Papers of Margaret S. Mahler,* vol. 2, ch. 1. New York: Jason Aronson, 1979.

——— (1965b). On the significance of the normal separation-individuation phase: with reference to research in symbiotic child psychosis. In *Drives, Affects, Behavior,* vol. 2, ed. M. Schur, pp. 161-169, New York: International Universities Press. Reprinted in *Selected Papers,* op. cit., ch. 4.

——— (1966). Notes on the development of basic moods: the depressive affect. In *Psychoanalysis: A General Psychology. Essays in Honor of Heinz Hartmann,* ed. R. M. Loewenstein, L. M. Newman, M. Schur, and A. J. Solnit, pp. 152-163, New York: International Universities Press.Reprinted in *Selected Papers,* op. cit., ch. 5.

——— (1968). *On Human Symbiosis and the Vicissitudes of Individuation, volume 1: Infantile Psychosis.* New York: International Universities Press.

——— (1972a). On the first three subphases of the separation-individuation process. *International Journal of Psycho-Analysis* 53:333-338. Reprinted in *Selected Papers,* op. cit., ch. 8.

——— (1972b). A study of the separation-individuation process and its possible application to borderline phenomena in the psychoanalytic situation. *Psychoanalytic Study of the Child* 26:403-424. Reprinted in *Selected Papers,* op. cit., ch. 11.

Mahler, M. S., Pine F., and Bergman, A. (1975). *The Psychological Birth of the Human Infant: Symbiosis and Individuation.* New York: Basic Books.

Searles, H. F. (1960). *The Nonhuman Environment in Normal Development and in Schizophrenia.* New York: International Universities Press.

Spitz, R. A. (1957). *No and Yes: On the Genesis of Human Communication.* New York: International Universities Press.

Winnicott, D. W. (1953). Transitional objects and transitional phenomena: a study of the first not-me possession. *International Journal of Psycho-Analysis* 34:89-97.

——— (1971). *Playing and Reality.* New York: Basic Books.

12

On the Expansion of the Affect Array: A Developmental Description

FRED PINE, PH.D.

How can we account for the progressive expansion in the array of affect states that a human being becomes capable of experiencing as development proceeds? Affective experience in the infant appears to consist of a relatively limited set of more or less automatic (built-in) responses to conditions triggered by inner or outer stimuli, responses which we on the outside can only describe as varying loosely along a pleasure-unpleasure series. But later, a full range of affects may include shame, guilt, longing, euphoria, awe, dread, excitement, loneliness, depression, nostalgia, glee, anxiety, fear, irritability, satisfaction, and more. Where do all these different affect states come from? How are they formed? In this paper, I shall make a preliminary attempt to discuss this question, at least from a descriptive-developmental point of view. Schmale's (1964) related attempt is different from but thoroughly consistent with the present one.

In Mahler's (1966) paper on the development of basic moods, she endeavors to show how depressive and elated moods, respec-

This paper appeared in slightly different form in the *Bulletin of the Menninger Clinic*, Vol. 42, 1978. I wish to express my appreciation to the editor, Paul Pruyser, Ph.D., for permission to republish. The paper was initially prepared for the first Spences Foundation Conference at the Menninger Foundation, October 1977.

tively, crystallize in relation to normal developmental events of the rapprochement and practicing subphases of the separation-individuation process. Her ideas on rapprochement and depressive mood in particular are seminal ones, and I shall herein attempt to enlarge both upon the understanding of the array of sad affects and the kind of developmentally-based thinking about affect that are in that paper. I shall proceed in three steps: First, following a few introductory remarks, I will discuss the familiar affects of anxiety and guilt in order to exemplify some of the developmental processes inherent in affect formation. I shall then turn to a group of affects, all of which I see as having origins in the rapprochement subphase, and will consider them in the developmental terms that will have emerged; these affects include sadness, longing, nostalgia, and mourning. And finally, I will conclude by applying the developmental approach to a few other selected affects outside this central domain.

Let me begin with a few preliminary remarks: there are inherent ambiguities in any discussion of affects. Because the expansion in the affect array is based in substantial degree upon cognitive specification and on the linkage of "feelings" and "ideas," it is often hard to know whether we are talking of an affect state or an idea (e.g., anticipation, awe). Indeed, human experience is not discontinuous, and most everything blends into most everything else; and I believe this to be true of affect and idea as well. Also, because the expansion of the affect array is based in substantial degree upon control and defense processes in human functioning, and because those control/defense processes tend sometimes to dominate the inner scene, obliterating much else, we ofttimes cannot tell whether our basic target of study, an affective state, even exists in a particular person (including ourself) at a particular time. And because affect states as experienced are subject to shaping by verbal-social-situational labels (that is, "naming" and the context shapes the experience), we cannot always be sure if we are talking of a psychobiological phenomenon or a sociocultural one.

These are among the reasons why a psychological theory of affects remains to be written. But the principal reason for uncertainty in a psychological study of the *development* of affects is the one that haunts so many other aspects of the study of the preverbal period—namely, that the infant cannot tell us what he or she feels. We are on the outside, looking, but not really even looking in. Additionally, in the realm of affects, where the reporting of an inner state is highly likely to alter that state (much of our theory of therapy rests upon that assumption, as do important aspects of our theory of development [Katan 1961]), the epistemological problem continues to be complex even later on. To *not* hear about an affect is to not know about it as a psychological phenomenon (at least not precisely, and not in others), but to hear about it is to participate in a process of alteration of the basic phenomenon under study.

How then can we proceed? Much as we do in all of psychoanalytic developmental theorizing. We learn what we can of inner life by self-observation and by verbal report from others; we trace this back in individual developmental history as far as memory allows; and then, beyond that period where memory and verbal report allow, we make inferences. The inferences have two overriding characteristics in common. First they have a certain "psycho-logic"—that is, they fit with and do not violate what we know of human functioning. And second, they are based on observations which, from the outside, look as though they bear on the phenomenon which we know later, and from the inside, to be relevant for us. Thus, Freud (1900), in discussing dreams of flying, asked how it was that such dreams (well before airplane flight was common) were accompanied by actual sensations of flying. His answer: every infant has experiences of being swooped up into the parental arms—hence, "flying." The match for the later-reported interior sensation (of flying) is found by inference from something that looks related to it from an exterior view. In our research on mother-child symbiosis and awareness of separateness (Mahler, Pine, and Bergman 1975) we worked similarly. Knowing both of these cognitive-affective states to exist in the older child and adult, and not assuming them to be inborn, we looked at early mother-infant interaction to see what inferences we could make regarding the way ideas of merging and ideas of separateness come into being. Specifically, we looked for behaviors which—in exterior view—were suggestive regarding the development of internal ideas of merging and separateness (and their accompanying affects). Beyond such inference in general, however, we have a particular advantage in the domain of affect. Namely, affects tend to show through. They are to a large degree expressive phenomena in infancy and they have at least some cue value for our inferences.

With these limitations, opportunities, and modes of inference in mind, I shall here undertake a descriptive-developmental approach to the understanding of the widening affect array, attempting to specify mechanisms of transformation or creation of affects along the way. I say "transformation or creation" because it seems to me that new affects come into being not only by differentiating out (transforming) from earlier affects but also by being newborn (created) at later stages in the developmental process when certain developmental conditions have been met. Shortly, I shall illustrate both of these affect-histories.

I will be suggesting that new affects are formed as a result of at least four broad sets of events that are inherent and omnipresent in the developmental process, and will discuss and illustrate (1) the cognitive specification, articulation, and differentiation of existing affect states; (2) the acquisition of new learnings that become permanent parts of mental life, having a "thing" or "entity" character (such as conscience, object constancy), and from which new affects flow; (3) control/delay/inhibition processes exerting an influence on current affects and thereby altering them; (4) and bodily processes that automatically trigger certain affects (the experiential accompaniments to the bodily events) and that become models for later, more purely psychological experiences as well.

To start with the familiar, consider Freud's (second) theory of anxiety (1926). Freud suggested that, early on, the infant suffers overwhelming experiences of distress (traumatic anxiety) at certain times of nongratification and frustration. The infant is helpless in the face of the distress; it is beyond what he can cope with—hence, "traumatic anxiety." (Clinically, it has often been suggested that the continuance of such states is a defining attribute of what gets called borderline pathology in childhood.) Later, the traumatic anxiety states are avoided via the development of what Freud called signal anxiety. That is, the person recognizes (or often, actually, has an inarticulate sense) that a situation is present or impending where traumatic anxiety may be experienced. This recognition sets off a mild degree of anxiety which in turn triggers flight or seeking of mother or (later) intrapsychic defensive operations, thus avoiding the fuller development of traumatic anxiety. This milder anxiety (which can still be quite uncomfortable) thus acts as a signal of danger—hence "signal anxiety." Such a signal can be reduced to near-imperceptibility with near-automatic triggering of defense in the smoothly (not necessarily healthily) functioning person. Clinically, excessive propensity to such signal anxiety, where too many things signal intrapsychically-defined danger or where there are marked rigidities or failures in the subsequent defensive processes, is a defining attribute of neurosis, though it is also relevant to all other psychological disorders to varying degrees.

Signal anxiety, then, has more or less replaced traumatic anxiety. What has happened? Essentially two things, and they are relevant in varying ways to the development of the entire affect array. First, the cognitive apparatus has come into play in relation to affect. In this instance, *perceptual* recognition of a danger, based on *memory* of previous distress, both of these organized by *thought,* permits an *anticipation* of impending distress. This process ordinarily becomes quite automatic and instantaneous, and does not necessarily involve effortful cognitive work. And second, the person has developed means of avoiding the danger situation; early on this means flight or seeking mother, but increasingly it comes to mean that there is an internal, entirely self-powered capacity for control, delay, and other intrapsychic alterations of the danger situation (which, broadly, we call "defenses"). The result is that the initial traumatic anxiety has been transformed, or, rather, a new affect state has been formed in relation to, and partially out of, the earlier one. Panic (helpless, without recourse, overwhelming) has been supplemented in the affect array by anxious anticipation (or call them what you will— disorganizing distress supplemented by functional anxiety, or traumatic anxiety by signal anxiety). The two states are now part of the psychic repertoire; that they have a functional relationship, the latter serving to ward off the former, is simply an added developmental nicety.

Now there is no question that to "explain" the development of a new affect (signal anxiety) in this way is an explanation at only one level and a nonexplanation at many others. In this paper, however, I shall not attempt to go beyond this kind of developmental description. Furthermore, I am aware that to mention anticipation, memory, recognition, control, or delay raises more questions (e.g., whence do *they* come?). But to pursue such questions would be to get involved in an infinite regress of questioning and to lose sight of the appropriate level of discussion for my topic. So let me simply say that a new affect (actually *itself* an array of affects, experienced differently at different times and by different persons—and including anxious anticipation, vague malaise or tension or uneasiness, acute but short-lived distress, etc.) has been formed out of the developmental mix of traumatic anxiety, cognitive recognition and anticipation, and control/defense options that have become part of intrapsychic life. Let us store *cognitive specification* and *control/defense processes* in our minds; they will come up again and again.

Let me backtrack, beginning again in a sense, this time working my way into another feature of this subject. Once again for the sake of familiarity I shall begin with a much-described affect—guilt. Obviously, with guilt as with all other affects, we cannot know whether the phenomenological experience of it in another matches our own experience. But when I say to children (when they seem to me to be in that affect state) that they are feeling badly inside about something they did or thought, they seem to respond with a marked feeling of relief that their state has been recognized by another, and often confirmation by verbal report. That will be my working definition. Where does such a feeling come from?

Freud (1923) suggested that guilt is the form that a tension emanating from the superego (or conscience) takes—that is, it is an indication of malfit between a person's standards, experienced as his own standards, and his self-perception of what he has thought or done in violation of these standards. Why that exquisitely unique feeling, that we call guilt, comes in such a circumstance is perhaps "in the nature of the beast." "Why" questions do not lead very far. But there are nameable forerunners. The young child's response to his discovered violation of parental standards appears (from his *appearance*, and additionally from spontaneous verbalizations) to be a mix of feared/anticipated loss of love, feared/anticipated punishment, and regret over having performed the violating act. But nonetheless, at least judging from those child verbalizations that inform us in this area, a new, more precisely articulated, more fully *inner*, feeling—that of guilt—comes into being somewhere from age 3 to 6. Again the affect array has been expanded. How?

This seems to me to involve less a transformation of an earlier feeling (as traumatic anxiety to signal anxiety) and more the creation of a new feeling when the inner psychological situation is right for it. Like many other things in development, both psychological and biological, it is organically programmed, even though not present at birth. The "right" psychological situation here is internalization of parental standards, what Freud called superego development. Perhaps this, too, can be conceptualized as a transformation of the earlier feared loss of love or punishment, and I do not want to make too absolute a distinction between "transformed" and "created" new affects, but there is at least a relative difference there. The cognitive participation in the formation of this new affect is of a very different order from that in the formation of signal anxiety—enough so for me to suggest that an additional developmental process is at work. In the case of signal anxiety, I described the role of inborn apparatuses, tools of mental life—perception, memory, joining together as antic- ipation, and allowing some degree of specification of an impending danger situation. By contrast, in relation to guilt, we see instead the acquisition *of a new cognitive entity,* an acquisition which has consequences for affective experience. In this case what is acquired is a not-too-clearly articulated, but still powerfully influential, set of standards for behavior and thought; the affect that we call guilt is an automatic (preprogrammed) consequence of such an acquisition. But such entities, permanent acquisitions of the person's mental life, are linked to the emergence of other affects as well (as I shall describe below) and so have relevance for other aspects of the development of the widening affect array. In any event, let us store this third process—*the formation of new permanent acquisitions in mental life,* acquisitions having "thing" character, new "entities." These too will reappear again and again.

Anxiety and guilt are, I believe, exemplar cases; and the modes that I have described through which new affects come into being have more general applicability. But before I go on to illustrate this in the case of a few selected affects, I should like to introduce one more influence upon the developing affect array—that is, *bodily events and their accompanying experiences.* The affect that I shall describe, less familiar in clinical writings but quite familiar in life, and highly suggestive for my purposes, is irritability. This name for an affect state is suggestive in its dual connotation. As a psychological state, irritability refers to a general low-level, often nonspecific, "both- eredness." It is generally a state where things keep nagging at us, though they often do not reach peak intensity or command sustained focal attention; in this it is different from anger or rage. But for the physical body we also refer to irritations, and their description is not dissimilar. Are the two connected?

An adult patient recently came in and said, "I'm feeling irritated; I'm just sore." ("Sore," like irritation, has a double meaning: sore as angry, sore as bodily soreness.) This was a patient whose body was an irritant to him and he wished to rid himself of almost all sensations emanating from it. With his emotions, as with his body, a chronic state of irritability was present. We have here a reminder that bodily states have accompanying experiences that achieve mental representation (quite automatically; this is inherent in the human thought process). I would add that those bodily-linked experiences can become models for more purely psychological experiences as well, and that irritability as an affect comes into being as an outgrowth of a *bodily experience* that has laid down a model for subsequent psychological experience, in this case an experience of negative tone though not of peak intensity nor commanding focal attention. As such, it can be experienced as a purely psychological phenomenon *(a)* when the source of the psychological distress has (in this case) *not* achieved clearly focused *cognitive specification*, and *(b)* when the quantity of the distress (in this case anger or frustrated need) has either not risen to intense levels or has been subjected to *control/ defense* processes. Incidentally, with something like irritability, we begin to introduce the issue of *mood* as opposed to affect per se— that is, a more general state which is characterized by a temporal spread (it lasts over time) and a spatial spread (it colors the reaction to *all* stimuli). This contrasts to a more time-limited and stimulus-specific state which might be called an *affect*.

To review the tools that I have highlighted for description of the modes through which an expansion of the early affect array comes about, we have (1) cognitive specification, (2) control/defense processes, (3) the achievement of new, internalized learnings, having an "entity" rather than a "process" quality in psychic life (internalized standards was my example), and (4) bodily experiences. Let us look at a few other affects to see how useful these four are in capturing aspects of their formation. I can say in advance that they have some usefulness, incomplete because of the many open questions about these processes themselves, yet they do provide a beginning conceptual language for working on affect development. In the following, I shall apply these four processes to a selected few other affects where I can see their applicability. In each instance I shall highlight the four processes by italics so that the reader can follow the flow of the argument. There are many affect states that I shall not attempt to grapple with here. This is not intended as a general theory of affect development; it is instead a descriptive mapping of a bit of psychological terrain so that we can become more familiar with it. And one last caution: I am well aware that these four processes (cognitive specification, control and defense, formation of new permanent acquisitions of the personality, and bodily models for affective experience) are processes of endless variability and uncertain form. To name them and draw upon them in an explanatory way is to advance our understanding only to a small degree.

Let us start with a group of affects, each of which has part of its developmental origins in the rapprochement period. In Mahler's (1966) important paper on the development of basic mood, she writes:

> In our studies we came across unmistakable evidence for the belief that a basic mood is established during the separation-individuation process. This basic mood or individually characteristic affective responsiveness is not due solely to innate factors but seems, at least to some extent, to be accentuated experientially and to counteract the constitutional characteristics of the individual child. This characteristic "base line" of the child's emotional responsiveness seems to derive from the preponderance and perpetuation of one or the other general emotional colorings that we found to be characteristic of one or the other of the subphases of the separation-individuation process (the practicing period or the period of rapprochement) [p. 156].

While for her purposes, in the quoted paragraph Mahler emphasizes individually *characteristic* moods, more to our purposes her paper also explicitly deals with the universal development of certain moods—elation in the so-called "practicing" period of toddlerhood (a period of expansive motor mastery from about 10 or 12 to 16 or 18 months), and depression (or perhaps, better, sadness) in the "rapprochement" period (a time from 16 or 18 to 22 or 24 months, wherein the child's awareness of self-other differentiation, especially vis-à-vis mother, and of his lack of participation in her power, crystallizes). Let me focus on the second of these first. (Incidentally, Mahler's paper introduces into the realm of affect development another general issue that is more often discussed in other areas of development—that is, the distinction between forerunners and a time of principal crystallization or synthesis of a given phenomenon. The practicing and rapprochement periods are the times of crystallization of elation and sadness, respectively, though normally each has earlier forerunners and pathological development might see variations in the timetable or even in the very presence of such crystallization.)

Whence sadness? By the time of the rapprochement period, the child has developed (through perceptual experience repeated again and again, and stored in memory) an understanding that one set of stimuli in the world are all aspects of one being—mother, and another set are all aspects of another—himself. And furthermore, he has learned (against affective resistance) that these two are separate. Self-other differentiation has taken place—cognitively, if not fully affectively. In the terms I introduced earlier, *a new internalized learning has been* established; it is a permanent acquisition; it has entity character. Specifically, the child is aware that he and mother are two different persons (something that has not been clearly "known" earlier). With a clearer (though still primitive) notion of causality, the child also comes to know that his wishes do not control mother's actions. This joint phenomenon, the loss of the earlier illusion of oneness with mother (as self-other differentiation takes place) and the loss of magical notions of causality ("I cry and food comes" equals "my wishes alter the reality"), is what Mahler calls the collapse of the illusion of omnipotence. This shift, involving cognitive clarification of real features of the external world (object properties and causality), changes the child's expectation-situation via gratification and mastery. Now he is small and alone in a big world, rather than sharing in the (imagined) omnipotence of the mother-child unit. Depressive mood is the automatic affective consequence of these developmental changes which force the child to see (albeit vaguely) the realities of his situation. The change has come about via the acquisition (ordinarily a permanent acquisition unless regressively and pathologically renounced) of the awareness of self-other differentiation (the new permanent learning) and simultaneously, the clear awareness that it is the specific mother (and not the generalized other) who provides gratification and relief (the *cognitive specification* of the conditions for affective satisfaction). The awareness of separateness from this specific provider culminates, in the rapprochement stage, in sadness or depressive mood.

In a paper that confronts problems of affect development parallel to those that we are dealing with, Spiegel (1966) makes closely related points with regard to the affect of longing. He contrasts desire and longing, suggesting that desire embodies the satisfaction/relief of some inner state through any object or means that works; it is thus self-oriented (oriented towards self-satisfaction by any means). Longing, in contrast, occurs when satisfaction/relief can only come through the constant/specific love object. Spiegel is discussing what

Piaget (1937) originally referred to as object permanence but which has come to be called libidinal object constancy (Hartmann 1952) in psychoanalytic writings (See Pine 1974, for a fuller discussion.) Blending Spiegel's description with my terms here, then, I would say that longing is the affect state that automatically comes into being after the internal image of the specific, loved other ("loved," here meaning the place of the person as a necessary feature in the gratification of wishes) is crystallized, has achieved entity character, *is a permanent acquisition in mental life.* (And, of course, this person must be absent at a time of need; hence, longing.) What both Mahler and Spiegel are discussing are the affect states that crystallize around the child's acquisition of self-other differentiation, the specific tie to mother, and (later) libidinal object constancy, wherein the differentiated other (ordinarily mother) is experienced as a necessary means to gratification. Sadness/depression reflects the first (self-other differentiation and loss of "oneness") and longing (in a state of need plus the object's absence) reflects the second (the specific tie to mother and libidinal object constancy).

Can we understand nostalgia as a derivative of these affects? Certainly, experientially, it includes qualities of sadness and of longing. I would suggest that two of the processes that I discussed earlier have come into play on top of the sadness and longing: *control processes* and a form of *cognitive re-specification.* What happens to sadness and longing in nostalgia is that the longed-for is placed in the past (a control process through a cognitive shift), arises as a general wistfulness without an experience of specific and imperious need (again a control process), and thus can be experienced as relatively (but only relatively) milder painful-sweet sadness rather than more fully painful longing. What is longed for in nostalgia, then, is the nonspecific past and the longing occurs without reference to a specific need-state requiring immediate satisfaction.

One last word about this cluster of affects: mourning, too, would seem to have roots here. Not only does mourning require the *cognitive acquisition* of object constancy (the permanence of attachment), but also the cognitive awareness of permanence of loss (a concept of death). Wolfenstein (1966) suggests that the slow process of normal adolescent mourning for the to-be-lost parents of childhood is a necessary prerequisite for the full experience of mourning. In my terms here, the extended duration of the adolescent mourning process, plus the very fact of its occurrence (with the adolescent's surviving and finding his way into new relationships), both serve as *control* processes, allowing for mastery of the experience of more sudden, painful, and complete mourning later on.

Let me turn now to the other end of the scale of affect qualities. I referred, earlier, to Mahler's (1966) discussion of elation as the characteristic mood of the practicing period, the period of new motor mastery from 10 or 12 to 16 or 18 months. It is not a totally new affect in the array at that age; both giddy excitement and blissful satiation seem visible much earlier in infant life. But the practicing period is a time of crystallization of that affect in its more sustained and complex form. What takes place? I believe it to be some combination of the following:

Hendrick (1942), White (1963), and others have discussed pleasure-in-function as a normal part of human experience. For the toddler, relatively suddenly able to move around (after months in which this was not possible), such function-pleasure must provide a basic groundwork for the elation of that period. But more would seem to be going on to account for the intensity of the apparent elated quality, a quality coupled with boundless energy in the constantly moving toddler. Lewin's (1950) work on elation, and its emphasis on the role of denial, is suggestive here and points us in particular directions. For the toddler, who can now crawl, walk, or run, we can sense that "anything is possible." It is as though all limitation has been removed. There is a temporary absence or suspension of cognitive specification of limitations, of reality testing—so that the movement made (in later life, the paper written, the thought that is thought) appears to approach perfection, to be free of limitation. Additionally, for the toddler, the former passivity (nonavailability of locomotion) is now reversed; the passive has been turned to active in reality, though in a limited way and whether or not the toddler is aware of this limitation. To generalize: elation, as an affect, may be built upon normal experiences of satisfaction in functioning (the *bodily* base), coupled with suspension of *cognitive specification* (having aspects of denial in it), and an imagined turn of passive into active—both this and the suspension of cognitive specification having *control/defense* functions. Developmentally, therefore, it is again useful to think in terms of the nature of the cognitive specification, of defense processes, and of built-in bodily experiences in coming closer to a description of the construction of new affects.

I would like to comment on just three more affects: anger, intense pleasure, and quiet satisfaction.

Anger—focused, modulated—has its origins in the diffuse, explosive rage of the infant. This change, too, represents a developmental process, here a transformation of an earlier state. How does it come about? The fight-flight reaction to danger, widespread in the animal kingdom, characterizes human behavior as well. Even early on, when motility is limited, infant "flight" from pain (physical or psychological) leads to withdrawal—reflexively, of a body part, or psychologically, into sleep or apathy (cf. Bowlby 1969). The "fight" reaction, more to my purposes here, consists of diffuse thrashing and crying in situations of need-frustration or some forms of physical constraint. Control over and direction of this process does not come simply through inhibition of rage. Rather, significant advances in cognition and motility change the whole psychological situation of the (now older) toddler and child. First a *cognitive specification* involving perceptual discrimination, and later understanding of causality, permits a more and more refined identification of, in the sense of targeting, the offending source of the pain/frustration. Second, advances in motor competence (including eye-hand coordination and locomotion) allow for possibilities of active struggle and for a change in the infant's essential helpless passivity, a major shift in the direction of greater *control* and *defense*. Together, the two advances (cognitive and motor) permit focused "fight" reactions— no longer diffuse, helpless rage—but reactions against a particular, identified source, understood to be the offending source. Such a reaction is accompanied by the new affect of anger (rather than diffuse rage). Still later, when there may be inhibition of the motor component, only the psychological experience of anger remains.

Kohut's work on the "transformation of narcissistic rage into mature aggression" (1973, p. 390) is also relevant for an understanding of the development of anger. He writes from his clinical experience with adult patients in whom the sense of self and of self-esteem is extremely fragile and is compensated for by grandiose fantasies of invulnerability. For these patients, an affront comes as a threat to the compensatory grandiosity, threatening to expose the vulnerable sense of self, which can only be preserved by imagined omnipotence. Thus their response to the affront is exteme (Kohut calls it "rage") and is powered by efforts to preserve the sense of self (hence "narcissistic rage"). Kohut suggests that direct interpretive therapeutic work on such rage leads nowhere; it can only be experienced as one more assault, an affront, thus provoking more of the same rage.

Clinical work must be directed towards the establishment of a more secure, less vulnerable and hence more realistic, less omnipotent sense of self. Only then will "mature aggression" emerge. Such aggression is characterized by its focused quality (anger at a specific other for a specific deed) and not the rage reaction induced by the threat to one's compensatory omnipotent invulnerability.

Kohut's is a clinical description, involving clinical technique. Viewed developmentally, in the terms I have used here, I would say that one route to the development of the affect of focused and limited anger is through new *acquisitions* of the personality, here the establishment of a realistic sense of self and of stable self-esteem. As this takes place, the rage reaction, defending against the experienced threat to one's inviolability, fades away and a new affect (anger directed at the other) automatically replaces it in certain specific situations.

The last two areas that I should like to discuss, briefly, are at opposite ends of the intensity scale: intense pleasure or relief from displeasure and, at the other extreme, quiet satisfaction. The former, intense pleasure or relief from displeasure, seems, like irritability that I discussed earlier, to be modeled upon an early bodily experience. I am referring to affects with a sudden termination quality, an orgastic character, a bursting-filling of the self or a sudden termination (relief) of such states. The early distress/relief/pleasure cycle of hunger, and later of bowel and bladder pleasure, lay down, through repetition coupled with intensity, a psychological experience that, as a *quality*, can become grafted onto any later need states, bodily or otherwise, which are then experienced as though having the old urgency and compellingness. Biological needs brook little delay. For some persons, the absence of delay (control), the urgency of need, becomes characteristic as a mode of experiencing *any* affect— modeled on early bodily experiences.

And finally, quiet satisfaction. Like sadness or elation, there are probably moments akin to this from infancy onwards. But it too undergoes a process of development which makes for a more specific and sustained state. Two streams flow into it. One, similar to what was described earlier regarding elation, is pleasure in the exercise of capacities; it involves what White (1963) calls effectance and competence. Again we see an experience that is inherent in bodily functioning, here the affective accompaniment to the exercise of capacities; this is most likely to be experienced in the absence of more imperious need states. In contrast to elation, however, quiet satisfaction requires no suspension of reality-testing, no suspension of awareness of limitation; instead it requires a focus on the actual acts performed in themselves. Additionally, and again unlike elation, it involves no redoing of an old conflict, pain, or disappointment. Quite the reverse, and here we see the second stream of influence, it is relatively conflict-free and involves a sense of safety that disappointment won't come. What am I referring to?

In a lovely paper on "the capacity to be alone," Winnicott (1958) writes of that capacity's developing out of the child's being "alone" in the presence of the mother. That is, the child who feels safe is able to be psychologically alone with his own thoughts and play precisely because he is not alone, because there is a background awareness of his mother's presence. That presence allows for a turning into aloneness, because aloneness is not absolute. Put otherwise, Benedek (1938) writes of the child's confident expectation of satisfaction from the mother. Such expectation of satisfaction restrains the development of more urgent, untrusting, need states.

Now, how does this link to what I have been saying about affect development? Simply this: two processes, to varying degrees, are contributory to states of quiet satisfaction. One, a psychobiological built-in process, an accompaniment to *bodily functioning*, involves pleasure in function. The other involves a *new acquisition of the personality* having "entity" character; it can be called basic trust, or expectation of satisfaction, but probably consists of a set of memory images of self-other relations wherein gratification was forthcoming. With the dual presence of built-in bodily pleasure in function and safety in the inner images of mother's (later others') presence and satisfyingness, quiet satisfaction can come into being as a complex and sustained affect.

To sum up: I have posed as my question: how does the diffuse and limited affective repertoire of the newborn, roughly classifiable on a loose pleasure-pain continuum, grow into the wide array of often highly differentiated affects seen in the human adult and seen already even in later childhood? Broadly, I have suggested that some affects represent alterations, transformations, specifications of earlier affect states whereas others are first born at later stages in the developmental process when the psychological conditions for their emergence are met. These psychological conditions involve new learnings, new acquisitions of mental life, that have consequences for affective experience. In pursuing my topic, I have drawn on a number of affects to develop and illustrate the argument. The affects discussed were: anxiety (both traumatic/overwhelming and functional/signalling), guilt, irritability, sadness, longing, nostalgia, mourning, elation, anger, orgasticlike pleasure or relief from displeasure, and quiet satisfaction. I have drawn on a number of "explanatory" processes (actually developmental descriptions) to detail how these affects come into being. The four processes with which I have worked (each actually a broad set of processes) are: (1) cognitive specification, articulation, and differentiation of affect states; (2) new learnings that are permanent acquisitions of the personality that have a "thing" or "entity" character, and from which new affects flow; (3) control/delay/inhibition processes; and (4) bodily processes that automatically trigger certain feelings and that become models for later fully psychological experiences as well. I am aware that these "processes" are only loosely defined and are themselves often in need of explanation.

Affects are complex processes. Their development in large part eludes us. I have attempted here to clarify, at least descriptively, a few aspects of that development.

References

Benedek, T. (1938). Adaptation to reality in early infancy. *Psychoanalytic Quarterly* 7:200-214.

Bowlby, J. (1969). *Attachment and Loss, volume 1: Attachment*. New York: Basic Books.

Freud, S. (1900). The interpretation of dreams. *Standard Edition* 4/5:1-622.

——— (1923). The ego and the id. *Standard Edition* 19:12-66.

——— (1926). Inhibitions, symptoms, and anxiety. *Standard Edition* 20:75-172.

Hartmann, H. (1952). The mutual influences in the development of ego and id. *Psychoanalytic Study of the Child* 7:9-30.

Hendrick, I. (1942). Instinct and the ego during infancy. *Psychoanalytic Quarterly* 11:33-58.

Katan, A. (1961). Some thoughts about the role of verbalization in early childhood. *Psychoanalytic Study of the Child* 16:184-188.

Kohut, H. (1973). Thoughts on narcissism and narcissistic rage. *Psychoanalytic Study of the Child* 27:360-400.

Lewin, B. D. (1950). *The Psychoanalysis of Elation*. New York: Norton.

Mahler, M. S. (1966). Notes on the development of basic moods: the depressive affect. In *Psychoanalysis—A General Psychology: Essays in*

Honor of Heinz Hartmann, ed. R. M. Loewenstein, L. M. Newman, M. Schur, and A. Solnit, pp. 152-168. New York: International Universities Press. Reprinted in *The Selected Papers of Margaret S. Mahler,* vol. 1, ch. 5. New York: Jason Aronson, 1979.

Mahler, M. S., Pine, F., and Bergman, A. (1975). *The Psychological Birth of the Human Infant.* New York: Basic Books.

Piaget, J. (1937). *The Construction of Reality in the Child.* New York: Basic Books, 1954.

Pine, F. (1974). Libidinal object constancy: a theoretical note. *Psychoanalysis and Contemporary Science* 3:307-313. New York: International Universities Press.

Schmale, A. H. (1964). A genetic view of affects: with special reference to the genesis of helplessness and hopelessness. *Psychoanalytic Study of the Child* 19:287-310.

Spiegel, L. A. (1966). Affects in relation to self and object: a model for the derivation of desire, longing, pain, anxiety, humiliation, and shame. *Psychoanalytic Study of the Child* 21:69-92.

White, R. W. (1963). Ego and reality in psychoanalytic theory. *Psychological Issues,* Monograph 11. New York: International Universities Press.

Winnicott, D. W. (1958). The capacity to be alone. *International Journal of Psycho-Analysis* 39:416-420.

Wolfenstein, M. (1966). How is mourning possible? *Psychoanalytic Study of the Child* 21:93-123.

Part IV

Rapprochement and Reconstruction

analysis. The careful and continuing evaluation of data and inferences is essential to psychoanalytic investigation and to the elucidation of controversy concerning genetic reconstruction and early development.

This paper focuses upon the early utilization of reconstruction in psychoanalysis and its relation to contemporary preoedipal reconstruction. In addition to conflict and defense, reconstruction now includes archaic ego states and object relations, reaction patterns and developmental consequences. Articulating with and amplified by the developmental concepts of separation-individuation (Mahler 1966, Mahler, Pine, and Bergman 1975), the reconstructions here are particularly relevant to the origins of structuralization, to preoedipal patterns and their later reactivation or persisting influence.

Freud (1937), having wrestled heroically with the problem of reconstruction, compared psychoanalytic work to the work of the archeologist in discerning, rearranging, and creatively synthesizing meaningful patterns out of the maze of piecemeal evidence provided by the patient in the analytic situation. Psychoanalysis may be said to have begun with an incorrect construction when Freud, believing the stories his patients told him of their childhood seduction traumata, assumed that neurosis was caused by parental seduction. The concept of defense was conceptualized at that time as a repressive force designed to keep painful memories of real traumatic experience outside of consciousness. When Freud made the momentous discovery that the fantasies of parental seduction were universal oedipal fantasies, he formulated the concept of the oedipus complex, and the analysis of the oedipus complex became the central issue. The libido theory was enunciated with its complex maturational sequences and developmental challenges, with the oedipus complex emerging out of important preceding developmental phases. Although he also uncovered preoedipal conflicts and related them to character formation, as in such early papers as "Character and Anal Erotism" (Freud 1908), the preoedipal contribution to and coloring of character was clinically isolated. The short analyses and techniques of the pioneer days did not permit character analysis. Analysis was symptom oriented, and symptoms and conflicts were mainly determined and evaluated in terms of the oedipus complex. The crucial elucidation of the oedipus complex overshadowed other discoveries. It is of interest that whereas Freud (1900, p. 245) referred to the preoedipal phase before age 3 as "the prehistoric period," he incorporated, over the years, the reconstruction of preoedipal reactions and influence, so evident in character, into psychoanalytic theory and technique. Today it is easily overlooked just how revolutionary the concept of early preoedipal influences in character formation was in those early years of this century when the formulations were introduced by Freud and Abraham. One cannot speak of character in the first and second year of life, and yet it was recognized that just such influences from the preverbal period in the case of oral character could decisively effect adult personality. The main traits and temperament of the oral and anal character were distinguished and placed in a biological and experiential explanatory framework. The forerunners of character were thus traced, even before character formation could be definitely identified, and these preoedipal personality components have become an accepted part of developmental theory. Considering the limited developmental knowledge of the pioneer days, these were extraordinary reconstructions which had immediate clinical and theoretical application and which were not considered to challenge, but to complement and supplement, the importance of oedipal phase issues. Preoedipal determinants and imprints were also discerned in psychic structure and oedipal conflict, in the form and content of the infantile neurosis.

But when did preoedipal reconstruction first appear in psychoanalysis and how was it utilized? Most of the preoedipal dimensions of Freud's reconstructions have been overlooked. The extraordinary reconstruction of the primal scene at 18 months in the Wolf Man case, probably the most famous of psychoanalytic reconstructions, was a preoedipal reconstruction. Freud (1918) gave an extremely detailed reconstruction of this scene, including the age of the Wolf Man, his illness—fever—the time of day, the position of the parents, the child's immediate reaction, and the developmental consequences. Freud regarded this single traumatic experience of the primal scene as a traumatic sexual seduction, but occurring in preoedipal infancy (Blum 1974).

At that time Freud did not regard the primal scene as immediately significant in the mental life of the 18-month-old infant. In the magnificent discovery and documentation of the infantile neurosis, such traumata as a protracted life-threatening malaria and pathological object relations were eclipsed and the focus was upon the primal scene. He then directly linked the primal scene with instinctual overstimulation, which explained the relation of the primal scene to trauma, but not to trauma that seemed to be tied to a later developmental phase. Invoking the concept of delayed trauma as a possible explanation, Freud proposed that the preoedipal primal scene became pathogenic as a phase-specific oedipal trauma at the time of the Wolf Man's nightmare on his fourth birthday. This preoedipal reconstruction, so daring in its conception and elucidation, was "reconstructed upward" to the oedipal phase. The preoedipal situation and the mode and timing of the reconstruction are often overlooked because of the phallic content, the shift in the significance of the reconstruction from 18 months to the phallic phase, and the close relation of the primal scene to Freud's discovery of the oedipal infantile neurosis as the precursor of the adult neurosis.

Freud's thinking encompassed developmental issues and the effects of traumatic overstimulation at different levels of development and on different areas of the personality. The unconscious gratifications and the threat of castration associated with the primal scene were evaluated in terms of oedipal progression and libidinal regression. The primal traumatic event of the single primal scene was reformulated as a universal oedipal configuration. The preoedipal primal scene was linked to pathogenic oedipal conflict (Esman 1973, Blum 1974).

Freud's complex discussion of the primal scene engaged different levels of memory, reconstruction, and personality organization. Freud also questioned whether he had reconstructed a phylogenetic memory, a dream equivalent of memory, a primal fantasy, or an actual experience—an animal or a human primal scene—and whether a reconstruction to 18 months was a retrospective falsification or whether the Wolf Man's nightmare at 4 years of age reactivated and organized the seduction trauma at 18 months in terms of the negative oedipus complex (cf. Eissler 1966).

The puzzling and vexing problems of such early reconstruction can now be understood also if considered in terms of Freud's simultaneous analysis of himself and his patients. Freud's analysis of the Wolf Man touched upon issues in his self-analysis (Kanzer 1972) which were in a continuing process of question, investigation, illumination, and extrapolation. In the Wolf Man, and in his self-analysis, Freud uncovered persistent early infantile influences which had profound consequences for later development.

Oedipal and preoedipal reconstructions actually make their appearance simultaneously, and long before the Wolf Man case. They are to be found in Freud's first analysis—his self-analysis—which can be traced in the Fliess correspondence (Freud 1887-1902). Freud reported his discovery of the oedipus complex to Fliess in September-October 1897 (letters 69, 70, 71, pp. 218-221) and also reconstructed what would now be regarded as important preoedipal influences; and most of the reconstructions in the Fliess letters are actually preoedipal reconstructions, (e.g., Julius Freud, the one-eyed Doctor, the Czech nursemaid). The presence of the first remarkable reconstruction by Freud (letter 70, October 3, 1897) of the period between 18 and 24 months—during his separation-individuation phase—has been essentially unnoticed in these terms. Freud reconstructed his relationship at this period of life not only to his one-year-older nephew, but to his one-year-younger brother, whom we now know died on April 15, 1858, after having lived for approximately six months. Freud, then, was approximately one and one-half years of age when his brother was born and just under two at his brother's death. Freud's brother Julius was, therefore, alive only during the rapprochement phase of Freud's preoedipal development. Lacking the sophisticated tools of contemporary analysis, Freud's initial reconstruction of his infancy is uncanny in its authenticity, complexity, and correlation with contemporary analytic and developmental observations. Freud, unraveling screen defenses, has given us an immediate and vivid picture of reconstruction to the period of rapprochement, with a rapprochement crisis complicated by the birth and death of his younger brother Julius.

Later, in the *Nonvixit* dream of October 1898 (Freud 1900, pp. 421-425), Freud's nephew John reappears as a revenant, an infantile object important in his own right, but also a screen object for his brother Julius, who is not directly mentioned in the associations to the dream, as Grinstein (1968) and Schur (1972) have noted. Freud (1900, p. 483) stated, "all my friends have in a certain sense been reincarnations of this first figure. . . . they have been *revenants*. My nephew himself re-appeared in my boyhood, and at that time we acted the parts of Caesar and Brutus together. My emotional life has always insisted that I should have an intimate friend and hated enemy." Referring to Brutus's speech of self-justification in Shakespeare's *Julius Caesar*, Freud proceeds to analyze the "prototransference" to Fliess, representing not only his father, but his brother Julius. Fliess, like Julius, was born in 1858 and thus younger than Freud. Brutus slew Julius Caesar, and Freud noted he was playing the part of Brutus in the dream. Freud and John really did act the roles of Brutus and Caesar during Freud's adolescence when John visited Vienna. Freud was identified with Brutus, and carried the "germ of self-reproach" for his death wishes toward Julius. The dream memorial bore the inscription *Nonvixit*, meaning he didn't live. In the day residue, the monument for the Kaiser Joseph refers to brother Julius (Kaiser=Caesar), father Jacob, and Freud's identification with the Biblical favorite son of Jacob, Joseph the dream interpreter and the other Josephs who were so important in his life.

The dream parapraxis of *Nonvixit*, or not having lived, rather than *Nonvivit*, not being alive, refers to his baby brother Julius, as do Freud's comments (1900, p. 484), "It serves you right if you had to make way for me. Why did you try to push *me* out of the way? I don't need you. . . ."

Freud utilized familial information in his self-analysis to help organize and test derivative dream reconstruction. In a scene described to him by his father as occurring when he was not yet two years old, Freud had been fighting with his nephew, John. Freud (1900, p. 425) asserted, "It must have been this scene from my childhood which diverted '*Non vivit*' into '*Non vixit*' for in the language of later childhood the word for to hit is '*wichsen*.'" This is the precise period of the death of Julius, when Freud was not quite two years old (cf. Grinstein 1968, p. 308). It is the anal phase of psychosexual development with all its problems of sadism, impulse and sphincter control and retention or loss of stool. From an ego orientation, it is also during separation-individuation, the rapprochement subphase, with continuing definition of self and object, animate and inanimate, male and female, with heightened separation anxiety and fears of reengulfment. The issues of disappearance and reappearance in this preoedipal period of Freud's life might possibly be related to the discovery, loss, and rediscovery of preoedipal influences in the development of psychoanalytic theory.

The enmity toward Julius was associated with the enmity toward his nephew John and his next sibling Anna, who was born December, 1858, some eight months after the death of Julius. As we know know (Schur 1972), sexual relations, birth, and death occurred in the same room during Freud's preoedipal development.

In *The Interpretation of Dreams* Freud's reactions to Julius and John and their parents are revived in an elaborate disguise in which the early sibling preoedipal material is condensed with oedipal fantasies. In a less disguised reconstructive letter to Fliess, Freud (1892-1899, p. 219) reported, "I welcomed my one-year-younger brother (who died within a few months) with ill wishes and real infantile jealousy, and that his death left the germ of guilt in me. I have long known that my companion in crime between the ages of one and two was a nephew of mine who is a year older than I am and now lives in Manchester; he visited us in Vienna when I was fourteen. We seem occasionally to have treated my niece, who was a year younger, shockingly [cf. Freud 1899]. My nephew and younger brother determined, not only the neurotic side of all my friendships, but also their depth."

Grinstein (1968, p. 315) has noted the series of deceased figures whom Freud survived with pleasure and guilt, tracing Freud's guilt over his father's death to the guilt over the death of his brother. Both Grinstein and Schur have enriched our understanding of Freud's dreams and the psychobiographical significance of *Nonvixit* and Julius Freud, without, however, a contemporary elucidation of the preoedipal dimension.

Schur (1972, pp. 119, 161, 241) emphasized the "guilt of the survivor" and documented the significance of this theme in Freud's life and work. In a letter to Fliess, Freud (1887-1902, p. 171) interpreted the dream, "You are requested to close the eyes," he had just after his father's death in October 1896. "The dream was thus an outlet for the feeling of self-reproach which a death generally leaves among the survivors." The request to close the eyes refers to denial as well as death wishes and punitive blindness. The *Nonvixit* dream, occuring just two years after his father's death, is a richly overdetermined anniversary dream. On the anniversary of the "request to close the eyes," the object is annihilated with a piercing look and *Nonvixit* words. The oedipal referents are clearly indicated in the associations. Freud has survived Brücke, Paneth, and Fleischl. A memorial had just been unveiled to Fleischl. Fliess, represented by "Fl" whose name was similar to that of the dead Fleischl, had just both celebrated his fortieth birthday and confronted serious surgery. The linkage of these figures with the series of Josephs, with whom Freud was also identified, is also clear and includes, ultimately, his father, Jacob, and his brother Julius (Shengold 1971). Fliess would soon "disappear" as had the others, and Freud recognized the unconscious childhood equation of separation, disappearance, and death. From the recent past of his professional life, Freud leaps to the infantile ghosts who return in the *Nonvixit* dream. In his early life John had not died, but he disappeared along with Julius, Freud's nursemaid, his half-brothers Emanuel and Philipp, and his first home (cf. Schur 1972, p. 173). However, Freud's reported affective reaction to the birth and death of Julius is not yet superego-derived guilt, but, in his own terminology, "the germ of guilt," or the "seed of self-reproach" (cf. Schur 1972, p. 164). The phrase "germ of guilt," translated from letter 70 of Freud's letters to Fliess was also translated by M. Schur as "seed of self-reproach." I shall utilize both translations[1] as complementary, and emphasizing the affective, cognitive, and structural processes consistent with the reconstructed infantile phase. The "germ of guilt" is analogous to a depressively tinged basic mood, and the "seed of self-reproach" to the developing sense of self and to a precursor of the superego. The basic mood and superego precursors develop during the rapprochement subphase of separation-individuation, the developmental period of Freud's *Nonvixit* reconstruction. Julius did not live, and if his brief life was denied and repressed, it would seem he never "existed": "*people of that kind only existed as long as one liked and could be got rid of if someone else wished it*" (Freud 1900, p. 421). And in the case of Julius, the wish for his elimination became a reality.

The references in the *Nonvixit* dream to birth, death, and rebirth occur in many forms of appearance and disappearance. The visual annihilation is reminiscent of infantile omnipotence, but also of the archaic primitive superego (Peto 1969). It is also possible, utilizing the developmental level of the Julius reconstruction, to reconstruct the significance of the visual gaze in terms of eye contact and its maintenance, and to wonder about peek-a-boo games and the denial and acknowledgment of object loss. The greater sense of separateness during rapprochement leads to a heightened sensitivity to object loss. As Mahler (1975) notes, the fear of object loss is then partly relieved by internalization, which includes the beginning internalization of the object's demands and commands. The fear of losing the object's love, now a relatively well-differentiated object, becomes an intensified vulnerability on the part of the rapprochement toddler, which manifests itself in a highly sensitive reaction to the

1. I am indebted to Drs. Mark Kanzer and Jules Glenn for indicating that the optimal translation should be "germ of self-reproach." This translation underscores Freud's avoidance of any confusion of the superego and guilt with the precursors of the superego and of guilt and self-reproach.

parent's approval and disapproval. By this time the child can already verbally evoke "Mama" during her absence, and can say "bye-bye" in anticipation of separation from mother. The capacity for delay, anticipation, reality testing, and symbolic substitution develops with object relations, and ego advances and drive development occur in the matrix of adequate object response. The achievement of representational thought and language is associated with a more enduring, internalized, and stabilized image of the mother, which permits the shift to active separation experiences characterized by volitional approach and detachment or distancing behavior (Mahler, Pine, and Bergman 1975, McDevitt 1975).

The reconstruction of the "prehistoric period" of childhood via dreams and screen memories is recorded in the Fliess letters for the first time in history. Transference, the return of "revenants," is co-discovered with reconstruction in *The Interpretation of Dreams* in the context of infantile object relations. In the evolution of the psychoanalytic process, this preoedipal reconstruction (of the rapprochement phase) was an object-relations model which actually preceded libido theory, and which returns as an important dimension of development in modern psychoanalysis. The reconstruction of the maturational phases of libidinal psychosexual development in childhood was one of the great achievements of Freud's analytic work with adults. The preoedipal reconstruction of early ego development and object relations was intimately related to libido theory, to the "libidinal object." Freud introduced dynamic formulations with a genetic viewpoint so that both dynamic and genetic viewpoints were interdependent and interrelated in the origins of psychoanalytic theory.

The *Nonvixit* dream is often used to indicate the revival and recapitulation of early object relations without indicating that the infantile object relations were indeed from the second year of life, so that such transference would be a preoedipal transference. Further, Freud's statements about his later relationships being determined by his brother Julius and his nephew John merit reevaluation, just as does his statement that his nephew was his partner in crime at 1 year of age. In *The Interpretation of Dreams* only John appears as the "inseparable" friend of his childhood until Freud's third year, and the revenants were said to be a series of reincarnations of this friend (Freud 1900, p. 485). How important were these companions, his one-year-older nephew and his brother who died at 6 months, probably even before he was able to sit up, and certainly before he had language and locomotion? Did not his "friend" represent a composite figure, *viz.*, his brother and other close relatives? As with the reconstruction in the Wolf Man case at 18 months of age, what may be most important would not be the validity of a specific content, but the methodology of reconstruction and the developmental level to which it pertains. The recapture of the infantile object relations in Freud's first reconstruction is associated with enduring preoedipal influences and a basic affective state. The therapeutic importance of reconstruction in the reorganization of memory and self-representation is implicit in Freud's formulation. The "friend" of his infancy becomes a screen memory to be analyzed.

Just as the primal scene, birth, and death fantasies are so significant in the case of the Wolf Man at 18 months, so were these issues bewildering infantile realities in Freud's self-analysis. The birth and death of his younger brother may have been at least as significant during Freud's rapprochement subphase as his ambivalent relation to play with John. Moreover, to follow Freud's reconstruction in his letter to Fliess, are the most significant relationships of that period of life likely to be the younger brother and the older nephew, or do these two figures really represent the most significant objects in the toddler's life, namely, the parents? (We do not have the data to indicate just how important a mother surrogate and how significant an influence his Czech Catholic nursemaid was, or his half-brothers.) Doubtless, the most important relationship at that period of Freud's life which is not delineated in his 1897 comments or in the analytic literature on his letters or dreams is the (rapprochement) relationship with his mother.

Freud's genius permitted this first reconstruction in psychoanalysis, a preoedipal reconstruction to 18-24 months of age. His "inseparable companion," his partner in life between the ages of 1 and 2 was his loving and adoring mother. His relation with his mother remains in the background of the father and brother associations of the *Nonvixit* dream, and, indeed, of Freud's (1900) dreams in *The Interpretation of Dreams*. The preoedipal mother in the dream book is hidden behind the pale shadow of his oedipal parent, usually the father. On October 15, 1897, Freud analyzes a haunting memory concerning separation from his nursemaid, also representing his beloved mother. "I was crying my heart out, because my mother was nowhere to be found" (1887-1902, p. 222), is a poignant expression of his separation anxiety and infantile grief.[2] The import of Freud's discoveries is to be seen in all later theoretical developments. His (1917) delineation of the predisposition to and mechanisms of depression, consonant with preoedipal reconstruction, took into account regression to orality and narcissistic object relations and pointed to the precursors and consequences of superego development. The loving and beloved superego (Schafer 1960) was also anticipated, along with the formulation of subsequent internalized self-criticism, conscience, and self-punishment.

Freud's nephew and younger brother ostensibly determined the depth of all future friendships. This can be reinterpreted, that is, his parents were the prototype of object relations and object love. This discovery of the origins of object relations would finally lead Freud to the differentiation of self and object and the primary significance of the mother/child relationship. He states (1940, p. 188), "A child's first erotic object is the mother's breast that nourishes it; love has its origin in attachment to the satisfied need for nourishment. There is no doubt that, to begin with, the child does not distinguish between the breast and its own body; when the breast has to be separated from the body and shifted to the 'outside' because the child so often finds it absent, it carries with it as an 'object' a part of the original narcissistic libidinal cathexis. This first object is later completed into the person of the child's mother, . . ." and then described, "the root of a mother's importance, unique, without parallel, established unalterably for a whole lifetime as the first and strongest love-object and as the prototype of all later love-relations—for both sexes."

Behind and beyond the ambivalent and complex relations to women Freud (1913) described in "The Theme of the Three Caskets," his 1897 remarks presage appreciation of the essential ingredient of a mother's love for the infant's development of "confidence" and "basic trust." (Confidence, basic trust, and self-regard were formally introduced and studied much later in psychoanalysis.) Freud (1917, p. 156) later observed: "if a man has been his mother's undisputed darling he retains throughout life the triumphant feeling,

2. His nursemaid was also used as a probable screen for his mother in the preceding letter (70), where Freud states, "I shall have to thank the memory of the old woman who provided me at such an early age with the means for living and surviving" (1887-1902, pp. 219-220). Freud, in reconstructing reactions to this obscure preoedipal mother surrogate, also cites her inappropriate mothering and dishonesty (cf. Grigg 1973).

the confidence in success, which not seldom brings actual success along with it. And Goethe might well have given some such heading to his autobiography as: 'My strength has its roots in my relation to my mother.'" Freud was identified with Goethe and would be awarded the Goethe Prize (1930); the observations apply to Freud as well as Goethe.

When Freud (1900) states that his emotional life requires an intimate friend and a hated enemy, as he does in association to the *Nonvixit* dream, ambivalence is apparent. The ambivalence and tendency toward splitting with displacement of anger and projection of aggression so characteristic of the normative rapprochement crisis can be suggestively discerned in his further associations: "and it has not infrequently happened that the ideal situation of childhood has been so completely reproduced that friend and enemy have come together in a single individual—though not, of course, both at once or with constant oscillations, as may have been the case in my early childhood" (p. 483). Freud's description and reconstruction to 18-24 months of age anticipates and is consistent with the modern conceptualization of the process of separation-individuation and the specific features of the rapprochement subphase. From that point in development, conflicts with the mother and other objects are no longer transitory, but persistent and ambivalent. The mastery of the conflicts of this period will be particularly observable in the wooing of the parent, and, intrapsychically, in terms of more cohesive, integrated self- and object representations with increasing stability and autonomy.

After being "inseparable" until the end of their third year, Freud's independence from his "companion" at that time is fully compatible with the achievement of object constancy (again translating his inseparable companion as his mother). The senior toddler tolerates longer periods away from his mother and demonstrates the capacity to function and play in her absence because of the security of her "constant" mental representation. Julius had a direct influence on Freud, but also on Freud's parents, who reacted to the birth and death of their baby. The birth of a new sibling during rapprochement is not uncommon, and parental reactions impinge upon the toddler just as the toddler also stimulates parental responses.

All development involves challenges and tasks, with normative crises and progression interrupted by expectable periods of regression. The birth and death of a sibling during rapprochement accentuates and complicates the cardinal conflicts of that period which, as Mahler (1966) delineated, include the additional trauma of toilet training and of the discovery of the anatomical sexual difference. The beginning deflation of the child's impervious narcissism and magic omnipotence is associated with the child's growing awareness of separateness and helplessness, and the beginning of verbal communication. The rapprochement proclivity to a negative affective response and to the feeling of ego helplessness, which Bibring (1953) characterized as the basic cause of depression, is heightened when the mother-child relation is skewed by maternal grief and depression consequent to the illness and death of their baby.

Bibring (1953), consistent with Mahler's formulations, saw the ego helplessness as a narcissistic injury. It is now possible to follow the evolution of affective dispositions during the separation-individuation process, with depression originating during rapprochement and replacing the intoxicated elation associated with the undiminished grandeur of the practicing period. The depressive proclivity may become a structuralized state, which, as Freud implied in his first reconstruction, may be reactivated in later life, depending upon constitution and later development. It is during and after rapprochement that such depressive reactions, differentiated from transitory grief and sadness in infancy, can be structurally related to depression at later ages. Preoedipal disappointments, narcissistic injuries, internalized rage reactions, oral and anal fixations and frustrations were identified in the classical literature on predisposition to depression. The newer formulations of a depressive basic mood proclivity and the development of superego precursors during rapprochement confirm, amplify and suggest phase specificity to the more global preoedipal hypotheses.

The "germ of guilt," which becomes guilt after the later consolidation of superego function, may also refer to the differentiation of other related affects. It is analogous to the depressive proclivity and the negative basic mood of the rapprochement period. The feeling of loss at that level of development, when validated by reality, reinforces the affective responses of helplessness, sadness, grief, and the *Anlage* of depression. The "seed of self-reproach" is indicative of the beginning of internalization, of "identification with the aggressor" with turning aggression on the self as a superego precursor which antedates and contributes to the formation of the superego.

That the guilt and self-reproach are not triggered only by the death of his father in the *Nonvixit* dream, and in the other dreams of the "Interpretation of Dreams," can be discerned in the specimen dream of psychoanalysis, the "Irma" dream which begins the book. This dream, in which Freud pleads not guilty and confesses guilt at the same time for a variety of sexual and aggressive transgressions, occurred on July 24, 1895, before the death of his father (1896). In his associations, Freud reproaches himself for the deaths of Fleischl and a patient with the same name of his eldest daughter, "Mathilde," and the near death of Irma at the hands of Fliess (Schur 1972). These self-accusations for adult "crimes" conceal the infantile sources of these reactions in his oedipal guilt, and his preoedipal germ of guilt and seed of self-reproach related to his death wishes toward his parents, his sister Anna, and his brother's death.

The death of Julius when Freud was two years old was the only actual death of a love object during his complicated and turbulent early life. The reconstruction of October 1897, is augured in letter 23 of April 1895 (Freud 1887-1902, p. 119). Preoccupied by the "Psychology for Neurologists," Freud writes to Fliess, "My heart is in the coffin here with Caesar." Later, August 1898, Freud (p. 261) reports the first understanding of a parapraxis, forgetting a name, that of the poet "Julius" Mosen. "The 'Julius' had not slipped my memory. I was able to prove (i) that I had repressed the name Mosen because of certain associations; (ii) that material from my infancy played a part in the repression." This example was never published, just as Julius disappeared from Freud's (1900) associations to the *Nonvixit* dream in *The Interpretation of Dreams.*

While the birth of his first sister, Anna, when Freud was $2\frac{2}{3}$ years old, doubtless triggered more complex "ill wishes and infantile envy," neither Freud's nor his parents' derivative grief reactions would be fully accounted for by reconstructing upward from the earlier dead brother to the later live sister. (This does not overlook the importance of later development and of regressive defense against oedipal conflict.) Reaction to the birth of Anna was not reconstructed, was not within conscious memory as indicated in his paper, "Screen Memories" (1899), and could have been displaced backwards to Julius (Schur 1972, p. 123). The hostility to Anna may also represent disguised aggression toward the older brother and father figures, and all the dangerous aggression may be displaced onto the younger weaker brother (Shengold 1971). But the birth and death of Julius, doubtless with traumatic effects, also colored later reactions. The telescoping of traumatic memories was probably associated with interweaving developmental influences on structuralization and oedipal conflict. Nevertheless, the reaction to the birth of another child is not at all identical to the reaction to the death of a child by the parents and the surviving sibling.

The traumatic infantile loss of Julius and his mother's mourning and new pregnancy appear to be significant roots of Freud's concerns with death and transience (cf. Atkins 1977). Fearing an untimely death, he repeatedly tried to time his death, and told Jones (1957, p. 279) he thought of death every day of his life. He had the disconcerting parting remarks of "Goodbye; you may never see me again." The theory of a death instinct is most probably linked to these problems. Further confirmation of Freud's preoccupation with separation and specifically with the death of Julius may be found in his symptoms and self-analysis, for example, the so-called Tilgner episode (Schur 1972, p. 100).

Months before Freud's father's death on October 23, 1896, Freud had written to Fliess (April 16) of a neurotic fear of death, on that occasion based upon an identification with the dead sculptor Tilgner. Schur has detailed a number of possible correspondences between Tilgner and Freud, including the intense longing of both to visit Italy. Reading the details of Tilgner's life and death in an obituary, and writing to Fliess in a letter conveying his great ambivalence and, it might be added, possibly concerned about his father's health, Freud suffered from the dread of death. What was not noticed, however, was the date of Tilgner's death and Freud's letter. Tilgner died on April 15, the same date as Julius Freud. Thus, the dread of dying on April 15 may be understood as an anniversary reaction, just as the *Nonvixit* dream was dreamt on the anniversary of the death of a love object.

Such "anniversaries" are overdetermined and may also express familial anniversary reactions. Tilgner died before the unveiling of his Mozart statue, and the *Nonvixit* dream associations refer to the monument to the Emperor and the unveiling of the monument to Fleischl, unconsciously to the deaths of Freud's father and his brother Julius. The Rome of Freud's dreams was the Catholic city of the forbidding father and forbidden mother, but also the pre-Catholic city of Julius Caesar. Freud's extraordinary preoedipal reconstruction of the life and death of Julius was instrumental in his self-analysis and led to deepening understanding of his symptoms and inhibitions. An appreciation of formative preoedipal influences was convergent with Freud's discovery of the nuclear oedipus complex and a cohesive psychoanalytic theory of neurosis.

Jones (1953, p. 317) recorded Freud's different and isolated levels of interpretation of pertinent oedipal and then preoedipal content. However, Jones did not compare and contrast the different levels of interpretation in different sections of the biography. Freud subjected to critical self-analysis his ambivalent relation to Jung, interpreting his fainting spells in Jung's presence in terms of the positive and negative oedipus complex, as well as his unconscious submission to, rivalry with, and guilty triumph over Jung, Fliess, and his father. It is significant that Freud, having analyzed his fainting, "expressed the opinion that all his attacks could be traced to the effect on him of his young brother's death when he was a year and seven months old" (Jones 1955, p. 146). Freud's giving this age is an interesting error or slip, for it refers to Freud's approximate age when Julius was born, not when Julius died, when Freud was just under 2 years of age.

Sibling birth, death, and new pregnancy are inevitably potential developmental disruptions in the mother-child relationship, and impose special challenges during the child's second year of life. The experience of intrapsychic loss is here compounded during rapprochement not only by anal-urethral and continuing oral problems and beginning castration conflicts, but by the real illness and loss of Julius. The proclivity to ambivalence will then be increased with abandonment anxiety and rage at the object, and possible splitting of the object world (Mahler 1975, p. 108). Hostility toward the mother may also be displaced and projected onto other objects or turned on the self. Fearful of aggression and retaliation, the child "survivor" may display more intense separation reactions, defensive reliance on denial, reparative undoing, restitutive ambition, and reactive goodness. A basic negative mood will be accentuated by the effect on both the mother and her toddler of the new baby's birth and death, and the mother's withdrawal, grief, sadness, etc. Mahler (1966) has noted that a negative-depressive mood may persist or may give way to an unchildlike concern which may indicate a precocity of superego structuralization. Freud's reconstruction anticipates and forecasts later developmental research, although what was missing from his knowledge of development at that time would be supplied by his own further research and by the pioneering contributions of his students.

The challenges and crises of rapprochement require maternal acceptance of the child's ambivalence and empathic responses to the child's hostile dependence and separation reactions. The child at this time is easily vulnerable to narcissistic injury and ego and drive regression. Freud (1926) formulated the great danger situations of early childhood, that is, of the preoedipal period, in terms of fear of loss of the object, and fear of loss of the object's love. The abstract "object" was the mother, returned to a pivotal position in psychoanalytic theory. In connection with the infantile separation experience, which he analyzed and reconstructed, Freud pondered the psychology of pain and mourning and observed (1926, pp. 169-170) of the infant: "It cannot as yet distinguish between temporary absence and permanent loss. As soon as it loses sight of its mother it behaves as if it were never going to see her again; and repeated consoling experiences to the contrary are necessary before it learns that her disappearance is usually followed by her reappearance. Its mother encourages this piece of knowledge which is so vital to it by playing the familiar game of hiding her face from it with her hands and then, to its joy, uncovering it again. In these circumstances it can, as it were, feel longing unaccompanied by despair." This is the first description of the peek-a-boo game in psychoanalysis.

Freud, to buttress and expand his theoretical constructs, utilized and recommended the direct observation of children. Starting from the consideration of traumatic repetitive dreams, he considered the functions of children's play, with the careful scrutiny of his grandson as his research subject. He noted (1900, p. 461) that all the child's toys were used in separation games, for mastery of separation anxiety by turning activity into passivity. These observations were of a child at eighteen months of age, the rapprochement period of his Julius and Wolf Man reconstructions. The child could express the concept of separation with the word "gone," one of his first words. Representation in thought, and symbolic play indicative of identification with the mother, convey ego-active modes of dealing with separation distress converging in a more differentiated internalized representation of the mother and the capacity for evocative memory.

The separation-individuation process at this time can be correlated with psychosexual phases with regressive and progressive swings. Psychosexual development and separation-individuation are interrelated developmental processes and frameworks having common roots in Freud's earliest observations and formulations. The concepts of oral incorporation and projection of the part object and retention and expulsion of the fecal object (or narcissistic object) were early correlations of libido and object relations theory.

I would parenthetically add that I do not believe that Freud's addiction to smoking, his lifelong battle against it, and his reliance on incessant smoking—twenty cigars daily—for creative and productive work can be understood mainly in terms of the masturbatory equivalent and father identification he originally implied (Schur 1972, p. 61), or as a nicotine drug habituation. The preoedipal roots of such a literally oral addiction, which led to Freud's oral carcinoma, are today much more clearly defined. In this respect, beginning with the examination of the oral cavity in the Irma dream, a preoedipal dimension can be inferred but not confirmed in many of his dreams and screen memories. Contemporary evaluation of addictive tendencies would include considerations of oral fixation and regression and archaic ego states, but also of conflicts related to symbiosis and separation-individuation. Such problems, when focal and attenuated, may coexist with many other areas of advanced personality development, and may also spur mastery and sublimation. Freud's unique capacity for developmental mastery and, later, self-analysis, were resources that fostered his insights into both personality formation and psychopathology.

The preoedipal reconstructions in the Fliess letters demonstrate self-analytic reconstructions related predominantly to the period of life before age 3. The Freud family left Freiberg when Freud was 3, a factor in his designation of the period before age 3 as "prehistoric," and isolating in time this period of his infancy. His apparent grasp of preoedipal attachment and ambivalence merged with the simultaneous discovery of the oedipus complex. Freud checked some reconstructions with his mother (1887-1902, pp. 221-222), a source of validation with the original object frequently utilized by contemporary analysands. His preoedipal reconstructions contributed to the development of psychoanalytic drive, ego, and object relations theory, to formulations of preoedipal character traits and patterns, and to the technique of psychoanalysis as a reconstructive therapy.

Reconstruction was always far more than a simple genetic interpretation of one segment of experience. It was a whole piece of mental life, as Freud illustrated in his letters to Fliess and described in "Constructions in Analysis." This "piece" of mental life can also be considered as a nodal point in development with both important antecedents and certainly significant consequences and ramifications for later development. The early tendency was to understand this in terms of the reconstruction of trauma with pathogenic consequences, but Freud's own reconstruction shows its general importance for the later development of object relations and both affective and character dispositions. What was reconstructed were not simple actual events, but the child's interpretation and reaction to his experience, in other words, the meaning attached to the experience: the ego state and developmental impact became more important than a consideration of actual history.

The historical reconstruction of real experience and of real traumatic episodes remains significant (Greenacre 1975), without diminishing the importance of unconscious irrational conflicts and fantasies which may never have achieved consciousness. The unrememberable and unforgettable (Frank 1969) would then continue to influence further development and the meaning attached to further experience. Even though early trauma might be telescoped into the appearance of the single shock episode, and even though earlier disorder might be overlaid with defensive and adaptive maneuvers and could acquire new meaning, it could be possible under favorable circumstances to reconstruct into the "prehistoric period" of separation-individuation. Analytic interpretation, via reconstruction, can be regarded as a reordering of the infant's misinterpretation of internal and external reality.

Freud's masterful use of dreams and screen memories to reconstruct the infantile past was demonstrated in his own self-analysis long before the development of many other areas of psychoanalytic theory and technique. Prescient of some of the modern debate and controversy about the value and validity of preoedipal reconstruction, Freud (1900, pp. 451-452) further observed, "It was distressing to me to think that some of the premises which underlay my psychological explanations of the psychoneuroses were bound to excite scepticism and laughter when they were first met with. For instance, I had been driven to assume that impressions from the second year of life, and sometimes even from the first, left a lasting trace on the emotional life of those who were later to fall ill, and that these impressions—though distorted and exaggerated in many ways by the memory—might constitute the first and deepest foundation for hysterical symptoms. Patients, to whom I explained this at some appropriate moment, used to parody this newly-gained knowledge by declaring that they were ready to look for recollections dating from a time *at which they were not yet alive*."

Many analysts were also sceptical, not only of phylogenetic memories or of elaborate fantasy in the first year of life, but of all preoedipal reconstruction. Regarding this controversy, it is clear that tentative preoedipal formulations and converging hypotheses were utilized by Freud and later pioneering analysts in the expansion of psychoanalytic theory. While inferences especially regarding the preverbal period have to be extremely cautious and careful, such efforts are consonant with Freud's own models and with continued efforts to trace pertinent earlier and verbalized memories to those preverbal and nonverbal phenomena that are isomorphic with the verbalizable clinical material (Mahler et al., 1975, p. 14). There have been many important examples of such efforts which in the long run have been richly rewarding to psychoanalytic understanding. Perhaps the most classic example of this kind of reconstruction to the earliest period of life is the Isakower phenomenon. This revival of very early ego states and attitudes was also reflected in the reconstructive studies of Greenacre (1950) on acting out, Lewin (1946) on the dream screen, and Spitz (1955) on the primal cavity to name a few.

Our expanding preoedipal knowledge and research exemplified in the concepts of separation-individuation should not be misunderstood to mean that initial psychic development and differentiation is accessible to psychoanalysis, that there are no limits or ambiguities to reconstruction, or that the earliest ego disturbances are reversible. The twin problems of the genetic fallacy about advanced development and adultomorphic myth about infancy have to be kept in mind. Anna Freud (1971, p. 147) expressed reservations about analytic work in the preverbal area of primary repression, but she also stressed the need for both analytic and observational studies (1971, pp. 24-25): "Where the imprint of more highly developed functions is superimposed on the remnants of archaic layers, the original simplicity of the primitive picture cannot but be distorted; this is true in particular where regression proceeds from verbal to preverbal phases . . . with regard to the study of the first eighteen months of life, direct observation is indispensable as a means to complement, correct, and verify the conclusions drawn from the analyses of later stages."

It is not to be expected that reconstructive efforts should be exactly parallel with the data of analytic child observation, but the two sets of data should be consistent, and accurate reconstruction should fit or articulate with our current knowledge of development. The formulations of separation-individuation which organize data derived from analytic reconstruction do not detract from an appreciation of psychosexual development and the role of the oedipus complex in adult neurotic disorder. Rather, these studies have enriched our appreciation of the epigenetic sequence of development wherein each phase is dependent upon the preceding phase for its impetus and solution; and at any point problems of irregular, arrested, or deviant development may occur. Our knowledge of the formative influences that impinge upon oedipal development and solutions have been greatly enriched. Analytic work should take into account all oedipal and accessible preoedipal problems that are encountered in a given case, not excluding the influence of later life. The picture, as we know from our own clinical work and from the dilemmas of many analytic students, can be very complicated and confused. Psychoanalysis is not for those who are looking for an easy solution or the use of some neat oedipal or preoedipal formula, or a conventional mold in which the clinical material can be artificially compressed.

The assessment of preoedipal influences and particularly of preoedipal disorder may be especially noted in the area of the patient's relation to the analyst: the transference, the therapeutic alliance, the attunement to reality, and the quality of object relations. In addition to the clinical history, the patient's use of the analytic process and analytic setting provides valuable information about basic personality function. The more serious the early preoedipal disturbance, with possible structural deficit, the less likely that the patient will demonstrate a classical transference neurosis or that there will be a stable therapeutic alliance. Preoedipal development will influence the formation and form of the oedipal infantile neurosis underlying later transference neurosis. I do not think there is an artificial isolation between preoedipal and oedipal analysis. Though an oedipal transference neurosis is central to analytic work, depending upon the personality structure and depth of regression, varying duration and intensity of preoedipal transference may be discerned or inferred. The analysis of a case of obsessional neurosis will eventually deal with symptoms and character traits related to anal-phase conflicts.

There is no reason to expect that any of the later normal developmental phases of life or pathological states will exactly replicate point by point any of the subphases of separation-individuation or psychosexual development. The early phases of development are not literally recapitulated; various consequences are inferred in terms of residue and influences, of forerunners which undergo further developmental vicissitudes, and which are subject to regressive transformations: "Certain configurations persist in transference or acting-out patterns which seem to be the outcome of unresolved conflicts in the separation-individuation process" (Mahler 1971, p. 415).

In the origins of psychoanalysis, Freud discovered reconstruction and transference, and immediately reconstructed infantile psychological reactions and patterns dating from his second year of life, and returning as "revenants." He returned to these fascinating complexities in his final paper devoted to this topic. In "Constructions in Analysis" (1937, pp. 266-267), Freud concluded "with a few remarks which open up a wider perspective." Referring to hallucinatory experience, he stated, "sufficient attention has not hitherto been paid that in them something that has been experienced in infancy and then forgotten returns—something that the child has seen or heard at a time when he could still hardly speak and that now forces its way into consciousness, probably distorted and displaced owing to the operation of forces that are opposed to this return."

Psychic history, which for Freud was preserved in its essentials and "present somehow and somewhere," tends to repeat itself. Freud's (1937, p. 261) last paradigm recapitulates his initial 1897 reconstruction: "'Up to your nth year you regarded yourself as the sole and unlimited possessor of your mother; then came another baby and brought you grave disillusionment. Your mother left you for some time, and even after her reappearance she was never again devoted to you exclusively. Your feelings towards your mother became ambivalent, your father gained a new importance for you,' . . . and so on." Reconstruction to that nth year (taking into account the most common age sequence in siblings) will most often require preoedipal reconstruction consonant with our expanding knowledge of psychological and developmental processes.

SUMMARY

Freud's first reported reconstruction was to the preoedipal period and referred to the psychological meaning and consequences of the birth and death of his younger brother, Julius. In the historical development of psychoanalysis, preoedipal and oedipal reconstruction were simultaneously utilized, and Freud's thinking encompassed preoedipal influences with the oedipus complex.

Reconstruction was one of the earliest discovered methods in psychoanalytic technique, reciprocally contributing to psychoanalytic theory, the uncovering of infantile amnesia, and awareness of the persistent influence of unconscious infantile conflict. Freud anticipated the importance of object relations in contemporary psychoanalytic theory before formulation of the libido theory. Reconstruction from dreams and screen memories converged in Freud's self-analysis in the discovery of the repression and revival of infantile object relations, leading to the concept of transference. Psychoanalysis was reconstructive, facilitating memory reorganization, and new ego synthesis.

Freud's self-analytic reconstruction concerning Julius, prototypical of preoedipal reconstruction, was to the protoverbal anal developmental phase, and the rapprochement subphase of separation-individuation. His reconstruction is remarkably consistent with modern knowledge of developmental processes. The integration of psychoanalytic reconstruction and direct child observation promises a deeper understanding of ego development and disturbance, character formation, and preoedipal determinants of oedipal conflict and the infantile neurosis.

References

Atkins, N. (1977). The analyst and transcience. Presented to the Psychoanalytic Association of New York as the M. Sperling Lecture, February 1977.

Bibring, E. (1953). The mechanism of depression. In *Affective Disorders,* ed. P. Greenacre. New York: International Universities Press.

Blum, H. (1974). The borderline childhood of the Wolf Man. *Journal of the American Psychoanalytic Association* 22:721-742.

Eissler, K. (1966). A note on trauma, dream, anxiety, and schizophrenia. *Psychoanalytic Study of the Child* 21:17-50.

Esman, A. (1973). The primal scene: a review and reconsideration. *Psychoanalytic Study of the Child* 28:49-82.

Frank, A. (1969). The unrememberable and the unforgettable: passive primal repression. *Psychoanalytic Study of the Child* 24:48-77.

Freud, A. (1971). *The Writings of Anna Freud*, vol. 7. New York: International Universities Press.

Freud, S. (1887-1902). *The Origins of Psychoanalysis*. New York: Basic Books, 1950.

——— (1899). Screen memories. *Standard Edition* 3:301-322.

——— (1900). The interpretation of dreams. *Standard Edition* 5:339-627.

——— (1908). Character and anal erotism. *Standard Edition* 9:167-176.

——— (1913). The theme of the three caskets. *Standard Edition* 12:291-301.

——— (1917). A childhood recollection from *Dichtung und Wahrheit*. *Standard Edition* 17:145-156.

——— (1918). From the history of an infantile neurosis. *Standard Edition* 17:3-122.

——— (1926). Inhibitions, symptoms and anxiety. *Standard Edition* 20:77-177.

——— (1937). Constructions in analysis. *Standard Edition* 23:255-270.

Greenacre, P. (1950). General problems of acting out. In *Trauma, Growth, and Personality*, pp. 224-236. New York: International Universities Press, 1952.

——— (1975). On reconstruction. *Journal of the American Psychoanalytic Association* 23:693-712.

Grigg, K. (1973). "All roads lead to Rome": The role of the nursemaid in Freud's dreams. *Journal of the American Psychoanalytic Association* 21:108-126.

Grinstein, A. (1968). *On Sigmund Freud's Dreams*. Detroit: Wayne State University Press.

Jones, E. (1953, 1955, 1957). *The Life and Work of Sigmund Freud*, 3 vols. New York: Basic Books.

Kanzer, M. (1972). Review of the Wolf Man by the Wolf Man. *International Journal of Psycho-Analysis* 53:419-421.

Kanzer, M., and Blum, H. (1967). Classical psychoanalysis since 1939. In *Psychoanalytic Techniques*, ed. B. Wolman, pp. 93-146. New York: Basic Books.

Kris, E. (1956). On some vicissitudes of insight in psychoanalysis. *International Journal of Psycho-Analysis* 37:445-455.

Lewin, B. (1946). Sleep, the mouth, and the dream screen. In *Selected Writings*, pp. 87-100. New York: Psychoanalytic Quarterly, 1973.

Mahler, M. (1966). Notes on the development of basic moods: the depressive affect. In *Psychoanalysis: A General Psychology*, ed. R. Lowenstein et al., pp. 152-168. New York: International Universities Press. Reprinted in *The Selected Papers of Margaret S. Mahler*, vol. 2, ch. 5. New York: Jason Aronson, 1979.

——— (1971). A study of the separation-individuation process and its possible application to borderline phenomena in the psychoanalytic situation. *Psychoanalytic Study of the Child* 26:403-424. Reprinted in *Selected Papers*, op. cit., ch. 11.

——— (1975). On the current status of the infantile neurosis. *Journal of the American Psychoanalytic Association* 23:327-333. Reprinted in *Selected Papers*, op. cit., ch. 12.

Mahler, M., Bergman, A., and Pine, F. (1975). *The Psychological Birth of the Human Infant*. New York: Basic Books.

McDevitt, J. (1975). Separation-individuation and object constancy. *Journal of the American Psychoanalytic Association* 23:713-742.

Peto, A. (1969). Terrifying eyes: A visual superego forerunner. *Psychoanalytic Study of the Child* 24:197-212.

Schafer, R. (1960). The loving and beloved superego in Freud's structural theory. *Psychoanalytic Study of the Child* 15:163-188.

Schur, M. (1972). *Freud: Living and Dying*. New York: International Universities Press.

Shengold, L. (1971). Freud and Joseph. In *The Unconscious Today*, ed. M. Kanzer, pp. 473-494. New York: International Universities Press.

Spitz, R. (1955). The primal cavity: a contribution to the genesis of perception and its role for psychoanalytic theory. *Psychoanalytic Study of the Child* 10:215-240.

14

The Origins of the Reconstructed in Psychoanalysis

Paulina F. Kernberg, M.D.

In this paper I shall use a series of clinical vignettes to present a developmental object-relations perspective of reconstruction. The noun "reconstruction" includes two components—the "reconstructing" stemming primarily from the analyst's interpretations, and the "reconstructed" emerging primarily from the patient's contributions to the psychoanalytic process and setting (Fraiberg 1967, Furer 1971, Furman 1971, Geleerd 1969, Greenacre 1975, Schimek 1975).

The definition of reconstruction given in *A Glossary of Psychoanalytic Terms and Concepts* (Moore and Fine 1967) may be viewed as including both the reconstructing and reconstructed. Moore and Fine describe reconstruction as an important type of intervention used in the course of psychoanalytic treatment: "It consists of the analyst's attempt—one of his chief tasks—to correlate, understand, and then convey to his patient (i.e., to reconstruct) forgotten, repressed but psychologically important early experiences from the traces that they have left behind. Such traces gradually emerge in the patient's *free associations*, behavior, *dreams,* and *transference* reactions" (p. 82). They also emphasize that reconstruction reflects the genetic and developmental nature of psychoanalytic psychology with its stress on the historical roots of behavior. Moore and Fine add that the recovery of repressed early experiences which are highly charged with emotional conflict remains an essential part of psychoanalytic therapy. Throughout the paper it will be necessary to keep in mind that the retrieval of early experiences is in the shape of a fantasy formation formed by those early experiences (a blending of what actually happened plus the subjective impact of the experience at the time) and the transformations of those experiences in the course of subsequent developments. Cognitive capacities such as perception, attention and memory structure further this reconstruction fantasy. Moreover, the reconstruction fantasy is elicited under the impact of the regressive pull of the analytic process, a phenomenon which adds the particular evocative and affective quality to the reconstructive interpretation.

SOURCES FOR RECONSTRUCTION

Greenacre (1956) has stressed the role of the reconstruction and recovery of real, traumatic, organizing experiences in development in the process of working through in some patients. Margaret Mahler (1971) and others (Escalona 1968, Escalona and Heider 1968, Kris 1956), however, have warned against simply extrapolating from child observation material of the separation-individuation process to clinical observations reminiscent of these phenomena. Indeed, the relation is not one-to-one; rather, various kinds of relations may link the developmental stages of symbiosis, and separation-individuation in the particular life of the individual, to their traces or markers as detected in the psychoanalytic situation.

In describing these traces or markers in terms of development, I shall use Margaret Mahler's outline of development (1972), with the reminder that each of her stages takes into account the development and maturation of drives, ego, and superego. I propose the following three hypotheses.

1. The evolving transference to the therapist, his physical surroundings, and routine may reflect not only the transfer of the patient's emotional reaction to the mother but also to her early surroundings and routines. The psychoanalytic setting may thus provide the possibility of evoking derivatives of early nonverbal developmental events such as symbiotic and differentiation stage with the greatest opportunity for achieving congruence between the early past and present.

2. The evolving transference may particularly facilitate the retrieval of derivatives of the practicing and rapprochement subphases of the separation-individuation process.

3. The termination process may recapitulate or reactivate the developmental stages of object constancy.

I shall discuss each of these hypotheses in turn.

THE ANALYTIC SETTING AND PROCESS

It seems to me that the psychoanalytic setting and process may serve as a vehicle for the evocation of nonverbal stages of development. I propose that two stages of nonverbal development—symbiosis and the differentiation subphase of separation-individuation—may be reexperienced by the patient and registered by the analyst not in their verbal interaction, but in the patient's reactions to the analytic setting and to the analyst's conduct of the psychoanalytic process. By the patient's relation to the psychoanalytic setting, I mean the patient's perceptions, reactions, and attitudes to the inanimate world of the office, including his sensitivity to the lighting, temperature, color, space, and constancy of environment, as well as his behavior at the beginning and end of sessions. By reactions to the psychoanalytic process, I include the patient's extreme sensitivity to the analyst's tone of voice and to his way of beginning and terminating the sessions, as well as the patient's reaction to the length, frequency, and timing of the interpretations, regardless of their content. Last but not least, I include the patient's reaction to the analyst's general attitude of constancy and predictability, as expressed in the schedule and length of sessions.

Clinical Vignette 1

In my analytic experience this particular episode comes the closest to early aspects of the separation-individuation experience and to a reconstruction of the differentiation subphase. The background of the office as a space containing both persons and objects became evident to Miss A as she seemed to reexperience psychologically the hatching from a symbiosislike phase. Previously, both the analyst and inanimate external objects in the office had been either not recognized or acknowledged by her as existing (possibly reminiscent of symbioticlike states), or not considered distinctly in the former global relationship to the analyst and her surrounding.

In fact she referred to these experiences only when she entered into the fourth year of her analysis. Miss A, then in her twenties, described her loneliness and diffuse longing for a nurturing relationship which she felt she had missed in her past. After a series of sessions interspersed with frequent silences, the patient one day described how she saw the room as becoming lighter and its contents—the windows, paintings, details of the rug, and other ornaments—as appearing more distinct and literally *acquiring* color. For the first time she perceived the analyst as someone who had been awaiting her awakening. During the same session Miss A reported a sensation of warmth extending from her esophagus down to her stomach, and simultaneously, a sensation of something good and fulfilling infiltrated her body. In her new perception of the office itself and of the analyst as an external object "available but separate," she understood, with a clear sense of conviction, that the analyst had facilitated her ability to perceive distinctly herself, including her body image, the representation of a mothering object, and the real external object—the analyst as analyst.

In this vignette the regression in the analysis may have facilitated the retrieval of a differentiation type of experience as in the case described above. Miss A began to experience anew the separateness of herself from the analyst who then became a clearer or external object. She became aware of the analyst's role as facilitator of this process. Concomitantly, she experienced a clearer differentiation between her self-image as a relaxed and alert person, and a pleasurable body image (warm milk flowing into her digestive system).

Clinical Vignette 2

In another case facets of the practicing and rapprochement subphases appeared without too many secondary elaborations. Bobby, a 9-year old adopted child, came to analysis because of severe learning disabilities, antisocial behavior, and various conversion symptoms, such as headaches and leg cramps. He was in analysis with me for almost five years. Toward the end of the first year of analysis he would play a game in which he was supposedly lost in my rather small office. With great skill, he managed to hide underneath the couch or behind the door so that he could not readily be located by me. I had to literally search for him and "catch him." Several months later he would go out of the treatment room, reemerge behind the window of the office and then talk to me from outside. I was supposed to stay in the office and wait for him to come back into the office or tell me that he would come back. He repeated this behavior in a rather compulsive way several times until I could interpret to him his need to leave me but to be sure to find me again when he needed to. The regression in the service of the ego had allowed for the reenactment of the early practicing phase, with the corresponding need for emotional refueling, in his game of "being caught." This game served multiple functions; reconfirmation of his sense of self as a distinct, individualized self accepted by adoptive mother, and allowing him to work through the early loss of a parent (the biological mother).

Clinical Vignette 3

The rapprochement crisis was brought up by a 4-year-old child who regressed to that fixation point as he started to express with marked anxiety his oedipal concerns. This regression in the session could be seen in his moving from oedipal fantasies of making babies and killing the enemies to a sitting child, fixed as it were in space, clamoring for his mother to come and protect him from danger.

Chris had been referred for treatment because his aggression was uncontrollable. He hit everybody, including his peers, and had already become a "kindergarten dropout." Chris began his analytic treatment with me at age 3. The session I will describe took place after a year of analysis at age 4 years, 3 months.

Chris was a stout, intense, disheveled boy, full of energy and extremely articulate. His vocabulary was equivalent to a child double his age. One day he kicked the walls of the corridor as he came in. He then entered the bathroom with a water pistol and shot at the various African animal designs on the wallpaper. He said he was making a baby zebra, a baby elephant, a baby kangaroo—he then left the bathroom in a state of omnipotent excitement. He repeatedly hit me, but I contained him—that is, I held him between my arms so that he would be unable to hit me, and yet would remain within my encircling arms. Chris began to cry and, while still whining in a subdued way, he stayed between my arms for a few minutes. Next he sat is the middle of the playroom and, with a shrill voice, screamed that he wanted his mommy (his mother usually waited in the reception room at the end of the corridor). As he screamed for his mother, he linked together pipe cleaners, building up a chain. Interestingly enough, this was precisely what he had done in our very first session. On that occasion, he mentioned he had had a dream of being locked in his bathroom and calling for his parents who never came. Although at the very beginning of treatment he had needed some refueling contacts with his mother—leaving the room to show her his products in the reception room and then returning to the playroom—later he was able to separate from his mother for the entire session.

In the session under discussion Chris showed a new behavior, namely, shrieking at the top of his voice that he wanted his mommy, while sitting relatively immobile in the middle of the room and making pipe-cleaner chains. I mentioned that he knew where his mother was and yet he did not seem to want to go to her. He replied in a very firm voice, pointing his little finger down to the floor, "I want my mommy here, not there" (out in the reception room). I said that he must be quite angry that his mother was not right here, in the place where he wanted her. I explained that he had become quite excited about the idea of making babies with water pistols, making babies of all kinds with me in the bathroom, and that this had made him feel frightened lest something bad should happen to him. I also told him that he needed his mommy not as a boy who wished to make babies, but as a boy who could not walk and needed mommy to comfort him and to be under his control. He did not want to feel out of control with all the exciting ideas about making babies with me or even with mommy. Amidst his tears, he looked at me and said, "Really?" Yet he continued to howl for mommy. I mentioned that he was not sure whether he could really go to his mother; he still kept sitting as if he had forgotten that he could walk. I then told him that he might be remembering the times when he really could not walk to his mommy and felt he needed her, and when it was terrible for him that he could not get hold of her. I said that he must have felt quite bad then; he must have felt the way he was feeling now, quite sad and angry.

His mother, in spite of her extreme need to do so (as she told me later), did not come in response to her child's shrieking. When Chris finally got up to fetch her, she came in. Chris brought his mother into the playroom under the pretext that he wanted to show her the chain he had made with pipe cleaners. He suddenly hit her, at the same time blaming me for hitting him. While he kicked at his mother, he told me that he hated me. I interpreted his being afraid to say to mommy how angry he had felt each time he had needed her and she wouldn't come right when he needed her—even a long time ago, when he couldn't walk. He left the session still shrieking, albeit less convincingly. Later, his mother reported that on the way home in the car he sang and whistled in a most relaxed mood.

Chris's mother was 18 years old when she had married and became pregnant. Her husband and she left this country to live abroad in rather impoverished conditions. She was depressed throughout the first year, and longed for the care and closeness of her own family. She was obese, having gained forty pounds during her stay abroad. During that time, she left Chris to his own devices. For the first eighteen months whenever Chris did not "obey her" or do exactly as she expected him to, she would literally leave him. In the park, for example, she would scare Chris into a panic by actually starting to drive away while the young toddler ran after the car and her in despair. In this way she tried to convey to him that whenever she said it was time to go, it was indeed time to go. In this case, the rapprochement crisis, reemerging in the regression from beginning oedipal wishes, seemed to appear in the analytic process with uncanny vividness.

Clinical Vignette 4

In another case, a derivative of a pathological symbioticlike relationship reemerged in the patient's accounts of her sexual life with her husband and also through her critical remarks about the contents of the office and the shape of her chair. Mrs. D was a married woman in her forties, diagnosed as psychotic depression in a borderline personality organization with hysterical features. In her twenties and thirties she had been in psychoanalysis and psychotherapy. In her third year of intensive psychoanalytic psychotherapy (three times a week), she told her therapist that her sexual life had become increasingly unsatisfactory. Mrs. D complained about her rare sexual contacts with her husband. For the first time in a month, she had felt "more romantic" and allowed her husband to approach her. In fact, she had become sexually aroused, a rare experience in the last few years of her marriage. As she allowed herself to be caressed and touched, she had an increasing sense of irritation which rapidly evolved into an intense emotional storm of "being angry and tearful." She felt her husband was not holding her "in the right way" and was not touching her breasts and body with the right pressure and exact quality of stroke she longed for. She felt disparaged, flustered, and abruptly ended the contact with him. She just could not understand what had suddenly interfered with her "initial good disposition." After only a few minutes, all of these affects—sexual arousal, irritation and sadness—disappeared, giving way to a sense of "anesthesia." During that session Mrs. D, who was very fussy about the orderliness and decor of the office, complained that the new armchair was stiff, uncomfortable, and did not hold her right.

As a young girl of 7 and through her midadolescence, she had had to wear a corset to correct a deviation of her spine in the dorsolumbar area. Throughout her childhood, her mother's behavior had seemed rather contradictory to her; her mother would provocatively expose her arms and neck by wearing sleeveless dresses with low necklines, and at the same time would avoid anybody's—including her own children—touching her.

I interpreted that in addition to her fear of experiencing full sexual involvement with her husband, the sexual inhibition due to conflicts over competition with her mother (she was free of sexual inhibitions with former married lovers or transitory acquaintances), she might be reliving her experience with her rejecting mother and her rage and frustration for not being able to cuddle against her as a baby girl. Instead of feeling good about being held and contained in her mother's arms, a longing now displaced onto her husband, she reacted as if her husband were as unsensitive and rigid as the corset she wore as a young child, or as she felt my chair was holding her.

This particular session illustrates the separate genetic aspects of the reconstruction (in the interpretation derived primarily from the patient's memories of the corset and of her rejecting mother) and the developmental aspects of the reconstructive interpretation (the longing of the baby girl to be held and contained by mother). Mrs. D's despair over the unavailability of her mother during early infancy was represented in the bad experience of the rigid and painful containment of the corset. The interpretation made a definitive impact on her, both in its genetic and developmental aspects. The sense of conviction in her understanding enabled her to resolve the reenactment, projected into the marital situation, of a past image of herself as frustrated in the arms of a corset-mother who did not hold or touch her as she wished. This whole experience in turn could now be understood as a defensive regression against oedipal wishes and conflicts.

Clinical Vignette 5

This case illustrates a traumatic event in the practicing phase and its possible impact on the rapprochement phase and subsequent character formation.

My last case example is that of a late adolescent girl who was an extremely gifted writer. Throughout her school years, until her first year of college, Susan had been a model student. Her black hair and slim figure conveyed an impression of fragility that was enhanced by her looking—when she entered the office—as if she had been literally beaten or was about to fall apart. She also attempted to control the analyst by frequent requests of schedule changes and by complaining that the analyst was not on her side.

Susan began analysis because of an intense separation anxiety that made her unable to leave the house to go anywhere without having her mother accompany her. Although she had managed, out of sheer will power, to attend college in a neighboring community, she had to be driven there by her mother. She was unable to drive a car; the very idea of driving threw her into a panic. In addition, because of an intense and severe condition diagnosed as an irritable colon, she had to eat special foods at home that she could not, according to her, have prepared for her exactly in the same way anywhere else. Her mother accommodated her every whim and made it practically impossible for Susan to express any aggression against her. The mother bent like a leaf under the wind to her daughter's frequent temper tantrums when Susan would wail that she had no boyfriends. During these violent storms, Susan would actually throw herself on the floor and scream in rage.

Susan's parents never denied her anything; in fact they had never even gone away as a couple for a vacation. In her second year of analysis, the patient acknowledged that she would be quite offended and furious if her mother were not available right when she needed her. What would happen to her if her mother went away on vacation and left her behind? The very idea that mother would not be immediately available to her was terrifying. She needed to know that her mother was at home where she left her. This need blended with her oedipal competitiveness with her mother for her father's attention, as she expected to be "included" in the parent's activities.

During the initial consultation period, I learned from Susan's mother that Susan had been involved in a automobile accident at an early age. Although Susan did not remember the specific incident, in her second year of treatment she described some residues related to this early childhood memory as she began learning to drive a car. She seemed obsessed with the possibility that the door would suddenly open and she would be thrown out. She was haunted by the idea that a policeman would be watching the inept way in which she had parked parallel to the sidewalk, and she would get a fine. In addition, she was obsessed with the idea that she would be lost on the highway and would not see her mother again, and her mother would be quite worried about any delay on her part.

I knew that when Susan was 18 months old, her mother had had an accident in the middle of traffic. The car had been cornered between the sidewalk and a bus, so that as the bus hit the side of the car Susan was forced out with her mother onto the sidewalk. The mother held the child in her arms, but they were abruptly separated when an ambulance picked up the mother, who had suffered a cerebral concussion and had to stay in the hospital for three months. During that time, Susan was shifted from paternal grandmother to maternal grandmother and various baby sitters until her mother was well enough to look after her again. Her mother had never shared this account with her daughter, for "she did not want to discourage her from learning to drive some day." Notwithstanding, the mother acknowledged that throughout the years it had been quite difficult for her to drive without being constantly apprehensive about having another car accident.

This traumatic incident during the practicing phase brought out a pathological rapprochement crisis with intense coercion of the mother, interfering with genuine individuation. Inasmuch as Susan as a young college student controlled her mother, she could separate— but only under the illusion that she carried the mother of rapprochement at all times within her.

REACTIVATION OF OBJECT CONSTANCY

My third and final hypothesis is that during the process of termination of psychoanalysis the stage and task of consolidation of object constancy may be reactivated. Positive and negative object and self-images are further integrated into a cohesive and stable self and the capacity for whole object representation (O. Kernberg 1976). In accordance with the criteria of Mahler, Pine, and Bergman (1975), separation, the distinction between the subject and the external object, and individuation, the differentiation between the self-representation and the object representation, are finally achieved. During his last session, after a successful analysis, a 10-year-old boy remarked that he knew every corner, every object in the analyst's room so well that if he were to return in a few years for a visit he would recognize every part of the office and every object even "if it was turned around." A 9-year-old boy who had the diagnosis of depression with borderline features stated upon termination that he would always recognize his analyst "even if he would shave his beard" or "would get very old." Thus, he felt confident of the continuity of his internal object and reassured by his anticipation of its ongoing psychological presence.

RECONSTRUCTION IN THE ANALYTIC SETTING

In presenting these hypotheses, I am implying that it is possible to reconstruct aspects of early development in the psychoanalytic setting. There are various reasons for this. First of all, the stages of development correspond to a series of self- and object representations linked by affective changes. Loewald (1972) has described that the object is internalized in conjunction with the subject's relation to the object. Thus this whole constellation of subject, his relation to the object and the object reemerge in the reconstructive process. Shapiro (1970) has pointed out that psychoanalysis is most apt to uncover these remnants because the analysis as a dyadic situation stimulates a replay of early developmental stages, mainly mother-child interaction. The dyadic units of self-object and affect components depend on the maturation of autonomous ego apparatuses; endowment as well as experiential factors are crucial here. Freud (1923) stated "that the character of the ego is a precipitate of abandoned object-cathexes and that it contains the history of those object-choices" (p. 29). It seems to me possible to extend this concept and to conceive of the ego as the precipitate of past representations of self and objects linked by affects, including primitive and indistinct forms of relations to both animate and inanimate objects. These internalized object relations can then be retrieved in the analytic situation in various ways.

1. The regression in the psychoanalytic process as conceptualized from an object-relations point of view, evokes earlier units of self- and object images linked by affect. A deep regression will elicit experiences of primitive relationships as far back as preverbal stages. These archaic forms of object relations to the animate and inanimate world may be reenacted. The case of Miss A illustrates the patient's responsivity to the physical aspects of the environment, to sound, noises, and feeling of warmth. A concomitant effect of regression is that memories are more easily retrievable if the ego state is similar to the state during which memory traces were established (Fine, Joseph, and Waldhorn 1971).

2. In terms of object relations theory, the repressed unconscious is partly structured or constituted by repressed bipolar self-affect and object units that reemerge in quite intact forms in the analysis, probably because they have remained unchanged and unchangeable due to repression and the timeless quality of unconscious contents. The image of the id as an ebullient cauldron becomes rather the image of a freezer preserver of past object relations contained in self-object-affect units.

3. The analysis of the transference neurosis sets free self- and object units, producing the closest version to the reenactment of these past object relations in the present, with their concomitant affective reenactments. The reenactment of early object relations is based on the reactivation of past self-representations, as in the case of Susan, who suffered from separation anxiety and looked beaten and frail in my presence (Clinical Vignette 5).

4. The joint participation of patient and analyst in the reconstruction of material serves in itself to elicit verbal and preverbal memories (Kris 1956). Fenichel believes reconstruction is experienced by the patient as an injunction to remember. I would like to underline that the patient's recovery of nonverbalized material in the analytic setting or rather, recovery of material from the preverbal stages of development, can be used in the analysis. It is, I believe, important to remember that material from the early years from Piaget's period of sensorimotor intelligence (birth to two years) and stage of preoperational representations (Flavell 1963), reflects simultaneously the af-

fective, cognitive, and motoric aspects of the child's behavior. Because of this close association of cognitive, affective, and conative features, the link between thinking, feeling, and acting in young children can be better observed than in the adult. In the child there is no dichotomy, where thinking can be to an extent separate from external behavior, because of the predominance of primary-process thinking and lack of repressive barriers. Bergman, Mahler, and Furer (1976) have described a case of autistic psychosis, a girl who at age 2 years, 4 months, related to the piano in ways that reflected aspects of the relationship to her mother who was a pianist, as well as her object representation of mother who responded (if at all) to the needs of her child in a stereotyped and rigid way, seldom holding her infant for comfort. Mother may well have felt like a wooden box of huge height to this young child. The child thus may have expressed symbolically what her experience of her relationship to the mother looked like to her as a toddler.

5. Returning once more to the analytic situation, through dramatization in play, one may reach facets of early stages of psychological development in which thinking, feeling, and doing are very close to surface behavior, as illustrated, e.g., in the play of children who hide in the room to be "caught" and found by the analyst or command and order the analyst around as a way of coercion.

6. Phyllis Greenacre (1956) suggests some clues indicative of real traumatic experiences under the effects of repression: "vacuoles of memory," areas consistently omitted or incongruously brought up, recurring discrepancies of age or place inappropriate to the events to which they are associated, somatic experiences, and screen memories which contain distorted elements of actual events. Acting out, especially the specific forms acting out takes, may also reflect events, sometimes traumatic, in the developmental stage of separation and individuation in which doing and thinking are parallel. Also, reeditions of previous stages emerge during the passage of one stage into another; for example, the transition from latency to early adolescence invokes derivatives from the anal stage.

7. Finally, vivid dream material (Fine, Joseph, and Waldhorn 1971) may also bring past, albeit distorted, self- and object images into consciousness in a special way. I would agree with Sharpe (1963) that some of the images contained in dreams may indeed correspond to actual aspects of the early life setting of the particular individual.

TRANSFORMATIONS OF DEVELOPMENTAL EVENTS

I shall now explore the counterpart of my previous proposal. Although we may have the opportunity to perceive derivative phenomena from the symbiotic and separation-individuation subphases in the analytic setting and analytic process, developmental events do not occur in a linear fashion and there is no "one-to-one" relationship of past to present. Escalona (1968, Escalona and Heider 1959) and Mahler (Bergman, Mahler, and Furer 1976, Mahler, Pine, and Bergman 1975), as well as others, indicate that developmental lines do not only occur separately, interacting with each other (A. Freud 1974), they also coalesce in more complex syntheses. These complex syntheses acquire particular organizations and structures at nodal points of development, the classical developmental stages. Fine, Joseph, and Waldhorn (1971) state, "More than repressed traumata are reconstructed in psychoanalysis. Not only are associated fantasies and affects also reconstructed, but so are independent repressed fantasies, connections between various psychic contents, and childhood object relations" (p. 123). Greenacre (1975) adds that the archaic ego state is not a separate aspect of the reconstructive process, but rather comes along with the rest of it.

It seems helpful to postulate that a certain developmental event, such as the rapprochement crisis, may be seen in the analysis in various kinds of transformation. A transformation is implied in even ordinary remembering as it is a reconstruction of the past rather than a simple reproduction of the past. Loewald (1972) and Kennedy (1950, 1971) have illustrated the role of ego development as well as that of wish fulfillment and displacement in a latency-age girl's memories of her infancy.

At times there is minimal distortion between the developmental event and its appearance in the analysis, as in the case of the 4-year-old boy who did not move while calling for his mother. More frequently what we see are distortions due to late developmental conflict (Kennedy 1950, 1971). Let us consider, for example, the traumatic experience of my late adolescent patient (Clinical Vignette 5). Her obsessive concerns about parking may have been due to the traumatic nature of the car accident ending in an abrupt separation from her mother at a point of vulnerability: the rapprochement period. It is important to remind ourselves that the traumatic experience probably "telescopes" multiple memories of a similar kind (A. Freud 1951). The same conflict or interpersonal interaction has been consecutively repeated, making it more difficult to trace it precisely in time (Greenacre 1956).

Another possible vicissitude of an event occurring early in the child's development is that of becoming condensed with other configurations. Such an event needs to be deciphered within the total emotional situation, as in the case of the married patient (Mrs. D) who condensed her heterosexual genital strivings with her oral symbiotic longings in which she needed her mother for soothing contact and integration. The reconstruction in her memory of the corset may be a reenactment of her identification with her mother (also inaccessible) so that the reemergence of the event comes as a projection of self-images onto the object (Greenacre 1956). In addition, the function of memory of events in development is such that not only do early memories affect later ones, but later experiences affect the recall of earlier ones (Kennedy 1971). Earlier experiences, moreover, may leave residues on later experiences by their form and not by a repetition of the content (Greenacre 1956).

A developmental transformation of an early event may be linked with regression, as in Chris's reenactment of his rapprochement crisis to protect himself from oedipal fears (Clinical Vignette 3). A developmental event may also be retrieved in a regression in the service of the ego occurring in the analytic situation. Here I would like to cite the case of a 16-year-old patient who felt helpless to deal with his pervasive sexual inhibitions. On one occasion he felt that he had a big head and a very small body and could not move. He literally compared this with what a baby, still in the crib, might feel like.

The process of sublimation may illustrate yet another transformation of a developmental event. For example, the relation of a self-representation (the child in the midst of a rapprochement crisis) to an object representation (mother) linked by an affect (angry coercion) may be integrated into a new, sublimatory configuration. This is illustrated in the case of a 24-year-old patient who at times presented psychotic episodes, during which he had the omnipotent fantasy that he could control all stars and all the universe. He would send messages to all distant planets. They would hear him and eventually reciprocate his call, although he would have to wait for a long time. He was able to relate this to his mother and himself as a child and to his sense of her unavailability and his trying to coerce her to respond to his sense of her as distant and unresponsive but omnipotently present inside of him wherever he went. As he progressed in his treatment, he became a computer analyst and was able to engage in very similar, but more realistic—sublimatory—experiences of "omnipotence" as a programmer for machines that, this time, did respond promptly and rewardingly to his messages.

Finally, a developmental event may only be observable vaguely "through a mirror, darkly" for the reconstruction by the patient and therapist. This category leaves room for the many complex and even unexplainable transformations that a developmental event may cause as it filters through character style. As Hansi Kennedy (1971) formulated it: "It is important to keep in mind that what is created by such early experiences are not conflict situations but attitudes which may not have specific fantasy or memory content attached to them," such as language and more specialized processes of adaptations (i.e., defense mechanisms) to the inner world and the outside world represented by analyst and patient in the joint effort of reconstruction. Lastly the patient's and therapist's reconstructions also change the content and structure of the memory which then includes the reconstructive process itself in its reorganization.

SUMMARY

In this presentation I have proposed that reconstruction of all developmental stages is a feasible task in the psychoanalytic situation from an object-relations point of view. Developmental material from the preverbal stages may be retrieved from the analysis of the relation of the patient to the psychoanalytic setting and to the person of the analyst in his nonspecific functions as a receptive listener, a predictable and integrating figure. Here the areas of early autistic and symbiotic stages with their respectively undifferentiated and fused forms of self-object-affect units may be tapped. In particular, the transference may evoke various stages of separation-individuation. Here self- and object units are distinct, and affective states are more differentiated. We may observe transitory fusions of self and idealized object, self and ideal self, transpositions of self and object, and lack of integration of positive and negative self- and object images. The differentiation between external and internal object, however, is now achieved. Termination in particular brings about stages of the transition to object constancy, with the integrations of positive and negative self- and object images, as well as positive and negative affects.

Finally, I have postulated the favorable factors for that reactivation analysis of retrieved relatively undistorted derivatives of preoedipal stages. More frequently, however, the transformation of these early developmental stages requires the reconstructive work of analyst and patient to decipher the original component of the experience recovered.

References

Bergman, A., Mahler, M. S., and Furer, M. (1976). Treatment of a childhood autism case. Presented to the N.Y. Psychoanalytic Society, March 29.

Bernstein, A. E., and Blacher, R. S. (1967). The recovery of a memory from three months of age. *Psychoanalytic Study of the Child* 22:151-161.

Burgner, M., and Edgcumbe, R. (1972). Some problems in the conceptualization of early object relationships. Part II: The concept of object constancy. *Psychoanalytic Study of the Child* 2:315-333.

Escalona, S. K. (1968). *Roots of Individuality: Normal Patterns of Development in Infancy.* Chicago: Aldine.

Escalona, S. K., and Heider, G. M. (1959). *Prediction and Outcome.* New York: Basic Books.

Fenichel, O. (1945). *The Psychoanalytic Theory of Neurosis.* New York: Norton.

Fine, B. D., Joseph E. D., and Waldhorn, H. A., eds. (1971). *Recollection and Reconstruction* and *Reconstruction in Psychoanalysis.* New York: International Universities Press.

Flavell, J. H. (1963). *The Developmental Psychology of Jean Piaget.* New York: Van Nostrand Reinhold.

Fleming, J. (1975). Some observations on object constancy in the psychoanalysis of adults. *Journal of the American Psychoanalytic Association* 23:743-759.

Fraiberg, S. (1967). Repression and repetition in child analysis. Presented at the Topeka Psychoanalytic Society. Discussant: P. F. Kernberg.

Frank, A. (1969). The unrememberable and the unforgettable: passive primal repression. *Psychoanalytic Study of the Child* 24:48-77.

Freud, A. (1951). Observations on child development. *Psychoanalytic Study of the Child* 6:18-30.

——— (1965). *Normality and Pathology in Childhood.* New York: International Universities Press.

——— (1974). A psychoanalytic view of developmental psychopathology. *Journal of the Philadelphia Association of Psychoanalysis* 1:7-17.

Freud, S. (1923). The ego and the id. *Standard Edition* 19:12-59.

Furer, M. (1971). Observations on the treatment of the symbiotic syndrome of infantile psychosis: reality, reconstruction, and drive maturation. In *Separation-Individuation: Essays in Honor of Margaret S. Mahler*, ed. J. B. McDevitt and C. F. Settlage, pp. 473-485. New York: International Universities Press.

Furman, E. (1971). Some thoughts on reconstruction in child analysis. *Psychoanalytic Study of the Child* 26:372-385.

Geleerd, E. R. (1969). Introduction to panel on child psychoanalysis (the separation-individuation phase: direct observations and reconstructions in analysis). *International Journal of Psycho-Analysis* 50:91-94.

Greenacre, P. (1956). Re-evaluation of the process of working through. *International Journal of Psycho-Analysis* 37:439-444.

——— (1975). On reconstruction. *Journal of the American Psychoanalytic Association* 23:693-712.

Heinecke, C. (1970). In search of supporting evidence for reconstructions formulated during a child psychoanalysis. *Reese-Davis Clinic Bulletin* 2:92-110.

Joseph, E. D. (n.d.). Sense of conviction, screen memories and reconstruction: A clinical note. Unpublished manuscript.

Kaplan, L. J. (1972). Object constancy in the light of Piaget's vertical decalage. *Bulletin of the Menninger Clinic* 36.

Kennedy, H. E. (1950). Cover memories in formation. *Psychoanalytic Study of the Child* 5:275-284.

——— (1971). Problems in reconstruction in child analysis. *Psychoanalytic Study of the Child* 26:386-402.

Kernberg, O. F. (1972). Early ego integration and object relations. *Annals of the New York Academy of Sciences* 193:233-247.

——— (1976). *Object Relations Theory and Clinical Psychoanalysis*. New York: Jason Aronson.

Kris, E. (1956). The recovery of childhood memories in psychoanalysis. *Psychoanalytic Study of the Child* 11:54-88.

Lampl-de Groot, J. (1976). Personal experience with psychoanalytic technique and theory during the last half-century. *Psychoanalytic Study of the Child* 31:283-296.

Loewald, H. (1972). The experience of time. *Psychoanalytic Study of the Child* 27:401-410.

Mahler, M. S. (1971). A study of the separation-individuation process: and its possible application to borderline phenomena in the psychoanalytic situation. *Psychoanalytic Study of the Child* 26:403-424. Reprinted in *The Selected Papers of Margaret S. Mahler*, vol. 2, ch. 11. New York: Jason Aronson, 1979.

——— (1972). On the first three subphases of the separation-individuation process. *International Journal of Psycho-Analysis* 53:333-338. Reprinted in *Selected Papers*, op. cit., ch. 8.

Mahler, M. S., Pine, F., and Bergman, A. (1975). *The Psychological Birth of the Human Infant.* New York: Basic Books.

McDevitt, J. B. (1971). Preoedipal determinants of an infantile neurosis. In *Separation-Individuation: Essays in Honor of Margaret S. Mahler*, ed. J. B. McDevitt and C. F. Settlage, pp. 201-226. New York: International Universities Press.

——— (1975). Separation-individuation and object constancy. *Journal of the American Psychoanalytic Association* 23:713-742.

Moore, B. E., and Fine, B. D. (1967). *A Glossary of Psychoanalytic Terms and Concepts.* New York: American Psychoanalytic Association.

Nagera, H. (1966). *Early Childhood Disturbances, The Infantile Neurosis, and the Adult Disturbances.* New York: International Universities Press.

Pine, F. (1971). On the separation process, universal trends and individual differences. In *Separation-Individuation: Essays in Honor of Margaret S. Mahler*, ed. J. B. McDevitt and C. F. Settlage, pp. 113-130. New York: International Universities Press.

Roiphe, H. (1973). Some thoughts on childhood psychosis, self and object. *Psychoanalytic Study of the Child* 28:131-145. New Haven: Yale University Press.

Schimek, J. G. (1975). The interpretations of the past, childhood trauma, psychical reality, and historical truth. *Journal of the American Psychoanalytic Association* 23:845-865.

Shapiro, T. (1970). Language development in young schizophrenic children: direct observation as constraint on constructions in analysis. Presented at the mid-winter meetings of the American Psychoanalytic Association.

——— (1976). Discussion of P. Kernberg's "The origins of the reconstructed in psychoanalysis: a developmental approach." Presented at the Annual Meeting of the American Psychoanalytic Association, December 1976.

Sharpe, E. F. (1937). The dream as a typical and individual psychological product. In *Dream Analysis*. London: Hogarth Press.

Part V

Rapprochement in Psychopathology and Creativity

15

Adolescent Psychopathology and the Rapprochement Process

AARON H. ESMAN, M.D.

The process of human psychological development resembles the elephant of the fable, described by seven blind men in vastly different ways depending on the part they touched. It can also be likened to a house with many windows; one's view will depend on the particular opening through which one looks. Thus, to the Piagetian, development is a succession of cognitive stages in orderly and invariant sequence; to the classical Freudian it is a complex progression through a series of overlapping psychosexual phases. Erikson sees it as a passage through a sequence of psychosocial crises, while the behaviorist observes a gradual accretion of learned responses and competences.

Over the past twenty-five years, another approach to the understanding of, at least, the early stages of psychological development has been propounded in the work of Margaret Mahler. As is well known, the window through which Mahler views the process is that of the evolution of self- and object representations, and with them, of mental life itself. I propose to explore in this paper the application of Mahler's ideas and, in particular, her thoughts about the crucial role of what she calls the "rapprochement" subphase, to the study of adolescence and the clinical care of disturbed adolescents.

It was Peter Blos (1967) who first developed the idea of adolescence as a "second individuation" phase. Granted, of course, that we
cannot speak of the normal latency or preadolescent child and his
parents as being involved in a symbiotic state akin to that of the first
few months of life, it remains true that there are distinct behavioral
parallels between the adolescent process (in our culture, at least),
and the normal separation-individuation phase and its several subphases, as Mahler has described them. There is, indeed, much
overlapping and the subphases are, perhaps, less distinct than in
Mahler's classic description of infantile development, but the parallels are surely there.

The early adolescent can be said to be involved in a massive
"hatching" or differentiation process, as he—in part defensively, no
doubt—seeks to establish psychological distance from the primary
objects of his preoedipal and oedipal longings. The first motor
efforts of the infant that initiate and accompany his emergence from
the symbiotic dual unity can readily be analogized to the beginning
gestures of independence and self-assertions displayed by the puber-
tal or postpubertal youngster. As he becomes more comfortable with
his new body image, his increased muscular strength, and the enhancement of his cognitive capacities through the development of
operational thought (as described by Piaget), the young adolescent
moves, like the junior toddler, into a "practicing" period in which he
tests out his newly-won powers and his greater range of freedom—
always assuming, of course, that his parents grant him both adequate
scope and adequate protection for such explorations of autonomy
and individuation.

Much of the "rebelliousness" and experimentalism of this period
has a quality analogous to the "love affair with the world" that
Mahler (citing Greenacre) ascribes to the practicing toddler as he
seeks to probe the limits of his world. Similarly, the "low-keyedness"
which Mahler and her associates have observed in the later practicing toddler as he senses the mother's absence is frequently mirrored
by the early adolescent's oft-described moodiness and irritability, as
he seeks to deal with the relative objectlessness and self-depletion
that result from his efforts at detachment.

Periodically, therefore, we see the early, and even the mid-
adolescent turning back for security and support to the parents from
whom he is ostensibly—and often noisily—seeking to remove himself. As with the toddler, however, such closeness to the parent may

evoke fears of regressive engulfment and dedifferentiation, leading to renewed assertions of autonomy and individuation, or desperate searches for substitute attachment objects. This rapprochementlike phenomenon, tinged with ambivalence (or, in Mahler's terms, "ambitendency") and frequently marred by turmoil, seems distinctly similar to that described by Mahler for the toddler. In both cases one can recognize the anxiety and insecurity generated by the process of distantiation, all the more so for the young adolescent because the unconscious conflicts around the reactivated oedipal and preoedipal wishes have not yet been resolved and truly integrated, and realistic mental representations of the self and of the parents, devoid of idealizations or defensive denigrations, have yet to be consolidated.

By late adolescence, however, this last work is normally well under way. Just as with the establishment of an at least relative self- and object constancy in the 3-year-old, its completion allows for a genuine, nonconflictual separation from parents, for the consolidation of character organization (Blos 1968), and for the undertaking of the age-appropriate work and object relations that characterize youth, on the one hand, and nursery and primary school life on the other.

It is true that, as Schafer (1973) has reminded us, "symbiosis" and "separation-individuation" concepts have as their referents mental representations rather than overt behaviors. Further, he points out that "only an already highly individuated person is capable of giving up his infantile relations to others (actually, of modifying these relations greatly)" (p. 43). It must be clear, then, that we are speaking here of analogies, rather than identities. Even so, it is possible, I believe, to use this schema as a framework for understanding certain clinical phenomena in adolescence. Blos (1967), in his discussion of the "second individuation process," points up the dialectic tension between ego growth in adolescence and the pull toward regression to more primitive, less differentiated modes of behavior. It is his view that the capacity to tolerate and master such regressive episodes is a central feature of normal adolescent development. While, like Gradolph (1978), I question the ubiquity or necessity of ego regressions in normal adolescence, it is surely true, unfortunately, that massive regressions to earlier levels of mental and behavioral function characterize much of adolescent psychopathology, especially in its severe forms. Differentiation between these grave disorders and the regressive shifts Blos describes sometimes represents a major diagnostic challenge, although one must bear in mind Masterson's (1968) observation that the burden of proof is on the psychiatrist who suggests in such cases that one deals with "normal turmoil" rather than psychopathology.

I believe that Mahler's schema proves to be of great value in meeting this challenge, in helping to conceptualize the nature of the pathology and in formulating a therapeutic program. Mahler and her associates suggest that "islands of developmental failure might lead to borderline symptomatology in . . . adolescence," but note that they "deliberately have not dealt with these vicissitudes in detail" (Mahler, Pine, and Bergman 1975, p. 229). I should like to do precisely that in the following case illustrations.

Case 1

Gladys was a 16-year-old girl of mixed Chinese and Puerto Rican ancestry admitted to a residential treatment center. She was sent there because of her long history of truancy and street activity dating back to age 14. According to Gladys, she had been sexually promiscuous and extensively involved with alcohol and drugs.

Gladys was born when her mother was 17. The father, an alcoholic, abandoned them when Gladys was 2, after the birth of her younger brother. The mother then returned to Puerto Rico where the maternal grandmother increasingly assumed the care of the children because the mother had lost interest in them, finally abandoning them when Gladys was 4. Grandmother was a rigid, fanatical, Pentecostal Christian who regarded all sensual indulgence as sinful. Gladys clung to her grandmother and was extemely compliant and submissive at home throughout her childhood, indeed, even while leading an active, rebellious street life for the two years prior to admission. Gladys explained, "I used to pick up men on the streets because of feeling lonely and because I wanted affection." Drugs and alcohol were clearly related to profound depressive feelings.

In the treatment center Gladys replicated this pattern. She was initially compliant, a "good girl," cooperative and well-behaved. Gradually, however, she became increasingly angry and aggressive, at first with peers, then with adults. She became especially agitated on weekends, when the child-care staff was depleted and when her therapist, to whom she became intensely attached, was absent. Unwilling or unable to attend school, she was at times left to wander aimlessly about the campus during the day, feeling detached, isolated, and abandoned to the destructive power of her own impulses and fantasies. In the absence of clear-cut structure and formal programming, she felt lost and helpless and her primitive affects and wishes asserted themselves. To her therapeutic sessions she began to bring a rubber rabbit as a combination alter-ego and transitional object. Gradually she became more disorganized and fragmented, with suicidal and homicidal thoughts and impulses, until it became clear that hospitalization was required. In hospital, she recovered quickly and was able to return to the treatment center, where she did well for a time. Weekend visits with her grandmother led to increasingly sharp regressions, culminating in a suicide attempt which was followed by violent assaults on staff. This necessitated her discharge into her grandmother's custody; the latter, thereupon, took her off to Puerto Rico, and contact with Gladys was lost.

This case is obviously complex and Gladys's pathology was multiply determined. Nonetheless, I believe that she clearly demonstrates a developmental failure at the level of the rapprochement crisis. In the absence of an adequate developmental history, there seems reason to think that her early symbiotic phase was fairly well established. Her intense, somewhat hypomanic street activity evokes images of the practicing period, in which the child tests out the possibilities and limits of his environment and of his own resources. What seemed unbearable to Gladys, however, was the absence of dependable, protective and nurturing figures in her life space. Under these conditions, she would lapse into primitive, regressive fantasies of symbiotic fusion or effusions of intense, unmodulated aggression. One can reconstruct that Gladys experienced the psychological loss of the mother at the time of rapprochement—around two or so—due first to the birth of her sibling and then to the immature, narcissistic mother's growing emotional and physical detachment and ultimate abandonment. Gladys was left with no secure sense of the availability of a protective object (her father having abandoned her, too), and no possibility to develop object constancy. The absence of her therapist meant to her total abandonment, with rage, panic and disorganized hyperactivity as the only recourse—or else a regressive restitution of symbiotic fusion with her grandmother, who had served, however, inadequately, as a substitute for the lost primary object.

It seemed clear, therefore, that a rational treatment plan for this girl would include the more or less constant availability of nurturing objects, and a structured program that left no gaps in which she could feel abandoned to the power of her own impulses. A rapprochementlike situation had to be feasible for her at all times, to avert disorganizing panic and self-destructive behavior—to prevent her from acting out in order to "obtain affection." In the absence of such a structure, her decompensation was inevitable.

Case 2

Jane was a 20-year-old college dropout when she came to me as her fifth therapist. She had been in treatment more or less continuously since age 14 when she began seeing a male colleague primarily because of school difficulties. At that time she was overactive, distractible, "the class clown." She had had social problems for years; usually she had one good friend, but was regarded by many of her peers as somewhat odd. At home, she was frequently in conflict with her mother, an unstable, impulsive woman who was alternately intensely possessive and harshly critical. The father, apparently something of a successful con man, had left the family when Jane was 11, and there had been only sporadic contact since, though he seemed to have provided adequately for them financially in Jane's early adolescence.

Over the years that had elapsed since her initial entry into therapy, Jane had had three more therapists—two women and one man—before coming to me. With none of them had any major changes in her behavior occurred; though she retained a tender affection for one of the women, who had been very supportive and maternal toward her and provided her with much intellectual insight, she acknowledged that little of substance had resulted from their work beyond what might be expected of normal maturation.

Jane presented herself as a pathetically appealing, attractive, somewhat disorganized young woman who described herself as "spacey." She was barely able to concentrate on anything related to school or work; she had lost a number of jobs because of her distractibility and erratic performance. She complained bitterly and intensely of a "talking problem" in which people who were speaking, such as lecturers, actors, or even social acquaintances, would appear to her to have distorted mouths and their words would seem similarly distorted and incomprehensible.

Her primary preoccupation, however, was her relationship with Jim, a young man who, she said, was cruel, unaffectionate, and manipulative, but upon whom she felt totally dependent and whom she could not give up. She had idealized him for years, and regarded her involvement with him as a triumph, since she had never really had a "boyfriend" before. She felt incapable of doing virtually anything for herself, relying on him, her roommate, or her best friend for help with many of the practical aspects of her life.

Or, of course, on her mother. She maintained a divided existence, spending some nights in her own apartment and some in her mother's—the latter rationalized on the ground that it was more convenient for her to come to her early morning treatment hours from her mother's home than from her own. She was beset with fears that her mother might die at any time and she would be left alone and helpless, and she had numerous rituals designed to ward off such thoughts. With her two-year younger sister she had a distant relationship; the latter figured little in her associations except as a sometime rival.

Much of the early work in treatment focused on her conflict about "breaking up" with Jim. Previous therapists had suggested she do so, but she could not. "Having him is like magic country," she said. "I don't know what would happen if I were alone—I'd probably be spaced out all the time." "My mother says I should hold on to him because it's terrible not to have a boyfriend." Her problems with concentration were in large measure the consequence of her immersion in fantasies about Jim or other idealized men. Jane's desperate clinging mirrored in many respects her relationship with her mother. Her profound separation fears represented the residues of unresolved ambivalent conflicts. She described her mother as cold, critical and unaffectionate, just as she did Jim. Her barely repressed rage at her mother seemed to me to be the legacy of her disappointment in the rapprochement period, when her efforts at establishing contact were met with rebuff or criticism. This served to intensify her feelings of helplessness and desperate need. It was as though she were involved in a continuous effort to establish a rapprochement position, from which she could move out into the world for brief periods, only to return for more support to the maternal object— mother, friend, roommate, therapist, Jim. In maintaining her attachment, she was able to cling to an illusion of magical, omnipotent control, without which she felt like a helpless, incompetent toddler.

From the therapist she expected magical intervention requiring no active efforts toward change on her own part, even to the extent of taking prescribed medication, which she usually "forgot" to do. Recurrently she accused me of acts of negligence or attitudes of disinterest or indifference, seemingly reactivating in the transference what she had experienced as her mother's affective unavailability in the rapprochement period. It emeged that she had a long-standing fantasy of being placed in a hospital, where she would be given "extensive therapy," that is, where she would be totally cared for.

Jane's "talking problem" remains an obscure and puzzling symptom. It is a fact, however, that the development of speech is roughly coterminous with the rapprochement subphase; indeed, speech is one of the primary means through which the process of rapprochement and its resolution—what McDevitt (1975) has called the "rapprochement crisis"—is carried on. In her quasi-hallucinatory distortions of both the visual and auditory aspects of speech, it seems possible that she might be projectively reproducing the experienced distortions of her own and her mother's speech in the angry, tormented exchanges of the rapprochement period. Such a reconstruction is unverifiable, at least at this time, but it has, for me at least, a measure of plausibility. It is certain that, as Sander (1978) has pointed out, the fate of the entire symbolic process is founded on the events of this early period; it is striking how for this borderline adolescent it is precisely the symbolic functions that are most grossly impaired.

Mahler (1971) has stated that "there is no direct line from the deductive use of borderline phenomena to one or another substantive finding of observational research." As I have suggested earlier, we deal here largely with analogies, rather than identities. The borderline adolescent reveals in his mental organization—or lack of organization—a bewildering range of regressions, fixations, developmental arrests, precocities, and islands of normality that bespeak a developmental process which, however skewed, makes him a far different organism from the "junior toddler" of Mahler's observations. Meissner's (1978) recent penetrating review of the literature on the borderline syndrome defines both the gains and the losses in considering it from the developmental (and other) perspectives.

It will be apparent that much of what I have discussed here is congruent in some respects with ideas presented by others—notably, Masterson (1973, 1977), Masterson and Rinsley (1975), and most recently, Edward Shapiro (1978) whose excellent review of the borderline syndrome merits careful study. Masterson and Rinsley have delineated what they consider to be a characteristic mode of mother-child interaction in the borderline syndrome.

> The borderline child has a mother with whom there is a unique and uninterrupted interaction with a specific relational focus, i.e., reward for regression, withdrawal for separation-individuation . . . the mother's withdrawal of her libidinal availability in the face of her child's efforts towards separation-individuation creates the leitmotif of the borderline child . . . the mother is available if the child clings and behaves regressively, but withdraws if he attempts to separate and individuate . . . [p. 167].

In my view, this picture comes dangerously close to what I have called "mother-baiting." The mother emerges as the unvarnished villain of the piece in this work, rewarding clinging submission, punishing separation-individuation, immersed in the satisfaction of her own narcissistic needs. That this may at times be a fair portrait cannot be denied, but Jane is typical of a group of borderline adolescents whose histories strongly suggest significant intrinsic deviations in the range of minimal cerebral dysfunction that have contributed substantially to the disturbed mother-child interactions. Jane is a virtual nonreader, in all probability a grown-up dyslexic (confirmed by psychological testing). This represents another aspect of the disturbance in her symbolic functions. Winnicott (1965) speaks of the normal infant's capacity, often in the face of massive traumatization, to derive enough "goodness" from the mother-child relationship to develop coherent self- and object images. This capacity, it would appear, Jane lacked; she could not extract from her mother's erratic behavior those elements of "goodness" that might have countered her own intrinsic tendencies toward object-splitting, unresolved ambivalence and self-fragmentation. It is the child's experience (Escalona 1963) of his interactions with the mother, not the mother's "actual" behavior, that is crucial for the laying down of self- and object representations in the separation-individuation phase; it is this process, not, as Masterson and Rinsley would seem to suggest, a person, that miscarries in the pathogenesis of borderline disorders.

Mahler and Kaplan (1977) and Kaplan (this volume, chapter 3) have sought to counter the tendency, explicit in Masterson's work

(1977), to identify specific diagnostic entities with specific subphase deviations. To quote Masterson,

> If the arrest occurs in the symbiotic phase, the self- and object representations are fused, and the patient's ego defenses are those of the psychotic. . . . The clinical diagnosis is schizophrenia.
>
> If the arrest occurs in the separation-individuation phase, the self- and object representations are separate but split into a good and bad object and self-representation. The ego defenses are still primitive. . . . The clinical diagnosis is borderline personality organization.
>
> If the arrest occurs late in the on-the-way-to-constancy phase or in the early phallic-oedipal phase, the self- and object representations are separate and whole rather than split. . . . Ego defenses are more mature. . . . The clinical diagnosis is psychoneurosis [pp. 446-477].

In challenging this categorical linkage of the borderline syndrome with the resolution of the separation-individuation phase in general and the "rapprochement crisis" in particular, Mahler and Kaplan emphasize the need to consider "subphase adequacy" on all levels. Kaplan seeks to relate subphase disturbances to Spitz's classic definition of "psychic organizers," and proposes to extend his concept beyond the three which he proposed—differentiation of self and object, recognition of the mother as a specific object, and the development of speech—to a fourth, the oedipus complex which, she contends, has crucial developmental impact on the formation of all human personalities, including the borderline.

One cannot, I acknowledge, seriously quarrel with these formulations or differ with Mahler and Kaplan's wish to avoid oversimplifications, dogmatic and simplistic one-to-one correlations, and exaggerated emphases.

Nonetheless, we have long been familiar with the concepts, imported into psychoanalytic developmental theory from embryology, of "epigenesis" and "critical periods." The idea that earlier "subphase inadequacy" will modify the evolution of later subphases and will cast a shadow on the oedipal configuration is, in essence, a restatement of the concept of epigenesis and, though a salutary reminder, adds nothing new to what is already known. That the oedipal crisis is central to psychic development is, of course, an article of psychoanalytic faith, and deserves restatement at a time when "separate developmental lines" and separate psychologies of the "self" are being advanced in some quarters and preoedipal development is, pendulum-fashion, being accorded what may be disproportionate attention. But we have long been accustomed to associate specific pathological formations with fixations at or regressions to particular developmental phases in the psychosexual line—for example, obsessional disorders with anal fixations—and have, therefore, come to view certain phase developments as *critical* ones. It does not, therefore, seem either artificial or grossly oversimplifying to propose as a heuristic hypothesis that the separation-individuation phase, and, specifically, the rapprochement subphase, may be such a critical period for the development—or transcendence—of borderline pathology, recognizing that on the one hand the transactions of this subphase will in part be shaped by the experience of earlier subphases, and that, on the other, they will color the child's manner and timing of entry into, experience of, and emergence from the oedipus complex. A growing body of clinical data, such as those presented here, would seem to lend support to this proposition.

Indeed, such cases as these demonstrate, I believe, the value of Mahler's conceptual framework for the psychiatric study and care of adolescents. Particularly in those cases of severe pathology with major elements of preoedipal fixation and regression, the specificity of her scheme of separation-individuation subphases often allows for a precise delineation of the locus of trauma and for a detailed prescription of object-related remedial intervention. It is through the processes she has so graphically described—differentiation, practicing, rapprochement, development of object constancy—that, in the felicitous title of her recent magnum opus, "the psychological birth of the human infant" occurs. Adolescence offers, as Blos has said, a "second chance" to rework some of the unfinished business not only of the oedipal conflicts but of some of these earlier developmental issues as well.

One must note a disposition in some quarters to designate such object-related conceptualizations as "social psychology," reserving the accolade "depth psychology" for formulations concerning the organization and experience of a "self system." Such invidious dismissals do not, I think, do justice to the richness and subtlety of Mahler's elaboration of the representational world of the child, or to the solid grounding of her observational research in hypotheses derived from clinical psychoanalysis. One is constrained, too, to recall Loewald's (1973) observation that "object-libidinal and narcissistic issues . . . are frequently blended or intermingled in such a way that each can be expressed in terms of the other, and it will depend on one's clinical acumen"—or, I should say, one's preconceptions—"whether one or the other aspect is chosen for interpretation" (p. 448). In any event, it is only through open clinical inquiry that we can, ultimately, assess these questions.

References

Blos, P. (1968). Character formation in adolescence. *Psychoanalytic Study of the Child* 23:245-263.

Escalona, P. (1963). Patterns of infantile experience and the developmental process. *Psychoanalytic Study of the Child* 18:197-203.

Gradolph, P. (1978). Developmental vicissitudes of the self and ego-ideal during adolescence. Presented at the Fall Meeting, American Psychoanalytic Association, New York.

Kaplan, L. (1978). Rapprochement and oedipal organization: Effects on borderline phenomena. This volume, chapter 3.

Loewald, H. (1973). Review of Kohut's *The Analysis of the Self. Psychoanalytic Quarterly* 42:441-451.

Mahler, M. (1971). A study of the separation-individuation process and its possible application to borderline phenomena in the psychoanalytic situation, *Psychoanalytic Study of the Child* 26:403-424. Reprinted in *The Selected Papers of Margaret S. Mahler*, vol. 2, ch. 11. New York: Jason Aronson, 1979.

Mahler, M., and Kaplan, L. (1977). Developmental aspects in the assessment of narcissistic and so-called borderline personalities. In *Borderline Personality Disorders*, ed. P. Hartocollis, pp. 71-86. New York: International Universities Press. Reprinted in *Selected Papers*, op. cit., ch. 13.

Mahler, M., Pine, F., and Bergman, A. (1975). *The Psychological Birth of the Human Infant.* New York: Basic Books.

Masterson, J. (1968). The psychiatric significance of adolescent turmoil. In *The Psychology of Adolescence*, ed. A. H. Esman, pp. 221-228. New York: International Universities Press, 1975.

——— (1973). The borderline adolescent. In *Adolescent Psychiatry*, vol. 2, ed. S. Feinstein and P. Giovacchini, pp. 240-268. New York: Basic Books.

——— (1977). Primary anorexia nervosa in the borderline adolescent: an object-relations view. In *Borderline Personality Disorders*, ed. P. Hartocollis, pp. 473-494. New York: International Universities Press.

Masterson, J., and Rinsley, D. (1975). The borderline syndrome: the role of the mother in the genesis and structure of the borderline personality. *International Journal of Psycho-Analysis* 56:163-177.

McDevitt, J. (1975). Separation-individuation and object constancy. *Journal of the American Psychoanalytic Association* 23:713-742.

Meissner, W. (1978). Theoretical assumptions of concepts of the borderline personality. *Journal of the American Psychoanalytic Association* 26:559-598.

Sander, L. (1978). New perspectives in early development: behavioral analysis twenty years later. The David M. Levy Memorial Lecture of the Association for Psychoanalytic Medicine, New York, October 3, 1978.

Schafer, R. (1973). Concepts of self and identity and the experience of separation-individuation in adolescence. *Psychoanalytic Quarterly* 42:42-59.

Shapiro, E. (1978). The psychodynamics and developmental psychology of the borderline patient: a review of the literature. *American Journal of Psychiatry* 135:1305-1315.

Winnicott, D. W. (1965). The effect of psychotic parents on the emotional development of the child. In *The Family and Individual Development*, pp. 69-78. New York: Basic Books.

16

The Borderline Syndrome: The Role of the Mother in the Genesis and Psychic Structure of the Borderline Personality

JAMES F. MASTERSON, M.D. AND DONALD B. RINSLEY, M.D.

The psychoanalytic literature is equivocal concerning the extent of the mother's role in the etiology of the developmental arrest peculiar to the borderline patient. Kernberg (1966, 1967, 1968, 1970a, b, 1971a, b, 1972) minimizes the role of the mother and emphasizes constitutional factors. Mahler (1953, 1963, 1965, 1968, 1971, 1972), Mahler and Furer (1963), Mahler and LaPerriere (1965), Mahler and McDevitt (1968) and Mahler, Pine, and Bergman (1970) stress the vital contribution of the mother's libidinal availability to normal ego development. Although she urges caution in drawing inferences concerning adult psychopathology based upon observations of childhood developmental phenomena, Mahler (1972) notes that there is considerable clinical evidence in support of the inference that the ego fixation of the borderline individual occurs during the rapprochement subphase (16-25 months) of separation-individuation, and in a case illustration she has pointed out the central theme of the patient's search for reunion with the "good symbiotic mother."

This paper describes the role of the mother's faulty libidinal availability in the development of the borderline syndrome. It describes

Reprinted from *International Journal of Psycho-Analysis* 56 (1975):163-177.

in terms of object relations theory the effects of alternating maternal libidinal availability and withdrawal, at the time of separation-individuation (rapprochement subphase), upon the development of the psychic structure of the borderline patient—the *split ego* and the *split object relations unit* (Fairbairn 1952, Guntrip 1961, 1969, Klein 1935, 1946, Parens and Saul 1971, Rinsley 1968, 1971a,b). It then demonstrates how these find expression and proceed to function in the therapeutic alliance, and in transference and resistance.

KERNBERG'S CONTRIBUTION TO THE OBJECT RELATIONS THEORY OF NORMAL DEVELOPMENT

Object relations theory may be defined as the psychoanalytic approach to the internalization of interpersonal relations (Kernberg 1971a). Kernberg (1972) postulates four stages in the development of normal internalized object relations. The earliest stage of development, roughly coincident with the first postnatal month of life, precedes the establishment of the primary, undifferentiated self-object constellation built up in the infant under the influence of his pleasurable, gratifying experiences in his interactions with the mother (Jacobson 1964). The second stage, roughly occupying the first to the third postnatal months, comprises the establishment and consolidation of an undifferentiated self-object image or representation (Jacobson 1964) of a libidinally gratifying or rewarding (= "good") type under the organizing influence of gratifying experiences within the context of the mother-child unit; concomitantly, a separate, primitive intrapsychic structure, comprising an undifferentiated "bad" self-object representation, is built up under the influence of frustrating and painful (i.e., traumatogenic) psychophysiological states. Thus, two sets of opposite primitive self-object-affect complexes are built up and fixed by memory traces as polar opposite intrapsychic structures. The third stage is reached when the self-image and the object image have become differentiated within the core "good" self-object representation; the differentiation of self-image from object-image within the core "bad" self-object representation occurs later and is complicated by early forms of projection, that is, intrapsychic mechanisms which attempt to externalize the "bad" self-object constellation (Kernberg 1966, Rinsley 1968, Spitz and Wolf 1946). This stage is said to occupy the period between the fourth postnatal month and the end of the first year. The fourth stage has its inception at some point between the end of the first year of life and the second half of the second year and continues to evolve throughout the remainder of childhood. During this stage, "good" and "bad" self images coalesce into an integrated self-concept; in other words, self-images establish coherence and continuity under the impact of polar opposite emotional-interpersonal experiences; affects become integrated, toned down and undergo further differentiation, and the child's self-concept and his actual presentation of behavior in the social field become closer. At the same time, "good" and "bad" object images also coalesce such that the "good" and the "bad" images of mother become integrated into a whole-object maternal concept which closely approaches the actuality or reality of the mother in the child's perceptual-interpersonal field.

Kernberg (1972) emphasizes the progressively integrative aspects of these stages for both ego and superego development, for the establishment of ego identity and for the development of the capacity for deep and consistent relationships with other persons.

KERNBERG AND THE EGO FIXATION OF THE BORDERLINE SYNDROME

Kernberg theorizes that the fixation peculiar to the borderline syndrome takes place during the third stage of this developmental scheme, when there yet remains a dissociation of libidinally determined (= "good") from aggressively determined (= "bad") self- and object representations, that is, "good" self- and object representations and "bad" self- and object representations are perceived as separate and unrelated.[1] He then outlines the structural consequences of this fixation, which determine the clinical manifestations of the borderline (Kernberg 1967, 1968): pathological persistence of the primitive defense of splitting; failure of development of

---

1. It will be evident that Kernberg's and Mahler's timing of the occurrence of the fixation underlying borderline personality development differ significantly, the former citing the period of 4-12 months and the latter the period of the "rapprochement subphase", coinciding with 16-25 months postnatally. No attempt will be made here to choose between these two differing schedules, although the preponderance of evidence would appear to be more favorable to Mahler's timing.

an integrated self-concept; chronic overdependence upon external objects; development of contradictory character traits in relation to contradictory ego states, resulting in chaotic interpersonal relationships. Superego integration suffers as a result of failure of the guiding function of an integrated ego identity, with persistent contradiction between exaggerated "ideal" object images and extremely sadistic "all bad" superego forerunners. Failure of development of an integrated object representation inhibits and ultimately limits development of the capacity for understanding of, and empathy for, other persons.[2] Ego strength depends in particular upon the neutralization of "raw" energies which occurs in intimate connection with the process of integration of libidinally derived (= "good") and aggressively derived (= "bad") self- and object images, and it is precisely this integration which fails to occur in future borderline personalities. Failure of neutralization in turn compromises specific aspects of ego strength, including anxiety tolerance, control of impulses and the potential for true sublimations (Rinsley 1968).

Kernberg's view of the etiology of this failure places predominant emphasis upon constitutional factors—an excess of oral aggression, a deficency in the capacity to neutralize aggression, or a lack of anxiety tolerance (Kernberg 1966):

> More characteristic for the borderline personality organization may be a failure related to a constitutionally determined lack of anxiety tolerance interfering with the phase of synthesis of introjections of opposite valences. The most important cause of failure in the borderline pathology is probably a quantitative predominance of negative introjections. Excessive negative introjections may stem both from a constitutionally determined intensity of aggressive drive derivatives and from severe early frustration.

A predominantly heredo-congenital view of the etiology of the

2. Associated failure to develop an integrated self-representation and an integrated object representation, normally accomplished during stage 4, may be viewed in terms of failure of development of whole-object relations from antecedent part-object relations. It may be noted that developmental fixation at stage 3 corresponds with fixation at Fairbairn's late oral stage of infantile dependence (Fairbairn 1952), during which the (maternal) whole object is characteristically perceived and treated as part object (breast). The borderline's cathexis of whole objects *as if they were part objects* leads in turn to a welter of later interpersonal depersonifications and appersonations elsewhere described (Rinsley 1971b).

developmental failure peculiar to the borderline personality would emphasize the infant's *a priori* propensity to form preponderantly negative introjections, which Mahler (1968) considers to be typical in infantile psychosis. Although, as Weil (1970) has recently stated, there is considerable evidence for a wide range of "basic core" variation, predominantly heredo-constitutional views can readily lead to underestimation of the importance of the mother's libidinal availability to the infant during the developmentally critical period of separation-individuation, which occupies the period from six to thirty months postnatally.

GENESIS OF THE FIXATION OF THE BORDERLINE: NATURE-NURTURE OR CONSTITUTION-EXPERIENCE

In discussing this often polemical issue with respect to infantile psychosis, Mahler (1968) suggests the complementary relationship between nature and nurture. She states:

> If, during the most vulnerable autistic and symbiotic phase, very severe, accumulated, and staggering traumatization occurs in a constitutionally fairly sturdy infant, psychosis may ensue. . . . On the other hand, in constitutionally greatly predisposed, oversensitive or vulnerable infants, normal mothering does not suffice to counteract the innate defect in the catalytic, buffering, and polarizing utilization of the human love object or mothering agency in the outside world for intrapsychic evolution and differentiation [p. 48].

Mahler clearly avers that, in her view, constitutional defect serves as the basis for infantile psychosis, the victims of which she describes as lacking or failing to acquire the capacity to internalize the representation of the mothering object as a guide for the differentiation of inner from external stimulation.

The presence of excessive oral aggression in the borderline leads Kernberg to favor a constitutional etiology for the borderline syndrome. Although undue degrees of oral aggression do indeed characterize the borderline individual, their presence does not *per se* justify a purely or predominantly constitutional view of borderline psychopathology, and Kernberg adduces no other evidence in support of his view. There is, to be sure, a parallel deficiency of libidinal cathexis of both self- and object representations which could as likely lead to a theory of deficiency of libidinal energy, constitutional or otherwise, a view originally put forward by Federn (1952) (Rinsley 1968). The issue becomes largely academic, however, in view of incontrovertible clinical evidence, drawn from reconstructive analytic psychotherapy and from intensive residential treatment, that both adolescent and adult borderlines demonstrate a full capacity for internalization once their abandonment depression has been worked through (Masterson 1971 1972; 1976 Rinsley 1965, 1971a,b).

Our contention is that the determining cause of the fixation of the borderline individual is to be found in the mother's withdrawal of her libidinal availability (i.e., of her libidinal supplies) as the child makes efforts towards separation-individuation during the rapprochement subphase;[3] and further that the fixation comes into existence at exactly that time because the child's individuation constitutes a major threat to the mother's defensive need to cling to her infant and, as a consequence, drives her toward removal of her libidinal availability.[4]

The twin themes *(reward* and *withdrawal)* of this interaction are subsequently introjected by the child, become the leitmotif of his psychic structure and reappear in his pathologic split self- and object representations as these are recapitulated within the therapeutic transference.

3. The normal developmental vicissitudes of the rapprochement subphase—i.e., the surge of individuation accompanying the acquisition of locomotion and speech as well as the increased awareness of the separateness from the mother which triggers the child's increased sensitivity and need for the mother—become unique vulnerabilities for the borderline child. The very surge of individuation which brings with it a greater need for the mother's support, actually induces withdrawal of that support—i.e., the vital process in which he is engaged produces the withdrawal that arrests that process and results in the stereotypical clinical pattern—individuation, depression, defense.

4. The early mother-child interaction is so complex yet so fateful for a child's development that it is both difficult and hazardous to try to tease out principal themes which can be generalized. Nevertheless, the stereotyped repetition of maladaptive themes in our patient's lives and in the transference impels us to undertake this task, in spite of its hazards and limitations, in the hope of unraveling some of its mysteries. It is essential if we are to understand our patient's problems and their therapeutic needs.

Since publication of this article in 1975 the point of view expressed above has been broadened as follows. The basic issue is the mother's libidinal unavailability to the

In view of these considerations, it may be argued that the child's excessive oral aggression becomes entrenched in consequence of the mother's withdrawal of supplies in the wake of the child's efforts toward separation-individuation, further aggravated by the latter's inability to integrate positive and negative self- and object representations, since such integration would require further separation-individuation, which in turn would provoke further withdrawal of maternal libidinal supplies. There thus comes about a situation in which aggression is repetitively provoked without any constructive means conducive to its neutralization.

MAHLER AND THE ROLE OF THE LIBIDINAL AVAILABILITY OF THE MOTHER IN THE DEVELOPMENT OF NORMAL OBJECT RELATIONS

Mahler's work is replete with references to the fundamental importance of the mother's libidinal availability for the development of normal object relations. In discussing Hartmann's view that infantile psychosis results from a defect in the ego's capacity for drive neutralization with ensuing interference with the development of other ego functions and of object relations, she states:

child's need for supplies for separation-individuation. In most of our patients that unavailability was due to the specific nature of the tie between the mother and that particular child—i.e., the mother's need to extend specific regressive projections on the child to defend herself against an abandonment depression. The child's individuation interfered with these projections, and exposed the mother to an abandonment depression and impelled her to withdraw as a defense.

We emphasized the unique, intimate and specific nature of that tie by stating that the mother had a borderline syndrome herself and required the child's compliance with her projections to defend against an abandonment depression. Although most of our mothers were, indeed, borderline, it now appears that mothers with even more serious disorders, including psychosis, can have a similar effect since they could also be libidinally unavailable for separation-individuation needs. Theoretically, this would also apply to mothers who are depressed as well as to those who are physically absent during this crucial period. The key issue again is the mother's libidinal unavailability for these needs which itself may be due to a variety of causes. The child would respond to the unavailability as an absence or withdrawal of a vital need and introject it as a withdrawing maternal part object. Nevertheless, the relationship stands out with the most clarity where the specific tie can be identified.

My theory places special emphasis, however, on the interaction of both these factors with the circular processes between infant and mother, in which the mother serves as a beacon of orientation and living buffer for the infant, in reference to both external reality and his internal milieu [1968, p. 229].

She also writes:

During the course of the normal separation-individuation process, the predominance of pleasure in separate functioning, in an atmosphere in which the mother is emotionally available, enables the child to overcome that measure of separation anxiety that makes its appearance at that point of the separation-individuation phase at which a differentiated object representation, separate from the self, gradually enters conscious awareness . . . [pp. 220-221].

In a quasi-closed system or unit, the mother executes vitally important ministrations, without which the human young could not survive. The intrauterine, parasite-host relationship within the mother organism . . . must be replaced in the postnatal period by the infant's being enveloped, as it were, in the extrauterine matrix of the mother's nursing care, a kind of *social symbiosis*. . . .
    The mutual cuing between infant and mother is the most important requisite for normal symbiosis . . . [p. 34].

It is the mother's love of the toddler and her acceptance of his ambivalence that enable the toddler to cathect his self-representation with neutralized energy [p. 222].

The question concerning the manner in which the mother's libidinal availability determines the development of the child's intrapsychic structure is answerable in terms of the child's internalization of his interactions with her to form self- and object representations, the nature of which will have profound consequences for ego integration (Jacobson 1964, Kernberg 1972, Mahler 1968). Functioning according to the pleasure principle, which both comprises and determines his initial orientation in the extrauterine field, the infant will draw away, or will attempt to expel or eliminate in the face of painful or unpleasurable interactions with the mother. Of critical importance, especially in early infancy, is the equation, *"good"* = *pleasurable* = *minimally stimulating*, as well as the equation, *"bad"* = *unpleasurable (painful)* = *overstimulating (traumatogenic)*, as they apply to the quality of the mother-infant interactions. These interactions are introjected to form scattered "good" and "bad" memory islands which proceed to integrate into the progressively differentiated self- and object images which Kernberg (1966) has described.[5]

Mahler articulates the mother's role as follows:

> It is the specific unconscious need of the mother that activates, out of the infant's infinite potentialities, those in particular that create for each mother "the child" who reflects her own *unique* and individual needs. This process takes place, of course, within the range of the child's innate endowments.
>
> Mutual cuing during the symbiotic phase creates that indelibly imprinted configuration—that complex pattern—that becomes *the leitmotif for "the infant's becoming the child of his particular mother"* . . .
>
> In other words, the mother conveys—in innumerable ways—a kind of "mirroring frame of reference," to which the primitive self of the infant automatically adjusts [1968, p. 19].

Mahler suggests the possible developmental consequences of the mother's libidinal unavailability to the infant. She asserts that in instances in which the mother in fantasy or in actuality fails of acceptance of the infant, the latter experiences a deficit in self-esteem and a consequent narcissistic vulnerability. She goes on to say:

> If the mother's "primary preoccupation" with her infant—*her* mirroring function during earlier infancy—is unpredictable, unstable, anxiety-ridden, or hostile; if her confidence in herself as a mother is shaky, then the individuating child has to do without a reliable frame of reference for checking back, perceptually and emotionally, to the symbiotic partner. . . . The result will then be a disturbance in the primitive "self feeling". . . . [1968, p. 19].

On the other hand, while emphasizing the importance of the mother's libidinal availability for optimal infantile ego development,

---

5. It should be noted here that, with reference to mother-infant interactions during the first postnatal year, and in particular during its first half, the term *mother* in fact has reference to the maternal part object (breast); thus the term *mother* is used here in this connection for convenience and simplicity.

Mahler also points out the normal infant's striking capacity to extract supplies from any available human contact. In support of this view, she cites Spitz's (1945, 1946, 1965) investigation of infants who experienced the loss of a symbiotic love object during the second half of the first year; although the infants perished if a substitute object was not found, they recovered when one was found.

Mahler also cites studies of children who spent their first year of life in a concentration camp (A. Freud and Dann 1951); she states: "While these experiences left their traces on these children's object relationships, the children developed strong ties to each other and none of them suffered from a childhood psychosis" (1968, p. 50). She further cites Goldfarb's (1945) studies of children placed in foster homes who

> amidst the most trying circumstances . . . were able to extract, as it were, substitutions for the actual loss of mothering. Although they may have paid the price for this object loss with neurotic disorders, character distortions, or psychopathic difficulties later in life, they *never* severed their ties with reality [1968, pp. 50-51].

Mahler's cited evidence may be adduced in support of her argument for a constitutional etiology for infantile psychosis, since the children studied did not develop such severe psychopathology despite having been subjected to severe stress, particularly as a result of having been deprived of their mothers. On the other hand, her evidence may indeed be taken as favorable to the concept of an environmental etiology of the borderline, particularly in view of her suggestion that these same children might well have later developed neurotic-characterological disorders typical for borderline personalities.

It is, in fact, impossible to compare the children reported on in these cited studies (A. Freud and Dann 1951, Goldfarb 1945, Spitz 1946, 1965) with borderline children. The former had lost their mothers at an early age and were subsequently able to "find" substitutes for them. *On the other hand, the borderline child has a mother with whom there is a unique and uninterrupted interaction with a specific relational focus, that is, reward for regression, withdrawal for separation-individuation.* As we shall attempt to show in what follows, the unique "push-pull" quality of this sort of mother-infant interaction becomes powerfully introjected and forms the basis for the progressive development of the borderline syndrome.

THE ROLE OF THE MOTHER'S LIBIDINAL AVAILABILITY IN THE DEVELOPMENT OF THE PSYCHIC STRUCTURE OF THE BORDERLINE

The mother's withdrawal of her libidinal availability in the face of her child's efforts toward separation-individuation creates the leitmotif of the borderline child, with the result that the child becomes the unique child of the borderline mother. The borderline mother, herself suffering from a borderline syndrome, experiences significant gratification during her child's symbiotic phase. The crisis supervenes at the time of separation-individuation, specifically during the rapprochement subphase, when she finds herself unable to tolerate her toddler's ambivalence, curiosity, and assertiveness; the mutual cuing and communicative matching to these essential characteristics of individuation fail to develop. The mother is available if the child clings and behaves regressively, but withdraws if he attempts to separate and individuate. The child needs the mother's supplies in order to grow; if he grows, however, they are withdrawn from him (Masterson 1971, 1972, 1976). The images of these two mothers are as it were powerfully introjected by the child as part-object representations together with their associated affects and self-representations. Thus is generated the *split object relations unit,* to which later reference will be made, which forms so important a part of the intrapsychic structure of the borderline case.

The evidence in support of this formulation and of what follows in greater detail is derived from several sources (Masterson 1971a,b, 1972a,b, Rinsley 1965, 1971a,b):

Observation. (a) Casework-family therapy on a once- or twice-weekly basis, for as long as four years, of the parents of in-patient and out-patient borderline adolescents; *(b)* Treatment of borderline mothers in private office practice; *(c)* Detailed observation and study of borderline mothers in conjoint interviews with their borderline adolescent children; *(d)* Long-term, intensive residential psychiatric treatment of borderline adolescents.

Reconstruction. The memories and associated affective responses of borderline adolescents in intensive psychotherapy as they worked through their underlying abandonment depression.

INTRAPSYCHIC STRUCTURE
OF THE BORDERLINE

As noted before, the terms "split ego" and "split object relations unit" are employed to define and describe the intrapsychic structure typical for the borderline personality; these terms require further definition.

Splitting (Kernberg 1967). Splitting is a mechanism of defense, the function of which is to keep contradictory primitive affective states separated from each other; the contradictory states remain in consciousness but do not mutually influence each other. Splitting also keeps apart the internalized self- and object representations mutually linked with these affective states. Used normally by the immature ego, splitting ordinarily becomes replaced or supplanted by repression. The ego of the borderline, however, retains splitting as its principal mechanism of defense, while the capacity for normal repression remains underdeveloped.

Split ego (Kernberg 1967). Along with its reliance upon the splitting defense, the ego of the borderline is itself split into two parts, one of which functions according to the pleasure principle, and the other according to the reality principle.

Split object relations unit (Kernberg 1972). The object relations unit is derived from internalization of the infant's interactions with the mothering object. The unit comprises a self-representation, an object representation, and an affective component which links them together.[6] The object relations unit of the borderline turns out to be split into two part-units, each of which in turn comprises a part self-representation and a part object representation together with their respective associated affects.

MATERNAL LIBIDINAL AVAILABILITY AND
THE SPLIT OBJECT RELATIONS UNIT

In the case of the borderline, the object relations unit remains split into two separate part-units, each of which comprises as it were a

---

6. The object relations unit, with its triadic representational-affective structure (Kernberg 1966) has been elsewhere defined as an ego state (Rinsley 1968).

part self-representation, a part object representation and an affective component which links the former two together. These two part-units are derived from internalization of the two principal themes of interaction with the borderline mother: the mother responds to the child's regressive behavior by maintaining her libidinal availability, and to the child's efforts toward separation-individuation by its withdrawal. Thus are produced, in effect, the two aforementioned part-units, which may be termed the *withdrawing part-unit* and the *rewarding part-unit*, each of which has its own component part self-representation, part object representation and predominantly linking affect; the withdrawing part-unit is cathected predominantly with aggressive energy, the rewarding part unit with libidinal energy, and both remain separated from each other, as it were, through the mechanism of the splitting defense. It will be recalled that this situation comes about through fixation at Kernberg's stage 3, with ensuing failure of integration of "good" (positive; libidinal) and "bad" (negative; aggressive) self- and object representations into whole (positive + negative) self-representations and object representations, which would otherwise be expected to have occurred during stage 4.

Table 1. *Summary of the borderline's split object relations unit*

Withdrawing or aggressive part-unit

Part object representation	Affect	Part self-representation
A maternal part object which is attacking, critical, hostile, angry, withdrawing supplies and approval in the face of assertiveness or other efforts toward separation-individuation	Chronic anger, frustration, feeling thwarted, which cover profound underlying abandonment depression	A part self-representation of being inadequate, bad, helpless; guilty, ugly, empty, etc.

REWARDING OR LIBIDINAL PART-UNIT

Part object representation	*Affect*	*Part self-representation*
A maternal part object which offers approval, support and supplies for regressive and clinging behavior	Feeling good, being fed, gratification of the wish for reunion	A part self-representation of being the good, passive, compliant child

The borderline's split object relations unit is summarized in Table 1.[7]

MATERNAL LIBIDINAL AVAILABILITY AND THE SPLIT EGO

Freud (1911) originally emphasized that in the beginning the child's behavior, under the domination of the primary process, is motivated by the pleasure principle, that is, to seek pleasure and to avoid pain. Governed "by the peremptory demands of internal needs" the child originally made use of hallucination to provide for their satisfaction. Freud added, however, that

> It was only the non-occurrence of the expected satisfaction, the disappointment experienced, that led to the abandonment of this attempt at satisfaction by means of hallucination. Instead of it, the psychical apparatus had to decide to form a conception of the real alteration in them. A new principle of mental functioning was thus introduced; what was presented in the mind was no longer what was agreeable but what was real, even if it happened to be disagreeable. This setting-up of the *reality principle* proved to be a momentous step.

Freud proceeds to trace the development of the use of the sense organs, perception, memory, consciousness and thought as agencies

7. The reader will immediately discern the similarity of the split object relations unit to Fairbairn's split internalized bad object, and Fairbairn deserves full prior credit for having perceived its basic structure in his analysands. Thus the withdrawing part-unit may be seen to correspond with Fairbairn's *rejecting object* (R.O.) while the rewarding part-unit may be seen to correspond with his *exciting object* (E.O.).

of the developing ego's capacity for reality testing. He goes on to say: "Just as the pleasure-ego can do nothing but *wish*, work for a yield of pleasure, and avoid unpleasure, so the reality-ego need do nothing but strive for what is *useful* and guard itself against damage." Of central importance is Freud's emphasis upon the gradual transformation of the pleasure ego into the reality ego in the wake of the child's increasing experience with the failure of hallucinatory wishfulfilment.

In the case of the borderline individual, the term *split ego* has reference to a persistent stunting of ego development such that a substantial part of the pleasure ego fails to undergo the expected transformation into the reality ego, with resultant pathological persistence of the former; thus a large part of the ego of the borderline continues, in effect, under the domination of the pleasure principle. It should be emphasized that, in the case of the borderline, the concept of ego splitting implies, not that a previously formed structure had undergone regressive splitting, but rather that a coherently functioning ego, operating in accordance with the reality principle, had failed to develop. Thus that part of the ego which Freud termed the pleasure ego could, in the case of the borderline individual, be termed the *pathological ego*, while the "remainder" could be termed the *reality* or *healthy ego*.

It is necessary now to inquire into the basis for the persistence of the pathological (pleasure) ego in these cases. To begin with, the future borderline child finds himself caught between his genetically determined drive toward separation-individuation and the perceived threat of withdrawal of maternal supplies in the face of it. As the child's self-representation begins to differentiate from the object representation of the mother, that is, as the child begins to separate, he now experiences the abandoment depression[8] in the wake of the

---

8. As here employed, the term "abandonment depression" refers to the core affect structurally linked to the part self- and part object representations which together comprise the withdrawing (aggressive) part-unit. The subjective state conveyed by the term includes a core anxiety component and a more differentiated component. The former is of an instinctual quality and corresponds with the primal experience of impending loss of the maternal stimulus barrier against endopsychic and external stimulation, with ensuing gross ego trauma. The latter, more structuralized, conveys the feeling of guilt which signifies the ego's anxiety over impending "abandonment" or sadistic assault by the superego, also perceived as a threatened loss or withdrawal of supplies. The basic feelings common to the state of abandonment depression thus comprise *a profound sense of emptiness* and, as an aspect of estrangement, *a sense of the meaninglessness of the "external" world.*

threat of loss or withdrawal of supplies; at the same time, the mother continues to encourage and to reward those aspects of her child's behavior—passivity and regressiveness—which enable her to continue to cling to him.

Thus the mother encourages and rewards in the child the pathological ego's key defense mechanism of denial of the reality of separation, which in turn allows the *persistence of the wish for reunion, which later emerges as a defense against the abandonment depression*. Thus part of the ego fails to undergo the necessary transformation from reliance upon the pleasure principle to reliance upon the reality principle, for to do so would mean acceptance of the reality of separation, which would bring on the abandonment depression.

The mother's clinging and withdrawing and the patient's acting out of his wish for reunion promote the failure of one part of the ego to develop, resulting in an ego structure which is split into a pathological (pleasure) ego and a reality ego, the former pursuing relief from the feeling of abandonment, and the latter pursuing the reality principle. The pathological ego denies the reality of the separation, which permits the persistence of fantasies of reunion with the mother, which are then acted out through clinging and regressive behavior, thus defending against the abandonment depression and causing the patient to "feel good." Extensive fantasies of reunion are elaborated, projected on to the environment and acted out, accompanied by increasing denial of reality. The two, operating in concert, create an ever-widening chasm between the patient's feelings and the reality of his functioning as he gradually emerges from the developmental years into adulthood.

Again, it should be emphasized that such an arrest of ego development in all likelihood reflects, not a sudden or acute occurrence at the time of separation-individuation, but rather a persistent, ongoing developmental failure, dating possibly from the mother's ambivalence toward the infant's earliest moves toward differentiation at about four to five months postnatally.

THE RELATIONSHIP BETWEEN THE SPLIT OBJECT RELATIONS UNIT AND THE SPLIT EGO

As already noted, the splitting defense keeps separate the rewarding and the withdrawing object relations part-units, including their associated affects. Although both the rewarding and the withdrawing maternal part objects are pathological, the borderline experiences the rewarding part-unit as increasingly ego-syntonic, as it relieves the feelings of abandonment associated with the withdrawing part-unit, with the result that the individual "feels good." The affective state associated with the rewarding part-unit is that of gratification at being fed, hence "loved." The ensuing denial of reality is, in the last analysis, but a small price to pay for this affective state.

An alliance is now seen to develop between the child's rewarding maternal part-image (rewarding part-unit) and his pathological (pleasure) ego, the primary purpose of which is to promote the "good" feeling and to defend against the feeling of abandonment associated with the withdrawing part-unit. This ultimately powerful alliance as it were further promotes the denial of separateness and potentiates the child's acting out of his reunion fantasies. The alliance has an important secondary function, the discharge of aggression, which is both associated with and directed toward the withdrawing part-unit by means of symptoms, inhibitions, and various kinds of destructive acts. The aggression, which gains access to motility through the agency of the pathological (pleasure) ego, remains unneutralized, hence unavailable for the further development of endopsychic structure (Rinsley 1968).[9]

The withdrawing part-unit (part self-representation, part object representation and feelings of abandonment) becomes activated by actual experiences of separation (or of loss), as a result of the individual's efforts toward psychosocial growth, and by moves

9. Again, the reader will discern the similarity of these formulations to those of Fairbairn. Fairbairn originally postulated a splitting within the infantile ego in correspondence with the split internalized "bad" object, and in effect postulated an alliance between their parts. He postulated, on the one hand, an alliance between the *exciting object (E.O.)* and what he termed the *libidinal ego (L.E.)*, and another between the *rejecting object (R.O.)* and what he termed the *anti-libidinal ego (Anti-L.E.)*. The *E.O.-L.E.* alliance fairly directly corresponds with that, here presented, between the rewarding part-unit and the pathological (pleasure) ego. For Fairbairn, the *Anti-L.E.* came to represent the punitive, sadistic aspect of the superego, allied with the *R.O.* as a split mental structure. The view of mental structure here developed presents no structural components analogous with Fairbairn's *Anti-L.E.-R.O.* alliance, in part reflective of the fact that Fairbairn had not developed a concept of the tripartite object relations unit. His profound insights, however, deserve further efforts to explore the possible relationships amongst his basic structural formulations and those presented here.

toward separation-individuation within the therapeutic process, all of which *inter se alia* symbolize earlier life experiences which provoked the mother's withdrawal of supplies.

The alliance between the rewarding part-unit and the pathological (pleasure) ego is in turn activated by the resurgence of the withdrawing part-unit. The purpose of this operation, as it were, is defensive, that is, to restore the wish for reunion, thereby to relieve the feeling of abandonment. The rewarding part-unit thus becomes the borderline's principal defense against the painful affective state associated with the withdrawing part-unit. *In terms of reality, however, both part-units are pathological; it is as if the patient has but two alternatives, that is, either to feel bad and abandoned (withdrawing part-unit) or to feel good (rewarding part-unit), at the cost of denial of reality and self-destructive acting out.*

THERAPEUTIC CONSIDERATIONS

It is necessary now to consider the impact which this intrapsychic structure exerts upon therapeutic transference and resistance. In brief, the transference which the borderline develops results from the operation of the split object relations unit—the rewarding part-unit and the withdrawing part-unit—each of which the patient proceeds alternatively to project onto the therapist. During those periods in which the patient projects the withdrawing part-unit (with its part object representation of the withdrawing mother) on to the therapist, he perceives therapy as necessarily leading to feelings of abandonment, denies the reality of therapeutic benefit and activates the rewarding part-unit as a resistance. When projecting the rewarding part-unit (with its reunion fantasy) on to the therapist, the patient "feels good" but, under the sway of the pathological (pleasure) ego, is usually found to be acting in a self-destructive manner.

THE THERAPEUTIC ALLIANCE

The patient begins therapy feeling that the behavior motivated by the alliance between his rewarding part-unit and his pathological (pleasure) ego is ego-syntonic, that is, it makes him feel good. He is furthermore unaware of the cost to him, as it were, which is incurred through his denial of the reality of his self-destructive (and, of course, destructive) behavior.

The initial objective of the therapist is to render the functioning of this alliance ego-alien by means of confrontative clarification of its destructiveness. Insofar as this therapeutic maneuver promotes control of the behavior, the withdrawing part-unit becomes activated, which in turn reactivates the rewarding part-unit with the appearance of further resistance. There results a circular process, sequentially including resistance, reality clarification, working through of the feelings of abandonment (withdrawing part-unit), further resistance (rewarding part-unit) and further reality clarification, which leads in turn to further working through.

In those cases in which the circular working-through process proves successful, an alliance is next seen to develop between the therapist's healthy ego and the patient's embattled reality ego; this therapeutic alliance, formed through the patient's having internalized the therapist as a positive external object, proceeds to function counter to the alliance between the patient's rewarding part-unit and his pathological (pleasure) ego, battling with the latter, as it were, for ultimate control of the patient's motivations and actions.

The structural realignments which ensue in the wake of the working-through process may now be described. The repetitive projection of his rewarding and withdrawing part-units (with their component maternal part object representations) on to the therapist, together with the latter's interpretative confrontation thereof, gradually draws to the patient's conscious awareness the presence of these part-units within himself. Concomitantly, the developing alliance between the therapist's healthy ego and the patient's reality ego brings into existence, through introjection, a new object relations unit: the therapist as a positive (libidinal) object representation who approves of separation-individuation + a self-representation as a capable, developing person + a "good" feeling (affect) which ensues from the exercise of constructive coping and mastery rather than regressive behavior.

The working through of the encapsulated rage and depression associated with the withdrawing part-unit in turn frees its component part self- and part object representations from their intensely negative, aggressively valent affects. As a result, the new object relations unit (constructive self + "good" therapist + "good" affect) linked with the reality ego becomes integrated into an overall "good" self-representation, while the split object relations unit linked with the pathological (pleasure) ego becomes integrated into an overall "bad" self-representation; both are now accessible to the patient's conscious awareness as are their counterparts within the person of the therapist. At this point, the patient has begun in earnest the work of differentiating good and bad self-representations from good and bad object representations as prefatory to the next step, in which good and bad self-representations coalesce, as do good and bad object representations. The stage is now set for the inception of whole-object relations, which marks the patient's entrance into stage 4 (Kernberg 1972).

The de-linking, as it were, of "raw" instinctual energies from the rewarding and withdrawing part-units renders these energies increasingly available to the synthetic function associated with the patient's expanding reality ego, hence available for progressive neutralization. With this, and concomitant with the progressive coalescence of good-bad self- and object representations, splitting becomes replaced by normal repression, with progressive effacement, as it were, of the personified or "unmetabolized" images associated with the disappearing split object relations unit (Kernberg 1966). The patient is now able to complete the work of mourning for these "lost" images, which characterizes his final work of separation from the mother.

CLINICAL EXAMPLES

The following clinical examples illustrate the foregoing considerations, particularly the operation of the rewarding and withdrawing object relations part-units, the pathological (pleasure) ego and the therapeutic alliance.

A 27-year-old married woman, a college graduate with a successful career as a television actress, came to treatment with a depression against which she had been defending herself through drinking, abuse of drugs, and by having an affair. She complained that her husband did not care for her because he spent too much time at his work.

The patient's history included an alcoholic mother who spent most of her time sitting at home drinking, and who rewarded the patient, at least verbally, for passivity, inactivity, and regressive behavior but who withdrew whenever her daughter demonstrated any form of constructive behavior; for example, when the patient, as an adolescent, cooked a meal, the mother would withdraw and assume a critical attitude; the same ensued whenever the patient attractively decorated her room or had success at school.

In what follows the patient clearly describes the withdrawing maternal part-image, that is, the mother's withdrawal from the girl's assertiveness, activity or need to grow up, with the associated feelings of abandonment and the accompanying part self-representation of being bad, ugly, inadequate, unworthy. She also clearly reports the rewarding part-unit: a rewarding maternal part-image, feeling "good" and the self-image of a child who is taken care of. The mother's commands and the patient's behavior are thus linked together as the basis for the alliance between the rewarding part-unit and the pathological (pleasure) ego.

Therapeutic progress had activated the withdrawing part-unit, which in turn activated the rewarding part-unit as a defense, with the patient's behavior coming under the control of the pathological (pleasure) ego, that is, passivity, drinking, the affair. As the patient improved, as if despite herself, every step symbolized separation-individuation and proceeded to activate the withdrawing part-unit with its feelings of abandonment. She experienced her improvement as a loss, a frustration of the wish for reunion, and each time she improved she became resistant and hostile, projecting her anger at the mother's withdrawal on to the therapist and the therapeutic situation.

After a year of individual therapy three times a week, during which she had gained control over the behavior motivated by the alliance between the rewarding part-unit and the pathological (pleasure) ego, she reported, "This week I pulled myself more into reality. . . . I felt you had left me but told myself it wasn't true and the feelings went away. . . ." (Note in what follows, however, the activation of the withdrawing part-unit and attendant resistance.) "Yet today I don't want to tell you . . . I'd like to report that I was fucked up all weekend . . . I guess I felt healthy over the weekend. Last night I made a big drink but threw it out rather than drink it." (Note that the improvement brings on further resistance.) "I woke up angry at you this morning. . . . I recognize I'm doing better and I'm afraid you'll leave me. When my work went well one side of me was pleased" *(Note: rewarding part-unit.)* "The other side said why did I do that and I wanted to drink. I don't think I can maintain a mature way of living ... when I have to do something responsible one side of me says no and wants to go out and get drunk." *(Note: wish for reunion.)* "The better I do the more I want to hang on to the fantasies of lovers and drink." *(Note: withdrawing part-unit.)* "If I'm grown up, independent, on my own, I'll be all alone and abandoned."

A little later the patient reports that, in effect, the alliance between the rewarding part-unit and the pathological (pleasure) ego has become ego-alien: "I had a fight with my bad side—the baby. . . ." *(Note: the rewarding part-unit and the pathologic (pleasure) ego.)* "I was enjoying myself reading and it was as if I heard a little voice saying have a drink. I could feel myself turn off feeling, then I took a drink. The bad side is my mother's commands. . . . I'm ten years old and I can't decide myself . . . I have to follow the command but as I become aware of the command I can now disregard it and decide for myself."

In the next interview the patient reports, "I had two successes— each time it was as if I heard my mother's voice get started but each time I overcame it and went ahead." *(Again, however, control of the rewarding part-unit activates the withdrawing part-unit, which is then projected onto the therapist as a resistance maneuver.)* "I wasn't going to tell you today as you'd think I was better and act like my parents. If I get better you'll leave me. I worry about this, especially when you go on vacation. I feel you're leaving me because I'm doing better. My image of myself is of a person who drinks and has affairs, or of a young little girl who has to be taken care of."

As another example of how improvement had activated the withdrawing part-unit and produced resistance, the patient stated, "I didn't want to come today. I saw my old boyfriend. The baby side of me made me feel angry that I didn't want those old satisfactions. I don't want you to think I'm doing too well or I'll want to leave you . . . as if I want to get back at you . . . angry at you, you're doing this, making me better to get rid of me . . . I'm losing you. The baby side of me is angry that you think I can handle myself. Whenever I have five good days the baby side of me gets angry at you but I can't verbalize it or you'll leave me for sure! I like to sit here and say nothing just to piss you off! I see getting better as your withdrawing affection. Last night as I saw I had fixed up my apartment nicely I got furious at you.

Mother used to resent any creativity in me. . . . I never imagined verbalizing this anger at mother . . . fantasies and the feeling were all action—hitting, stabbing, killing her!"

As illustrated by this case, the alliance between the rewarding part-unit (rewarding maternal part object representation) and the pathological (pleasure) ego had as its objective the restoration of the wish for reunion and the relief of feelings of abandonment (separation anxiety and resultant rage), the latter being acted out, hence discharged in behavior. Thus aggression otherwise available to build intrapsychic structure gains access to motility via self-destructive behavior.

The second case example concerns a 20-year-old man who had dropped out of college because of severe depression and a work inhibition; he reported that he felt unable to perform, study, or even think. The patient's frankly paranoid mother had openly attacked him throughout childhood, both verbally and physically, for any assertion or expression of individuality; the father, rather than come to his son's aid, demanded that the boy submit to the mother's assaults as the price for the father's approval.

Analysis of the patient's withdrawing part-unit revealed the following structure: a part object representation consisting of a condensed image which included elements of the attacking mother and the withdrawing father; the predominant affect was, as expected, that of abandonment; the part self-representation was that of a person who had caused the abandonment, who had leprosy, was no good, inadequate, "crazy" and "bad." The rewarding part-unit included the affect of feeling "good" and the part self-representation of an obedient child, both dependent upon the pathological (pleasure) ego's use of avoidance, inhibition and passivity with denial of reality in pursuit of the wish for reunion. The patient's efforts to assert himself, to study and to learn activated the withdrawing part-unit, which in turn activated the rewarding part-unit, leading to the defensive use of avoidance, inhibition and passivity.

As the patient improved in treatment and attempted to resume studying he would block; however, he was now able to report the maternal part-image, the part self-image and the abandonment feelings (the withdrawing part-unit) as well as the results of activation of the rewarding part-unit, that is, inhibition, avoidance, passivity, and blocking. He stated, "When I sit there trying to study I feel hurt, stepped on, crushed, and I want to give up. I never felt any support or connection with my mother. It's a feeling of complete loss, helplessness, inability to cope with reality. . . . I feel adrift, alone . . . mother has no love for me. My image of mother's face is one of an expression of disgust like despising, criticizing, mocking me. I want her to love me but she hates me and she acts as if I did something against her and she wants to get back and she attacks me. I haven't done anything for her to hate me . . . she used to discourage my interest in girls or in my taking any activity in the home or outside. When I appealed to my father for help he was never home and he would tell me to cut it out because I was upsetting his relationship with my mother.

"When they left me alone they took part of me with them. They take something with them that leaves me empty. They double cross me

. . . no feeling of worth or meaning . . . the feeling of being deserted kills me. I can't handle the aftermath of asserting myself or speaking out, studying or learning. I feel it's wrong to be myself and I can almost hear my father's voice telling me to cut it out, that if I don't he will leave me. Mother told me that father didn't care about me . . . she was the only one who cared . . . if I didn't stay with her she'd leave me.

"Trying to learn is tempting fate, risky, treacherous. It brings them down on me . . .I can almost hear their voices . . . I can't break their hold . . . I feel I'm dying. I can't think and not feel hurt so I give up. I feel they don't care and they're laughing at me. I can't fight them every second. I have to block out. When I sit down to study it's as if I hear my father saying, 'Don't you see the anguish you're causing me?'

"I feel completely abandoned and I yell: Help me out! Where is everybody? And they say, 'He's crazy!' Father tells me it's my fault . . . the way I see things is all wrong. They feel sorry for me. I say: Please forgive me for having leprosy. I can't scream or beg any more because they think I'm crazy. I'm so afraid if they don't protect me I'll die!"

As the above communicative sequence reveals, the activation of the withdrawing part-unit in the wake of the patient's efforts toward self-assertiveness leads the patient into a condition of abandonment which brings him close to experiencing delusions, somatic delusions and auditory hallucinations. The untrammelled operation of his split object relations unit could be seen to have brought him close, at times, to regression into stage 2, with consequent blurring of the distinction between self-representations and object representations.

The third case example concerns an unmarried, 19-year-old girl, a freshman in college who had been an outstanding high-school student and who had subsequently dropped out of college because of depression and "panic."

The patient's father, a manic-depressive professional man, had had an explosive temper. Throughout the patient's childhood the father had behaved as a dependent child in his relationship with the mother, had openly attacked the patient for her "childhood inadequacies" but had envied her achievements. The major role obfuscations within the family found the mother playing the role of the father's mother and demanding that the patient not only submit to the father's attacks but also serve in the role of her own (the mother's) mother (Rinsley 1971a,b).

The patient's withdrawing maternal part-image was that of a mother who exploited her and who was deliberately cruel and enjoyed the patient's helplessness and dependency; the associated affect included abandonment depression and the fear of engulfment; the part self-image was that of being inadequate, worthless, guilty, an insect, a bug. The patient harbored cannibalistic fantasies and fears throughout childhood, relieved during that time by masturbation; in the fantasies she was at times the victim and at other times the cannibal. The rewarding maternal part-image was that of a strong, idealized ("all-good") mother who would save her from death; the associated affect was that of feeling "good" and the part self-image was that of a helpless, clinging child.

After some five months of treatment, the patient had begun to separate, with emergence of the withdrawing part self-image (withdrawing part-unit), which precipitated her into near-panic. She reported, "I feel everybody's angry at me. I'm about to be attacked. I feel like an insect, a bug. It's all because I don't want to be like my mother, I don't want to hold on to her. The role she puts me in fit her needs but also gave me security. She would love me no matter how bad I was. I want her and I want to be taken care of and I can't breathe without her. I don't have a separate existence and I feel guilty if I try. I can't stop wanting my mother like a baby. I can't seem to make a life of my own."

Whenever the withdrawing part-unit was activated as a result of a move toward separation-individuation, the patient projected her resultant anger at the withdrawing maternal part-image and became resistant to treatment, which she then viewed as conducive to abandonment. Thus she expressed her wish to kill the therapist, her mother, and herself: "Over the weekend I felt completely independent but cut off. I talked about my job very self-confidently, then I got frightened and went into a rage. I wanted to tear myself apart, rip my mother apart or you apart and I felt terribly depressed. I realize I'm getting better and I don't want to admit it. I don't need my mother. I lost my motivation, my desire to go on. I feel humiliated, defeated, dead and cold, I hate you! I don't think you can help me and I want revenge on my mother and you!"

This patient's pathological (pleasure) ego, shaped by her mother's "rewarding" responses, comprised regressive-defensive behavior, such as acting helplessly, clinging, a variety of somatic symptoms, and carrying out the mother's assigned role of an inadequate, hysterical child.

The fourth case example concerns a 22-year-old unmarried college graduate who lived alone. She complained of anxiety, depression, and hysteriform fears that her legs "might not work" and that she might be unable to eat or swallow; she had, in addition, experienced several episodes of impaired consciousness. There were also feelings of helplessness and inability to cope, and she almost constantly contacted her mother for reassurance.

The mother had idealized the family unit and had rewarded infantile-compliant behavior, which she viewed as a religious virtue; conversely, she vigorously attacked her child's efforts toward self-assertiveness or originality, an example of which had been her refusal to attend the patient's high school graduation exercises when she had learned that the girl had participated in a demonstration against the war in Vietnam. The mother had particularly attacked heterosexual relations as "the work of the Devil." The father, an emotionally distant man, served in the role of the mother's figurehead.

The patient's withdrawing maternal part-image was that of an angry, punitive, and vengeful mother who would kill her; the associated affect was a compound of fear and abandonment depression; the part-self image was that of being guilty, worthless, despicably bad. The rewarding maternal part-image was that of an omnipotent, godlike mother; the associated affect was relief from anxiety and feeling "good"; the part self-image was that of a helpless, compliant child. The pathological (pleasure) ego, which functioned to maintain the wish for reunion, abetted the fulfillment of the mother's wishes by being helpless, dependent, unassertive, clinging, and asexual. Again, therapeutic progress activated the withdrawing part-unit, which then triggered off the rewarding part-unit with ensuing helpless clinging, passivity, and phobic and hysteriform symptomatology.

Following resolution of the patient's initial resistances, she reported, "I think I'm destined to die because I'm growing up. I can envisage no life outside of my mother or family. I'm made up of two parts—one me, one her. The part that she has worked on, taken care of and given to me. . . . If I move away from her the part of her that's in me would turn against me. . . . Mother will make it turn against me and it will punish me. I don't feel strong enough to battle in spite of myself. Mother insists that I remain helpless and not grow up."

The patient continues: "I'm afraid if I grow up I'll lose her. I will take away her reason for living. I carry out what mother says—I'm an empty shell. Mother puts in the values, otherwise I will be nothing. I'm empty except for her. Mother sees me as a tool for herself. She instructed me in the one thing I can't do—grow up and leave her—or I'll be punished for it."

The patient experienced intense guilt over her hostility toward the mother: "I feel dirty and disgusting! Mother equates growing up with stealing and murder. Defying her is like defying God—you feel guilty and frightened. I've been frightened into believing that growing up is wrong. If I do anything that mother doesn't approve of, like have sex or smoke grass, I'm throwing myself to the winds and anything can happen to me. Mother suggested that sexual intercourse before marriage would make me mentally ill. If I smoke or have intercourse I'm violating the bargain I made with her not to leave her. I'm afraid she will leave me. When I assert myself rather than complying I feel nasty and impudent and that everybody will be angry with me. I'm just beginning to realize the extent to which I carry out Mother's wishes. If I don't do what she says it's wrong. . . . If I reject one thing it's like rejecting all. In other words, having sex is like lying, stealing, or rejecting my mother. She would rather I die than go out and do something she didn't want. Mother wanted me in order, just like she wanted the nice, clean bathroom in order. When I go and do something that is not in order she goes into a rage and would like to kill me."

In this case the alliance between the rewarding part-unit and the pathological (pleasure) ego engendered the patient's feeling of panic over anticpated punishment if she attempted to grow; the punishment she expected would take the form of her "going crazy," and of paralysis of walking, talking, and swallowing. In her case the pathological (pleasure) ego discharged aggression by means of autoplastic symptom-formation.

SUMMARY

This paper describes the contribution of maternal libidinal availability and withdrawal to the etiology of the borderline syndrome. It underscores Mahler's emphasis upon the mother's vital contribution to normal ego development and relates the effects of deficiency in that contribution to the development of the intrapsychic structure of the borderline: *the split ego* and *the split object relations unit*. The latter, which develops from internalization of the two major themes of interaction with the mother, produced the leitmotif of the borderline's intrapsychic structure: *the rewarding* and *withdrawing object relations part-units*. The rewarding part-unit becomes allied, as it were, with the pathological (pleasure) ego to defend against the withdrawing part-unit, but at the cost of failure to cope with reality.

The relationship of these borderline intrapsychic structures to each other and to the therapist's intrapsychic structures, as developed in the therapeutic transference and resistance, is described and illustrated by means of clinical case examples.

References

Fairbairn, W. R. D. (1952). *Psychoanalytic Studies of the Personality*. London: Tavistock. Reprinted as *An Object-Relations Theory of the Personality*. New York: Basic Books, 1954.

Federn, P. (1952). *Ego Psychology and the Psychoses*. New York: Basic Books.

Freud, A., and Dann, S. (1951). An experiment in group upbringing. *Psychoanalytic Study of the Child* 27:621-625.

Freud, S. (1911). Formulations on the two principles of mental functioning. *Standard Edition* 12: 213-226.

Goldfarb, W. (1945). Psychological privation in infancy and subsequent adjustment. *American Journal of Orthopsychiatry* 15:247-255.

Guntrip, H. (1961). *Personality Structure and Human Interaction*. New York: International Universities Press.

——— (1969). *Schizoid Phenomena, Object Relations and the Self*. New York: International Universities Press.

Jacobson, E. (1964). *The Self and the Object World*. New York: International Universities Press.

Kernberg, O. F. (1966). Structural derivatives of object relationships. *International Journal of Psycho-Analysis* 47:236-253.

——— (1967). Borderline personality organization. *Journal of the American Psychoanalytic Association* 15:641-685.

——— (1968). The treatment of patients with borderline personality organization. *International Journal of Psycho-Analysis* 49:600-619.

——— (1970a). A psychoanalytic classification of character pathology. *Journal of the American Psychoanalytic Association* 18:800-822.

——— (1970b). Factors in the psychoanalytic treatment of narcissistic personalities. *Journal of the American Psychoanalytic Association* 18:51-85.

——— (1971a). New developments in psychoanalytic object relations theory. (Paper read to the American Psychoanalytic Association, Washington, D.C.)

——— (1971b). Prognostic considerations regarding borderline personality organization. *Journal of the American Psychoanalytic Association* 19:595-635.

——— (1972). Early ego integration and object relations. *Annals of the New York Academy of Sciences* 193:233-247.

Klein, M. (1935). A contribution to the psychogenesis of manic-depressive states. In *Contributions to Psycho-Analysis, 1921-1945*. London: Hogarth Press, 1948.

——— (1940). Mourning and its relation to manic-depressive states. *Contributions to Psycho-Analysis, 1921-1945*, op. cit.

——— (1946). Notes on some schizoid mechanisms. In *Developments in Psycho-Analysis*, ed. J. Rivere. London: Hogarth Press, 1952.

Mahler, M. S. (1953). Autism and symbiosis, two extreme disturbances in identity. *International Journal of Psycho-Analysis* 39:77-83. Reprinted in *The Selected Papers of Margaret S. Mahler*, vol. 1, ch. 9. New York: Jason Aronson, 1979.

——— (1963). Thoughts about development and individuation. *Psychoanalytic Study of the Child* 18:307-324. Reprinted in *The Selected Papers of Margaret S. Mahler*, vol. 2, ch. 1. New York: Jason Aronson, 1979.

——— (1965). On the significance of the normal separation-individuation phase: with reference to research in symbiotic child psychosis. In *Drives,*

Affects, Behavior, vol. 2, ed. M. Schur. New York: International Universities Press. Reprinted in *Selected Papers,* op. cit., vol. 2, ch. 4.

——— (1968). *On Human Symbiosis and the Vicissitudes of Individuation volume 1: Infantile Psychosis.* In collaboration with M. Furer. New York: International Universities Press.

——— (1971). A study of the separation-individuation process: and its possible application to borderline phenomena in the psychoanalytic situation. *Psychoanalytic Study of the Child* 26:403-424. Reprinted in *Selected Papers,* op. cit., vol 2, ch 11.

——— (1972). On the first three subphases of the separation-individuation process. *International Journal of Psycho-Analysis* 53:333-338. Reprinted in *Selected Papers,* op. cit., vol. 2, ch. 8.

Mahler, M. S. and Furer, M. (1963). Certain aspects of the separation-individuation phase. *Psychoanalytic Quarterly* 32:1-14. Reprinted in *Selected Papers,* op. cit., vol. 2, ch. 2.

Mahler, M. S., and LaPerriere, K. (1965). Mother-child interaction during separation-individuation. *Psychoanalytic Quarterly* 34:483-498. Reprinted in *Selected Papers,* op. cit., vol. 2, ch. 3.

Mahler, M. S., and McDevitt, J. B. (1968). Observations on adaptation and defence *in statu nascendi:* developmental precursors in the first two years of life. *Psychoanalytic Quarterly* 37:1-21. Reprinted in *Selected Papers,* op. cit., vol. 2, ch. 7.

Mahler, M. S., Pine, F., and Bergman, A. (1970). The mother's reaction to her toddler's drive for individuation. In *Parenthood: Its Psychology and Psychopathology,* ed. E. J. Anthony and T. Benedek. Boston: Little, Brown.

Masterson, J. F. (1971). Treatment of the adolescent with borderline syndrome. *Bulletin of the Menninger Clinic* 35:5-18.

——— (1972). *Treatment of the Borderline Adolescent: A Development Approach.* New York: Wiley.

——— (1976). *Psychotherapy of the Borderline Adult: A Developmental Approach.* New York:Brunner-Mazel.

Parens, H., and Saul, L. J. (1971). *Dependency in Man: A Psychoanalytic Study.* New York: *International Universities Press.*

Rinsley, D. B. (1965). Intensive psychiatric hospital treatment of adolescents: an object-relations view. *Psychiatric Quarterly* 39:405-429.

——— (1968). Economic aspects of object relations. *International Journal of Psycho-Analysis* 49:38-48.

——— (1971a). Theory and practice of intensive residential treatment of adolescents. In S. Feinstein et al. (eds.), *Adolescent Psychiatry,* vol. 1: *Developmental and Clinical Studies.* New York: Basic Books.

——— (1971b). The adolescent in-patient: patterns of depersonification. *Psychiatric Quarterly* 45:3-22.

Spitz, R. A. (1945). Hospitalism: an inquiry into the genesis of psychiatric conditions of early childhood. *Psychoanalytic Study of the Child* 1:53-74.

——— (1946). Hospitalism: a follow-up report. *Psychoanalytic Study of the Child* 2:113-117.

——— (1965). *The First Year of Life*. New York: International Universities Press.

Spitz, R. A., and Wolf, K. M. (1946). Anaclitic depression: an inquiry into the genesis of psychiatric conditions of early childhood. II. *Psychoanalytic Study of the Child* 2:313-342.

Weil, A. P. (1970). The basic core. *Psychoanalytic Study of the Child* 25:442-469.

17

Homosexuality and the Rapprochement Subphase Crisis

Charles W. Socarides, M.D.

THEORETICAL AND CLINICAL BACKGROUND

It is well known that clear-cut and accurate distinctions may be made in psychoanalysis decades in advance of the theoretical understanding of the structure of the phenomena described. Freud (1905), for example, clearly perceived the early intense fixation to the mother in homosexuals long before its theoretical comprehension. I shall here attempt to further elucidate the psychopathology of the homosexual through the application of theoretical concepts of primary psychic development, especially that of the rapprochement subphase of the separation-individuation process.

My clinical experience with adult homosexual patients has led me to conclude that oedipal-phase conflict in certain homosexual patients is superimposed on a deeper, basic preoedipal nuclear conflict (Socarides 1968). My view was that in certain cases of homosexuality object relations pathology contributed more to the development of homosexuality than the vicissitudes of the drives—in other words, that the central conflict of the homosexual was object-related rather than structural. These views applied to relatively pronounced cases in which the perverse development was clear and definite. In these patients, nonengagement in perverse practices induced severe anxiety. Because the perverse acts were usually the only avenue for the attainment of sexual gratification and were obligatory for the alleviation of intense anxieties, and because the intensity of the need for such gratification was relatively pronounced, I referred to these cases as the "well-structured" perversion. In this paper, I am restricting myself to this type of (male) homosexual, who is, I believe, developmentally arrested and, hence, structurally deficient.

The following psychopathology appeared in all preoedipal cases, although it varied in degree from patient to patient. A lifelong persistence of the original primary feminine identification with the mother results in a pervasive feeling of femininity or a deficient sense of masculinity. The patient is symbiotically attached to the mother, has fantasies of fusing with her, but is also intensely ambivalent toward her. A severe degree of narcissistic vulnerability is manifest, especially in relation to the mother, to whose attitudes and behavior the patient is unduly sensitive. Attempts to establish sexual relatedness to a woman are followed by a regressive reenactment of a fear of engulfment and extreme anxiety. A deficit in the body-ego boundaries is accompanied by fears of bodily disintegration, an unusual sensitivity to threats of bodily damage by external objects—explainable, in part, as a manifestation of castration anxiety—and destructive aggressive impulses which threaten to destroy both the self and the partner. Homosexual acts are intense and imperative, and their effect can be likened to those of the opium alkaloids and their magical restorative powers—the optimum "fix"—reinstating the sense of self against the threat of dissolution and regressive experiences. Mental mechanisms are archaic and primitive, characterized by splitting, incorporation, and projection, and by the presence of unneutralized libidinal and aggressive energies, by a failure to construct intrapsychic representations of the self and of objects, especially of the mother as a stable, need-satisfying, trustworthy object with symbolic value. A search for love from the father or father-surrogate and a concomitant wish to wreak vengeance upon him seem to lie beneath the homosexual's apparent devotion to men. The end result is a chronic distrust, rage, and resentment toward men, often masked by feelings of an opposite nature. The patient fears retaliation from both parents and suffers from a deep sense of inferiority, worthlessness, and guilt, consciously or unconsciously—the aggression toward mother, and secondarily the father, having been drained off into a psychic masochistic state. The homosexual behavior constitutes an erotized defense against this more threatening masochistic position. Anxiety and aggression derived from preoedipal sources have undergone erotization. The dramatic reappearance of severe anxiety, tension, depression, and other revival during analytic therapy of intense archaic ego states in which activities underscores the function of the homosexual symptom, an outcome consistently seen in the course of treating these patients (Socarides 1968, 1978).

These clinical distinctions were made well in advance of their satisfactory theoretical understanding. Increasing clinical experience and refinements of therapeutic techniques led to alleviation of many of the symptoms of these patients, but their psychopathology could only be incompletely understood without the application of a gradually expanding theory of earliest psychic development. Combining clinical data and theoretical propositions which relied heavily on the early separation-individuation theories of Mahler, I tentatively proposed a preoedipal theory of causation of homosexuality (1968), placing the fixation at the symbiotic phase because of the revival during analytic therapy of intense archaic ego states in which there was a threat to ego cohesion and a threat of loss of object relations.

I subsequently observed that, although some patients reenacted and relived fears and wishes derived from the earliest period of life (even of the oral phase), they did not suffer an irreversible loss or destruction of object relations and other ego functions. In other words, they did not regress to the symbiotic phase whose "essential feature . . . is hallucinatory or delusional somatopsychic *omnipotent* fusion with the representation of the mother and, in particular, the delusion of a common boundary between two physically separate individuals" (Mahler, Pine, and Bergman 1975, p. 45). Furthermore, even in the depths of regression, they maintained a transference relationship to the analyst, and, despite florid transference reactions of even a transitory psychosislike character and a vivid reenactment of oral/anal fantasies, they did not become psychotic.

Preoedipal homosexuals of the type I am describing have developed sufficient ego structure and sufficient differentiation between self and object, and possess enough capacity for object relations, to indicate that they have successfully traversed earlier phases, that is, the symbiotic phase, the differentiating and practicing subphases of the separation-individuation process. They had been less able, however, to resolve the challenges of rapprochement, that subphase of the separation-individuation process leading to the successful development of object relations. As noted by Mahler (1968), "the state of object constancy develops gradually and may be regarded as having been attained when, by contrast with the previous stage, the firmly established object image is available, the cathexis of which persists regardless of the stage of instinctual need" (p. 223). The homosexual cannot, because of the absence of successful internalization, accept someone else as a substitute for the mother in her absence, or in the context of a threat of her loss.

Mahler's later discoveries (Mahler 1971, 1972a, 1972b, McDevitt and Settlage 1971, McDevitt 1975, Mahler, Pine, and Bergman 1975), as well as advances in object relations theory, new concepts of narcissism and the pathology of internalized object relations (Kohut 1971, Kernberg 1975), together with another decade of clinical observation, led to a considerable elaboration of my ideas—to a classification of clinical forms of homosexuality, the delineation of differentiating criteria separating perversions and perversions in psychotics, and an increased understanding of the difference between oedipal and preoedipal forms of the same perversion (Socarides 1978).

Homosexuality serves to repress a pivotal nuclear conflict: the urge to regress to a preoedipal fixation in which there was a desire for and dread of merging with the mother in order to reinstate the primitive mother-child unity.

The preoedipal theory of homosexuality rests on three pillars: the first is the presence of a fixation in the first three years of life; the second is the early disturbance of gender-role formation (sexual identity); and the third is the disturbance in synchronicity between maturational (physical) compliance and its counterpart, developmental (psychological) compliance (Spitz 1959), producing a traumatic impairment leading to developmental deficiencies. Viewing the well-structured perversion as a preoedipal disorder helped me to perceive that we are dealing with a developmental disorder in which object relations are maintained and deep anxieties relating to both mother and father are lessened through a short-circuiting technique or erotization. The erotic act (facilitated by the Sachs [1923] mechanism) functions to neutralize overwhelming anxieties, helps maintain threatened and precarious object relations, buttresses and reinforces self-representations and body-ego boundaries, and neutralizes destructive aggression threatening both the object and the self.

Having been unsuccessful in traversing the separation-individuation phase, the patient has a fear of reengulfment which continually threatens his insufficient differentation. The primary stage of unity and identity with the mother is no longer constructive for the evolution of an ego in an object world, and the homosexual's fixation leaves him prone to a defensive ego regression to this period. Furthermore, his fixation has exerted a decisive influence on the structure of his psyche, so that there is inadequate structuring of superego, ego, and id in the oedipal period, a disturbance in the patterning of drives and of defenses (Greenacre 1967). This disturbance leaves imprints on the later nature of genitality and in particular on his capacity for pleasure.

Other theoretical constructs, especially those by Roiphe (1968), Abelin (1971), Edgcumbe and Burgner (1975), Galenson and Roiphe (1973), Galenson et al. (1975), when applied to my own clinical material, helped to explain the disturbance in sexually defined gender-identity found in these patients. Roiphe (1968) noted that an early period of genital arousal occurs during the preoedipal years. The differentiation of the self from the object and the internalization and solidification of the object representation, that is, the consolidation of object representations and self-representation, are intimately connected with a primary genital schematization. There is an early castration anxiety (a "nursery castration," if you will) which is soldered to the anxiety of object loss so that early experiences which tend to challenge the child unduly with the threat of object loss or body dissolution, result in a faulty and vacillating genital outline of the body at a time when the genital schematization normally undergoes a primary consolidation (Roiphe 1968, Roiphe et al. 1975). Furthermore, the entire process of acquiring a differentiated sexual identity lies in the child's ability to identify with the parent of the same sex. Abelin (1971) noted from direct observational studies that, as important as the role of the mother is in allowing the child to separate and individuate, the father also serves a vital function. It "might be impossible [for either mother or child] to master [intrapsychic separation] without having the father to turn to" (p. 248). Both "dis-identifying from the mother" (Greenson 1968) and forming a counteridentification with the father are seriously impaired. The absent, domineering, hostile, detached father will not allow the child to identify with him and thus become a bridge in the latter's achieving both an individual sense of self and a gender-identity sense of self. This is later dramatized in the continuation of the lifelong poor relationship between father and son. The acquisition of sexual identity begins during the child's second year, continues through the anal phase, and reaches its peak during the phallic phase (Edgcumbe and Burgner 1975). Theoretical explanations of this type led to a further appreciation of the nature and meaning of distorted sexual identity in homosexual patients. The homosexual was unable to pass through the developmental phase in which he would have established a separate identity and individuality. This deficit in development led to profound difficulties, for example, faulty identification, disturbance in both the sense of self and in the development of appropriate sexual identity, a fluidity of ego boundaries, and a continuation of the primary feminine identification with the mother.

Mahler (1972a p. 495) describes the "dramatic fights with the mother" as characteristic of the rapprochement subphase, conflicts between the child's individual interests as opposed to his love for the object, and a painful and precipitous deflation of his "delusion of his own grandeur." The failure to resolve these issues produces a centrum or nidus of intrapsychic conflict which may later lead either to neurosis or to faulty or incomplete structural development, setting the stage for later narcissistic or borderline disorders (Mahler 1972a, pp. 492-504). Although not mentioned by Mahler, I believe there is sufficient evidence to add perversions to this list of conditions which arise from the second group of disorders, those associated with arrested or deficient structural development.

PREOEDIPAL RECONSTRUCTION AND HOMOSEXUALITY

In a recent paper, Settlage utilized our expanding theories of early psychic development in an effort to cast light on the psychopathology of narcissistic and borderline personality disorders in adults and children. He suggested that if we are to define the pathogenesis, the "pathological formations," and the means of treatment of narcissistic and borderline personality disorders, we must make a "precise correlation of traumatic experience during the first years of life" (Settlage 1977, p. 806) with the phases of early psychic development.

While theoretical formulations of early psychic development "are based primarily upon the process of reconstruction" (p. 803), a much closer view of the "beginnings of formation of psychic structure and function" can be obtained by direct observational studies. Both reconstructive and direct observational approaches have merits and limitations; they are "complementary to rather than in conflict with each other and . . . both of them are valuable and essential to a full psychoanalytic understanding" (p. 807).

Blum (1977, this volume, chapter 13) has comprehensively reviewed the reservations psychoanalysts must have with regard to preoedipal reconstruction. He noted Mahler's cautionary comment that we should not be led into the belief that "preverbal . . . phenomena . . . are isomorphic with the verbalizable clinical material" (Mahler, Pine, and Bergman 1975, p. 14), and Anna Freud's earlier warning (1971, p. 24) that more highly developed functions are always superimposed on more archaic layers and "the original simplicity of the primitive picture cannot but be distorted." Blum observed that "there is no reason to expect that any of the later normal developmental phases of life or pathological states will exactly replicate point by point any of the subphases of separation-individuation or psychosexual development. The early phases of development are not literally recapitulated; various consequences are inferred in terms of residue and influences, or forerunners which undergo further developmental vicissitudes, and . . . are subject to regressive transformations" (p. 781). We may conclude, with Blum (p. 783), that "the integration of psychoanalytic reconstruction and direct child observation promises a deeper understanding of ego development and disturbance, character formation, and preoedipal determinants of oedipal conflict and the infantile neurosis."

Thus, we may speak of the "potential for defining the psychopathology" (Settlage 1977) in severe borderline and narcissistic disorders and say that analytic reconstruction profits by its articulation with our current knowledge of development. In this connection it should be noted that as early as 1937 Freud perceived the uncertainties attendant on preoedipal reconstruction when he said that an infantile psychological reaction and pattern dating from a time when the child could barely speak may force "its way into consciousness, probably distorted and displaced owing to the operation of forces that are opposed to this return" (p. 267).

In treating cases of homosexuality, my aim is to discover the location of the fixation point and to make it possible for the patient to retrace his steps to that part of his development which were distorted by infantile and childhood deficiencies. Following the lessening of compensatory reparative moves in the adaptive processes that had distorted and inhibited his functioning, and the analysis of self-perpetuating defenses, I have repeatedly encountered head-on what seemed to be reenactments of rapprochement subphase conflicts and vicissitudes, complicated by oedipal and other subsequent experiences. In almost all instances, anxieties relating to separation from the mother were revived and relived. Maturational achievements, for example, the successful taking of career examinations in a patient previously unable to do so, activity undertaken without the mother's approval, etc., all produced anxiety and guilt of varying degrees as they were unconsciously equated with *intrapsychic* separation.

In the case I am about to present, the precipitating factor was a premature attempt to effect separation from an engulfing mother. The precipitating event itself was merely a small act of self-assertion. The patient, in what seemed to be an effort to comply with the father-analyst's wishes, was thinking of establishing himself in an apartment of his own—certainly something his mother would view with disfavor.

CLINICAL ILLUSTRATION

The extensive case history of this patient and an account of his psychoanalysis may be found in my book, *Homosexuality* (1978), "The Case of Campbell" (pp. 245-277). My major emphasis here will be on the derivatives of the rapprochement crises as they occurred during analytic therapy.

The patient was a 30-year-old, highly intelligent, attractive, and cultured man who experienced periods of confusion, depression, and anxiety which could be alleviated only by having a homosexual experience.

Campbell was an only child. His mother was highly cultivated, his father a rugged explorer, an alcoholic, contemptuous of what he deemed his wife's ultrarefined tastes. She treated him with a condescension born from her conviction of her social, aesthetic, and moral superiority. After years of dissension, the mother instigated a separation when Campbell was 14, after which the father resided nearby, contributing intermittently to the support of his wife and son. In effect, the mother's depreciation of the father forced his withdrawal from the family.

Campbell had been born within ten months of the marriage. It was a difficult birth requiring extensive surgery for the mother in order to repair a severe perineal tear. Because of the mother's long convalescence and a series of secondary physical complications, the child was placed in the care of a nurse. Periodically during the first year and a half postpartum the mother went on several long trips lasting one to two months. The child was not breast-fed; early on he developed a mild to moderate degree of feeding difficulty. He suffered repeated ear infections around age 2. From age 1½ to 4 he had protracted "screaming fits" when he was separated from the mother—for instance, if the nurse or anyone else attempted to supplant the mother in wheeling the carriage.

In early childhood, when mother went on one of her frequent vacations, she left him with a Scots maid who was a strict disciplinarian. Upset by the boy's masturbation, she continually punished him for it.

Campbell had numerous childhood fears. One was that if he left his hands outside the covers when he went to sleep, someone would cut them off. Another was that there was someone, especially his father, at the foot of the bed who had come to murder him. Often, upon going to sleep, he would suddenly be awakened with a terrifying sensation that his legs were going to drop off.

Memories of his early childhood included recollections of having liked dolls—he had a family of Teddy bears with which he played until he was nine—of dressing up in his mother's clothes, of his marked interest in clothes. He could recall over many years a particular costume either his mother or her friends had worn. He always felt that his mother wanted to "keep me home." Her attitude toward her husband led Campbell to view his father as insubstantial and weak. The father habitually demeaned his son for his lack of athletic abilities, openly referring to him as a "sissy."

As a small boy, he hated sports and felt awkward. His mother pushed him into going to dances, told him where to stand and with whom to dance. He did everything possible to stay away from girls, but became increasingly close to mother, who undressed in front of him, sharing with him discussions of her social and personal life, her clothes, etc. As an adolescent, he gradually became her escort to social events.

Ever since he was about 8 years old, Campbell had daydreams in which he planned to "eradicate" his father. Alongside his aggression against the father was a great need to be loved by him.

In adolescence, Campbell always felt depressed after his weekly outings with his father. The father sent him home punctually in a taxi, but Campbell felt he was curtailing their time together. During adolescence, he was terrified of his mother's touch, for it stimulated sexual feelings. At age 13 he began asking her not to kiss him goodnight. When he was 14 or 15, she invited him to sleep in the same bed with her the night before he left for boarding school, to insure his remaining faithful to her. "Mother was very stupid about coming into the bathroom when I was in there. I was rather offended that I didn't seem to have any sex at all to her."

When Campbell went off to boarding school he fell in love with the first in a series of beautiful blond boys a few years older than himself, realized he was homosexual, and was seized by an intense need to dye his own hair blond. Later, in college, he was seized by another "compulsion"—he shaved off all his body hair, except for that in the pubic area. The enactments of his "compulsions," which represented both his identification with the all-powerful (blond) mother and the defeat of his masculinity, and which protected him against the anxiety of not being loved by men, were often followed by a "kind of hysterics" in which Campbell sobbed, felt intensely confused, and occasionally wished for death.

In college, he was increasingly unable to adapt adequately to environmental demands, feeling that he was "not enough of a man." Frightened and weakened by these reality stresses, homosexual urges became more conscious and terrifying. He resisted their enactment until, unable to study, he failed the academic requirements of graduate school and was drafted into the Navy. He then engaged in a "calculated career of homosexuality" which continued away from home. He commented, "Homosexuality saved my sanity. Before, at college, I had reached the end of the world, an awful fear. Then I suddenly failed my exams." In the Navy, homosexuality quieted his general distrust and relieved his projective anxieties which bordered on paranoidal symptomatology, although no psychotic symptoms developed. It furthermore defended against extreme outbursts of aggression.

Early in therapy, Campbell felt that his homosexual problem must somehow be tied up with his mother and his feelings toward her. "There's a big 'voltage' toward my mother . . . a strong resentment against her and a tremendous dependency." His homosexuality was also a way of controlling men so that they did not attack him, especially when he felt vulnerable—following the loss of a job, for example. Furthermore, he felt that the homosexual act sometimes saved him from a strange sort of chaotic, mysterious fragmentation of himself: "I will fall apart if I don't have it." Magically, after homosexual intercourse, he felt relieved, whole and strong. He sometimes experienced a split in himself, "like two selves existing," and that he did not know who he was. He noticed that homosexual feelings came on whenever he was afraid of his mother "turning around and engulfing me." By late adolescence, he frequently experienced a weird excitement when his mother approached him suddenly, particularly if he was half asleep and she unexpectedly walked into his bedroom. This excitement proceeded on several occasions to overt sexual feeling toward her of which he was "terribly frightened." At the same time, this had an admixture of aggression: he didn't know quite what he would do to her, "either have intercourse with her, or perhaps murder her."

The onset of homosexual desire was often ushered in with severe shudders and chills. "I have to run to the Turkish bath for sex and then I suddenly feel better. I have a feeling that I'm acting like a girl. I'm like my mother. The anal business is the only thing that satisfies me. Before I go I feel, somehow, I'm going to be engulfed, or that I may lose my mind. This reestablishes me."

Intermittently and frequently during the first three years of the analysis, when weak and defenseless, the patient underwent regressive experiences with sensations of being engulfed and losing himself in the mother. He had experienced these on numerous occasions for seven or eight years previous to his beginning therapy—agonizing episodes of overwhelming anxiety, rolling on the floor, various psychosomatic complaints—stomach pain, short stabbing pains in his lower spine, loss of all energy, overwhelming depression and withdrawal, fears of being physically attacked, fears of loss of parts of his body. These attacks of "confusion" began with extremely severe tension headaches, occasionally one-sided and migrainous in nature. At these times, he felt he might "crack up" or fragment into a "million pieces." He felt a loss of direction and orientation. Lights became exceedingly bright. The room sometimes appeared to shift somewhat and he became frightened. "It's sort of terrible fright, then a compulsion to homosexual activity."

In these dramatic regressive episodes, he experienced severe autonomic reactions: a feeling of generalized collapse, pervasive panic, loss of identity, and fears of engulfment. "These feelings disorganized every thought I have, and homosexuality is my only outlet. They go all over my body and seem to sweep through my nerve centers. I feel it everywhere. It can be compared to water rushing through the rooms of a house. It activates certain things first, like certain centers, first my stomach, then my head, and I don't feel two things simultaneously. Within an hour or two my hands are trembling. There's tension in the pit of my stomach, I have a diarrhea feeling, a terrible feeling at the base of my spine, a pain. Also, strangely enough, a feeling of intense genital excitement. My headaches then begin and are very intense, and I'm almost in a state of hysteria. I feel aches and pains, and I feel mad and disgusted with myself, but I can't calm my mind. I am completely dead, too, completely automatic, a robot."

The relationship between the regressive phenomenon, its precipitants, and the homosexual solution to the dangers of regression could be readily discerned. The regression was activated by any attempt to seek closer contact with the mother. The danger of an intensification of his closeness to her was that he would be forced into the affective state of his preoedipal fixation. Any desire to get closer to her than the guarded optimal distance that allowed partial satisfaction produced a cataclysmic and catastrophic fear of merging with her.

To illustrate: in the third year of his analysis, I received a call from Campbell on Sunday, asking for an immediate appointment. When he arrived at my office, he was distraught, flushed, severely agitated, and complained of an excruciating headache. He was nearly screaming, and alternated between crying and a bitter, childlike half-laughter. Tears streamed down his face. He was unkempt, complained that he felt "paralyzed," and did indeed fall from the couch to the floor. He had, in effect, lost a characteristic behavioral concomitant of the rapprochement phase: the mastery of upright locomotion. Regressive material appeared when the patient, aided by the positive transference, attempted a premature separation from his mother, openly defying her.

He had spent Friday and Saturday with his mother, but when, on

Saturday, he told her he was planning to leave earlier than usual on Sunday, she was enraged, especially as she was thereby losing her escort to a cocktail party on Sunday night. "I felt as if mother was saying that if I left her she'd leave me to daddy. She compared me to him, how thoughtless I was. Last night, I had dreams in which my teeth were all knocked out and were rotten and falling." Campbell frequently had dreams of losing his teeth. Not only did this signify his fear of castration and his wish to become an infant, it also indicated that his self-representation was being severely threatened. It was a harbinger of an oncoming severe and imminent regressive reaction.

He felt apprehensive on his drive back to the city. His mother had misplaced her automobile license and, just before he left, had angrily asked him to look for it in her bureau drawers. Upon entering the bedroom of their city home, he opened the drawers only to find lingerie and underwear mixed up as if they had been thrown in there. He compared it to a garbage can fantasy he used to have up to adolescence. In this fantasy (a childhood correlate to fears of engulfment), he was immersed in garbage up to his mouth. This always aroused disgust and extreme fright. "This is the garbage can, the underwear thrown into the drawers; this is like being inside her. I began breathing very hard as if I were inside her, and I felt sick at my stomach and as if I would be compressed and choke and die. I think I'm going to faint now, like I'm going under an anesthetic." Campbell began to scream and cry uncontrollably, his hands clenched, his body rocking back and forth. He felt better crying, as if somehow that restored him to himself. He recalled that he had felt like this numerous times before. He suddenly began to roll on the floor. When I helped him to rise, he slumped and collapsed on the couch. "I'm a child, I'm a child. Mommy is coming back to the room. She's got to come back. I think I'm yelling; it's a funny yell, like a child's yell. I think it's rage."

The patient could quite easily be brought back to reality in the midst of such episodes. "I have a terrible ear abcess and the pain, it's terrible, and I'm yelling now, a terrible abcess and the pain won't go away. This happened when I was two, I was told. It is mommy, if only she would come back to me." Campbell's voice was now that of a baby. "If she'd only understand me, protect me." He was pleading, whimpering, crying, face contorted, eyes glaring and wild-looking. "She must protect me. She said this morning she'd leave me to daddy. Yes, this is what I've been afraid of, that daddy would kill me and that she would leave me. I was never allowed to chew the blanket. My mother saying, 'Don't chew the blanket—something to do with losing my teeth. Last night I felt some of this, some of her disapproval. I must be under an anesthetic. It's as if I was under ether. The picture I have is of a wish to lie in mother's arms and her loving and enfolding me, but it scares me. The conflict is I want to love her terribly, but we can't because of the sex business. When I went into her drawers, a childish impulse . . . I see the drawers, and I feel a terrible impulse to get inside her, not intercourse-like. I thought of totally entering her. I remember I would never open her pocketbook or any of her drawers. I actually was rejoining her and I couldn't do it. Before I came here, I tried to stop it all. I bought some peroxide for my hair and then I realized I shouldn't do this any more, and I washed it out. Then I felt terribly depressed, and I can't change my sex. I thought I'd then go back to lie on her bed and I'd die there, die there like in her arms . . . and I looked at myself in the mirror and was shaking, and I thought, 'Oh, you bitch.'"

The reenactment of this strong affective state led to a gradual cessation of the patient's overwhelming anxiety, and he became restored to his former self. While a running commentary on the meaning of his experience was given during the experience, what was vitally important was the presence of the analyst so that object relations were reinforced and were ultimately restored. In support of this, he telephoned me the next day as an attack began, and, as he talked, the threat of personal dissolution vanished.

DISCUSSION

Campbell was unable to pass through the developmental phase in which he could separate his identity from that of the mother and achieve object constancy. Out of the inability to separate and the need to identify with the mother came a threat of merging with her. The preoedipal fear that crystallized was then augmented by the later castration fears of the oedipal period.

Campbell entered later childhood with an inhibition of self-assertion and a pronounced feminine (maternal) identification. He had a strong inhibition of all male sexuality to avoid his fear of merging. He achieved a spurious masculinity, acquiring a penis and affection from men, thereby avoiding the dangers connected with his mother, but he still wished to maintain a close tie with her. In his homosexuality, he tried to rid himself of his damaging, destructive urge toward union with her and attempted to ward off his incorporative needs. When the pressures of adaptation and appropriate masculine-role functioning became too strong in adulthood, he regressed to a less demanding state of maternal closeness fraught with more primitive unconscious fears, which led to urgent needs for homosexual experiences. They reassured him against ego dissolution, were a substitute for a reunion with the mother, and allowed the expression, alleviation, and discharge of severe aggression aroused by the imperative need to merge with her. It was a lesser danger compared to merging with the mother. He established masculine identity by uniting with a male and his penis in homosexual intercourse, thereby reconstituting his ego. If he was unable to have homosexual relations, he felt "somehow I'm going to be destroyed, that I'm in terrible danger." For example, his mind suddenly "felt fatigued"; his body reactions became uncontrolled. "The idea of something jumping all through my body as if my heart suddenly hits a bit harder, as if I'm terribly hungry, and suddenly I'm conscious of all the blood in my stomach." This was quickly followed by impulses to act irrationally "like I might want to kill you. I know you're not going to attack me, but I somehow fear this, and I'm frightened also of myself." An explanation for these bursts of aggression may well be that the breakdown of formerly partially effective fusion and neutralization processes led to an abrupt awareness of a defusion of libido and destructive aggression. When regression occurred, deneutralization followed, with resultant reinstinctualization. This led to a striking phenomenon: the experiencing of intense aggressive, destructive feelings alternating with equally intense libidinal impulses, reminiscent of the splitting and ambitendency of rapprochement. The patient exclaimed: "I want to hug you and kiss you and then, just as suddenly, I want to hurt you and crush you."

He had strange feelings that he would swallow parts of his body such as his hand or foot (primitive incorporative anxiety); felt he would lose part of his face or be separated from his face, or that in "separating" from his face, another face would be found to exist beneath it. Splitting of the ego was also evident in less dramatic forms during his daily life on numerous occasions.

The patient felt that he actually became a baby. He revived memories of the pain and screaming due to a chronic mastoid infection. He enacted fear of abandonment, loss of his mother, and his inability to separate from her. Concomitantly, he had a desire to merge with her, but this was mixed with fears of personal dissolution and self-destruction. His mother's threat to give him back to "daddy," with the implicit threat of loss of the mother and castration by the father, caused an intensification of his wish to be close to her, with an ultimate joining and merging with her. This gave rise to severe anxiety. The wish to merge became a fear of merging, the fear of exploding, the fear of dying, the fear of personal annihilation.

The attacks occurred in the general setting of insecurity, feelings of weakness, loss of power, threats of loss of mother, her anger of disapproval of him, and her "coming at me," and anything perceived as a threat from the external world. This inordinate sensitivity to parental disapproval and threats resembled a manifestation of a rapprochement crisis. When these crises occurred, he at first was unwilling and then afraid to move. His affective life underwent a progressive decline in terms of his control over it; extreme anxiety, with its psychosomatic accompaniments, depression, feelings of loss of self, and emptiness made their appearance. Similar to the rapprochement child of 15 to 22 months, he was attempting to effect increasing psychical separation from his mother, induced by the analysis. Increased separation anxiety, however, began to appear with the fear of object loss. Increasing independence from mother was changed suddenly into a constant concern, and he was both afraid of and resented the attempt at separation from her.

Attributing the patient's homosexuality to preoedipal factors does not minimize the importance of the oedipal period and its castration fear. Campbell suffered severe castration anxiety. Upon entering the oedipal period, he was assailed by many fears related to his "cruel" father, in part a consequence of allegiance to his mother and murderous wishes and guilt feelings toward his father. Campbell expressed this fear of his father in his negative oedipal attitude, in which he unconsciously offered himself sexually to the father in place of the mother. At the same time, he could be more like his mother, exaggerating and emphasizing his feminine identification, with the hope of gaining safety and narcissistic supplies. Unconsciously, he was not only castrated by the father, but also attained sexual pleasure from him masochistically through substituting male partners. This led in part to a desire for and dread of anal rape. He successfully fought off conscious awareness of this dread of anal rape by attacking other men anally and by transforming them from threatening figures into "love figures." But above all, his homosexuality served the repression of a pivotal nuclear conflict: the drive to regress to a preoedipal fixation in which there is a desire for and dread of merging with the mother in order to reinstate the primitive mother-child unity: The homosexual object choice was crucial to the repression of this basic conflict between the wish for and dread of the mother-child unity.

Campbell suffered severe ego defects, deficiencies in reality testing, and a disturbance in body-ego boundaries. Although his thinking was clear, his behavior was dominated by the pleasure principle. This, combined with poor impulse control, led to actions which seemingly denied reality. His thinking also reflected his projective anxieties. Alternating with an elevated sense of self-esteem bordering on omnipotence were feelings of self-depreciation, need for narcissistic supplies and for narcissistic restoration. Ego boundaries were impaired but remained mainly intact, except under conditions of severe stress. He was intolerant of external frustrations which aroused anxiety, and action was substituted for normal anxiety or depression. These ego deficits, though severe, suggested that the mother-infant relationship was not hopelessly destroyed during the first half-year of life, that is, during the symbiotic phase. His tendency to respond to anxiety and depression with object-directed or self-directed aggression connoted a disturbance and exacerbation of both primary and secondary aggression due to frustration. Libidinal unavailability and absence of helpfulness on the part of the mother during the rapprochement subphase, due to her frequent absences, posed a threat of intrapsychic loss. This alternated with an overweening closeness, dependency, and mutual clinging. His partners for sexual relations were representatives of his self (narcissistic) in relation to an active phallic mother. Furthermore, he identified with and incorporated the partner's masculinity in the sexual act. What he was unconsciously enacting was a mother-child role via the breast-penis equation. Splitting processes of ego, superego, and object were prominent.

The patient's failure to achieve age-adequate ego autonomy, gender-defined identity, a separation of self from object, body-ego delineation, a structuralization of psychic functions played a vital role in the pathogenesis of his homosexuality. From the soil of his preoedipal disorder the well-structured perversion arose; its mechanism was erotization. A fundamental observation is that, when a homosexual's insufficient self- and object representations are threatened, he develops anxiety and is faced with the necessity to shore up his precarious or "imperiled representational world" (Stolorow 1979). Early psychosexual experiences are utilized to this end. It is not the fixated erotic experiences per se, that is, the instinct derivatives, that have been regressively reanimated in the perversion: it is the *early function* of the erotic experiences that is retained and regressively relied upon. In this way, through erotization, the homosexual, like other perverts, attempts to maintain structural cohesion and stability in the face of a disruptive or disintegrating self- and object representation. Ego survival is thereby insured.

A reconstruction of the childhood experiences could be achieved through their revival in the transference. The disruption in the successful traversing of the rapprochement subphase produced difficulties in the transference and therapeutic alliance. Since self- and object representations were merged, he could not tell the source of his feelings and frequently accused the analyst of not believing him when a serious or incisive comment was made; he thought that the analyst might laugh at him behind his back after he left the consultation room. The analyst was viewed as fluctuating between being all good and all bad. The splitting was due to a developmental deficiency in his self-object boundary maintenance, with a confusion between self and object. He wished to see his narcissistic self mirrored in the approval of the analyst and distrusted the latter's observations. A positive working alliance could be maintained only intermittently, and the patient frequently missed sessions during the first two years of therapy, before sufficient structuralization of his ego had taken place. The absence of the analyst during periods of vacation led to severe separation anxiety. Similarly, the mother's absence produced separation anxiety.

At the other pole of the dyadic relationship, his mother reacted to his attempted acts of independence with a lack of empathy, rage, threats of castration, threats of abandonment to the father, threats of loss of the object (mother), and a disruption of the symbiotic unity which still remained in the archaic layers of his mind. What ensued was a further regressive impairment of object relations, an exacerbation of splitting processes, separation anxiety, and dangers of annihilation together with fears of reengulfment. In several such instances, he experienced and regressively reenacted (1) the early trauma of the mastoid infection at age 2, at the height of the rapprochement subphase; (2) severe separation anxiety upon attempting to leave the mother; (3) overwhelming fears of father; (4) the fear of losing ego differentiation (the threat of further ego regression into an amorphous phase, with further loss of ego functions). His homosexuality was a prophylactic device, preventing defensive regression of the ego and helping him to maintain the optimal distance from and closeness to the mother through substitution (male in place of female, penis in place of breast).

During therapy, the patient's mother demonstrated a complete lack of receptivity to his nascent individuality or an understanding of his need to be independent. To emphasize what I have already stated: upon attempting intrapsychic separation, severe castration anxiety was experienced at both the mother's and father's hands, together with deeper preoedipal anxieties, fears of maternal reengulfment, and a severe deflation of his own feelings of self-esteem. In essence, he reproduced a rapprochement crisis in which he was once again unsuccessful. The mother did not wish for him to separate both in childhood and adulthood, used him as an object for her own ends, endlessly manipulating, controlling, and keeping him a part of her. The regression produced a further impairment of object relations, a threatened dissolution of his self-representation, and the fear of merging into the symbiotic mother-child unity. It stimulated aggressive responses of intense severity and castration fears of an overwhelming nature, in part derived from superimposed oedipal fears and in part due to object loss which was associated with an earlier faulty genital schematization (Roiphe 1968). The father was absent, cold, showed a lack of empathy and understanding. He was devalued and diminished by both mother and son. The end result was a powerless and impotent male figure with whom the patient could not identify. An identification with a powerful, strong, and loving male figure could only be provided later in the analysis through the transference.

As a result of the transference and working alliance induced by the therapeutic relationship, Campbell attempted prematurely to effect separation from his pathological attachment to his mother and was catapulted into a crisis that had all the characteristics of a rapprochement crisis. He experienced incorporation anxieties, projective anxieties, fears of loss of self and loss of the object. In effect, what resulted was a threatened dedifferentiation of psychic structure and of object relations.[1]

While there is no "direct line" (Mahler 1973) between the patient's adult psychopathology and his developmental fixation, it is my belief that the revival of primitive ego states and their essentially hallucinatory reenactment found so frequently in homosexual patients of the preoedipal type are a confirmation of the enormously valuable developmental data of the earliest phases of human existence, thoroughly documented by Mahler. These episodes have enormous relevance for the ultimate solution to the etiology and problem of homosexuality and other sexual perversions. It is my further belief that the significant incidence of homosexuality in the general population is due to the necessity for all human beings to traverse the separation-individuation phase of early childhood, which is decisive for gender-defined self-identity. A substantial number of children fail to successfully complete this developmental process and therefore are unable to form a healthy sexual identity in accordance with their anatomical and biological capacities.

We still do not know why one person develops the perversion of homosexuality while another chooses another type of perverse activity or eventuates with a narcissistic character disorder. The solution to this problem may well lie in careful observation of the early development of perverse acts in children and a careful clinical description of perversion occurring in adult patients. Long-range studies of individual cases from infancy to adulthood are likely to prove especially valuable.

SUMMARY

I have attempted to cast light on the psychopathology of well-structured cases of homosexuality of the preoedipal type by utilizing

---

1. Campbell was in analysis for nine and a half years, at which time he procured highly desirable employment in Europe. His overall psychological functioning was vastly improved and rapprochement crises completely disappeared by the third year of analysis. He was able to function heterosexually but continued to depend (when under severe stress) on homosexual activity. Several follow-up interviews during the ensuing five years revealed that he has maintained the progress achieved, but that under severe emotional strain he engages in infrequent and isolated homosexual encounters. All in all, he has profited greatly by increasing his performance and functioning in the major areas of life and he has felt increasing confidence and pleasure in living.

our expanding knowledge of primary psychic development as it pertains to the rapprochement subphase of the separation-individuation process. Analytic reconstruction is enriched by its articulation with current knowledge of development, especially when correlated as precisely as possible with earlier traumatic experiences which have caused developmental interferences.

I have focused on mainly the rapprochement subphase origin of clinical phenomena observed and on the three great anxieties of the rapprochement subphase: fear of object loss, fear of losing the object's love, and the undue sensitivity to approval/disapproval by the parent. Reenactments of rapprochement crises in the transference were depicted.

References

Abelin, E. L. (1971). The role of the father in the separation-individuation process. In *Separation-Individuation: Essays in Honor of Margaret S. Mahler*, ed. J. B. McDevitt and C. F. Settlage, pp. 229-253. New York: International Universities Press.

Blum, H. P. (1977). The prototype of preoedipal reconstruction. *Journal of the American Psychoanalytic Association* 25:757-786. Chapter 13, this volume.

Edgcumbe, R., and Burgner, M. (1975). The phallic-narcissistic phase: a differentiation between preoedipal and oedipal aspects of phallic development. *Psychoanalytic Study of the Child* 30:161-180. New Haven: Yale University Press.

Freud, A. (1971). A discussion with René Spitz. *The Writings of Anna Freud*, vol. 7, pp. 22-38. New York: International Universities Press.

Freud, S. (1905). Three essays on the theory of sexuality. *Standard Edition* 7:135-243.

——— (1937). Constructions in analysis. *Standard Edition* 23:255-270.

Galenson, E., and Roiphe, H. (1973). Object loss and early sexual development. *Psychoanalytic Quarterly* 22:73-90.

Galenson, E., Vogel, S., Blau, S., and Roiphe, H. (1975). Disturbance in sexual identity beginning at 18 months of age. *International Review of Psycho-Analysis* 2:389-397.

Greenacre, P. (1967). The influence of infantile trauma on genetic patterns. In *Emotional Growth*, vol. 1, pp. 260-299. New York: International Universities Press, 1971.

Greenson, R. R. (1968). Dis-identifying from mother: its special importance for the boy. *International Journal of Psycho-Analysis* 49:370-374.

Kernberg, O. (1975). *Borderline Conditions and Pathological Narcissism*. New York: Jason Aronson.

Kohut, H. (1971). *The Analysis of the Self.* New York: International Universities Press.

Mahler, M. S. (1968). *On Human Symbiosis and the Vicissitudes of Individuation, volume 1: Infantile Psychosis.* In collaboration with M. Furer. New York: International Universities Press.

——— (1971). A study of the separation-individuation process and its possible application to borderline phemonena in the psychoanalytic situation. *Psychoanalytic Study of the Child* 26:403-424. Reprinted in *The Selected Papers of Margaret S. Mahler,* vol. 2, ch. 11. New York: Jason Aronson, 1979.

——— (1972a). The rapprochement subphase of the separation-individuation process. *Psychoanalytic Quarterly* 41:487-506. Reprinted in *Selected Papers,* op. cit., ch. 8. Also this volume, ch. 1.

——— (1972b). On the first three subphases of the separation-individuation process. *International Journal of Psycho-Analysis* 53:333-338. Reprinted in *Selected Papers,* vol. 2, ch. 8.

——— (1973). Discussion comments. Margaret S. Mahler Symposium, Philadelphia (unpublished).

Mahler, M. S., Pine, F., and Bergman, A. (1975). *The Psychological Birth of the Human Infant: Symbiosis and Individuation.* New York: Basic Books.

McDevitt, J. B. (1975). Separation-individuation and object constancy. *Journal of the American Psychoanalytic Association* 23:713-742.

McDevitt, J. B., and Settlage, C. F. (eds.) (1971). *Separation-Individuation: Essays in Honor of Margaret S. Mahler.* New York: International Universities Press.

Roiphe, H. (1968). On an early genital phase. *Psychoanalytic Study of the Child* 23:348-365.

Sachs, H. (1923). On the genesis of sexual perversion. *International Zeitschrift fur Psychoanalyse* 9:172-182. Reprinted in *Homosexuality,* C. W. Socarides. Trans. Hella Freud Bernays. New York: Jason Aronson, 1978.

Settlage, C. F. (1977). The psychoanalytic understanding of narcissistic and borderline personality disorders: advances in developmental theory. *Journal of the American Psychoanalytic Association* 25:805-834.

Socarides, C. W. (1968). *The Overt Homosexual.* New York: Jason Aronson, 1972.

——— (1978). *Homosexuality.* New York: Jason Aronson.

Spitz, R. A. (1959). *A Genetic Field Theory of Ego Formation.* New York: International Universities Press.

Stolorow, R. D. (1979). Psychosexuality and the representational world. *International Journal of Psycho-Analysis* 60:39-46.

18

Some Aspects of Aesthetics in the Light of the Rapprochement Subphase

GILBERT J. ROSE, M.D.

Because of the historical development of psychoanalysis, as well as Freud's personal tastes, the analytic view of aesthetics has traditionally been that of defense. Aesthetics was a way of paying a bonus to the censor in order to gratify a forbidden wish in a somewhat attenuated form. Scarcely, if at all, distinguished from a neurotic symptom, dream, or joke, art became trivialized as a diversion. While this did no lasting damage to art, it impeded the development of psychoanalysis, isolating it from much of contemporary creative thought. If the aesthetic experience was essentially a regression of one kind or another and aesthetic form primarily a defense against content, much of the challenge of aesthetic experience and the constructive elements of aesthetic form—in short, what was most creative about creativity—must necessarily leave the psychoanalyst untouched, as indeed Freud said he was. Abstract art held no interest for him. Impressionism, symbolism, pointilism, cubism, etc., swirled in the air, revolutionizing man's view of reality while Freud, revolutionizing along different lines, remained attached primarily to classi-

This paper draws on a full-length work, *The Power of Form: A Psychoanalytic Approach to Aesthetic Form. Psychological* Issues, Monograph 49, to be published by International Universities Press.

cal art of antiquity like his old master, Professor Brücke. (Spector 1972). The essentially aesthetic quality of form, including, of course, musical form, was ignored.

This is still largely the case, as it was twenty-five years ago when Kris (1952) remarked that the psychology of aesthetic form was as yet unwritten. Ego psychology, however, particularly perception, early object relations, and the elements that go into the construction of reality, can begin to bridge the gap between psychoanalysis and aesthetics, and prove illuminating to both. In trying to put forth some tendrils to connect our field with others, one relies on the scientific spirit of exploration for encouragement, setting aside the quasi-juridical judgment, "Is it analytic enough?"—which can only prove fatal at an early stage to many a promising inquiry. It was Alfred North Whitehead, I believe, who said that the test of an idea was not its ultimate "truth" but its ability to stimulate new and interesting thought.

In this paper we will consider (1) the interactional quality of the aesthetic experience and (2) the temporal aspect of aesthetic form, both from the point of view of early object relations—specifically, the rapprochement subphase of childhood. Finally, (3) we will suggest that aesthetic form may carry an unsuspected significance far removed from the pleasure of peripheral diversion—namely, a biological function of aiding orientation in a fluid reality—as did the quality of mother's disappearance and reappearance in the rapprochement phase. This is not, however, intended to imply a "source" for either specific characteristics of art or of the aesthetic experience.

SEPARATION AND FUSION IN AESTHETIC FORMS

The ongoing interplay between an artwork and a responsive audience is like the balancing of closeness with distance, the child's "shadowing" and darting away from mother characteristic of the rapprochement subphase. In this stage (15-24 months or beyond) there is a deliberate search for, and avoidance of, intimate bodily contact, an alternation between pushing mother away and clinging to her, an incessant watching of mother's every move and ducking out from her hugs. The child both exercises individuality to the limit and demands mother's constant involvement, wishing for reunion and also fearing reengulfment. Rapid mood swings, tantrums, and sadness may accompany this growing realization of separateness. The invention of play (along with the development of language and internalization) helps him master the fact of the disappearance and reappearance of things. Peekaboo games and games of imitation, social interaction and symbolic play make it possible to function at a greater distance from mother. At the same time many transitional phenomena also develop; for example, having stories read while mother is absent is of particular interest (Mahler, Pine, and Bergman 1975).

The child's emergence from primary narcissism occurs in its own gradual time. Ideally, it prefigures the eventual development of a creative relation to the world. This has been described as an essential, recurrent search (whether in mystical, aesthetic, religious or empathic terms) for harmonious union with the universe (Milner 1952). It also implies the capacity for separateness.

This double aspect of harmonious union alternating with separateness corresponds with the way in which aesthetic experience has traditionally been described. Stokes (1955) has suggested that aesthetic form organizes and combines the imagoes of the two prototypical experiences of separation from, and fusion with, the mother. This fundamental dichotomy can be elaborated in many ways: objective and subjective, thought and feeling-action, tension and release, present and past, as well as other ways—all corresponding more or less to secondary and primary process (Rose 1976).

Whatever else a particular art object may represent it is above all something special, unique, perhaps strange in its own individual right. But, simultaneously, it remains an example of something general and familiar. Like the mother or the transitional object, it bridges between the new and strange and the good, old familiar. The emotional tie to the latter, as to the mother or the transitional object, encourages the recognition and acceptance of its unique aspects. By selecting forces common to the unique and the general, art balances the polarities and at the same time sharpens the dialectic between them. It heightens the appreciation of the unique as well as the general. In this it differs from science which abstracts from the general and in so doing tends to water down the emotional weight of the unique (L. Friedman 1965).

This description of art as a transitional bridge between the strange and the familiar implies a two-way contract between art and audience. This is more easily demonstrated with the *content* of a literary work. For a real act of reading to take place, a reader must be reciprocally active and creative, allowing the content of the work to awaken "harmonic resonances" within him (Barchilon and Kovel 1966, Barchilon 1971). Holland (1975), for example, has demonstrated that a reader uses material from the work to match and balance his own defenses, and builds fantasies in line with his own identity theme. Out of this transaction he recreates a literary interpretation compatible with the work and his own personal style.

Aesthetic *form* also calls for an active contract with the audience. To begin with, we might say that it requires on one part the capacity to trust and from the other side that it be trustworthy. A readiness to participate responsively calls for assurances of safety. The theatre, for example, warrants that for a limited time, a new yet familiar experience will be offered, recasting and rearranging thoughts and feelings—round trip, safe conduct guaranteed. Serious breaches of this contract can be disastrous. When opera singer Leonard Warren sang fateful lines about the capriciousness of life, then collapsed and died on stage, newspaper accounts described panic among parts of the audience.

The theatre also counts on the audience to fulfill its part of the contract. Its reality testing must be dependable and it must be able to take a safe, neutralizing distance from the drama being depicted. Without these safeguards, a strong specific resonance between an unconscious fantasy in the drama and one in the unconscious of the audience can even lead to fatal consequences. For example, after seeing Dürrenmatt's play, *The Visit*, a man felt both deeply disturbed and enraged. The play was too vivid a portrayal of his own specific sadomasochistic fantasies. He secretly took unknown amounts of sedatives from various hiding places, cajoled his wife into giving him more, and thus, unbeknownst to her, succeeded in making her administer the final fatal dose—repeating in this private performance the tragic ending of the previous night's play (Rose 1964).

The aesthetic experience might be described in terms of this reciprocal performance of a working contract. In poetry, for example, semantic ambiguity is punctuated by islands of discursive meaning which again drift off into ambiguity. The rising tension of discontinuous meanings is contained within the control of the overall structure of the poem. In the meantime, the reader must be able to tolerate the tension and function independently of meanings within easy reach until he can refind them or discover new ones for himself.

In addition to having to reach for meanings, rhyme and rhythm may also be withheld altogether, offered obliquely, or intermittently. (Rhythm is being used here in its most general sense of periodic recurrence, including accent, meter, time, tempo.) Free verse abandons both meter and rhyme. Blank verse gives up rhyme but not regular meter. Most modern poets do not eliminate rhyme but rather work to vary it through consonantal, assonantal, and approximate rhyme. They all seem to set up an expectation of regularity which they then vary in metric and nonmetric ways (Ciardi 1960). (Some of the ways of modifying pace are through the manipulation of pauses, visual patterns, punctuation, and grammatical structure.)

The dictionary definition of musical rhythm stresses that psychologically it is based on felt muscular response rather than upon mere exactness and regularity or measured time units. It is this priority of personal responsiveness that makes possible the various subtleties and fluctuations in rhythm and tempo known collectively as "tempo rubato." When a beat is left out it is understood to be present by the responsive listener. In the meantime, a stronger beat may be provided elsewhere in the music, supporting the listener's continuing participation. In the same way, the silence of a rest in the music, a pause in the poetry, is filled and integrated into the unified perception of the work by the listener's participating responsiveness.

Rhythmic ambiguity is, of course, only one aspect of the controlled ambiguity of musical form. It also involves the control of melodic and harmonic or chromatic ambiguity. Only a brief exposition of the latter will be undertaken.

The tonal structure or scale of a culture is one of the most powerful forces which condition and control the sense of melodic completeness. It establishes a system of order, of expectancies, and is probably the most important single facet of style of even the most primitive musical organization. It describes the relationship among tones within the context of a particular style system. In the major mode of Western music, for example, the tonic tone is the one of ultimate rest towards which all other tones tend to move; next to the tonic are the third and the fifth (dominant) of the scale.

Moving from one key to another (chromaticism) delays or blocks the expected motion to the normally most stable tones. Used in connection with other types of deviation, like rhythmic delays and dissonance, it helps produce ambiguity. But this ambiguity of moving from one key to another classically takes place within the control of a stable relationship of tonics and dominants (fifths) based on the universal phenomenon of the harmonic series. The overtones of the harmonic series make possible a circle of fifths; that is, one may move from the key of C to its dominant, G, and from the key of G to its dominant, D, and the key of D; thence to its dominant, A, and the key of A; thus on to the keys of E, B, F, and back to C. Wandering from one key to another is thus firmly supported by this underlying tonal organization of tonics and dominants.

The favorite harmonic ambiguity of romantic composers was the diminished seventh chord because it is capable of at least four different resolutions to the tonic, and each in either a major or minor key. The augmented fourth was considered so unstable that it was outlawed by early Church Fathers—a *diabolus in musica.* Debussy, however, was able to make this his basic musical principle, dividing the scale into six whole tones, or two tritones. Since it cannot produce tonic-dominant relations, no traditional modulations are possible from one key to another. This produces an enormous ambiguity, but still within classically stable, interrelated keys and clear resolutions.

The growing tendency in musical history to move from one key to another (chromaticism) is based on the accretion of more and more remote overtones of the harmonic series as they were gradually accepted into common practice. Schoenberg devised a whole system based on rootlessness from the harmonic series. Alban Berg created a new ambiguity which counterposed tonality with atonality. And Stravinsky pushed chromaticism as far as it could go, expanding the triad into seventh, ninth, eleventh, and thirteenth chords, all making for new tonal dissonances (Bernstein 1976).

During the ambiguity in the music, the negative space in the painting, the loss of discursive meaning and regularity in the poem, the audience is on its own. If the art form has stimulated needs as well as encouraged the participating ego to join in forming new integrations, if it has provided a favorable proportion of freedom and control, the audience will be able to put up with the discontinuities and continue to respond in resonance. It will be able to intensify and enrich the carefully withheld ingredients with its own sympathetic, supplementary vibrations. During chromatic wanderings from one key to another the absent tonic will be understood as immanent if not obvious, until it appears later in time. As in a painting the composition will introduce it in another place, and the art work trusted to bring us back safely to the home key.

Ordinarily some ambiguity represents a relaxation of boundaries and a freeing of the energy used to maintain them. Some tension is associated with unpleasure and stimulates thought and searching to bridge the gap, restore some pattern. In the near absence of familiar meaning—a total emptiness or discrepancy in space, unresolvable gap in time or ordinary logic, a total irregularity in the expected pattern—tension mounts to the point which incurs anxiety about loss of structure altogether, including fear of loss of self. Some contemporary art may have led us by the hand to abandon us at such a void. Words belie meaning, meanings are systematically dismantled, articulateness conceals senselessness. "One has only learnt to get the better of words," wrote T. S. Eliot. We are returned to the beginning, but without its safeguards. The art that mirrors such a world without mitigation is rejected when not ignored altogether. Some reunification in space, some resumption of the beat, some recurrence of the patterns of sense and expectation are needed to overcome separation and make the tension bearable.

Concealed recurrence within variety has traditionally provided such stability and unification for music. The mind hears the polyphony of constancy within variety. The transformations of thematic, rhythmic, and harmonic material are varieties of repetition of the same material. Melodic material, for example, can undergo almost endless transformations by inversion, augmentation, retrograde diminution, modulation, the opposition of consonance and dissonance, various forms of repetition like canon and fugue, rhythm, meter, harmonic progressions, dynamic changes, etc. But these are all varieties of repetitive constancy (Bernstein 1976).

Traditional psychoanalytic theory argued that since many of these transformations can be shown to be analogous to the primary process in the dream work, music thus offers a temporary regression in order to achieve a sense of mastery over early anxiety mobilized by the music (Friedman 1960, Kohut 1957). This overlooks the distinction between the formal features of primary process, based on mobility of cathexes, and its primitiveness, which reflects the demand for immediate drive discharge. Bach's fugues can be shown to be organized according to the primary process (Ehrenzweig 1953). This does not demonstrate that Bach is less than we thought but rather that primary process is more and that the formal features of primary process can undergo elaborate development.

The alternative view suggested here is that the mastery that music offers does arise from the earliest experiences of separation but contemporaneously has to do with the nature of time itself. Music works with variations of sameness to reconcile time's change with its constancy. Like the rapprochement phase child who invents forms of play and transitional phenomena which bridge between mother's disappearance and reappearance, music continues to integrate the everlasting tension of change with the ever-welcome release of return to constancy. (The balance of tension-release has been called the specific dynamic of musical form [Toch 1948, p. 157].)

PERMANENCE AND CHANGE

These two aspects of time—permanence and change—have been debated since antiquity. The enduring constancy of time, that is, the fusion of separate moments into a unity, and the fact that it also consists of ever-changing separate moments of change, never to be repeated, is a paradox ineluctable to logic. Both science and art have concerned themselves with time. We think now, in the light of modern physics, that both permanence and change are real, though precise present location of a particle in motion will be uncertain if its ultimate destination is known, and vice versa. For the Greeks, who employed space as their thought form, time is a line upon which one stands with gaze forward, facing future. Western thought, with its need to believe in progress, adheres to this convention, despite the fact that we cannot see into the future but only into the past; so that, if we are indeed marching forward it is with our backs turned— marching forward while facing the rear. For ancient Hebrew thought, the future is not what lies before us but what comes after us. The reality of time is the rhythm of beginning, continuation, and return to the beginning. The so-called end of the year is the return of the beginning. This notion of recurrence coincides with duration. Time is something qualitative, determined by content; the reality is movement, dynamic change. All things come back but the recurrence keeps changing (Boman 1960).

By the timelessness of the unconscious Freud meant to indicate the

permanence of unconscious wishes. The wish for timeless permanence is clearly a manifestation of the primary process and involves
fusion—the fusion of disparate units into a seamless permanent
whole. Contrariwise, the objective knowledge that time is transient
and change inevitable is a secondary phenomenon involving separation—the delineation of separate moments of everchanging time. In
his paper, "A Note Upon the Mystic Writing Pad," Freud (1925)
mentions his suspicion that it is the discontinuity between these two
systems which "lies at the bottom of the origin of the concept of
time" (p. 231).

Each aspect of time—successivness or change, and constancy or
permanence—can be grasped only in relation to the other. Considering time only as constancy turns it into something timeless like
eternity; and if it is considered only as a succession of present
moments there is neither history nor future (Seton 1974). Successiveness lends flexibility to constancy, and constancy mitigates the
inexorability of change and successiveness. When the passage of
time is not rejected, scattered, successive time is collected; and when
constancy is not clutched, rigid and enduring time is made more
malleable (Kummel 1966).

Ritual stops time. Perhaps in no culture has timelessness been more
central than in ancient Egyptian death cults. The aim was to guaran-
tee that the good fortune of life be carried on in perpetuity in death.
The recital of a ritual formula had to be exact and undeviating to
magically stop time and ensure permanence; ritual narration must
always remain the same as ever so that time, itself, by sympathetic
magic be frozen solid.

A wall painting in the judgment hall of Osiris, now in the British
Museum, depicts the "weighing of the heart." This was a common
chapter included in the papyri forming the *Book of the Dead* which
was placed in the tomb with the deceased. The deceased is led into
the judgment hall before Osiris, the supreme judge of the dead, and
forty-two other gods. His heart is placed in a balance opposite a
feather, representing Maat, the goddess of Truth. While Thoth, the
god of writing and wisdom records the results, the deceased recites
the ritual formula in which he denies any guilt against the moral law.
The lengthy catalogue includes: "I have committed no injustice
against man, I have not maltreated animals, I have not killed anyone
. . . I did not deny bread to the hungry, or drink to the thirsty, or
neglect to console the widow and orphan . . . ".

It is the faultless recitation of this negative confession which keeps the heart exactly balanced with the feather of truth and satisfies the judges that the dead person should be admitted into the kingdom of Osiris. "There is no record of any judgment ever going against the deceased, or of his seizure by the monstrous animal waiting for those found wanting. The efficacy of the proper recital is all that is required . . . " (Sewell 1968).

The act of narration helps to turn the *it was* into the *it is*. Narration in ritual observance aims at transforming the transitoriness of past history into the permanence of living tradition. The "talking cure" of psychoanalysis attempts to reverse the flow, rendering intractable present symptoms into their historical antecedents and, hopefully, mere memory. Thus, narration can be the medium of exchange between past and present as well as permanence and change.

The narration of literature transforms time's changing into time's enduring. The child's excitement at story-telling ("Tell it again! And exactly the same way!") represents in part the triumph of mastering time's flow by reversing it. Literary narration suggests that the past is not only that which came before but also what, in the retelling, exists now and will again. While it *was*, it also *is* and *will be*, forever after, so long as it is "once upon a time." (Perhaps a dim echo of this magical control of time is exercised by any reader in being able to pick up a book and put it down at any point, even beginning at the end or ending by rereading the beginning. Reading at bedtime to fall asleep may not be unrelated to this control over time flow.)

It is the fact that narration represents a *recurrence* which correlates permanence with change. Recurrence in all the arts succeeds in presenting an image and a reminder that the essence of time is that it *is* by always *becoming;* or, as Nietzsche said, the endless recurrence of difference is what constitutes sameness.[1]

In addition to the act of narration, through recurrence, reflecting the dialectic of time, the style of writing may do the same. Faulkner's style slows down and makes explicit the split-second recurrences in mental functioning. He makes the clear, hard boundaries of conscious discrimination and separateness once again negotiable, blurred, and flexible. The senses merge, self and objects fuse, the

---

1. Irwin (1975, p. 94) points out that this idea is linked with Freud's that the repressed inevitably returns via the repetition compulsion but necessarily disguised through displacements. Thus Freud (1920, p. 22) quotes Nietzsche: "This 'perpetual recurrence of the same thing.'"

tenses are flattened out and become inseparable, active and passive modes alternate, and the genders struggle within the same body. And then order is restored, reality reconstituted with experience replenished and the moment expanded. Faulkner's style mirrors the rhythm of the mind which, like music, follows recurrent time.

In both music and mind, recurrence in time permits the changing material to be worked through into patterns of aesthetic form on the one hand or meaning on the other. Changing thematic material in music may be worked through many elaborations while rhythm combines constancy in the midst of change. Endless personal vicissitudes may be worked through and navigated successfully while a reliable sense of identity provides inner stability despite change. Faulkner's style of rhythm, recurrence, progression is peculiarly satisfying, both musically and psychologically, and we will examine it briefly with examples from *Light In August* (Rose 1979).

Faulkner's sentences often appear to flow forward and ebb back: "So often our deeds are not worthy of ourselves. Nor we of our deeds" (p. 382).[2] As in music, an idea may be stated, then restated with a partial inversion which elaborates the theme: "He will have no more shame than to lie about being afraid, just as he had no more shame than to be afraid because he lied" (p. 407). In addition to the restatement with inversion, this example begins with the future tense and moves back to the past.

Sentences may overlap in describing an action, ebbing part of the way back, then driving further forward. As in perception or thought, as well as in music, there may be a first, fast scanning and summarizing sweep, then a series of fragmented, discerning examinations from various angles until, feelings mobilized and reflections gathered, the action moves forward.

In the confrontation between the scoundrel Lucas Brown and the pregnant woman he abandoned, Lena, with her newborn, Faulkner describes his eyes darting around the room, Lena watching him, till he brings himself to look at her, and they look at each other, till he breaks off the contact and flees. "Ceaselessly here and there about the empty room went his harried and desperate eyes. She watched him herd them by will, like two terrified beasts, and drive them up to meet her own." (p. 406). We see the action, then we observe Lena

2. Faulkner, W. (1932). *Light in August*. New York: Random House. Page references to the Modern Library edition.

watching the action, then we examine the scene with the help of a simile. His eyes are like two terrified beasts herded together and forced against their will in her direction. The simile sets up an anticipation. How might two terrified beasts behave when herded? The action is repeated, the anticipation is made explicit, then broadened: "She watched him, holding his eyes up to hers like two beasts about to break, as if he knew that when they broke this time he would never catch them, turn them again, and that he himself would be lost" (p. 406). The image of the darting eyes and the herded beasts who break and flee is turned back upon their owner: "He himself would be lost." The owner of the beasts, the two wild eyes, finds this thought intolerable and his observation of the unwelcome scene is immediately disowned, attributed to his eyes only, and then further away: "His eyes watched her. It was as though they were not his eyes, had no relation to the rest of him" (p. 408). Then he fled.

Faulkner's style of interchanging the tenses and active passive modes parallels an oscillation in gender identification. Certain imagery suggests a purposeful blurring of other distinctions which are first made in early life. The merging of self with outside objects rolls back time to the earliest period before the establishment of a sense of reality. Likewise, when various sensations are confused and condensed, memory is returned to its origins in raw sensory data. Both have to do with the obliteration of separateness and the return to early fusion states when the rudimentary sense of time was scarcely discriminated from the ebb and flow of physical needs.

If an unconscious memory of these early states should come close to consciousness it imparts a sense of uncanny foreboding as of impending truth. The feeling of conviction which accompanies it precedes and outlasts conscious understanding, actual recollection, or imagining.

He puts it as follows: "Memory believes before knowing remembers. Believes longer than recollects, longer than knowing even wonders." Faulkner continues in a sentence as long as a third of a page which, abstracted, reads: "Knows remembers believes a corridor in a . . . building . . . surrounded by smoking factory purlieus and enclosed . . . like a penitentiary or a zoo, where . . . orphans . . . in and out of remembering but in knowing constant as the bleak walls, the bleak windows where in rain soot from the nearly adjacenting chimneys streaked like black tears" (p. 111).

Faulkner is describing the experience of Joe Christmas in his earliest years in the orphanage. Christmas knows remembers believes the black tears of rain soot on the bleak windows. This image forcefully fuses Christmas's face with the window, his tears with the rain, the sense of his blackness or perhaps a dirty face with bleakness and soot. The black tears running from his eyes down his face is like the rain running down the sooty windows of his orphanage and scarcely distinguishable. This is an imagist picture of the feeling of early childhood depression before the establishment of the sense of separateness from the outside world.

Many years later Joe Christmas enters Joanna Burden's window like a cat. He moves unerringly towards some food and eats something from an invisible dish, with invisible fingers. "His jaw stopped suddenly in midchewing and thinking fled for twenty-five years back down the street . . . I'll know it in a minute. I have eaten it before, somewhere" (p. 217).

Faulkner then describes how Christmas struggles to reconstruct a memory from bits of raw sensory data buried alive years ago and now stirred up, just barely teased out, and now finally linked to the smell and taste of the unseen food in his fingers, his mouth, at last given a name and identified by the words on his tongue as field peas. An interminable sentence tells us physically that waiting to eat them must have felt like an eternity. Weeping with his eyes, and waiting to taste with his tongue, he smells the steam from the dish of peas. Faulkner writes: "I smelling my mouth and tongue weeping the hot salt of waiting my eyes tasting the hot steam from the dish" (p. 217). Weeping and waiting to taste, tears and saliva and hot steam merge, eyes and tongue become fused, so that tears might as well be coming from weeping tongue, and saliva from drooling eyes in the experience of waiting, weeping, smelling the steam and wanting to taste the field peas on the plate in front of him, but not being able to as long as his foster father droned on saying grace. In trying to match the present taste and smell with lost memory, all these old sensations come up at once with their confused registration and organs of origin; past and present are joined together till Christmas speaks the words, "It's peas," and probably simultaneous with hearing himself speak, identifies the unseen food he's eating and reenters the present.

Thus painting and overpainting with words, the senses are mixed and spread and stroked over the canvas until a feeling experience is made to emerge from the depths of past body memory and freed to live again in the present. This condensation of the senses in a kind of synesthesia to be sorted out and made into recognizable sense which can be finally labeled and communicated to himself describes some of the micro stages in the process of perception, thought, and memory. Like gender uncertainty and loose boundaries of time and mode, images of synesthesia and of fusion between self and outside objects all have the effect of returning us to an early, relatively undifferentiated phase of psychological development, and thus evoke a sense of timelessness.

"If only we could repeat time, change it, set it back," Faulkner's characters keep saying. Against this theme of recurrence, undoing or negation of time there is the insistent beat of causal time and accountability. The insistent beat of God's own judgment time which can be neither hurried nor delayed sounds through Doc Hines, speaking as though with the voice of a ventriloquist in the next room, puppetlike, without inflection. Instead of inflection there is the drumbeat of immutable rhythm: "And old Doc Hines went when God told him to go. But he kept in touch with God and at night he said, 'That bastard, Lord,' and God said, 'He is still walking My earth,' and old Doc Hines kept in touch with God and at night he said, 'That bastard, Lord,' and God said, 'He is still walking My earth,' and old Doc Hines kept in touch with God and one night he wrestled and he strove and he cried aloud, 'That bastard, Lord! I feel! I feel the teeth and the fangs of evil!' and God said, 'It's that bastard. Your work is not done yet. He's a pollution and a abomination on My earth'" (p. 365).

The next line is: "The sound of music from the distant church has long since ceased." There follows Mrs. Hines wishing that time could be set back for one day, that present consequences could be undone with an alibi. The chapter ends with: "Beyond the open window the sound of insects has not ceased, not faltered" (p. 370).

What does not falter is time's unchanging circular rhythm of seasons and perpetual recurrence, as well as human time with its linear progression of cause and effect and certain death.

We would like to believe that because the generations renew themselves and because the rhythm of the seasons recurs endlessly so do we; and because each day dispels the night, what is done can always be undone, or at least somehow mitigated. But while nature is cyclical and the mind, too, functions according to the principle of mastery through repetition and adaptation, the relation of cause to consequence is inexorable and cannot be rescinded.

While bringing the harsh message that all things have their price, and the consequences of time flow cannot be undone (although we must think, act, and feel as though they might), Faulkner's style, like mental processes, is that of recurrent time. He evokes timelessness by recalling early periods of one's life: interchanging the tenses and modes, treating the genders as ambiguous, using images of synesthesia, oxymoron and of fusion between the self and outside objects. His rhythms express endless recurrence and thus stimulate the illusion that the individual, like Nature itself, is timeless. There is an ebb and flow, statement and reversal, image and inversion, as if an individual's time, like his mental rhythms or phrases of music, could be reversed, not "irremediable."

Faulkner presents us with no "solution," no synthetic interpretation. The universal dialectic between man's finiteness and his imagination is reflected in the narrative style which orchestrates time with timelessness, change with constancy.

REFLECTIONS OF RAPPROCHEMENT

The foregoing sketched the outlines of a congruence between aesthetic form on the one hand and the dual nature of our sense of time on the other. We perceive time as both linear and circular. It consists of separate moments of change and of constantly recurring timeless cycles, both of which we call time. I have attempted to show that musical form reconciles both by appearing to represent change while the various transformations of music are really concealed recurrences of underlying constants. The same can be shown in some literary styles, that of Faulkner, for example, which present the message of the inexorable passage of time but in a "musical" way which belies it.

One might also show that our perception of space is likewise double, consisting of differentiated, focused, delineated perception of separate objects, and an unconscious undifferentiated fused space (Ehrenzweig 1953). The structure of aesthetic form reflects this, offering a second congruence.

One might go on to show that the dichotomy between a person's logical thoughts on the one hand and his motor-affective impulses to action on the other, is similarly reflected in the structure of aesthetic form, for example, the discursive message of a poem, contrasted with its physical sounds, rhythms, silences. If this were shown one could suggest a congruence exists between the structure of aesthetic form and the mind in respect to time, place, and person—the three coordinates of orientation. The congruence between these two structures provides an area within which the ego can test its capacities in respect to orientation.

In the fluid reality which characterizes the situation of the child in rapprochement, darting away from and shadowing of the mother succeed in internalizing more than his location in respect to her and the unexplored world outside. Location implies a host of subjective and objective aspects: that balance of closeness and distance, inner tension and prospects for release, tolerable separation and change and needed degree of constancy.

To the extent that reality always remains complex and somewhat fluid, the coordinates of orientation remain in need of renewal, as they were in the beginning. The structure of aesthetic form facilitates this. The experiencing person in the present, and the memories of himself in the past are brought into a thinking-feeling association with the art object which resonates with both. In so doing, time, place and person are melted down and re-formed, resharpening the coordinates of orientation in the broadest sense.

We read novels, look at pictures, go to the theatre in order to interact and take a position in relation to them. At the least they act like magic rituals reassuring us that nothing is new, nothing has changed, all is safe and well, we never left home. At most, our sensibilities are refreshed by an exciting and sometimes anxious trip, from which we return safely but forced to look at our familiar self and world in some new ways. Not only have separation and reunion been relived, but the ordinary divisiveness between thought and feeling, as well as present and past, has been anulled. Old and new are redelineated and brought into fresh balance.

A second effect of the congruence between the structure of aesthetic form and that of the mind, in addition to possibly serving the function of orientation, is that of fostering a sense of fusion between one's self and the art object. The art work externalizes the moment-by-moment activity of the mind, in slow motion, magnified and abstracted. Moreover, since it does it far more harmoniously than our own mental operations are capable, the art object not only stands for the working of the mind, but the mind *idealized*. Thus, a partial fusion with the art object is with an idealized self-object (to use Kohut's 1971 terminology). The recurrent merging and re-separating from an art object standing for the harmonized workings of the mind enhance self-esteem. Early fusions and separations are re-experienced as the first steps in the construction of reality are repeated, with self-esteem replenished at the same time.

At this point it is necessary to add some clarifying remarks to avoid misunderstanding. The coexistence of primary and secondary processes on all levels, in moment-by-moment functioning, and the two-way traffic between them, implies that fusion and dedifferentiation take place continuously and not just once upon a time at a certain developmental stage. What was initially a fragility of early ego boundaries may become an adaptive flexibility, and one that functions autonomously. Though this may recall the earliest fusions and separations it does not signify that the aesthetic experience involves a regression, a nostalgic journey. It is precisely the close experience of the past without regression, the sensuously textured past contemporaneous with the present, expanding the moment with greater dimensionality and a heightened sense of transience, that distinguishes the aesthetic experience from the merely sentimental.

Secondly, many developmental mother-infant interactions occur from birth onward. Some studies (Sander et al. 1976), for example, suggest that the regularity of infant-caretaker interactions during the first ten days of life may be critical to the infant's temporal organization—his nighttime sleeping and daytime activity patterns.

The choice of the rapprochement subphase as a genetic focus of this paper is not to claim it as a "source" of the aesthetic experience or to suggest that characteristics of art correspond specifically to that period. It is rather a strategic vantage point in early childhood from which to view the lifelong active process of self-differentiation. The period of the beginning of the self reverberates throughout the life cycle, and the latest aspects of self-differentiation resonate with the earliest.

Towards the end of the rapprochement subphase each child becomes individually very distinct in his own characteristic ways of coping (Mahler, Pine, and Bergman, 1975). It is when play and originality become apparent. The first steps in the construction of reality take place in the space between the mother and the rapprochement subphase child. The child both searches for and pushes the mother away, watches her every move and ducks away from her hugs, plays peekaboo, listens to fairy tales and begins to develop an unmistakable individuality. The space between them is analogous to the intermediate area of Winnicott (1953, 1967) where the interplay between separateness and union, originality and tradition gives rise to creative imagination.

What began in relation to the mother and her resilient availability becomes internalized in the course of time as trust in the reality of the self and the reliable constancy of one's identity in respect to a broadening world. The forces of constancy and change are in dynamic interaction. As with any ongoing process of growth, some ambiguity remains inherent in the nature of human experience and stimulates the creative imagination to reorder the data of reality into revised forms, as it did in the beginning.

We must admit that we do not yet have a satisfactory language to elucidate the area or process we are attempting to illuminate. Clumsily at best, we might describe the interaction involved as the prototype of an ongoing "transitional process" which outlasts the transitional object itself, lying behind the ego's integrative and abstracting ability in perception, memory, etc., to make possible the "creativity of everyday life" (Rose 1978). It might be conceptualized in genetic, structural, and economic terms. From the genetic (and object relations) point of view this space is the site of an alternating progression and regression: the rising tension of unfamiliarity and strangeness of the new that once went with separating from mother, controlling feelings and transforming impulses via long-circuiting them into thought; the release of tension that goes with giving up thought and separateness and yielding to the feelings and impulses towards reunion with mother as in the past. From the structural point of view, there is some heuristic value in speculating that it is this separating and rejoining behavior between mother and child which gradually becomes internalized within the ego as an alternating cathexis between a core of certain key ego functions such as reality testing, and the boundaries of the ego (Rose 1964); or as an oscillation between self- and object representations within the ego. From an economic point of view the tension of change, control, thought, and separateness corresponds to the child leaving the mother and reflects present secondary process functioning with bound energy; the discharge of feelings and impulses towards action, the surrender of separateness and change for the fusion and constancy which characterized the union with mother in the distant past correspond to the primary process and mobile energy.

CONCLUSION

I have tried to suggest that the "transitional" type of interaction between the rapprochement subphase child and its mother in Winnicott's intermediate area may be discerned in the interplay of the aesthetic experience as well as some aspects of aesthetic form. It would seem plausible that the structure of aesthetic form continues to fill an adaptive, biological need first served in the rapprochement subphase by the quality of the mother-child interaction. So long as imaginative growth continues and the boundaries of awareness do not congeal, the structure of aesthetic form invites identificatory participation and interplay. In so doing it sustains the continuing need for sharpening orientation in an ever-expanding reality, while offering what is subjectively felt as an aesthetic experience.

It is the hypothesis of this paper that both the aesthetic experience and the biological function it may subserve are illuminated by the rapprochement subphase. Early mother-child interactions such as occur then may help account for the contradictory feeling that Levi-Strauss notes (1969, p. 17) is aroused by aesthetic enjoyment, namely, that it subjects us to impossible challenges at the same time as it provides us "with the marvelously unpredictable means of coping with them." They may help account for the unique combination of feelings which traditionally describes the aesthetic experience: a simultaneous force and calm (Nietzsche), vitality and ease (Berenson 1948), energy and repose (Stokes 1955). They may also help account for why the recipient of a truly artistic impression experiences, as Tolstoy said, a sense of recognition that something has been understood and felt which he already knew but had been unable to express;[3] further, that he understands and feels something which in the form of an argument might have remained incomprehensible and inaccessible.

References

Barchilon, J. (1971). A study of Camus' mythopoeic tale "The Fall": with some comments about the origin of esthetic feelings. *Journal of the American Psychoanalytic Association* 19:193-240.

Barchilon, J., and Kovel, J. S. (1966). Huckleberry Finn: a psychoanalytic study. *Journal of the American Psychoanalytic Association* 14:775-814.

3. In his essay, *What is Art?* (1897-1898). See *Aesthetics*, ed. J. Stolnitz. New York: Macmillan, 1959.

Berenson, B. (1948). *Aesthetics and History*. New York: Pantheon.

Bernstein, L. (1976). *The Unanswered Question*. Cambridge, Mass.: Harvard University Press.

Boman, T. (1960). *Hebrew Thought Compared With Greek*. New York: Norton.

Ciardi, J. (1960). *How Does A Poem Mean?* Boston: Houghton Mifflin.

Ehrenzweig, A. (1953). *The Psychoanalysis of Artistic Vision and Hearing*. New York: Julian Press.

Freud, S. (1920). Beyond the pleasure principle. *Standard Edition* 18:7-64.

——— (1925). A note upon the 'Mystic Writing-Pad.' *Standard Edition* 19:227-232.

Friedman, L. (1965). Fact and value: new resources for esthetics. *Psychoanalytic Review* 52:117-129.

Friedman, S. M. (1960). One aspect of the structure of music: study of regressive transformations of musical themes. *Journal of the American Psychoanalytic Association* 8:427-449.

Holland, N. (1975). *5 Readers Reading*. New Haven: Yale University Press.

Irwin, J. T. (1975). *Doubling and Incest/Repetition and Revenge: A Speculative Reading of Faulkner*. Baltimore: Johns Hopkins University Press.

Kris, E. (1952). *Psychoanalytic Explorations in Art*. New York: International Universities Press.

Kohut, H. (1957). Observations on the psychological functions of music. *Journal of the American Psychoanalytic Association* 5:389-407.

——— (1971). *The Analysis of the Self*. New York: International Universities Press.

Kümmel, F. (1966). Time as succession and the problem of duration. In *The Voices of Time*, ed. J. T. Fraser. New York: Braziller.

Levi-Strauss, C. (1969). *The Raw And The Cooked*. New York: Harper and Row.

Mahler, M. S., Pine, F. and Bergman, A. (1975). *The Psychological Birth of the Human Infant: Symbiosis and Individuation*. New York: Basic Books.

Milner, M. (1952). Aspects of symbolism in the comprehension of the not-self. *International Journal of Psycho-Analysis* 33:181-195.

Rose, G. J. (1964). Creative imagination in terms of ego 'core' and boundaries. *International Journal of Psychoanalysis* 45:75-84.

——— (1976). Towards an aesthetic theory: the mirroring of some primary-secondary process interactions. Paper presented at the Fall meeting of the American Psychoanalytic Association.

——— (1978). The creativity of everyday life. In: *Between Reality and Fantasy. Transitional Objects and Phenomena*, ed. S. Grolnick and L. Barkin, pp. 345-362. New York: Jason Aronson.

——— (1979). The orchestration of time in Faulkner's *Light In August*. In *The Psychoanalytic Study of Society*, vol. 8. New Haven: Yale University Press.

Sander, L. W., Stechler, G., Julia, H. and Burns, P. (1976). Primary prevention and some aspects of temporal organization in early infant-caretaker interaction. In *Infant Psychiatry*, ed. E. N. Rexford, L. W. Sander and T. Shapiro, pp. 187-204. New Haven: Yale University Press.

Seton, P. (1974). The psychotemporal adaptation of late adolescence. *Journal of the American Psychoanalytic Association* 22:795-819.

Sewell, B. (1968). *Egypt Under The Pharaohs*. New York: G. P. Putnam.

Spector, J. J. (1972). *The Aesthetics of Freud*. New York: McGraw-Hill.

Stokes, A. (1955). Form in art. In *New Directions in Psychoanalysis*, ed. M. Klein, P. Heimann, R. Money-Kyrle, pp. 406-420. New York: Basic Books.

Toch, E. (1948). *The Shaping Forces in Music*. New York: Criterion Music.

Winnicott, D. W. (1953). Transitional objects and transitional phenomena. *International Journal of Psycho-Analysis* 34:89-97.

——— (1967). The location of cultural experience. *International Journal of Psycho-Analysis* 48:368-372.

Part VI

Rapprochement in Clinical Practice

19

Unresolved Rapprochement Conflict and the Infantile Neurosis

J. Alexis Burland, M.D.

The importance of the past was one of Freud's earliest psychological discoveries. As he listened to his emotionally troubled patients, something their previous physicians had not thought to do, he learned from them that their current complaints could be understood dynamically as reflecting ongoing attempts at coping with unresolved issues from childhood (Freud 1893-95, 1909a, 1909b, 1911, 1918). Reconstructive work has therefore been central to psychoanalysis from its inception. Whether limited to the analyst's private meditations, shared with the patient, or formulated by the patient himself, reconstructions linking past and present lay at the heart of the analytic process.

Reconstructive work is aided by developmental models, an important part of the analyst's theoretical armamentarium. Freud's discovery of infantile sexuality led to the formulation of a developmental model based on its phase-by-phase unfolding; this model has served psychoanalysis well for three-quarters of a century, and continues to do so, particularly in understanding the psychogenesis of neurotic structures.

Research over the past quarter of a century, normal infant observation in particular, has greatly expanded our understanding of the psychical events of the first years of life. We now know that there is more to the mental life of the infant than psychosexuality. Accordingly, reconstructive work has available to it a much broadened developmental model, and clinical data hitherto inadequately understood can now be conceptualized and interpreted in a way not previously possible.

The researches of Margaret S. Mahler and the developmental models she has formulated have contributed greatly to this deepening of our understanding of early psychological development (Mahler 1966, 1968, 1972, 1975; see also Burland 1975). Her concepts are currently in the process of being collated with earlier psychoanalytic developmental theories. Well within the mainstream of psychoanalytic thought, her writings contain a minimum of conceptual and terminological idiosyncrasy, thereby requiring little in the way of translation into traditional psychoanalytic terminology or theory. Nevertheless, the task of integrating her discoveries with ideas more familiar to analysts goes on; this is particularly true with respect to clinical application.

The clinical report which follows is offered as part of that task. It concerns a girl whose symptomatology reflected both rapprochement and phallic-oedipal conflict, and whose analysis dealt with each in its own time and in its own way. After the case report, some thoughts will be offered concerning the influence of rapprochement issues upon the infantile neurosis.

HISTORY

Presenting symptoms. Beth was brought for analysis at the age of 6 years 1 month. Hinting at the centrality of mother-daughter conflict, the mother's opening words to the analyst were "I'm a nervous wreck, I'm in tears, my nerves are shot!" She then described Beth as being equally overwhelmed emotionally, despite the fact that at the same time she could be provocative, controlling, and often imperious in her behavior.

For some three or four months, Beth had increasingly been behaving in a manner incomprehensible to her parents. She was agoraphobic. She complained her clothes were either too tight or too loose "around the middle," and demanded her mother iron and reiron them to make them absolutely wrinkle free. She repeatedly asked seemingly pointless questions of her mother. Sometimes she asked her questions that had obvious answers only to complain angrily that her answers were "too obvious," "stupid," or "simple-minded." At other times she would force her mother to repeat her answers and then berate her if she did not use the identical words. The phobia, the concerns with looseness and tightness, the anxiety about wrinkles, and the questioning were readily identifiable as symptomatic of a phallic-oedipal conflict.

But there were also symptoms identifiable as dyadic in nature. She was hostile toward her mother yet clinging; insulted her yet insisted she never leave her. Her mother was unable to comprehend the basis for Beth's distress, while Beth insisted she should be able to. As Beth's panic would mount, it would become pointedly directed at her mother, who would grow confused and frightened and then pull away. On several occasions confrontations led to physical assaults upon one another. Most confrontations ended with both of them in tears. Her mother complained of the assaults, as well as of Beth's intense dependency and demands that she perform "magic" to ease her daughter's distress.

The father saw less of the problem. Beth's most anxiety-filled behavior was directed at her mother; she was much less symptomatic with him. He tended to dismiss his wife's distress as excessive, although he had witnessed at least some of what she described. He felt as unable to comprehend the problem as did she.

The symptomatic behavior was in evidence only at home. When visiting relatives next door, for instance, an infrequent event during these weeks, she seemed totally symptom free—"her old self." This suggested a degree of ego strength, or at least ego resiliency, not at all visible when she was engaged in her most intense confrontations with her mother.

Past history. Beth's mother, in her mid-thirties, and her father, in his mid-forties, came from different sociocultural backgrounds, though both were Catholic. Around their dating and the marriage there was much interfamilial ethnic bickering. A few days before the marriage, the mother's father died, and two years later her mother. These were difficult years for her, and she was not helped by the fact that their next-door neighbors on one side were her husband's parents, and on the other his sister and her family. The mother felt in alien territory, and unsupported. Although they all said that these difficulties had largely been resolved, in point of fact the affect accompanying their description of the situation indicated that the issue was still alive.

The mother's pregnancy with Beth was planned and uneventful. An older sister had been born two years before. Both parents had the impression that Beth was precocious and hyperindependent "from birth." Birth itself was described as "very quick." She was early in the development of all skills. She "weaned herself" at the age of eight or nine months. Because of her precocity, Beth was allowed independence at an earlier age than her sister, and earlier than the standard books for parents suggested. As independent activity increased, her apparent need and desire for affectionate hugging by her mother disappeared—again, her mother felt, precociously.

No stranger anxiety was noted. The parents described their home as so populated by relatives and friends that Beth "must have learned not to fear others" at an early age.

But there were also instances of anxiety and inability to cope, reflecting aspects of Beth's funtioning the parents could never understand. At age 1½, Beth commenced a certain pattern of behavior that came to be known as "Beth's way" in the family: when away from her mother and "on her own," she would run into some obstacle that would send her screaming back to mother, who would be unable to learn from Beth what had happened. Although inconsolable, Beth would almost immediately struggle to break free from her mother to return to whatever it was that had just upset her. It seemed evident when the history was taken that this pattern was a paradigm for much of the mother-daughter conflict: Beth in acute distress, running in panic to mother, mother's inability to understand or help and Beth's inability or refusal to help her understand or help, and finally Beth's departure, only later to return once again. This pattern was recognizable also as evidence of rapprochement crisis behavior, although more intense and more persistent than usual.

At age 2½ Beth was briefly hospitalized because of dehydration resulting from an acute febrile gastrointestinal infection with vomiting and diarrhea. As the analysis later revealed, this was a critical event. Interestingly enough, the parents did not mention this hospitalization at first, and informed me of it only after several months of analysis and only because her father's sister recalled the incident and suggested they inform me as she thought it might be significant.

Beth persisted in both her precocity and in her episodes of "Beth's way" when she would involve herself in things beyond her ability to cope. Her friends tended to be a year or two older. Her closest friends were her cousins, a girl ten years older and a boy eight years older, who lived next door. They themselves were precocious, both of them a year ahead of their peers in school. All three enjoyed their reputation for "precocity" and often talked of it. Little, it seemed, was made of the large gap between the ages of Beth and her two co-prodigies.

At age 3, several fears appeared, some of which persisted to the time of the start of the analysis. Her initial fear was of loud noises, such as from vacuum cleaners and lawn mowers. She was also afraid of loud crowds, like at the supermarket, though she insisted her mother take her when she went shopping. Several fears were transient, including fears of dogs and of the dark. Beth's mother thought little of these fears at the time. They seemed to be a part of "Beth's way," which was by then more or less tolerated and an accepted behavior pattern, and she did not understand them and offered Beth little help. Beth would complain, or scream, but seemed somehow to cope on her own.

When Beth was four, her mother gave birth to a baby sister, the family's last and youngest child. At the time of the pregnancy, Beth asked many questions about it, in contrast to her older sister who was silent on the subject. For a few weeks, Beth expressed concerns somewhat similar to those which brought her to treatment two years later: the tightness and looseness of such things as dresses and shoes and her blankets when tucked in at night. Any analyst would recognize the phallic-oedipal content both in the most likely precipitating event, the birth, and in the symbolism of the symptoms.

At 5½, Beth was enrolled in kindergarten in the local parochial school. She had expressed an eagerness to go to school like her older sister did, but within a few days complained of being "bored." One day she put it in her typical precocious manner: "I can color and take naps at home." The parents thought the point was well taken and withdrew her from kindergarten. The teacher was astonished; from what she saw in the classroom, Beth was well adjusted and happy to be there. We later learned in the analysis that it was phobic anxiety that propelled her home; but it was not identified at the time, in keeping with Beth's facade of hypercompetence.

It was also later learned that while at home during the ensuing months she watched television most of the day out of range of mother's supervision. She especially watched the "soap operas." She described her fascination with and fear of one show in particular, in which an unwed pregnant woman is informed her unborn child is dead, and "goes crazy" and kills herself after trying unsuccessfully to kidnap another woman's baby.

Just prior to the onset of the presenting symptoms, Beth and her older sister were given goldfish. Beth asked many questions about how mother goldfish have baby goldfish, how the babies come out of the mother and whether it hurts. Beth's goldfish died in a few days; her father explained that it went blind and killed itself battering its head against the side of the bowl.

In summary, Beth presented both acute symptoms of a clearly neurotic nature as well as dyadic problems with her mother reflecting unresolved rapprochement issues. The *content* of her symptomatology particularly reflected conflict over primal scene curiosity and castration-penetration anxiety. The *form* spoke for ambitendent behavior vacillating between the demand that mother be an omniscient and omnipotent symbiotic partner and the demand that she, Beth, be totally separate and individuated. The form also suggested vacillations between feelings of helplessness associated with primary narcissistic yearnings, feelings of secondary narcissistic competence, and feelings of near hypomania.

Description of family members. Both parents revealed their humble backgrounds in unsophisticated view of themselves and Beth. Both seemed to be basically quite intelligent, but hampered by characterological inhibition of thinking. Beth's mother, a high-school graduate, clearly had ambitions for herself and her family. She dressed as stylishly as her budget allowed, believed in a good education, and wanted the best for her children. She tried to cooperate with the demands of the analysis, and to understand it. She was conscientious in all things, but intermittently beyond her emotional capacities, so that one sensed chronic disappointment with herself. Her religiosity seemed similarly more of a burden than a support. Her anguish, as described in the beginning, was over her sense of failure, and her feeling alone and unsupported in her hour of need. She did not know what she had done "wrong" as a mother. She could not understand her daughter, and never felt she had. She did not know how to respond to Beth's provocative behavior; she assumed that what she did was wrong. When finally she would explode at

Beth, she was intensely self-recriminatory. When not under such pressure, she seemed warm, affable, and attractive. She was liked and well regarded in her community.

Beth's father, an accountant, although also at his best warm and affable, when under pressure was tense and rigid. In one of the early parent conferences it was mentioned that Beth was refusing to wear a certain pair of socks. Although in the ensuing discussion the issue was broadened to be seen as a symptom of her neurosis, etc., as he was leaving he was still mumbling under his breath that she had to wear those socks. He did not convey hostile passive-resistance as much as fearful rigid constriction. He, too, was conscientious, yet also impulsive. Twice during the analysis there were minor problems with the bill that were readily resolved. Yet both times he grew confused and argumentative, and voiced the conviction the analysis would have to immediately end.

Description of patient. Beth gave the impression of being small for her age. That her clothes were purchased a size too large lest she grow out of them added to this impression. She had straight, dirty-blond hair and gray-blue eyes. She was perky, sassy, and always engaged in interpersonal process with the analyst. There was a feminine, narcissistic, exhibitionistic quality in her manner that combined with her vivacity to make her seem more attractive than her rather plain features allowed. She gave the impression of superior intelligence with her precocious verbal skills, subtle sense of humor, capacity to think psychologically, and ability to deal—if not to play—with ideas. As might be suspected, she tended to throw herself into all things, and at least occasionally during the first eighteen months of the analysis her unpredictability demanded that the analyst be ever on the alert. This was emotionally draining to some degree, and afforded the analyst the opportunity to empathize with Beth's mother. The analyst could feel the extent to which Beth demanded that he be an auxiliary ego, operating as an extension of her own mental equipment and performing self-regulatory functions for her. This transference from the early dyadic mother-child relationship contrasted with the transference manifestations of object-directed oedipal cathexes, as the clinical material will later reveal.

Her exhibitionistic bent was noted in her sense of theatre. Her pantomimes and play-acting were sufficiently skillful that one had to be on guard against being distracted from what she was communicating. She even spoke of her interest in a career in "show biz" (her words). Her ego skills in this area also added to the impression of her superior endowment.

From the start of the analysis she revealed a capacity to enter into and participate in the analytic process. She carried over activities and themes from one session to the next; she connected current with past material; she attended to and recalled what had been said. She observed and commented upon her own and the analyst's behavior. One could say she threw herself into the analysis in a manner simultaneously adaptive and maladaptive.

Her anxiety level at the start of the analysis was high. Her initial method of dealing with it was by constriction and by exerting rigid control of the interaction in the office. As this abated during the early months of the analysis, she revealed two other methods of coping with anxiety. When the level was high enough to be distressful but still tolerable, she would "dive in" to the anxiety-laden material with increasing intensity, so that her play took on a driven counterphobic quality; then, as though a critical mass of anxiety had been reached, play would cease. She would move to the part of the office distant from the play area, and lie down on the couch, suck on her tongue in a manner similar to an infant sucking on a nipple, and stroke a soft piece of clothing (usually her cotton undershirt). As the analysis progressed these behaviors decreased in frequency and intensity, remaining in her repertoire until the final months of treatment.

COURSE OF THE FIRST YEAR OF THE ANALYSIS

Beth coped with her first analytic session by sitting almost totally mute, perched guardedly on the edge of the couch, hands folded on her lap, eyeing me obliquely but intensely. There was a sparkle to her evident even as she sat still. She did not acknowledge my questions or statements, and declined my invitation to explore the office and the toy cabinets. After some thirty minutes, much of it in silence on both our parts, she got a deck of cards from the cabinets and announced we were to play poker. However, she sat and stared at the cards as though she did not know how to play the game. I commented on her wish to play such a grown-up game, yet her inability to do so.

During the first hours, she emerged from her anxious self-containment by defensively ritualizing, and thereby controlling, the sessions—saying the same words, playing the same games, and playing them in the same manner. In the games themselves she flamboyantly and imperiously broke the rules. At checkers, for instance, she would have her piece fly back and forth over my pieces, and take several of them with each turn. This contrasted with her obvious fearfulness. The defensive dynamic—her need to control in order to cope with her feelings of helplessness—was pointed out to her.

She began to verbalize more. She claimed that children controlled their parents. She bragged of being able to do grown-up things, such as play games her teenage cousins played, or watch adult television shows, or even enter school directly into the third or fourth grade. But at the same time revealing her insight and psychological minded- ness she alluded to how frightening the TV shows really were, how afraid she was of being spanked, how really she did not know how to play grown-up games. She confessed that she had asked to be dropped from kindergarten as she missed her mother; however, she claimed she was eager to start first grade in the Fall.

At home in these first weeks there was a marked symptomatic improvement. The phobias and anxiety-driven behavior almost disappeared. Instead, for the first time, she talked of her fears to her mother, something mother found increasingly distressful. She asked about "morbid" (mother's word) things, such as babies dead *in utero*, surgery, and death. She described fears of the crucifix in her bed- room, saying it looked as though it were coming towards her, especially at night. It was though she were attempting to adopt an "analytic" means of coping, talking out instead of playing out. But her mother could still not effectively deal with her.

In the 15th session, Beth said she would like to marry the analyst. She had proposed to her father, she explained, and he had said no because he was already married to mother. I commented on how grown-up a wish that was. She said she was in a hurry to grow up; children have to go to school, and she was afraid of school because the boys tease the girls. She also deprecated "childish" ideas, at the end of the session laughing at her little sister for believing that babies "pop out of their mother's belly-botton."

In the 19th session she insisted we play chess. However, she seemed ignorant as to how to play. She stared at the chess pieces and at the board in a confused manner. She then suddenly leapt into my lap and asked again to marry me. She then froze as if in fear. The parallel was drawn between her wish to play chess and her wish to marry me, both of them being grown-up things that confused and maybe even scared her, and about her tendency to jump into things that were upsetting for her. I suggested she might feel better if she got off my lap as I was sure it was upsetting for her to be there. After a moment she did. She sat silently, in deep thought, for the rest of the session.

The phallic-oedipal theme of "marriage" was to continue to be central to the *content* of Beth's symptom picture as one would have expected from the presenting complaint and the history. But the *form* in which this material was presented, in keeping with "Beth's way," pointed to other unresolved infantile issues dealing with separation-individuation. It was therefore not surprising when in the twenty-second session she first revealed in the office the separation anxiety that lay behind her counterphobic pseudo-precocity and restitutive hauteur. She suddenly said she missed her mother and wanted to go home. This was what she was afraid would happen in school. That it occurred in the office suggested the transference was operative. In the next session she returned to her phallic-oedipal fears as she introduced a new theme: her fear of injections from her doctor. At the end of that session, she asked personal questions about me (my age, my first name) and then interrupted herself when the thought of mother once again came to mind and she wanted to go home at once. In other words, phallic-oedipal transference activity stimulated separation anxiety. Her need to be with mother indicated the vulnerability of the material introject, a vulnerability pointing to an inadequately negotiated separation-individuation phase.

Over the subsequent weeks, she continued to play out these issues with the building blocks. She built a tower starting with the smallest block on the bottom, adding increasingly larger blocks until the structure finally collapsed. She then built a staircase that led upstairs to the bedrooms. The members of a family then proceeded up the stairs, one at a time, starting with the children. The entire structure would collapse before the second parent (the father) could climb the stairs. Her curiosity about, and fear of, "upstairs bedroom things" was clear. But also to the point was the little block struggling unsuccessfully to support the bigger blocks, and the collapse of the staircase which reflected the same theme. This was likened in the running comments to how she felt about all the worries on her mind. She responded by making a swimming pool out of the blocks, and referred to the deep pool in her older cousins' back yard, and the shallow wading pool in her own. She boasted of swimming in the deeper pool, but admitted how scary it was. She ended the play opting for the shallower wading pool. During this game, she made odd, high pitched sounds of laughter. It was several sessions before she identified this as "witch's laughter," referring to the witch in the Hansel and Gretel story. She said that sometimes she was afraid there was a witch under her bed at night; she looked "fearfully" under the couch in the office to see if there was a witch there, pointing again to the transference—i.e., the office where the nighttime bedroom fantasies and anxieties also arose.

During one of these sessions she talked about bikini bathing suits, and what they revealed of the body; but she then stopped herself, and said she wanted to go home to her mother. I reprised her curiosity about grown-up things, her tendency to get into water too deep for her, and how then she gets worried and wishes to be with her mother. She mentioned her fear of the witch, pointing under the couch and then said: "I remember from before (the younger sister) was born, when I was in her room, I saw a finger, in a white glove shaking 'no' at me. Because of noises I was making." This was her first reference to masturbation.

Two sessions later she again referred to both the oedipal and the separation-individuation issues as she built and contrasted two structures. One was a castle in which lived a king, a queen, and a princess; the other was the moon (this was the time of a lunar landing). She said how scary it would be on the moon, so far away from earth, and how alone she would feel. She made other references to long trips, and expressed her fears, at first indirectly by referring to her younger sister asking for "mommy." In mock imitation, she lay on the couch, and talked baby talk. But then for the first time in the analysis, she sucked her tongue and stroked her cotton undershirt. This now became her method of expressing her regressive longings, and appeared where she would frighten herself with her fantasies, situations in which previously she had asked, or demanded, to go home. A transitional phenomenon now replaced the actual presence of mother (Winnicott 1951).

Over ensuing months the material in the sessions continued to flow as before, pushing forward into infantile neurosis material, then rushing back to the couch to "mother herself" as Beth grew to call it. Among the elements associated with the former were husband and wife quarrels, bathing beauties, the mysteries of reproduction, a large beach scene painting where "by mistake" she kept drawing three legs on the bathers, fears about losing her baby teeth, and broken and missing parts of things (play equipment or toys she would bring in). She pantomimed honeymoons as wild up-and-down plane flights followed by the man chasing the woman up and down hillsides in order to stab her with a knife.

This material was presented, however, in a tense, frenetic and pressured manner so that I could feel in the countertransference her unspoken demand that I serve as an ego-auxiliary helping her to contain the impulses implicit in the blatantly transparent material. The very transparency of much of it, accompanied usually with a certain look in her eyes suggesting she "knew" what she was talking about, continued the thread noted earlier, relating to the issue of in *vs.* out of control. Clinically there was no question that at this stage in the analysis problems of form took precedence over matters of content.

Beth awoke each morning refusing to go to school. Her mother would start to argue at once, and the argument would eventually focus on trivialities—which dress to wear, which socks, what kind of sandwich to pack, was the breakfast right, etc. Over each issue Beth would demand her mother advise her, but then she would reject the advice. There were many changes of clothing, last second ironing, changes of menu, etc. As the moment for the actual departure neared, Beth's distress intensified, and therefore her demands upon her mother also intensified. Mother felt overwhelmed. She felt pushed and pulled, as in rapprochement crises which, indeed, this behavior resembled. Father was either uninvolved, or, since he had little problem with Beth, attempted to mollify his wife, whom he saw as a major provocateur. In school, Beth was quiet, reserved, and shy. She took eagerly to the school work itself, and received "100's" on all her assignments (except "handwriting"). The teacher saw nothing in her behavior out of the ordinary other than her slight shyness.

In the analysis, the content remained focused on infantile neurosis material, but the intensity of her distress seemed greater. Two new themes emerged whose significance became clear only in the second year of the analysis—the contents of things, and nurses and hospitals. Though the readily recognized references to female internal organs and sexual activities were noted, in fact these were her first references to her early hospitalization.

Also another significant theme began to appear: *time.* From first appearance, it related in particular to *control* over the passage of time, or rather, her lack of it. It was at that point in the session when she would suddenly need to evoke mother that she now said, "How much *longer* do I have?" or "How many more minutes?" or, eventually, "Only five minutes to go!" (when there were fifteen or twenty to go). She also bemoaned the fact that she, and others, were the ages they were, and grew older at a set rate, in spite of her wishes to the contrary.

Session 71 conveyed her vulnerability and painful sense of separateness from mother. It also showed how she used time as a theme in her efforts to cope with primary narcissistic deflation.

Beth came into the waiting room from school, with her book bag. She looked out of the waiting room window at her mother who was parking the car. "I can leave my book bag in here," she announced, "as my mother will be in to guard it." She then entered the office, but within a few seconds noted through the window that her mother was sitting in the parked car. She was in instant distress, screaming "she's supposed to be in the waiting room! I want my book bag! It'll be stolen without mother there! Can't I go get it?" She ran into the waiting room, got her book bag, ran back into the office and, sobbing unconsolably, she curled up on the couch clutching the book bag in her arms. Her intense distress, and collapse in the face of it, was most moving. Slowly, over some ten to fifteen minutes, her sobbing ceased and she lay there as if asleep. She softly sucked her tongue.

I identified her distress at her mother's not being there, and pointed out how sucking her tongue was like silently holding onto her as if she were there. I related the analysis to her frequent use of the couch and the tongue sucking by suggesting that what we talked about often made her feel her mother wasn't there. I also contrasted closeness with mother to growing up—that is, school, which is grown-up, means less time with mother. She listened intently to all I said. By the end of the session her spirits had brightened some. She went over to the clock, and said: "How long have we left? Five minutes? Five hours? Five years? Five thousand years?"

Shortly thereafter Beth had a severe case of bronchitis and had to stay home. At first, it was thought she would not miss many analytic sessions, but her fever rose to 103° and she ended up missing three sessions over six days. Although her behavior at home had been improving, I learned during one of my calls to check on her progress that it had reversed itself severely. Many of her initial symptoms returned, and her mother was frantic again. With much guilt the mother admitted that during one of their arguments she had chased Beth through the house, shouting at her in utter exasperation while Beth screamed in fear. In her rage she threatened to suffocate her daughter with a pillow. The argument ended when Beth's mother grew suddenly breathless and dizzy, and staggered out of the room. Since that incident, Beth had been quiet and docile. It was clear that the mother had frightened herself as well as Beth with her actions, but that she needed to deny it. "Anyone would be frantic with *her!*" she insisted. I suggested, diplomatically, that that might be so but that her reaction was a bit unusual and suggested that perhaps Beth was touching upon some particular sensitivity. I suggested we get together to discuss it, and she agreed reluctantly.

In our sessions, after insisting that it be understood that Beth was the patient, not *she*, talked sincerely of her frustrations with Beth. She felt intimidated by Beth's obvious distress, and therefore felt a keen responsibility to relieve it. Beth's rejection of her help not only confused and angered her, but hurt her deeply, and made her feel incompetent as a mother as well as powerless as a person. That episodes indicating acute rapprochement crisis were occurring could not have been more evident. I explained Beth's ambivalence about dependency, and her mother seemed to understand it for the first time. She had already, with her friends, worked out a solution: She was to disengage herself not just from Beth but from the other children as well, feel "less responsible for everyone else's problems," get out of house more, and maybe even get a job. She followed this prescription.

Subsequent sessions with Beth focused increasingly upon being good and being bad. There were many references to pleasing her mother, or trying to please her. She made no direct reference to the confrontation between her and her mother when she had been ill, nor did I at first, though we dealt with their "fights," and Beth's wish to be with her mother when she was scared but her need to fight with her when they were together. Being bad in relation to her mother was discussed in terms of her *sisters* being the bad ones, never Beth. In the sessions, however, her "badness" was much in evidence: she threw her coat on the floor and ordered me to pick it up, refused to clean up her toys at the end of the sessions, wouldn't answer questions, teased me with muttered phrases she would not repeat or vague allusions she would not explain. This was done with hauteur, not with anger; the issues seemed to be narcissistic ones. There were a few references to the devil—and ex-angel—as the cause of all badness. Sometimes she insisted it was I who had made the mess she left. She related curiosity and knowing about things to badness. The references to toilet training seemed clear, both as to anality and as to rapprochement subphase mother-daughter conflict.

Over the next few months her functioning at home and in school improved so markedly that friends and relatives now realized in retrospect how anxious and unhappy she had been for years. In the office, the intensity of the transference, however, did not abate. The following sessions, 82 and 89, convey the continuing blatant infantile neurosis material as well as her provocative precocity in her bantering with me, a style of behaving that seemed to strive to conceal and deny the underlying anxiety—but with little success.

She showed off her new pants suit. She noticed that a decorative button was broken. She got very upset, and asked that I fix it. I did. At first, she couldn't believe it was fixed. She then rewrote a story she had written the previous hour for her mother; she rationalized that she had to because her mother had thrown out the earlier version as the pages had been stapled out of sequence. But she interrupted herself and threw the new story out as it was "too messy" (which, in fact, it was: she had written it out purposefully sloppy). She started the story once again, alternating between being neat and sloppy. When sloppy, she called herself "stupid." I asked: "'Stupid'?" She replied: "I don't know what I mean. I'm too stupid to know." I pointed out that that was a very smart answer. She finished the story, about a relative who found some money on the street and returned it for the reward money, and read it. She said: "I tease you so much in here you probably don't believe the story." She wanted to take home the pen she used, first because it was broken and I didn't need it, then because it worked so well. I commented that she didn't seem to know whether she was smart or stupid, neat or sloppy, broken or not. She started a pantomime that looked like a drunken person staggering. I asked about it, and she answered: "If I'm too stupid to know why I'm stupid, I'm surely too stupid to know why I'm drunk!" At the end I said: "Sometimes smart girls learn about things that scare them, and they wish they *were* stupid."

In a session two weeks later, she told me she was to sleep over at her aunt's, who had two teenage sons ages twenty-six and twenty-eight (sic!), and she was excited about seeing them. She drew a huge tulip—a series of drawings of tulips in recent hours were referred to as generations of a family, the oldest being dead—then threw it out as "wrong." She then drew a queen, but very carefully. "I'll give her four fingers!" she giggled. As she drew, she started to stagger, acting "stupid" as she had done before. She said: "Five plus four equals ten!" She then added the queen's tenth finger. I underlined the recurrent theme: "Broken and missing parts. . . ." She then asked to play fish. She got the cards, but rushed through the game. However, she made an elaborate act out of putting the cards away, which seemed to be what she wanted to get to. The cards didn't fit in their box because it was "too tight." She then made a series of confusing and contradictory statements. I commented that she seemed to be trying to mix me up because there was something on her mind mixing *her* up. She then asked to be taught how to play dominoes. She alternated between being smart and learning with ease, and being "stupid" and learning nothing. I commented that some of the things she wants so much to learn about are scary and confusing, things that have to do with queens with missing fingers and boxes that are too small, and so she doesn't know whether to be smart or stupid.

The parents informed me that at home Beth had become increasingly preoccupied with "doctor shows" on television. In the office, she finally approached the subject directly, again eventually referring to the theme of time. She came in the office and showed me her knit hat, first claiming it was really her older sister's; she added that it was stretched all out of shape. She then showed me the *beautiful* pictures inside a toy kaleidoscope. She said school had gotten out early, and she had watched TV. Then, for the first time, she told me in detail about the TV shows she had watched the previous year while not in kindergarten. She pantomimed some of the scenes: a bitter fight between a man and a woman having a stormy love affair; she had thrown an ashtray at his head, and knocked him out. Then a woman was screaming with pain in labor; she then was told her baby was dead. She didn't believe it, and went "crazy," running into the nursery and trying to pick up the babies. She finally threw herself out of a window, and died. Beth then described "scary" mystery shows. "Those shows turn my afternoons into *nights!*" she said. She alternated then between asking, "Is it time to go?" and continued pantomime. I pointed out how hard it was to stop, as it must have been hard stopping to watch the TV shows though they were scary. She was thoughtful, briefly, and then complained that her father would be fifty years old when she was eight. She reviewed the arithmetic: he'd be sixty when she was eighteen, sixty-one when she was nineteen, etc. "That's not romantic!" she complained. She was sure it was more romantic for *my* daughter, who was seventeen while I was fifty (a statement based purely on fantasy). I started to reprise the session, but she interrupted. "I *like* romantic things." She sang a song about love and peace. "Is it time to go?" she asked, looking at the clock; there were five minutes yet. "I wake up five minutes before mother calls me in the morning, too."

Her references to masturbation grew more transparent, suggesting the extent to which she was "having symptoms" into the office, that is, throwing herself into subject matter beyond her ability to adequately cope. For example, in session 132, she came in hiding something from me—it was gum her father had given her. She ate a piece, dropped the wrapper on the floor, eyed it, but then picked it up and threw it away. She played typewriter repairman, giving a complex (incomprehensible) explanation of what was broken, saying it would be *very* expensive to fix (the cost rose each time she mentioned it); it would have to be in the shop for at least a week. As she fixed it, she used a long pencil, sticking it into the works of the machine, so as not to get her fingers dirty. The pencil reminded her of the mechanical pencil she used to use as a hypodermic needle, and she wondered if I'd fixed that one (i.e., replaced the lead). She talked softly, and said "Can you hear me?" She put the pencil up her sleeve, so far up she "lost" it. She scribbled on her pants, and said "Mother'll kill me!" She interrupted herself, and said it was time to go. I pointed out the theme of fixing things, and about that she wanted to talk about the things that worried her but it was hard for her to find the right way without getting so upset she wanted to leave. At the door, she touched the latch in the middle of the knob, and said: "All I have to do is push the bottom and I'm off!" and she fled. It was not surprising that at times she needed to blame the *office* for her sexual thoughts, for instance, playing that the office was a lending library with "shocking" books in it.

As her seventh birthday approached the passage of time became even a more prominent theme. She made clear her ambivalence about growing up. Old age, with its facial wrinkles and loss of "romance" had been a previous theme, and was related to her disappointment over becoming a year older. The following session was on her birthday:

"Now you're seven years old!" I said, in a rather factual tone of voice, as she entered the office. She showed off the new dress and shoes which she wore that day because by coincidence it was the day class pictures were taken in school. She was sure her picture would be awful; the photographer would make her smile, so her missing teeth—the "hole"—would show. She showed me a library book from school entitled *Hole in the Hill*. It was about a caveman and his family. She said they had a wolf for a pet—or, she wondered, was it just a dog? She showed me her new purse and its contents. She then described her other birthday presents, and her birthday party in an uncomplicated happy and pleased way. She was particularly grateful for her older sister's gift, as she knew it was expensive. Then her mood changed. She complained that I had said nothing about her birthday. I reminded her that I had, and said that I knew birthdays were special but that she had mixed feelings about her own. She agreed and said she didn't want to be a year older. She wanted to be one year old. Her little sister wanted to be older and imitated her older sisters, even imitated her father's curses. "She wants a birthday every day; then she'd be 365 years older every year!" She went to the couch, lay down, and started to suck Ler tongue. "Don't look!" she said, "because I have to lift my dress to reach my undershirt."

Over the next few sessions she complained that the teacher at school was moving too slowly, that the work was too easy: in one session she complained of the "same old baby toys" in the office. This material was followed by transparent references to her sexual anxieties, and this was followed by the "time to go" theme. It was possible to point out to her that she was as curious as a ten-year-old but then as afraid as a two-year-old, and that her curiosity was about marriages and honeymoons, the insides of things, and having babies.

In session 167 she showed me her math book, saying it was too easy. She then showed me a library book she was taking home—a fifth grade book. She read a page, with some difficulty. "See page 36!" she said, and then turned to that page. On it was a drawing of a recumbent princess. "She's dead," she said (actually, she was sleeping). "Now look at page 127!" she said. She turned to that page, and on it was a picture of the princess surrounded by a dozen young men with wings. "See? She's dead." Then she asked that I read the page opposite the picture. I did. In the story, the princess was to be killed

by a witch, but was rescued by eleven swans that changed into
princes. She was quiet and deep in thought. I reprised the session,
and referred to her fifth grade curiosity, but her fear that makes her
feel like two. "I'd rather *be* two" she said. "I'm afraid of being old,
and wrinkled. Like a hundred years old. Ugh!" After another moment of thought, she said "And time flies so *fast*. A hundred years . . .
how many seconds in a hundred years?" (We did the arithmetic—3
billion, 206 million, etc.) "Is that all? So few?!" After a few more
minutes of deep thought, she told me two stories she had heard in
school that day. In the first, a man and a woman marry. She has a gold
finger. On their honeymoon night, she dies. He cuts off the finger.
She's buried. Her ghost returns, recovers the finger, and kills the
man. In the second story again a man and a woman marry. She
always wears a black ribbon around her neck. He is told never to
touch that ribbon. On their wedding night, he unties it and her head
falls off. Her ghost comes back and kills him. I alluded to her many
questions about what goes on between men and women, and her
conviction that it is something scary and hurtful, with parts of the
body missing, and death. She added, "And don't forget about what's
in there!" pointing to the closed bookcase on top of my desk,
referring to what had become a shorthand for her concerns about the
insides of things. As she listened intently, I thought out loud about
how little girls have many theories about how what they have that
makes babies is inside, and can't be seen, while boys have a penis that
is on the outside and can be seen; and they wonder how those parts of
the body are used to make babies. "I know how the baby gets in
there!" she said, but then was silent again. After a pause, I went on:
"I'm sure you have ideas, and you've told us what some of those ideas
are in your games, and they seem to be scary like the man who
stabbed the lady." She said, "And don't forget the needles!" "Yes," I
agreed, "the needles that hurt." After some more silence, at the end of
the session I added: "As you're a smart girl you want to know all
about these things, even though they are frightening at times, and
even though sometimes you think you're not supposed to know
about them."

  Two sessions later, she came in and showed me her nail polish, and
told me its poetic name. She pointed out that she had gotten more on
her fingers than on her nails. She had used her Easter money to buy it.
She said her little sister was taking a nap even though it was 5:15 in the
afternoon! Then she said: "I almost cried yesterday! Well, actually I

did cry, but I'll say I almost cried!" and she went on to describe how a white horse, that belonged to neighbors, was moved to a distant stable so that she would never see it again. "Never again in my *whole life*," she said. For the rest of the session she was deep in thought, sucking her tongue, stroking her undershirt. She seemed a little sad, a little in awe of the ideas she talked of. She seemed to be struggling hard to settle something in her mind. After a while she said: "Do numbers go on forever? Or is there a last number? . . . I'll never be six again! . . . Will it ever be May 12 again? or 1972? In a *million* years, will it be 1972 again? . . . Maybe if I make myself small, by cutting off my arms, shrinking my legs—no, that wouldn't make me really younger, it'd be fake. . . . When my father is a hundred years old, how old will I be? My sisters?" (We did the arithmetic.) Then she asked the same questions for when her mother would be a hundred years old, and then how old others would be when she was a hundred. Each time as the arithmetic was done she offered to "change numbers" with her younger sister. She then asked how many seconds before her father was a hundred years old. Then, after a pause, she asked why I wore a wrist watch *and* had a table clock, and how I decided when to start the appointments, and when to end them. I commented that maybe she wondered if I had found a way to be in control of time—for she felt that time was in control of her. She looked at the clock. Even though there were five minutes left in the session, she kept saying "It's time to go!" (I said that at birthdays we see how time moves on, and it makes us want to find a way to control it.)

The next day she showed me a little bottle of eau de cologne she'd received as a gift from her aunt. She dabbed some behind her ears in a feminine manner. While doing so, she "accidentally" spilled a drop or two on the couch. She then threatened to spill more, or just leave the bottle uncorked, and "smell up" the office unless I said my ABC's twice. She commented that it's woman's perfume but that it smelled like a man's after shave lotion. Proudly she stated that next year she'd be in the second grade, and would be a Brownie. In March she'd be able to wear her Brownie uniform to school. She described the uniform in detail, and pointed out that it included a necktie "just like for a boy!" Therefore, she concluded, she could use the perfume again! She asked me why I always sat in the same chair (i.e., "my" chair, at the desk) and then wanted me to join her in the play area to play school. I pointed out that it seemed she had something else on her mind. "You *guessed*," she said. "I just wanted to get you out of your chair so *I* could run and sit in it." Then she went to the couch, and returned to the same thoughtful mood she'd been in in the previous session. I reprised, after a minute or two: the difference between men and women, and something about being in charge. She asked: "How long have I been coming here? The reason I ask is that *all* you've said all that time has gone right in one ear and out the other! And, it's *all* been wrong!" She grinned from ear to ear. She was silent for a while, occasionally directing a warm and tender grimace towards me. Then she started slowly: "I know . . . that you know . . . that I know . . . that you know that I know that you know that I knowthatyouknowthatIknow," etc. And then, pointing to various objects around the office, "and *they* know that *it* knows that *it* knows that *you* know that I know that *you* know." Then she had me say it while she pointed: "The lamp knows that the windows know that the bookcase knows," etc., that I know that she knows that she knows that I know. Then she added: "The whole *world* knows, everybody knows!" Her tone of voice became happier, even triumphant. I commented: about men and women. She looked at the clock. There were two minutes left. She announced: "I won't hurry, I'll go slowly. I'll even stay over! I'll take my time buttoning my coat buttons . . . or tying my shoe. . . ." When the two minutes were up, however, she scooted out.

These three sessions were a turning point in the analysis. The issues she confronted in them reflected both rapprochement and phallic-oedipal ones, and exemplified the interrelationship of these two aspects of her intrapsychic conflict.

The passage of time had come to be the arena in which she fought out her sense of vulnerability, the loss of her belief in her, and her mother's, omnipotence. She could not control time both as to growing up—which meant old age, wrinkles, and death, but also meant oedipal and eventually adolescent sexuality—nor, in the transference, could she control time as to her comings and goings to and from the office. In these sessions she seemed to resolve this fear of recognizing limitations to her own power and autonomy. From this session on there was a striking diminution in her rapprochement behavior. In the countertransference in particular I could sense a lessening of the drain upon me, a greater calm in the sessions, a diminution of her helpless frenzy that demanded I hover protectively over her. In this way she was letting go of me as a dyadic mother transference part object, as indeed she had largely dropped the dyadic mother as a topic in the content of her communications. Her forays into frightening material and the retreats that followed decreased in intensity, and changed from minute-to-minute swings to week-to-week swings. Her ego growth was most evident, particularly in terms of the greatly improved stability of the supportive dyadic maternal mental representation.

At the same time as these changes in form were noted, the content of these sessions pointed to how she was now ready to confront the infantile neurosis as she felt no longer so handicapped by the developmental interruptions from earlier phases. She could now acknowledge the fact of anatomical sexual differences: "The whole *world* knows about it." Separation anxiety gave way to castration anxiety, penis envy of a relatively pure sort took the place of penis envy contaminated with infantile megalomanic longings. The submission to the autonomy of time, with its implied primary narcissistic loss, paved the way for acceptance of the equally autonomous "facts of life." In the second year of the analysis, then, she was able to deal directly with what had been central in the content of her communications from the start, namely, the infantile neurosis. But it had been necessary first for her to confront and master the challenges that had been revealed in the form of her communications.

COURSE OF THE SECOND YEAR OF THE ANALYSIS

During the second half of the analysis the struggle to enter latency, to cease infantile masturbation with its primal scene content and to relinquish oedipal aims, ran side by side with the recovery of memories and fantasies of her hospitalization at age two and a half. With the waning of the hostile-dependent dyadic rapprochement transference, with its demand that I function as an auxiliary ego, the more object-related oedipal transference came to the fore, giving the analytic sessions a more relaxed affective quality. The focus naturally shifted from form to content.

In a session about two weeks following the ones just described, Beth indicated the relationship between the change from dyadic to phallic-oedipal issues quite graphically.

She brought in gum from her father, and put three sticks of it in her mouth, commenting on how that was too many. She combed her hair, and was very concerned about getting the part straight. She made passing comments about the shoes that she and I were wearing. She showed me gymnastics she was learning at school and tried to demonstrate a "split," something she claimed she had already learn-ed from her teen-age cousin, but she cried out in mock distress: "Ouch! I'm hurt! I sprained my toe! Call an ambulance! Momma-mia, poppa-pia!" She suddenly stopped, and was thoughtful. "I used pocket, that she couldn't believe was real, and that maybe she to say that when I was three. . . ." She lay down on the couch, deep in thought. I began to reprise the session, and when I got to "three years old" she interrupted. "No, when I was two! No, I was one! No, nine months! Do you know how *fast* I was? I was walking when I was nine months old! I was so fast in everything!" After a minute, she asked: "Are those plants *real?* They *look* fake. . . ." (They were real, and she knew that.) "Is there a safe in the wall behind that picture? Where you hide jewels and money? What's that in your jacket? Is that a *pocket* on the inside of your jacket?"

I reviewed the material and said that a memory from long ago came to her mind, about discovering something, like a safe or a pocket, that she couldn't believe was real, and that maybe she wondered if she'd been hurt; that she must have been quite scared and confused, that being such a precocious child she often learned things that only older girls knew about. She pantomimed "in one ear and out the other," while nodding "yes," and then pantomimed: "I know that you know that everyone knows." She lay silent for a while, rubbing her cotton t-shirt. She then rubbed harder and harder. She switched to rubbing her sock, then her shirt, then her glasses. She then put her finger in her mouth. There was little if any anxiety; she was communicating. She then got a piece of kleenex, placed it on her t-shirt and, by rubbing the kleenex, tore it. "Rubbing too hard will break it," she said. I commented that that must be part of the memory too, believing that rubbing things too hard might break them. She smiled. After a few moments of silence, she started a new game of imitating me—how I was sitting, etc. "A new game?" I asked. "A new game!" she said. It was the end of the session. As I moved towards the door to open it, she ran ahead and said *she* would open the door.

During this time her parents, in a phone contact, informed me that Beth was trying very hard to stop "habits" of wanting things in even numbers; she likened breaking this habit to stopping smoking. Also in subsequent sessions she began increasingly to refer to "God's wrath" and Holy Communion. When school ended, she reminisced about her experiences in first grade, pointing out how she would miss her teacher, but also looked ahead to second grade with mixed feelings. "In second grade I have my first Holy Communion, so I have to worry about *that* all year!" Indeed, it did seem as though that event in her life acted as a focus for many of her productions over ensuing months, and as an organizer of the psychological events of her life.

Although the various aspects of the infantile neurosis were dealt with simultaneously, certain specific themes seemed predominant at different times. But she returned most often to the ambivalent issue of seeking a more feminine identification as opposed to her jealousy and envy of boys. She pantomimed "Miss America" contests, talked of bridal veils, imitated very feminine television actresses. There were references to "missing" items, and to whether various objects looked broken. She spoke scoffingly of boys who were "bad," rough, or "stupid" in school. There were references to the themes of "needles" (i.e., injections), spaceships and boys' toys; she referred to hospitalization for the delivery of babies.

The transference increasingly became the arena in which the issue of the differences between the sexes was worked through. She compared herself and her possessions with me and my possessions. Her shoes, for instance, in contrast to mine, had broken laces and holes. She sat in "my" chair, gave injections to me or my plants, or insulted items in the office. She attempted to "put down" or "tease" me, by behaving in a "hard to get" fashion. This material was interpreted in terms of her mixed feelings about being a girl, her curiosity about boys and men, and the ways in which these same issues influenced what she thought about me.

The parents saw Beth as "symptom free" at this time, and happier and more outgoing than she had ever been in her life. They reported, however, that she vaguely alluded to certain fears that she was planning to soon conquer. Almost as an afterthought, they said that Beth was also talking a lot about a Teddy bear that had been lost at the beach shortly after her hospitalization, when she was two. It had never been replaced because her parents thought she was "too old." Beth now said she wanted it replaced as a Christmas present.

In the office, in one session, she pretended she was my secretary in a company that repaired washing machines and automobiles. She drew a complex chart of the inside of a washing machine, with many tubes and pipes. She asked me to draw the chart of the car, for she was a girl and I was a man, and only men understand about the insides of cars. Further associations in this session were to favorite "romantic" fantasies. In another session that symbolically but blatantly dealt with genital union, she made reference for the first time to her mounting anxiety about her first communion, six months away.

Shortly thereafter she introduced a new game. With checker and chess pieces she play-acted a parade. In the audience were children and their parents. In the parade were kings and queens, engaged in leap-frogging kinds of activities, or dancing with one another. In one session while playing this game she announced it was based on a real memory, from when she was about two and a half, when her father took her to see a parade. In the play she had the children desirous of joining in with the activities of the parading kings and queens. She interrupted this play, and switched to one in which she had the chess and checker pieces coming out of their boxes and wondering how they ever got into them in the first place. I related this material to questions she must have had around the time of her younger sister's birth—how babies get into their mothers, and how they get out.

It was in early December she mentioned to me for the first time her wish that her long-lost Teddy bear be replaced at Christmas. After announcing this, she played the "nurse game" in which she have "shots" to plants to make them grow.

In session 269 she started to make Christmas decorations. While doing so the central themes were old and familiar ones: being clumsy with her hands, and not knowing how to do things she obviously did know how to do. (I pointed out the familiar themes.) She attempted to make a cut-out pair of gingerbread men such that they were holding hands. She commented on her "butter fingers" as she dropped pencils and scissors. She then changed to playing "nurse." Almost at once she announced: "You know, I was in the hospital once. When I was two. It was *awful!* It was all dark, and gloomy, and there were big spiders and worms and dirt on the walls." In response to my wondering why she was in the hospital, she said she had been "dehydrated." I asked her what that means. "I don't know," she said, "something to do with my water." I reprised the session, wondering what it was about making the decorations, and being clumsy with her hands that brought the memory of the scary hospitalization back to her. She was thoughtful, but silent. She then got the scissors, and pantomimed cutting her hair. I said I wondered if that told us that, as a scared little girl who didn't know why she was in the hospital, she had the idea that it had something to do with cutting something off. After another minute of silent thought, she made a paper airplane, put a girl doll in it, and had the airplane crash. She then took the gingerbread men, referred to their being separated or connected, and said one of them was a "dumb-dumb" while the other one was "smart." In closing, I commented how she was remembering and telling us her ideas about her hospitalization when she was little.

In the next session she brought her report card. She received half "A"s and half "A-pluses" but only a "C" in handwriting. School awards for "courtesy" and handwriting marks were contrasted with "first honors" and academic awards, the latter two success areas for her, but not the others. Interspersed with this material were references to being "pretty" or "ugly" and broken or unbroken.

For Christmas she requested that I give her a small toy blackboard so she could play school. Her first response to the gift was to state her mother would be angry as she was allergic to chalk dust. In the session she used the little blackboard to teach a class in penmanship. Her "students" had very poor penmanship, and were angrily reprimanded. She referred to her teacher from first grade, a young lay teacher, and spoke with derision of her "micro-mini" skirts, and of how she got married. Beth insisted that she would never marry. In the next session she played at the doll house. She took such a long time arranging the doll house furniture that she announced that she would never get to the story—a defense that had been previously interpreted. The story touched lightly on "bored" children who end up doing what their parents do; this ended up as a game of wrestling and falling off of a cliff. At the end, parents and children went to bed and *immediately* awoke in the morning. It was morning so quickly, she announced, because they slept right through the night.

In a session shortly thereafter, she showed off a "diamond" ring her father had just given her. She was not sure which finger to wear it on. She complained it was too tight. With a girl doll she played Miss America, using the ring as a crown. Then Miss America wondered whether she should get married. She said she wouldn't as "he waited three years before asking me," but finally decided she would marry him . . . only to divorce him *immediately*. Up to this point in the session, Beth's interaction with me was warmly positive, totally devoid of the teasing, narcissistic quality that had predominated until recent sessions. I pointed out her ambivalence about marriage because of her fear of honeymoons, and of what happens between grooms and brides on them. She interrupted, becoming increasingly imperious, and said: "Now listen! There are ten rules in here you are supposed to follow! First, *never* talk when Beth says not to. Second, always play fair at games. And third, stop staring at me!" I started to comment about her anxieties in the transference, and again she interrupted. She went to the office door that led to the adjoining house and listened for sounds of a TV set, or dinner being prepared. She then asked me to get out of "my" chair. When I asked her why, she reluctantly admitted she wanted to sit in it. I commented that sitting in my chair made her feel better when she was worried about what happens in the office.

After several more sessions dealing with her ambivalence about marriage, she came in with her "Suntan Barbie" doll, complaining her sisters have "wrecked" it. Using Barbie and a doll from the office she began a queen and princess story. The daughter was whiney, nagging her mother, clinging to her such that mother was angry at her. The daughter wouldn't go out as she was afraid of the boys, who teased her. The mother went out. The daughter stayed home and did "naughty, fun" things, like "hula dances." The mother returned. The daughter was sleepy, and cuddled up with mother. At this point Beth announced they were no longer queen and princess, just mother and daughter. They went to an amusement park and rode on what looked like a roller-coaster; the ride was exciting, but scary.

In the next session she picked up the story where she left it, at the amusement park. The girl fell off the roller-coaster, and was sent to the hospital where she got "four I.V.'s just like when *I* was in the hospital." Then she had "surgery"—her arm was amputated. Her mother was furious, and punished her by making her go on the roller-coaster ride again. She again fell, and returned to the hospital. She died. No, she corrected herself, it was her little sister who died. "Yay!" she shouted, "she was such a pest!" But no, she said, she wasn't really dead, just faking. At the end, she had mother go on a date, and announced that in the next part of her story they marry, and *he* dies. I pointed out how in her story she was telling us what she thought her hospitalization was for when she was little.

A week later she briefly play-acted a story about climbing a mountain and flying in a plane, material that in earlier sessions stood for honeymoon fantasies. She then told a long story about nighttime, and sleeping so deeply that night passes in less than a second. The story ended with the mother and father angry at the noises that came from their daughter's bedroom. In the next session she showed the contents of her purse, which were mostly broken items and a torn poster of the teenage idol, David Cassidy. She "tore" and "stretched" the purse as she showed its contents. "What was I playing yesterday? Oh, yes! Nighttime!" She promptly changed the game to playing school. She was a strict teacher, and at the end she changed from a lay teacher to a nun. I commented on the change of game, and the implication that something about "nighttime" stories worried her about being good and being bad. In another session she play-acted a scary TV show, and struggled with the decision as to whether to change channels to a less frightening show. I added that this was like two years ago when she quit kindergarten and watched soap operas all day, and how hard it had been for her then to turn them off.

Two weeks later, she started the session intensely play-acting a story about a mother and father who were asleep, while their children wrestled and fought in a pool. She stopped, and went to the couch. "It's a night," she said, "and I'm asleep." She and her sister sometimes wrestled at night, she said, and there were scary noises they didn't understand. When I wondered what a frightened child might do to feel less frightened, Beth quickly said her sister sucked her tongue, and quickly changed the subject.

Two sessions later she talked about a picture of Jesus in her mother's bedroom, with eyes that follow you as you walk around. It smiled at you when you were good, and frowned at you when you were bad.

In the next session, after saying something unclear about "bad boys" she play-acted going on a hectic, frightening honeymoon flight, then with exaggerated gestures collapsed on the couch. "*I'm* never going to marry," she said. I commented on her ambivalence. She said she was too exhausted to talk. I referred to her opening comment about what some "bad boys" did, and mentioned how she was sometimes afraid her worries about marriage were "bad," and might make the picture of Jesus frown. I referred also to a screen memory talked about in the first year of analysis, of a gloved finger shaking "no" at her. "That was God's finger," she said, "telling me to stop sucking my tongue." I asked if that's bad to do. "Well," she said, "maybe I was sticking it out a bit, too." I commented that little girls in bed who are worried try to find something to do to feel better, like suck their tongue, or rub their t-shirt, or suck their thumb, or find other parts of their body to hold on to or rub. "All my *sister* does is suck her thumb, only that *one* thing," she said, then was thoughtfully silent for a while.

In the next session she showed me her infected finger. "It's like that because I pick at it," she announced. She asked if she should see a doctor. We played Candyland, but mostly she talked about how she eats too much candy and that gives her cavities. She then play-acted a situation in which if she said "five" she would die. "One . . . two . . . three . . . four . . . I can't stop myself . . . five! Bang! I'm dead!" She fell to the floor. But then she got up, and said "Gee! I'm *not* dead!" She started counting again, repeating the sequence several times.

Later, associating to two recent dreams, she realized that she expected something would go wrong at her first communion. She then alternated between pantomiming a sexy hula dance and communion. She put her shawl over her head, and prayed—but then put her hands under the shawl and pretended she had breasts. I pointed out how she was still playing "change the subject," and it was between "romantic" things and religious things, between things that make the picture of Jesus frown and smile.

The theme of good versus bad was most prominent over the ensuing weeks. The mother reported that at home Beth was again asking her parents to tuck her in "very tightly" at night, with her arms above the covers. She was critical of others for using bad English, showing off, and reading "bad" magazines. She was again preoccupied with doctor shows on television, and was remembering more of her hospitalization. For instance, she recalled she had to be fed because of the arm restraints used with the I.V.'s; she recalled one time when her mother fed her the jello the nurse had forgotten to feed her. She also was talking more about the Teddy bear she had lost at the beach right after her hospitalization, and wondered if the whales and sharks might have eaten it.

In another session at this time she put on a "performance" of alternating "silly" and religious poems. I commented on the two kinds of poems, linking them to the good-bad theme of recent sessions. "Alright," she announced, "I'll be bad." She threw paper on the floor, talked loud, said fresh things. She said she didn't believe in "J.C." or God. "After all, who made *Him?*" She drew many sloppy pictures and threw them on the floor. She then said she would be *good*. She cleaned up the mess she had made. She took a piece of paper, rolled it up, and looked inside. She poked her finger in it, and said "Ow! I've hurt my finger! My hand is paralyzed!" Before I could say anything, she said "Don't say it! I won't listen anyway!" She then started to ask me silly and pointless questions. I commented that that was what she was doing two years ago when she had these same worries on her mind and didn't know how to ask about them.

It should be mentioned that, increasingly, Beth now presented herself in parts of almost all sessions, and in many sessions from start to finish, as a most "normal," "average" latency-age girl, reporting on her day-to-day activities in a manner such that I could see how her social skills were improving and her repertoire of activities was broadening. At these times the interaction was devoid of conflict or tension, with none of the push-pull, teasing qualities of the past, or the more recent overly "romantic" qualities.

In the next month, she brought in her report card to show me that, along with her usual "A"s and "A-pluses," she had received for the first time a "B" in handwriting. She was very pleased, and excited that "at last" she had accomplished something she thought impossible.

It was at this time, too, that Beth first expressed the wish to stop the analysis as it interfered with her after-school play with friends, activity that she had only relatively recently begun. In her sessions she showed me some of the new games she had learned, such as card games and "Chinese jump rope." In one session the theme seemed to be her wish to pretend she was not Beth and I was not me. When I started to say something about this she said she was "bored" with my talking. I suggested that she seemed to want things to be different in the office between us, that she wished to be different, wanted me to be different, and wanted different interaction between us. Two sessions at that time indicated some of these differences.

In one session she pantomimed a new Lipton tea TV commercial. She wanted/didn't want me to watch. I referred to a previously identified theme, namely, her ambivalence about exhibitionism; as we had put it: she wanted to perform on a stage but without an audience. She then changed her activities to a classroom in which we had to name a state or country that begins with each letter of the alphabet. At "O" she said "Operation—oops! That's not a state!" She then pantomimed being in a bathtub, and being concerned at what I might see. "If you see the bubbles you'll want my bubblebath, as they're pretty bubbles!" She then went to bed. She said she sleeps oddly, and tossed and turned, snored, put her legs up over the back of the couch, etc. She was very self-conscious as to what I might see. I commented that even in bed she felt "looked at" and so had to be careful about what she did. She tried to adjust the bed to get it "just right," but without success. I said that I agreed that that is why she needed to be tucked in just right, because she felt looked at and therefore self-conscious, and hoped that if the bed were just right it would keep her from doing things that might make the picture of Jesus frown or God's finger shake "no." She was quiet and thoughtful for a while. I reminded her of the word "operation" from earlier in the session, and said it came to her mind as she believed at the time that she was in the hospital because of the things she did at night in bed. After a pause she said she remembered now all about the hospitalization and that really it wasn't so bad. The nurses were nice and played games with her, and her mother and father visited often and gave her presents. But she didn't like the needles the doctors gave her.

In the next session she told me of the beautiful veil she was to wear at her first communion, and described details of the rehearsal, party, etc. She mentioned a classmate with whom she had had a "feud" all year, and decided to draw a picture of her and then "smash" it! She changed the picture to that of a king. She said that the picture first reminded her of a queen she'd like to smash, and that reminded her of a king she liked. She said the queen was Queen Mary . . . whose daughter is Princess *Elizabeth!* As she made her drawings, she said: "Don't look as they're not finished yet. They're being born. You don't know what it'll be until it's born." I asked her if she had her little sister's birth in mind. She said she first thought she was a balloon under her mother's dress. Her parents had asked her whether she'd like a brother or a sister, and she said she'd rather have a dog. I commented that children have many theories about babies. She then played school. She was a teacher teaching how two parts of words can be put together to make a new word, such as "pull" and "ed" becomes "pulled," etc. I commented on the theme of knowing/not knowing, and how two different parts that combine to make a new word is like conception. The teacher scolded those students who didn't know the lesson. She had Princess Elizabeth be a student who *does* know.

A month after her first communion, her father called me on the phone and announced that he and his wife had decided therapy was to stop the middle of July when the family was to leave for their summer vacation. They both felt that Beth was "totally cured," and that the expense and inconvenience was too great to continue. They also saw her first communion as a "new beginning." Father felt that the summer break was an "ideal" time to stop as therapy would be stopping then, anyway. Further, he and his wife had realized how much their own problems had contributed to Beth's problems, as well as those of their other daughters, and because they were working on them successfully, this, too, was a reason therapy was no longer needed. It seemed clear to me that Beth's father was firm in his conviction. Further, from the clinical material it did not seem that unreasonable. I elected to join Beth's father and work with him towards a compatible joint termination of treatment.

In subsequent sessions almost all the themes from the analysis were briefly recapitulated by Beth. I commented on this, and shortly she was commenting on it herself. There was a nostalgic reminiscence about our work together. She also put certain issues in perspective. For instance, when replaying the secretary of the repair shop who knew about washing machines but not cars, she said "After all, I *am* only eight, and I *am* a girl, so how could I know all about cars?" There were also repeated references to her progress in dancing school with demonstrations that indeed confirmed her increasing grade and comfortable feminine identity.

In the following session she recounted the history of the analysis: the conflicts of two years ago, the transference neurosis of eight months ago, and its current resolution. Then, in the next session, she thanked me for my efforts on her behalf, not without a pointed reference to the transference.

She surveyed the assortment of toys in the cupboard and commented how each game was marked as appropriate for a certain age child. She chose to play Candyland as it was for four to eight-year-olds, and she was eight. We played it twice, then she used the board and the men to play-act a story. There were two couples, Bob and Louise, and Rick and Laurie, visited with one another and had a nice time together. After the second couple, whose men were manipulated by me, left Beth's couple, the hosts, discussed what a nice time they had. I was instructed to have my couple do the same. Then time changed to two years ago. At that time Beth had the couples fighting with one another. The women complained the men spent too much time watching sports; then men complained the women spent too much money. "It's *awful*," Beth said. Then the time changed to eight months ago, and Beth had *her* couple visit *my* couple. My couple were "very rich." Beth interrupted the story and asked me if I were rich. She said her father said I was. In her story, her couple asked my couple about their thick rugs, jewelry, etc. Her couple left, and fought on the way home, especially when they got back to their bedroom. They were noisy and up all night, eating snacks and drinking. She explained their fights made them thirsty and hungry. Her eye was on the clock, so she knew the session was about to end. I commented on the time, and said her story had to be interrupted. She said it was alright, as there would be plenty of time to finish it in the next session.

She came in the next day saying she didn't know what to do. Draw? Play school? Play a game? I commented that she had ended her previous session with plans for this one. "I know," she said, "I remember." She announced she would end the story by making a report card for me. The rest of the session was involved with this activity. I recieved "A"s and "B"s in my various academic subjects (reading, math, etc.), and an "A-plus" in courtesy. But I got a "D-plus" in handwriting, so I earned only *second* honors. Her sense of humor, her friendly warmth towards me, and her pleasure in this activity, were striking.

In a phone conversation, the mother said that Beth was now engaging in activities she had previously feared, such as playing with the neighborhood dogs or riding her bike on the street with her friends.

Beth spent all of one of our sessions showing me what she had learned in dancing class, and telling me of the pleasurable activities she and her friends engaged in. She added at the end that *now* she really could swim in the deep pool as she could hold her breath, swim under water, etc., and that she was no longer afraid of dogs. She interrupted herself twice to lie on the couch and suck her tongue and stroke her t-shirt. I commented that that was something she used to do when she felt her mother wasn't there. "I know what you're going to say next," she said. And I said she was doing it now as she was thinking that soon I wouldn't be there. "Yes," she said. She was quiet and thoughtful for a while. At the end I said that she probably felt both excited and pleased about stopping, as well as sad about saying good-bye. She pantomimed "in one ear and out the other" while smiling and nodding "yes."

In our last session, the 381st, Beth came in, thoughtful and low-keyed. She said, "Cartwheel time!" and proceeded to show me how she had learned to do them in dancing class. She then wanted to play chess, showing me how she was now learning from one of her cousins. She then used the chessmen to play parade, commenting that the "kings" and "queens" in the parade were really just people dressed up to look like royalty. In these references to rapprochement and oedipal material from the analysis she communicated her view that she was ready for termination. Affectively, to this point she was holding herself back, avoiding interaction with me. I commented that it was our last session, and that maybe like the people in the parade she was pretending to be something that she wasn't by acting so calm. "Did you say something?" she commented with a sly grin. "Who ever heard of an idea like *that!*" She was quiet and thoughtful, eyeing the clock. In the last few minutes she repeated: "It's time to go" over and over though it was not yet time. I commented that that was something she did a lot early in the analysis, when she felt time was moving against her wishes and she wanted to be in control of time rather than feel time was in control of her; and I said this was related to her feelings about our last session. At the end, she looked a little sad, but not really that distressed. I said good-bye, that I enjoyed knowing her and working with her, and wished her the best for the future.

DYNAMIC FORMULATION

Constitutionally Beth was mismatched with her parents. Her superior endowment and the relative strength of her drive structure made her not the best sort of child for her well meaning but somewhat limited parents. Their reliance upon superego put them in opposition to instinctual expression, but more reactive to than in command of it. Mother's presumed situational depression during Beth's first years left her less libidinally available than she might have been, limiting an important source of supplies that contribute to the maximal neutralization of aggression and ego structuralization.

Beth's excellent endowment made possible—in fact, may have made necessary—the precocious exercise of independence. She felt, therefore, torn between a push for separate, autonomous functioning and a heavily conflicted regressive wish for the gratifications of symbiotic yearning she felt had not been adequately met.

The challenges of separation-individuation presented a stress with which she could not successfully cope. This was seen clinically in the persistence of certain behavioral phenomena characteristic of the first three subphases of separation-individuation. She revealed abortive miniature anaclitic depressions in response to mother's absence, with a need to withdraw into herself to hold onto mental images of mother. She revealed, in part defensively, the hypomanic "world is my oyster" activity of the practicing subphase, but with limited capacity to seek out mother for refueling. Beth's rapprochement crisis was unresolved at the time of the start of the analysis, as seen in her alternating independent and dependent behavior, contradictory messages to her mother, and the hostile dependency seen where there is uncertainty as to the libidinal availability of mother. Object constancy vis-a-vis her mother had not been achieved to an age-appropriate extent. She was also still reacting to the mortification engendered by the deflation of infantile omnipotence and clung stubbornly, though ambivalently, to the illusion of symbiosis recaptured.

Characteristically, she threw herself into phallic-oedipal issues as psychosexual development proceeded. As the final year of psychoanalysis revealed, real life experiences dovetailed with her developmental conflicts, influencing the shape of her infantile neurosis. The hospitalization at age two and a half was felt as punishment for primal scene curiosity and infantile masturbation. It was interpreted by her subsequently as the time when she was castrated as a punishment for her sexual fantasies. The loss of the Teddy bear shortly thereafter can be seen as reflecting the equation: transitional object equals penis, and, therefore, was another event felt as castration.[1] The birth of the sibling when Beth was four was psychologically traumatic as it implied another anxiety provoking separation from mother, stimulated further phallic and oedipal wishes which increased her castration anxiety, and resulted in greater conflict-laden regressive wishes.

Her symptoms reflected her unsuccessful attempts at resolving her multiple intrapsychic conflicts: staying at home, and her hostile

1. I am indebted to George Kochis, M.D., for this intriguing hypothesis.

dependency upon her mother reflected her anxiety filled attempts at a regressive solution to her phallic-oedipal wishes, but only intensified her still unresolved rapprochement crisis. The tight clothes reflected her penetration fears and castration anxieties; her obsession with soap operas reflected both primal scene curiosity and counterphobic defensive operations. Her interest in the medical content of these shows reflected the return of the repressed memories and fantasies concerning her own traumatic hospitalization; her repeated "meaningless" questions, and the criticism of the answers she received, reflected her inability to ask the questions she wanted to ask and her disappointment that she was not given the answers she *really* wanted. Bedtime difficulties and the "shaking gloved finger" reflected her masturbatory guilt and her efforts at seeking external help in controlling both the activity and the accompanying fantasies. But the intensely emotional push-pull behavioral interaction with her mother—which was mother's primary concern at the start of treatment—reflected the unresolved rapprochement issues that underlay the phallic-oedipal conflicts. The start of school meant a further separation from mother; and it meant contact with boys and, therefore, the stimulation of phallic-oedipal anxieties. It served as a double precipitating influence.

RELATIONSHIP BETWEEN UNRESOLVED RAPPROCHEMENT CONFLICT AND THE INFANTILE NEUROSIS

The adequate resolution of the rapprochement subphase of the separation-individuation process brings about certain developmental accomplishments which make more likely the adequate resolution of the infantile neurosis, with which it overlaps. These developmental accomplishments can be discussed under three headings: the nature of the mental representations; the level of ego structuralization and the neutralization of aggression; and the vicissitudes of infantile omnipotence.

The nature of the mental representations. The "mother of separation," the rapprochement mother who remains omnipotent in the eyes of her child but now seems suddenly to be unwilling to share this omnipotence as she had in the past, is qualitatively different from the oedipal mother. There is an affective charge and cognitive style unique to the interaction with each. The former, dyadic relationship is experienced by the child in the context of separation, if not annihilation, anxiety, and with still unstable self-boundaries. Object constancy has not yet been achieved, and accordingly the intra-psychic object world is prone to collapse. The oedipal mother, on the other hand, in the triadic relationship, is perceived in the context of castration anxiety primarily, with a far more stable sense of self and some degree of object constancy. The *dyadic "good mother" mental representation* from the adequately mastered earlier separation-individuation process, as a constant internal object, is available to the oedipal child at moments of intense conflict with the *oedipal mother*.

Where the separation-individuation process has not been ade-quately surmounted, there is a relative failure to develop a stable, positively cathected maternal introject to buttress the ego against anxiety, to act as a nidus around which identity can crystallize, and to allow for episodic regression in the service of the ego, should the need arise. Instead, the maternal introject is ambivalently cathected, and a source of greater rather than lesser anxiety as the narcissistic mortification of rapprochement is revived and the fear of the dis-solution of the self is aroused in response to heightened symbiotic yearnings.

The level of ego structuralization and the neutralization of aggres-sion. The narcissistic deflation the child experiences when cognitive development makes necessary the perception of separateness from mother during rapprochement mobilizes infantile rage. The "bad mother/bad self" mental images laid down as memory traces from past occasions when mother's ministrations failed to immediately quell the infant's distress are also mobilized, and are contrasted to the comforting images of the "good mother/good self" memory traces. The "splitting" of rapprochement occurs, a splitting expressed not only in terms of positively versus negatively cathected images of mother but also of self as mental image and of subjectively experi-enced affect states. The healing of this split is an essential accom-plishment of the adequate resolution of the rapprochement subphase, and involves blending the split images into more or less homogenized images of mother and self, with positive and negative affects attached but of a less extreme, all-or-nothing sort. This is a developmental phenomenon clinically observable, but not yet ade-quately explained theoretically, perhaps due to shortcomings in theoretical conceptualizations at this time.

Nevertheless, for the oedipal child who has not yet adequately healed the split, the affect of unpleasure and hostile wishes directed against the mother abound, relatively unmodified by the "split off" positive affects. The ambivalent attachment to the mother impedes the development of self-reliance because distance between mother and child intensifies the separation anxiety and thereby the hostility. Primary rather than secondary narcissism remains the child's predominant mode of seeking relief from the mortifications of separateness from mother. The development of object constancy is impeded.

For such a child the phallic-oedipal stage of development cannot easily be mastered. Castration anxiety is intolerable, defenses are unstable, the tenuous sense of identity cannot tolerate the inevitable conflicts with his parents. Unpleasure and hostility are experienced too intensely to be contained, and the capacity for triadic object relationships is lacking.

The vicissitudes of infantile omnipotence. The narcissistic pain engendered by the discovery of separateness in rapprochement is a forerunner and preliminary to the narcissistic mortifications inevitable in phallic-oedipal conflict. The relinquishment of the symbiotic part object can be viewed as a process similar in many ways to the task of relinquishing the oedipal objects; both involve a loss just as both involve a narcissistic deflation. There is, however, a qualitative difference between the narcissism of infantile megalomanic omnipotence and phallic narcissism. The former is primitive in affect and cognitive style, dealing with issues of total annihilation and total dominance, and with a poor sense of ego boundaries or reality. Where the infantile yearnings for the omnipotence of the symbiotic bond have not been adequately relinquished, the primitive qualities of infantile omnipotence contaminate phallic narcissism in the infantile neurosis. Phallic wishes are overidealized, phallic activity is charged with relatively unneutralized infantile sexual and hostile wishes, and castration anxiety brings with it the threat of annihilation. The oedipal scenario takes on a larger than life quality, and such a child's already handicapped ego is confronted with more than even an adequately developed ego can cope. The resultant sense of ego helplessness only aggravates the situation by intensifying regressive wishes, further mobilizing omnipotent yearnings.

In Beth's analysis can be traced the developmental progress of her capacity for object constancy, the stability of her ego, and the shift from primary to secondary narcissism. Initially, her capacity for libidinal object permanence was so deficient that she required the physical presence of mother. The internalized object was unstable, particularly when threatened by intense rage mobilized by her narcissistic mortification. Ego defensive maneuvers were insufficient. She seemed to fear her own destruction.

It was an important step forward when she was able to give herself mothering with her transitional object—her cotton undershirt—and by means of autoerotic stimulation (sucking her tongue). The regressive excursions made necessary by her ego's inability to tolerate the anxieties mobilized by phallic-oedipal conflict became free of mother-connected ambivalence; the good-mother substitute object was also constantly and readily available, supporting her fragile sense of autonomy.

There followed in the analysis a lengthy and painful delayed rapprochement subphase, with relinquishment of and mourning for the lost symbiotic partner, using the passage of time as the main metaphor. The injured primary narcissism was compensated for by the gradual development of secondary narcissistic supplies. The split was finally healed.

It was then possible for Beth, psychologically now equipped, to confront the phallic-oedipal challenges. At this point, through defense and content analysis, using the transference, the repressed traumatic core of her infantile neurosis was brought into consciousness. The oedipal complex was resolved sufficiently to allow for her entry into latency.

Beth's analysis was, then, both *a classical analysis of the infantile neurosis,* as first described by Freud three-quarters of a century ago, and an *ego developmental process.* The latter a facet of the analytic situation, it is increasingly appreciated as ego developmental psychology widens our perspectives and deepens our understanding of the human mind.

SUMMARY

The psychoanalytic understanding of the psychical events of the first years of life has deepened, particularly as a consequence of the researches and developmental theories of Margaret Mahler and her co-workers. Reconstructive work in psychoanalysis has reaped the benefits of the expanded developmental models, in keeping with

Freud's early discovery of the importance of the infantile past in the psychogenesis of mental conflict. The psychoanalysis of a child is recounted in some detail in an attempt to explicate with clinical material the interrelationship between unresolved rapprochement conflict and the infantile neurosis. This interrelationship is then discussed in terms of the nature of the mental representations, the structuralization of the ego and the neutralization of aggression, and the vicissitudes of infantile omnipotence. The treatment was both a classical analysis of the infantile neurosis, and an ego developmental process.

References

Burland, J. A. (1975). Separation-individuation and reconstructions in psychoanalysis. *International Journal of Psychoanalytic Psychotherapy* 4:303-335.

Freud, S. (1893-1895). *Studies in Hysteria. Standard Edition* 2:1-306.

——— (1909a). Analysis of a phobia in a five-year-old boy. *Standard Edition* 10:5-149.

——— (1909b). Notes upon a case of obsessional neurosis. *Standard Edition* 10:158-249.

——— (1911). Psycho-analytic notes on an autobiographical account of a case of paranoia *(Dementia paranoides). Standard Edition* 12:9-82.

——— (1918). From the history of an infantile neurosis. *Standard Edition* 17:7-122.

——— (1937). Constructions in analysis. *Standard Edition* 23:255-269.

Mahler, M. (1966). Notes on the development of basic moods: The depressive affect. In *Psychoanalysis: A General Psychology: Essays in Honor of Heinz Hartmann,* ed. R. Loewenstein et al. New York: International Universities Press. pp. 152-168. Reprinted in *The Selected Papers of Margaret S. Mahler,* vol. 2, ch. 5. New York: Jason Aronson, 1979.

——— (1968). *On Human Symbiosis and the Vicissitudes of Individuation,* vol. 1. Infantile Psychosis. In collaboration with M. Furer. New York: International Universities Press.

——— (1972). On the first three sub-phases of the separation-individuation process. *International Journal of Psycho-Analysis* 53:333-338. Reprinted in *Selected Papers,* op. cit., ch. 8.

Mahler, M., Pine, F., and Bergman, A. (1975). *The Psychological Birth of the Human Infant: Symbiosis and Individuation.* New York: Basic Books.

Winnicott, D. N. (1951). Transitional objects and transitional phenomenon. In *Through Paediatrics to Psycho-Analysis,* pp. 229-242. New York: Basic Books, 1958.

20

Residues of Split-Object and Split-Self Dichotomies in Adolescence

SELMA KRAMER, M.D.

The applicability of Mahler's symbiosis and separation-individuation theory has been documented in many ways. The series of programs at the American Psychoanalytic Association on the reverberations of separation-individuation throughout the life cycle, the demand for her books and papers, and the growing number of articles in adult and child psychoanalysis, psychiatry, psychology, and pediatrics referring to Mahler's work all attest to the ever-increasing awareness of the importance and usefulness of her concepts.

Mahler's papers have made me increasingly sensitive to the difference between dyadic and triadic transference in patients of all ages, and have aroused a special interest in reconstruction of very early childhood pathology in the analysis of adolescent and adult patients.

Her formulations of the separation-individuation phase, especially the rapprochement subphase and its vicissitudes, have helped me to conceptualize a treatment plan for a group of adolescent patients, for the most part girls,[1] who have had experiential or constitutional

---

1. Colleagues in Philadelphia raised interesting questions about male patients with similar problems. I feel that they should be the subject of continued study.

problems, or both, which have seriously impaired their object relationships and sense of self. They are the subject of my paper. As I
shall describe, very early conflicts intensify or recur in adolescence;
their problems pertain especially to intrapsychic separation from
primary love objects, attainment of heterosexual object choice, and
ultimate culmination of a well-defined sense of identity. In an earlier
paper (Kramer 1971), I wrote:

> Mahler, through her investigation of infancy and early childhood,
> has opened doors to a new understanding of the evolvement of entity
> and identity in the child. On the basis of careful clinical study of long-
> term interaction in mother-child pairs, and of observation and treat-
> ment of psychotic and ego-defective children, Mahler has formulated
> certain well-documented theoretical concepts that spell out the intra-
> psychic process in the child, as he slowly moves from the original
> undifferentiated union with his mother to the achievement of a sense
> of personal identity.

She emphasizes that object and self-constancy are only partially
achieved by 36 months, and describes the lifelong regressive desire
for reunion with the primary love object (Mahler 1966). When there is
a persistence of problems stemming from the preoedipal phase of
development, the oedipus complex and the ensuing infantile neurosis will be compromised (Mahler 1975, Ritvo 1974).

In 1968 Peter Blos published an outstanding paper, "The Second
Individuation," in which, within the framework of Mahler's theories,
he conceptualized normal and inevitable regressive phenomena in
adolescence to preoedipal developmental phases, and he described
the adolescent's need to experience a "second individuation." As I
will describe in greater detail, my patients could not attain a "second
individuation" in adolescence nor attain a well-defined sense of
identity. Unable to achieve sound secondary narcissism, they rely
too much on opinions of others for their own sense of worth. As a
most important problem these adolescent patients demonstrate,
basically, a persistence of or regression to preoedipal splitting of
self- and object representations. I feel that the split of the self-
representation is the more noxious split and determines the course
that treatment must take. This is the theme of my paper.

THEORETICAL FORMULATION

The following leans heavily upon Mahler's developmental concepts, particularly those concerning normal and pathological splitting. I will demonstrate what I interpret as evidence of pathological splitting of self- and object representation in these adolescent patients, and raise questions about certain requisites for treatment, using clinical material.

First I will present some of Mahler's thinking about the epigenesis of normal splitting of self- and object representations, and its vicissitudes. Although I will not refer to them here, I wish to state my indebtedness to Jacobson (1954) and Kernberg (1967), among others.

Mahler (1955) disclosed her concept of the origins of splitting of self and object, each into "good" and "bad," when she and Gosliner described expulsive mechanisms used by the young infant to rid himself of unpleasurable tension; these mechanisms, together with the mother's ministrations, help the infant to distinguish eventually between pleasurable and unpleasurable experiences. At differentiation, predominantly "good" and predominantly "bad" memory islands become vaguely allocated to self and the nonself (Mahler 1968), as scattered part images of both self and nonself are beginning to be formed. (See also Jacobson 1954)

Mahler emphasizes (1968, p. 45) that part *self-images* [my italics] are endowed with the same qualities of . . . 'good' and . . . 'bad' as are scattered part images of the mother." In the course of normal development (after 12-18 months) there is a unification of split images of objects and self, and a united object representation becomes demarcated from a unified self-representation; however, "solid integration . . . is not achieved during the symbiotic phase . . . nor is it completed during the . . . separation-individuation phase" (p. 46). Mahler feels that "object constancy can be said to have been reached when one particular defense—the splitting of object images—is no longer readily available to the ego" (p. 224).

What starts as a mechanism to rid the very young infant of unpleasurable tension becomes for a while a normal defense, the purpose of which Mahler feels, as does Kernberg (1966), is to protect the beloved good object from the derivatives of the child's aggression which is directed toward the bad or absent mother (see also Mahler 1966). Normally splitting, a temporary defense, is then replaced by repression which enables the child to handle his anger toward the loved object and to tolerate his ambivalence.

Vicissitudes of the developing self-representation are similar but more difficult to follow. Mahler (1966) has alluded to the need for love by the mother and to her acceptance of the child's anger for the synthesis of "good" and "bad" self into a unified self-representation—for her "love and acceptance of the toddler and even of his ambivalence which enable the toddler's ego to cathect his self-representation with 'neutralized energy'" (p. 161). She further connects the failure of the mother to provide such emotional supplies especially at the rapprochement subphase (Mahler 1971) with the "collapse of the child's belief in his *own omnipotence* [which] with his uncertainty about the emotional availability of the parents creates the so-called 'hostile dependency' upon and ambivalence toward the parents" (my italics).

This is often followed by a "feeling of helplessness which creates the basic depressive mood." The latter negative depressive affective responsiveness or mood may persist or give way to a "premature earnestness, a kind of unchildlike concern which may possibly indicate a precocity of superego structuralization" (p. 163-164). This type of unchildlike precocity was seen in my patients.

Mahler (1971) discusses the failure of integration of "good" and "bad" self as she alludes to

> sequelae of the failure of internalization, increased separation anxiety, and other clinical signs that indicate, for example, the following: that the blending and synthesis of "good" and "bad" self- and object images have not been achieved; that ego-filtered affects have become inundated with surplus unneutralized aggression; that delusions of omnipotence alternate with utter dependency and self-denigration; that the body image has become or remains suffused with unneutralized id-related erotogeniety and aggressive, pent-up body feelings, and so on.

She also suggests that "the child might not have taken autonomous, representationally clearly separated possession of his or her own bodily self, partly because he or she did not experience the mother's gradual relinquishing possession of her toddler's body" (p. 416).

My clinical experience with analysis of this group of adolescents led me to raise some questions:

1. Just as persistence of splitting of the object representation protects the mental representation of mother from the child's fury, does splitting the self-representation similarly protect the self from an overwhelming amount of aggression turned against it?

2. Just as the existence of and inability to modulate aggression are related to splitting, might the apparent "basic" or "constitutional" passivity I have encountered in my patients have relevance to the maintenance of splitting to problems in separating from the mother, to depressiveness, and to precocious superego formation?

3. Are the mothers of these children excessively afraid of their own aggression, and therefore convey this to a susceptible child?

The histories of my patients give almost uniformly the picture of the "good child" who very early was overly attuned to the mother's need for closeness, quietness, and controlled behavior. In questioning why the child has been "good," "undemanding," and "compliant," we must consider constitutional, experiential factors (interaction with the parents, their needs and make-up) and stress traumatic factors. It is quite possible that more than one factor must be present to create the need to be and to remain the "good child."

Returning to "basic passivity" as a constitutional factor, I should like to cite the work of Weil (1970), Alpert, Neubauer, and Weil (1956), who have described some infants who reveal a preponderance of passivity as compared to aggressive reaction. I feel that the interaction between an infant's passivity[2] and the maternal temperament, as well as the mother's needs for a less, rather than a more reactive child, must be of considerable significance in the creation of the compliant child who is "always good."

Mahler described mother-child pairs in which the mother's needs and especially her depressive affects have considerable influence upon the child's temperament, especially insofar as early depressiveness in the child is concerned. She suggests that this is encountered more often in girls, both because of the boy's greater aggressiveness which enables him to "get out from under" the mother's influence and because of the girl's need to turn back to the mother, whom she blames for what she perceives as her inadequate genitals and from

2. The concept of basic passivity was questioned in the Philadelphia presentation of this paper. However, Dr. Joseph Rudolph, who had been a pediatrician for years, stated that he observed many variations in activity-passivity levels of newborns, which did or did not jibe with the activity type of the parents as well as their needs for a particular type of child.

whom she expects amends. Rapprochement crises may ensue (Mahler 1966, 1975).

My patients did not, to the recollection of their parents, have overt temper tantrums nor disturbing crises during rapprochement. As with Mahler's research subjects, my patients were clinging and coercive, but as one mother put it, "nicely so." Could it be that the precocious islands of superego development in my patients joined with a constitutional temperament and with needs of depressive mothers, whose influence and expectations produce a low-keyed rapprochement without open crisis, and with continuation of splitting, now as a pathological phenomenon?

Certainly in adolescence, evidence of depression, harsh superego, low self-esteem, and problems with aggression were all present. Reconstruction suggests that all of these problems existed at least in rapprochement, when most of these emotionally precocious children were considered happy by their parents because they were good and quiet, even placid.[3]

As for stress traumata, one patient had very serious medical problems during infancy and toddlerhood. A number of patients experienced the birth of a younger sibling during their rapprochement subphase.

CLINICAL MATERIAL

I should now like to discuss my patients as a group. Their histories bear an extraordinary resemblance to each other. The presenting problems are of dependency, separation, autonomy, and their inability to tolerate even minimal aggression. In some, with puberty, dormant problems come to the fore. Others may show anxiety symptoms and depression when they are about to go to college; occasionally there may be anorexia (see Sours 1974). The awareness

3. While only one mother in my series was sufficiently clinically depressed to need hospitalization during her child's infancy and toddlerhood, most of the mothers of this group could be considered "depressive" and many had problems with aggression.

Mahler (personal communication) speaks of an "infectiousness" of the depressive affect from the depressed mother into her child (especially her daughter). Parens (personal communication) sees much evidence of "contagion of affect in young children."

of their psychic pain, dependency, and especially of depression leads them to seek counseling which results in the recommendation for psychoanalysis.

It is difficult to get an accurate history of very early development in these patients because the history is eminently undramatic.[4] Symbiosis and differentiation are reported as having gone well. They had a rather subdued practicing subphase although in some there was pleasure in mastery. Even then the girls were described as solemn "little owls," "cautious," and "very good." There were no reported rapprochement crises; outstanding features were rather of closeness, compliance, and overalertness to, or great empathy with, mother's moods. In a few cases there was a history of early feeding difficulties. Many of the patients had transitional objects or sucked their thumbs for prolonged periods of time. Neither of these behaviors seemed to have created conflict with the parents. Toilet training, as one might expect, went well.

As some parents were questioned in greater depth, they reported shadowing by the patients, firm and persistent coercion of the mother, and more than average separation problems during the rapprochement subphase. This was not particularly troublesome because it seemed to gratify the needs of the mothers as well. I was led to question whether these mothers were of the type who tie but who do not really love. Later I will discuss the mothers more completely.

The continuation of rapprochement phase conflicts suggests that object and self-constancy were not fully achieved. The oedipus complex is affected substantially. The girls remained too close to their mother, and couldn't show or feel the typical triadic hostility or competitiveness during what was for many of them a most distorted oedipus complex. In latency they were good girls with, however, a verbalized fear of school and of teachers and serious problems in making friends with peers. In spite of their dislike of school, school difficulties were seldom recognized. The patients were good students, reported as "a pleasure to have in class" or "my most reliable helper" by teachers who did not recognize the anxiety behind this behavior, instead picked it out as model behavior. As I suggested

4. Dr. Robert Prall reminded me that early developmental history is very hard to elicit. I feel that there may have been a greater than ordinary difficulty eliciting history in these patients.

earlier, puberty or later adolescence ushers in evidence of real trouble, as the girl finds herself less and less able to function. Her school performance often drops, or if maintained, it is with great effort, with much anxiety and depressiveness. School is really intolerable, and although the high I.Q. of these patients may enable them to continue to do good work, they may refuse to attend school altogether; some may start college only to drop out, return home, or move to a commune where there is "always a family to surround you." They may join a group such as the "Moonies" where they are comfortable in accepting authority without questioning it, and where relationships with peers similar to themselves do not push them to the formation of a mature self.

The earlier discomfort with peers of both sexes is intensified. The patients rationalize this on the basis that their peers represent all that is bad, "fresh, sloppy, sexy and rebellious." When one investigates the problems with peers it is apparent that these patients have a wistful yearning to be like the peer group, of whom they are very envious. They feel that their mothers (and they) cannot permit friendships with peers who typify all they have been raised to think is so bad.

Because these patients are adolescents, some far from home, caught up in serious problems as they attempt to attend college, I do not know many of the parents well. I have had the opportunity to analyze one such mother whose child was treated by a colleague; in other cases reconstruction has given me a picture of the mothers of these girls.

DESCRIPTION OF THE PARENTS

I assume that there has been mutual clinging between mother and child even before the rapprochement subphase. I say "mutual" because the mother did not promote separation; instead she permitted as normal and to be expected the child's great need for exclusive closeness with herself, often with deliberate exclusion even of the father—going so far as to devalue or denigrate him.

For a variety of reasons the father could not act as "the father of separation," or, as Loewald describes (1951), could not function as the Rock of Gibraltar protecting the child against reengulfment. The fathers warrant further study.

It is possible that the mothers had excessive need for closeness with their daughters because they could not find closeness with their husbands; sometimes the mothers were, in addition, schizoid or friendless. Many of these mothers appear to have had excessive dependency on and great hostility toward their own mothers. Their clinging and hostile relationship with their adolescent daughters showed up very clearly in the course of analysis. Cindy's mother tried to seduce her away from the peer relationships which she was finally able to make after two and a half years of treatment by telling her what fun she would be missing if she went out with friends and offering to come drive her home if she felt bored. When Sandy finally went away to college, her mother called her daily, dropped in to see her without forewarning, and wrote long guilt-inspiring letters, asking how Sandy could leave her alone to suffer so. ("Alone" meant living with her husband.) A further reference to Cindy's analysis was made at the Panel on Transference in Child Analysis (Van Dam 1966).

CLINICAL CASE

I will present clinical material from the analysis of one of my patients, C, a 19-year-old college student who originally came for "short-term" help because of uncertainty over changing careers. A ballet dancer with some promise, during her first college year as a dance major she had increasingly severe pains which did not respond to competent medical treatment, and which made her unable to dance.

An interesting aside, which I understood only later, was that although I agreed to see her only for consultation, I accepted her for treatment in spite of a full schedule. Her quiet coercion had been, in fact, forceful and pushed me to accept this very interesting adolescent for treatment.

C was a rather pretty and delicate girl who appeared to be 14 instead of 19. She dressed in too-young looking clothes, and yet was always much more carefully put together than the average female student of the early 1970s used to be. (In general, the girls were pretty, fragile, and feminine in appearance.)

In preliminary appointments the patient complained somewhat

about her painful legs, but spoke much more about her personality problems that made life so joyless.

"I have no confidence; I'm so insecure; I have no friends; I am lonely; I am a high-strung person who has always been over-protected. Although I have achieved whatever I have set out to do, I never feel that I do well enough. Every performance, every exam is so frightening. I'm basically unhappy; maybe I'm depressed."

C was the second daughter of middle-aged academicians. Her father was a well-regarded professor; her mother never achieved a significant rank in her field, and gradually withdrew from professional work, seemingly rationalizing that her children needed her at home; even after they were of advanced school age she did not return to her work. The family had early stabilized into two pairs, the father and the eldest daughter forming one pair while the patient and her mother were the other, and had been overly close as far back as the patient could remember. The sister and father were strong, bombastic, and argumentative and had fought constantly until the sister left for college. My patient was known as the good child, "compliant, cooperative, and close." In spite of the fact that both girls received equally good school marks, family legend had it that the older sister was brilliant while my patient was "so-so but sweet." C remembered pervasive feelings of dread all through school, often staying home with her mother's consent. She feared and hated teachers although they made her their pet. As a child she had very few friends. If a friend was criticized by her mother, C immediately dropped her. When the patient's talent was discovered, she decided to pursue dance as a way out of the competition of academia; of course she soon found ballet to be as competitive. Ballet teachers caused her to experience the same hate and fear that she encountered with teachers anywhere. In other words, the mother-image at home was all good while the out of family mother-image was all bad.

When I first saw the patient, she had no friends. She was consciously contemptuous of and avoided male and female peers. "They don't love classical music or ballet as I do. They are interested in clothes, noisy parties, stupid things, rock and roll, drugs, sex, and violence. We have nothing in common." She could not see how much she yearned to be like them. She dated only occasionally. She said, "I guess I'm messed up, sex-wise" but she added with pride that she was the only 19-year-old virgin she knew.

When treatment started the patient was superficially overly compliant to me; she coerced me for rules and regulations to which she could comply both in treatment and in her "outside life." Otherwise she felt bereft, "without an anchor" to hold her from experiencing overwhelming anxiety. When I did not give her instructions the patient became anxious and querulous.

Material about her mother and her teachers revealed the phenomenon of the split object, that about herself and peers revealed the phenomenom of the split self. Early in treatment her mother was sweetness and light, while other adults in authority were ominous and threatening. Later it became apparent that she had to maintain the mechanism of splitting the object representation in order to protect the love object from (her) rage, and to avoid separation between them. Much further work led her to recognize the depth of her rage. While the rage was deep, and largely unconscious, I feel that for the most part, the rage—and also the ambivalence of these patients—was not excessive. The child's fear of aggressiveness makes the ambivalence seem terrifying.

The split self was evidenced by a continuing need to be the good girl, while she projected and displaced what she experienced as her own unacceptable impulses on to her sister and her peers. Keeping peers at a distance prevented C from using them in the service of healthy and realistic reappraisal of the parents and achieving age-adequate distance from them, physically and, more importantly, intrapsychically.

In dreams and in hesitantly described masturbation fantasies, elements of what she experienced as her own "bad self" slowly emerged into the transference. Slowly she allowed herself to recognize and say that masturbation was exciting, but very worrisome and guilt-provoking. Sexual fantasies, although upsetting, were less upsetting than evidence of hostility toward her mother which crept ever so gradually into the transference where only very slowly could it be analyzed.

For a long time she continued to shop for clothes with her mother, professing that only Mother had good judgment in selecting clothes for C. She and Mother, in a frequently repeated ritual, shopped in another city, for only there could they find a large selection of clothes in C's size. At times Mother's plans for shopping threatened to interfere with C's analysis. When, instead of changing appointments, I said that her request should be analyzed both as a resistance and because it was important for C to know why she and her mother needed to maintain the shopping ritual, C became angry with me, insisting with apparent anxiety that I could cause a rift between Mother and her. However, as we persisted, C began to sense mounting anger at her mother, feeling that she was being used as mother's "baby doll" who should and could know nothing, and that her mother unduly criticized whatever C bought on her own. For a while, C used her sister as a mother substitute when shopping and recognized within herself the same feelings toward her sister as those she had recently been feeling toward her mother. Some patients had a similar experience with another adult woman or, rarely, with a peer whom they use as a mother substitute. C felt unable to depend on her own judgment, experiencing that her mother and sister knew everything and that she knew nothing.

After a while, C began to recognize that she felt she *should* know nothing, because to *know* meant that she would come into conflict with her mother, as her sister had been. As the blanket denial of hostility toward her mother gradually lifted and her earlier use of projection and displacement gave way, C could tolerate and test the feelings and fantasies she had ascribed to the "bad self," and had projected onto others—her sister, whom she experienced as "cold, mean and rotten" (which meant that she was critical of their parents), and her classmates who were openly competitive, aggressive, and sexual.

After about one and a half years of analysis, C's attempts at coercing me served to help synthesize her "good" and "bad" self-representations in the following way. She would begin an hour in a friendly, chatty fashion, speak for about ten minutes, and then stop after saying "Now it's your turn." With that, her affect changed to apprehension and tension. My silence resulted in C's experiencing increasing anxiety and then panic as she implored me to take my turn. I then asked what she expected me to do on "my turn." She answered, "You'll tear me down. You should." And then, "You're the only one who has found out that I get angry. I've never shown anyone else. They'd hate me for it." I commented that she, too, was finding out what she had been unable to let herself know all along, that she got angry and that she hated herself for it.

The patient thought about my statement and wept, "But I am supposed to be nice and sweet. I've always seen myself that way . . . nice and sweet and not angry or sexy. You're taking it away from me." I said that her analysis was helping *her* to see that she was more complicated than she had thought herself to be, that in addition to being nice and sweet, she was also angry, competitive and sexual.

The patient soon brought in a dream about going into a strange apartment; someone was urging her to go into it. Maybe it was I. There was something about a cat and about a mongoloid child. In her associations, she thought of her anticipated move from her parents' home. Although I had not promoted the move she felt that I favored it. She was not a cat lover. Cats were like her sister, sneaky and independent and cannot be controlled. C prefered dogs. Cats were sexy and are creatures of the night, hence the term "catting around." Her sister is criticized and yet admired by her parents for her independence. "They criticize her so much, how can they admire her?"

To the mongoloid child the patient associated to a borderline retarded cousin who speaks in a high-pitched voice. C said, "That's the way I speak to my parents. I talk to them as if I'm a child, a retarded child at that!"

I said that she felt her alternatives were to be the cat (evil, cold, smart, sexy, and uncontrollable) or the "good, compliant baby" even to the point of dreaming that she was retarded, but that she found it hard to admit that all of these traits coexisted in her.

The patient continued to be in conflict, and struggled against accepting the two sides of herself as one. Gradually she could see herself as more like her peers—as competitive, boot-licking, and materialistic as they were. Her school major, no longer dance, became more focused with a realistic career aim. And in school, although studying remained conflicted, she began to do well. For the first time in her life she made close friends, joined them in their causes and rebellions and shared confidences with them, even staying overnight to do so.

One day she breezed in, bursting to tell me that she had received the only "A" in a class. However, her happiness in telling me that was quickly replaced by depressive ruminating over whether she really deserved it. She had filled the exam book with an awful lot of "bull." And she covered the "A" so her classmates would not see it. After a while the patient realized that she had been depressed since she received her grade. Suppose she is expected to get an "A" on the next test. If she did not it would be awful. How can she count on doing it? It was like in dance. If she had one good performance it made it worse for the next one. As she spoke she sounded like a simpering, whining little girl, pushing at me to give her the answers.

I told the patient that getting the "A" seemed to carry the threat that her relationship with me might change. I pointed out the change in her affect from early elation when she wanted to share with me the fact that she received the "A" to the almost immediate high-pitched whining of the dependent little girl. The patient replied that she never felt that she belonged in a place that could lead to success, for she was not sure she wanted to be a successful woman. Successful women have unisex haircuts (short and curly) and dress in tailored clothes. She said then, "You're a success and you have regular hair." "Hair" led to associations concerning sex. "To be feminine means you can be wishy-washy and indecisive." She felt that the analysis threatened to make her assertive and that she would lose the qualities that she felt make her feminine. She could not bear to think that she would become aggressive and assertive, even if such qualities could lead to success.

The struggle over unifying the good and bad self-representation continued for many months. The good self-representation was that of the sweet, unknowing, and compliant child; the bad self-representation was the hostile, knowing, and increasingly independent individual. The infantile nature of her good and bad self-concepts was increasingly apparent during this time.

Much work had to be done in the analysis to help her achieve a sufficient integration of the heretofore split between the good and bad self. Among other manifestations, integration was evidenced by an increased comfort with what she had considered bad traits in herself, by increased self-esteem and a much diminished need to project and displace to the peer group forbidden aggressive and sexual traits. Friendships with same-sex peers, and then a heterosexual affair strengthened her own ego identity, for now she was truly "good and bad."

When improved consolidation of the good and bad self had been achieved the analysis focused more consistently on, first, the recognition and, finally, the fusion of good and bad aspects of her mother and of the transference object. This fusion enabled her to separate emotionally and to be much less clinging and dependent. However, in the process fear mounted that she might hurt her mother or me by growing up and away. She was guilty as she saw her mother (and me, in the transference) as less capable, less all-knowing, as imperfect, infantilizing, or interfering.

In the transference, she began to question the near-perfection she had hitherto attributed to me. She complained one day that I was forcing her to be less dependent on her mother, but how could she? She had no role models, or if she had them, she did not want to know what they were. She referred to a successful woman bank director who is effective, feminine looking ("no unisex haircut") and who has a husband. C could not fantasize that she had sex or was vulnerable. After she spoke about the bank director for a while, there were many pauses and a build-up of tension. I commented that she was also wondering about me. The patient said, "I could never fantasy about you; I can't think of your private life. The idea that there's another side of you (different from the 'cool' of the office), sexual, or angry, threatens me. I get embarrassed by any such thoughts. It's better if I keep your two lives separate. I really mean that I can't bring it together . . . you as good and competent, with you as angry or sexy." Later she went on, "I can't see them together. I don't know which is best. I had two mothers. I couldn't figure out which [mother] was supposed to be and which was not. If you have a mother given to moods, one minute she's nice and then the next minute she was screaming, you know after a while that she's moody, and you adjust. But if you have a mother who always gives the impression of control, the lack of control is threatening. She gave me the impression of one [facet of her personality] and when she changed I got disoriented. So I only thought of her as nice and controlled. It stopped me from being disoriented. My sister was mean. Was that mother's meanness? My mother's sexuality is missing here, I know, just as yours is."

The separation struggle which followed upon the bringing together the good and bad real and transference mother now stirred up great anxiety, and fear of loss in C, the ultimate loss carrying with it a dread of "emptiness."

"It's like she's sitting on top of my brain. She's part of me. All the guilt. All the fears she instills in me. She told me such stupid things.

"I can't get rid of her unless I get sick of being sick. I can't compromise, I have to get rid of mother or capitulate to her completely.

"When I was little I thought she was perfect—one hundred percent. It was too painful to see her any other way. If I acted like my sister I was sure I'd get no love. I could never criticize mother and I had to show I needed her." The patient was quietly crying now and after a pause said, "Empty, that's what I'm afraid of." I asked, "Empty?" The patient said, "It's the awfullest feeling . . . since I was very little, I hate that emptiness. I did everything to avoid it. There's such a feeling of loss now, almost like mourning. Why should I do it (make a break from mother), except I have to. I see mother as shrivelling up. She looked that way yesterday when I didn't agree with her. It's like the end of the *Wizard of Oz*—they threw water on the wizard and he shriveled up." (At that moment I had taken a sip of water.) Her condensation of the witch, upon whom the water was really thrown, and the wizard reflected her anger at both of her parents.

Primal scene fantasies were now more explicit, and oedipal conflicts ensued, mixed with affect-laden material concerning disappointment in mother and in me. She continued to be angry because I did not give her advice or fulfill other wishes. Sometimes she came early in the secret hope that I would dismiss the earlier (male) patient and see her. When I did not, she felt dejected, as though I had not fulfilled my half of a bargain. Yet she was glad that I did not fulfill these wishes, for *she* would have become powerful and manipulative, as in retaliation to a powerful older woman who would "shrink." She thought of the mother in the film, *The Graduate,* who shriveled when she found out that her young lover was sleeping with her daughter. At the same time she had primal scene fantasies in which my male patient and I were involved.

Further analysis was concerned with continued integration of both good and bad object representations, and with conflicts over separation from the more unified object.

A few weeks before I was to go on a vacation the patient said that she was afraid again to tell me that to her surprise she got the highest marks in her class. She said that she now saw what I meant when I once had commented on her inability to know that she is intelligent and capable unless she is told by an outside source.

But she could not understand her reluctance to tell me. She knew I would be going away soon and she was sure that she would do badly in her next exam while I'd be on vacation.

She told her parents about the marks. They showed little enthusiasm. She had a "separation feeling." "That awful emptiness." They loved her when she was a little girl and dumb. She's not dumb now but still too dependent. She could earn some money but doesn't. She

feels she's hurting herself by being too dependent because she has
such low self-esteem, but she's hurting herself to hurt them. She's so
angry at them. They didn't think she was worth anything. "Their
disapproval terrorized me as a child. I can see myself crawling into
bed and pulling the covers over my head because they disapproved
of me. How can I stop overreacting? I have to look at them objectively. But I can't stop overreacting to the way they act towards me."
She was crying now. I wondered what she would lose if she could
have good regard for herself without her parents telling her she was
worthwhile.

The patient paused a moment and said, "The vision is of being on a
train and saying 'good-bye' to someone and that person gets smaller
and smaller. The train is not horizontal, it's vertical. I go away and I
may not see them again. Maybe I can say 'Maybe they're right'; but
that makes me judgmental and on a par with them, and I lose their
warmth and affection."

She paused and now laughed and said, "Oh, oh! and if I can do well
when you're away, you're not so essential to me. Then you might give
me up."

Discussion

I have presented some formulations based on Mahler's developmental concepts, especially those concerned with the derivatives of
splitting, and with her descriptions of normal developmental problems which the rapprochement subphase girl may encounter which,
together with experiential problems, may contribute to later borderline phenomena or depressiveness.

The continuation of splitting as a pathological defense interferes
with formation of normal object relations and with attainment of
healthy self-concepts, as well as with the child's ability to modulate
aggression. In the patient under consideration, aggression (or apparent lack of it) posed important problems from the start. Possibly
these patients are constitutionally endowed with too little aggression
to permit them to extract mothering as effectively as better endowed
children might, especially since their relatively depressed mothers
who were not given to spontaneous stimulation of these "quiet"
children, were at least adequately responsive to the needs of their
lustier, more demanding infants. By the same token these patients
did not "escape" from their mothers who, afraid of their own

aggression, welcomed the dependency and passivity in their children rather than encouraging individuation.

The combination of constitutional and these experiential factors made it extremely difficult for my patients to tolerate in themselves even moderate amounts of ambivalence and aggression, and equally difficult to accept them in the object. By taking aggression toward self- and object representations out of the purview of the ego, splitting prevented the ego from developing adequate and healthy defenses to handle aggression, and resulted instead in the persistance of naked, unmodulated aggression displaced to the "bad" self and object. Love and compliance, which had to be maintained toward the "good" object and the reassuring comfortable feelings of being the "good self", were sustained at great cost to the child's autonomy, for the increased sense of identity that parallels object constancy did not take place, nor did the improved sense of worth that derives from mastery occur. The ego ideal suffered greatly, and was often chameleonlike.

Just as object constancy did not ensue because of the continuation of split object cathexis, self-constancy which is even more precarious (Jacobson 1965) did not develop. Mahler and Kaplan (1978) say,

> self constancy, that is, individual entity and identity, should be achieved at the end of the rapprochement subphase, in addition to a level of object constancy that facilitates triangular whole-object relations cathected with neutralized libido and aggression. In the psychosexual sphere an emerging and flexible narcissistic genital orientation should be evident. Repression is the main defense mechanism in these important developments. . . .
>
> In contrast to progress in object relations, the building of a cohesive, separate and *whole* [my italics] self-representation is elusive [p. 72].

The patients have an insufficient source of appropriate self-esteem and sound secondary narcissism. Consequently, they do not build up an adequate ability to appraise themselves. Later in life, past competence gives them no promise of future achievement, and they constantly seek from outside sources a sense of worth.

SUMMARY

I have described cases where there is a continuation of split self- and object representations in adolescence; and I now wish to allude to the therapeutic implications of these concepts.

My patients compare and contrast to those described by Peter Blos (1976), who addressed himself to adolescents who *are* able to use the peer group to unify residues of split good and bad object representations and in the service of separating from primary love objects. He says that "preoedipal object relations are relived in adolescence; in the process infantile libidinal and aggressive dependencies are given up and replaced by extrafamilial object involvements with age-mates, and by new identifications within the wider world of personalities, values, ideas, ambitions, or generally speaking, by mature ego-ideal formation" (p. 9).

Blos postulates (p. 20) that reliving of preoedipal object relations in adolescence with age-mates serves the important purpose of unifying residues of split-object dichotomies, for via the process of externalization of the split good and bad object representations onto the peer group, which Blos calls the *autoplastic milieu*, intrapsychic harmony and increased independence from primary objects are brought about.

Blos adds (p. 29) that "the incapacity to use the environment for [this] self-development is considered pathognomonic . . . for the adolescent." I agree with him, and I hope I have demonstrated the degree to which my patients were unable to use the peer group and were therefore handicapped in the unification of split-object dichotomies. In trying to understand why they could not do so, it seemed to me that the additional and, I thought, more pathological, continuing split between good and bad self compromised development and adaptation *even* more than did the influence of the continuing split between good and bad object representations. The split in self-representations results in displacements and projections of attributes of the bad self-representation to the peer group. Consequently, these adolescents cannot use the peer group, in spite of their envy of them, in the service of unifying the split object imagoes and in eventual separation from them until the good and bad self- representations have been sufficiently integrated through analysis into a single entity.

In the technique of analytic treatment of adolescent patients with split parental and self-imagoes, I feel, therefore, that it is necessary to aim first at unifying good and bad self-representations. Once well under way, this unification permits the peer group, no longer standing for all that is bad, to be used by the now stronger ego in the service of further adolescent development, as Blos said, in "extrafamilial object involvements with age-mates, and new identifications" in the service of mature ego-ideal formation, and especially in the service of mature and age-appropriate separation from the primary love objects whose strengths and weaknesses must be recognized and dealt with.

References

Alpert, A., Neubauer, P. B., and Weil, A. P. (1956). Unusual variations in drive endowment. *Psychoanalytic Study of the Child* 11:25-163.

Blos, P. (1968). The second individuation process of adolescence. *Psychoanalytic Study of the Child* 22:162-186.

——— (1976). Split parental imagos and adolescent social relations: an inquiry into group psychology. *Psychoanalytic Study of the Child* 31:7-33.

Chess, S., Thomas, A., and Birch, H. (1958). Characteristics of the individual child's behavioral responses to the environment. *American Journal of Ortho-Psychiatry* 29:791-802.

Jacobson, E. (1954). *The Self and the Object World.* New York: International Universities Press.

Kernberg, O. (1966). Structural derivatives of object relations. *International Journal of Psycho-Analysis* 47:236-253.

Kramer, S. (1971). Adolescent recapitulation of a childhood psychosis. In *Separation-Individuation: Essays in Honor of Margaret S. Mahler,* ed. J. McDevitt, and C. Settlage. New York: International Universities Press.

Loewald, H. (1951). Ego and reality. *International Journal of Psycho-Analysis* 32:10-17.

Mahler, M. S. (1966). Notes on the development of basic moods: the depressive affect. In *Psychoanalysis: A General Psychology. Essays in Honor of Heinz Hartmann,* ed. R. Loewenstein, et al. New York: International Universities Press. Reprinted in *The Selected Papers of Margaret S. Mahler,* vol. 2, ch. 5. New York: Jason Aronson, 1979.

——— (1968). *On Human Symbiosis and the Vicissitudes of Individuation, vol. 1: Infantile Psychosis.* In collaboration with M. Furer. New York: International Universities Press.

——— (1971). A study of the separation-individuation process and its possible application to borderline phenomena in the psychoanalytic situation. *Psychoanalytic Study of the Child* 26:403-424. Reprinted in Selected Papers, op. cit., ch. 11.

——— (1975). On the current status of the infantile neurosis. *Journal of the American Psychoanalytic Association* 23:327-333. Reprinted in Selected Papers, op. cit., ch. 12.

Mahler, M. S. and Gosliner, B. J. (1955). On symbiotic child psychosis: genetic, dynamic and restitutive aspects. *Psychoanalytic Study of the*

Child 10:195-212. Reprinted in *The Selected Papers of Margaret S. Mahler*, vol. 1, ch. 6. New York: Jason Aronson, 1979.

Mahler, M. S. and Kaplan, L. (1978). Developmental aspects in the assessment of narcissism and so-called borderline personalities. In *Borderline Personality Disorders*, ed. P. Hartocollis, pp. 71-84 New York: International Universities Press.

Mahler, M. S., Pine, F. and Bergman, A. (1975). *The Psychological Birth of the Human Infant*. New York: Basic Books.

Ritvo, S. (1974). The current status of the infantile neurosis: implications for diagnosis and technique. *Psychoanalytic Study of the Child* 29:159-181.

Sours, J. A. (1974). The anorexia nervosa syndrome. *International Journal of Psycho-Analysis* 55:567-576.

Van Dam, H. [rep.] (1966). Panel on problems of transference in child analysis. *Journal of the American Psychoanalytic Association* 14:528-539.

Weil, A. (1970). The basic core. *Psychoanalytic Study of the Child* 25:442-460.

21

The Rotten Core: A Defect in the Formation of the Self During the Rapprochement Subphase

Ruth F. Lax, Ph.D.

A MYTHIC EXPRESSION OF IDENTIFICATION WITH THE AGGRESSOR

The Balinese myth about Rangda, the blood-thirsty, child-eating demon queen (Covarrubias 1974, Hoefer 1974), illustrates the universality of certain early mother-child interactions, and highlights the vicissitudes of identification with the aggressor, which results in a split of the self.

In one version of this story the queen, Dewi Kunti, for reasons unknown, had to sacrifice Sadewa, one of her sons, to Rangda. This made Dewi Kunti very sad since she was a good and loving mother. She could not bring herself to sacrifice her son. However, when the witch, Rangda, entered into Dewi Kunti, she became bewitched and transformed into an angry Fury. In this state Dewi Kunti commanded her Prime Minister to take Sadewa to Rangda's forest. The Prime Minister, who loved Sadewa, did not want to sacrifice him and was saddened by this terrible command. However, the witch, Rangda, also entered into him. This transformed the Prime Minister, and he became angry and violent. He took Sadewa to the forest, tied the boy to a tree in front of Rangda's abode and abandoned him.

Shiwa, the most powerful of all the gods, took pity on Sadewa and gave him immortality. When Rangda arrived, eager to kill and eat Sadewa, she was unable to do so. Admitting her defeat, Rangda asked Sadewa for redemption so she could go to heaven. Sadewa granted her wish and killed her, thus enabling her to go to paradise.

Rangda's most important disciple, Kalika, begged for a fate identical to that of her mistress. Sadewa, however, refused. In the ensuing battle Kalika was twice defeated, but when Kalika transformed herself into the powerful Rangda, Sadewa could no longer vanquish her.

In the dance-drama enactment of this story[1] the dagger dancers attack Rangda. The attack, however, fails. Rangda, the embodiment of evil, cannot be destroyed. Finally, to give vent to their anger and, I believe, helpless despair, the Kris dancers turn their daggers upon themselves and in a frenzy repeatedly stab themselves.

Vicissitudes of the child's early fantasy and reality interactions with mother and father are dramatically depicted in this tale. The different personages in the story represent split-off good and bad objects. The destructive element predominates, changing the good mother and also the good father into raging, unfeeling demons. Mother, however, is seen as the prime evil-doer since she—as Rangda (the bad mother)—not only demands the sacrifice of the child, but also as Dewi Kunti (the seemingly good mother) sacrifices him. Expression is thus given to the early *experiential* struggle in which mother is perceived as the potential destroyer. Father—as Prime Minister—at first is seen as weaker than mother. However, as Shiwa, he subsequently becomes the rescuing all-powerful figure onto whom the child projects his omnipotence, which he then reintrojects as the gift of immortality. Made invulnerable, the child's fury at mother and his wish for revenge find expression in Sadewa's killing of Rangda.

The changes in Sadewa's attitude toward killing Rangda can only be understood when one realizes that the plot condenses various versions of the same act, thus reflecting the changing dynamic balance of psychic forces. In the tale different fantasy elements are combined and allowance is made for the conflicting attitudes of the child. Thus:

1. The Barong and Kris dance. A Kris is a dagger often having magical powers. A Kris dancer is a man in a ritual trance.

—The mother is killed but the murder undone by her redemption and immortality in paradise;

—no guilt need belong to the child for it is mother who asks to be killed as an act of atonement for her wrong-doing toward the child;

—the child's unforgiving, vindictive and destructive anger, disguised in the killing of Rangda at her own behest, is apparent in the savage interaction with Kalika, who is killed twice and denied salvation;

—Kalika's final transformation into Rangda, who cannot be defeated, represents the child's awareness of the "bad" mother as an ever-present threat.

The myth describes the intensely affect-laden, internalized object relations of early childhood as they are experienced, projected, and expressed primarily in interaction with mother. The Kris dancers who turn their daggers against themselves because they are unable to vanquish Rangda, the "bad" mother, depict one possible resolution of such mother-child strife. They represent the child whose fury has merged with mother's experienced rage and who, having succumbed in the futile struggle with mother, also identified with the self-destructive elements in her (Rangda pleading to be killed). Thus, the Kris dancers dramatically portray the ultimate consequence of an identification with the aggressor (A. Freud 1936).

I suggest that the turning of aggression against the self (as victim) is based on an identification not only with the aggressive but also with the self-destructive elements in the aggressor (mother).

THE ROTTEN CORE: CLINICAL EXAMPLES

Every discussion of a specific aspect of pathology constitutes a delimitation which results in an artifact since it is an exploration of but one strand from the interwoven fabric comprising the harmonious and discordant elements of the human psyche. Mindful of such qualifications, I shall nonetheless make use of this method to highlight a specific form of self-pathology, which is central and gravely disturbing in some personalities.

The women to be described presented a puzzling picture. Each sought treatment after one or two previous therapeutic experiences, and each complained of great suffering in spite of leading an apparently adaptive social and professional life and even enjoying at least partially gratifying object relations.

As far as I could ascertain, there was no uniformity in the causes which brought these patients into treatment initially. On the basis of my work with these women, I did surmise that their previous therapeutic experience was partially successful. It did not enable them, however, to resolve the underlying cause of their recurrent, deep depressions, nor did it enable them to overcome their feeling of discontent with themselves.

In the course of treatment with me, though pained by anxiety, depression, and physical symptoms, each of these patients insisted that the real cause of her suffering stemmed from "something rotten within her" which comprised her innermost self and which filled her with a pervasive sense of doom. One patient said: "It is the sensation of something bad within which makes me feel bad." The patients were convinced that nothing they could do or become would change this fundamental fact. The "rottenness" was their essence and made it impossible for them to like and accept themselves.

The patients felt as if they had two selves, thus experiencing a sense of duality. In contrast, outsiders only perceived their well-functioning capable self. The patients sometimes responded to such an appraisal with a modicum of pleasure and sometimes with a feeling of being a "fake." Though the patients enjoyed their achievements they frequently looked upon them as a "way to survive." In general, achievements, accomplishments, and love were only a solace. They mitigated the anguish but did not change its fundamental nature. Good feelings and praise expressed by love objects were appreciated, sometimes even sought actively. They filled these patients with surprise, made them sad and ready to cry. The patients explained these reactions as due to their awareness that good feelings expressed by others neither depicted nor related to their "real self," that is, to their "inner rottenness."

The analyses of these patients' "outer self," which they considered a sham, did not reveal any significant pathology. Were it not for their reported suffering, it would appear that one was dealing with individuals functioning autonomously in a chosen sphere of ego interests, interacting quite adequately with others, and obtaining narcissistic gratification from goals syntonic with their conscious wishful self-image. Ego strength seemed sufficient for the achievement of well-sublimated aims pursued energetically. These patients even appeared to experience pleasure from their achievements. Such gratification, however, was short-lasting. Without any apparent cause, these women again and again would become depressed, filled with suffering, and complain, ascribing their pain to a "bad feeling." The patients insisted that a feeling of inner rottenness interfered with their having a sense of well-being.

I have observed this type of pathology, though it may have differed in degree of severity, in quite a number of patients. Analytic reconstructions indicate that it develops as a consequence of a specific form of interaction with a mother who becomes severely depressed during the patient's toddlerhood.

In the last ten years, chance had it that I worked with four patients whose mothers suffered from a severe reactive depression while their daughters were in the rapprochement subphase. Family anecdotes acquainted my patients with this historical material which they claim to have known all their lives. They told it to me as a bit of life history, in a manner which indicated that it was totally isolated or split-off from their conscious emotions or psychic reactions. I stress this point to emphasize that the patients initially had no conscious awareness of their reactions to mother's depression, nor did they recognize that it had any effect on them. The consequences of their childhood interactions with the depressed mother only became apparent in the later phases of treatment from the analyses of dreams, fantasies, and specific transference manifestations.[2] Analytic work also revealed that the selection of specific types of object relations was unconsciously motivated by this mother-child paradigm.

In my patients, the sense of inner rottenness became a focal aspect of their pathology. The analyses of this malformation led to the understanding of the processes by which it developed and the consequences to which it led.

I have chosen to discuss three of these cases to illustrate, via "extreme" examples, the dynamic interactions following maternal libidinal unavailability due to severe depression, and to demonstrate how such mother-child interaction leads to the development of self-pathology.

I do not mean to imply by presenting these three cases that such pathology develops only when mother's depression is reactive. It is also possible that the trauma which evoked mother's reactive depression triggered a latent chronic state. I did observe, however, that the

2. These aspects will be discussed in detail in a subsequent paper dealing with treatment techniques for these patients.

self-pathology which manifested itself by a profound sense of inner rottenness varied in severity depending on the extent of mother's unavailability due to her depression.

The following vignettes will serve to illustrate some of these points, and throw light on specific genetic factors and developmental malformations.

Case 1

Nina, a very successful kindergarten teacher, married and with many friends, could neither accept nor emotionally integrate the love and esteem in which she was held. She would frequently say: "I am 'hatable' because mother hated me. Since it was mother who had these feelings, they must be correct. I always feel I somehow fool all who love me, only mother knew the truth."

When Nina was 18 months old, her grandmother, a daily visitor in the parental household, suddenly died of a stroke. Mother, as Nina learned from family anecdotes, became deeply depressed following this event.

Nina pictured her mother as angry and morbid, a compulsive cleaner and housekeeper. Mother accused the family of making her into a workhorse and slave. Nina was a special target of mother's endless accusations. She felt that mother favored her younger sister and looked upon her as a Cinderella. Nina could not become reconciled to mother's lack of loving feelings toward her; she recalled long hours spent in her room tearfully reassuring and consoling herself that, nonetheless, mother really did love her.

Nina was fortunate to have had, and been able to make use of the love she experienced from her maternal grandfather, aunts and uncles. She contrasted their attitudes and lives with the hell she experienced at home. It is not surprising that in her early teens Nina decided that "mother was crazy." She stood alone in this belief, however, since mother capably pretended to the world that "all was well, and she was loving and reasonable." No one but Nina recognized mother's false facade, and even Nina wavered in her conviction.

The feeling of craziness, however, did not apply to mother only. There were times when Nina felt she also was "crazy inside and hid behind the pretense of an outer normal shell." She kept saying, "I feel like a freak. I raised myself to look normal but inside I am crazy.

Others tell me I handle things well but this is not how I experience it. I feel I know nothing." These convictions about herself were so powerful that Nina refused to have children. She feared that in her relationship with her child she would reenact the hateful interaction experienced by her with mother. She feared she would curse her child to reexperience her own fate.

The patient said: "I cannot believe I am okay because I was not okay with mother. I am very angry but I learned to cover it up. I sometimes have a feeling of not being there while I smile and talk and everything goes on. That is how I survived my childhood: by not being there so that what mother did and said would not hurt. I feel everything is wrong with me though everyone praises me. Now all of them say I do such a wonderful job, but mother humiliated, ridiculed and destroyed me. I feel sometimes the 'I of me' no longer exists. I feel, most of the time, that the praise I now receive does not relate to me. I can't relate to it and enjoy it. I devalue it."

The patient had broken off contact with mother in her mid-twenties and had not seen her for many years when she started her analysis.

Case 2

Professionally successful, married, and the mother of four, Irene was an anthropologist associated with a leading university. Though she seemed to enjoy life, she complained about a sense of doom and a belief that she was damned to eternal hell. She acknowledged these ideas as irrational but could not free herself of their effect. Irene looked on her personal and professional achievements as not related to her real self. Her depression was well-hidden from the outside world but she was fully aware of it, reporting the onset at about age 5 when she began to pray for death at 100. The ensuing long life span seemed to reassure her; it seemed like eternity. As a child Irene felt guilty though she did not know her crime. Irene grew up to be self-righteous. She had an almost compulsive need to rescue those in distress.

Mother was a beautiful, self-absorbed, empty woman. Though middle-class, Irene remembers her as an avid practitioner of preventive voodoo, engaged in rituals to "undo the evil eye." She recalls mother scrupulously collecting her nail parings and cut-off hair, packing them into little bundles and making sure they were completely burned. This procedure was necessary—so Irene learned—to prevent evil-doers from causing her harm. Irene, in spite of her seemingly secure environment, grew up always having a sense of foreboding. Her attempts in later life to refute mother's warnings of an evil around her did not free her of an inner sense that it was always present.

Irene recalled many days of her childhood when mother was silent, distant, and ignored her. On those days Irene felt that mother's behavior was her fault, proof of her wrong-doing. There were other days when mother would clutch her and hold her tight; such behavior made Irene want to get away from mother. Yet, when she succeeded, the sensation that something terrible was going to happen would intensify and overcome Irene. She would feel evil. She would run back to mother only to find her once again distant and silent.

Since late adolescence Irene knew that, during the eleven years following her birth, mother miscarried five times. The first of these miscarriages occurred when Irene was about 22 months old. The significance of these facts, however, only became clear during treatment. Analysis of dreams, memories, and free associations made the specific mother-child interaction more understandable. Via reconstructions it became clear how these events, so traumatic for her mother, incomprehensible to Irene as a child, contributed to her sense of foreboding and doom. Following each miscarriage and intensifying as the years passed, Mother expressed her ambivalence on the one hand by possessively holding onto her only living child, and on the other hand, by ignoring her for long periods of time. Mother seemingly became more and more depressed and could not stop mourning for her lost babies. This supposition was confirmed by the fact that Irene recalls that the feelings of foreboding and the sense of being evil intensified as she grew older.

Irene described her self-feelings when she came for treatment as follows: "A time came when nothing good about me felt real. All I knew was the pain of never feeling well. When I made good, kind and friendly gestures to which others responded by grateful, loving acceptance, it did not make me feel good. I knew that I was only propitiating and warding off their evil intents. I did not extend the good gesture out of love but rather out of fear of their evil, to placate them, to buy their good intent, perhaps even love. Thus, the success of my gesture did not ameliorate my sense of inner evil. The knowing, doing, succeeding belongs to the outer part of me. It does not change the rotten core inside. However, as an adult I no longer feel that my rotten core causes others evil, rather it seems to be sapping my life."

Familiar with analytic theory, the patient added: "The evil my mother projected into the world and then tried to undo with her rituals got into me anyhow. It was her hatred."

Case 3

Anna, a Hindu social worker, came to New York from India as a scholarship student to obtain an advanced degree. Extreme anxiety, however, soon interfered with her ability to study. The patient complained about loneliness; analytic work indicated she had difficulty tolerating her separation from mother.

Anna's father had developed Hodgkins disease when she was almost 2. Though her mother was acclaimed to have special healing powers,[3] father refused her help. Mother's anxious depression apparently started at that time.

Mother wanted to make sure that Anna, at least, was protected. To forestall all possible dangers to her daughter, Mother purged Anna once a week with a mixture of herbal laxatives. During these sessions a struggle would ensue. Anna would try to run away. In vain, Mother always triumphed. Anna, exhausted by the ordeal, finally would crawl onto mother's lap. She would feel mother's body enfolding her, "like a spider's web: safe and suffocating." She would fall asleep.

These experiences contributed to the conviction Anna developed that there was something rotten within her. She believed the purgings must have been to "cleanse her from within." Anna said: "I am stuck with it, and there is nothing that can touch it, this feeling of 'I am rotten'. No matter what happens on the outside, I still feel this way. It is like a homunculus in me, black and in flame. I should go to a sorcerer so he could exorcise it and expurgate it. That is what mother tried to do with the purgatives she gave me. It did not work, it is still in me."

DISCUSSION

The term *rotten core* evolved to denote my patients' awareness of an aspect of their psyche which simultaneously is a part of, and yet

3. Mother was a respected homeopathic practitioner.

also is alien to, their self. Grossman and Simon (1969) discuss the causes which lead to the description of inner experiences in anthropomorphic terms. The rotten core should be understood along these lines of reasoning, as a metaphor depicting a specific inner feeling, "a sense of rottenness," known to my patients throughout their lives.

I have used this term in two ways: to provide a phenomenological description of a certain group of observable psychic data and, also, to categorize them. In this latter sense, the term is employed as a hypothetical construct on a level of abstraction corresponding to, but not identical with, such concepts as the bad or good introject and the self-image. Consistent with the structural delineation of the psychic appartus, the rotten core, along with other self-images, can be conceived as one of the components of the self-representation.

Balint's description of the *basic fault*, as well as Winnicott's observations regarding the *true* and *false self*, will be mentioned briefly since, phenomenologically, patients suffering from each of these deviations appear to have certain similarities with patients manifesting rotten core pathology.

Commenting on the basic fault, Balint (1968) states: "The patient feels there is a fault within him that must be put right. The fault is something wrong with the mind, a kind of deficiency" (p. 21). "A basic fault can perhaps be merely healed provided the deficient ingredients can be found; and even then it may amount only to a healing with defect, like a simple, painless scar." According to Balint, the origin of the basic fault lies in the "lack of fit" between the biopsychological infant needs and the physical, psychological and affectionate care he receives (p. 22).

According to Winnicott (1956, 1960), the origin of the split into true and false self takes place in early infancy. Differences in the degree of this type of pathology are determined by the stage of development at which the greatest pressure for conformity occurred. Winnicott claims that the true self which arises from the vital, creative, subjectively genuine aspects of the individual rooted in the biological givens, becomes stilted, distorted, or completely obliterated, depending on the extent to which the infant is deprived of a "holding" environment provided by "good enough" mothering necessary for unencumbered growth.

Thus the false self develops in proportion to the absence of such mothering and results from premature accommodations to the demands of external reality. It is serviceable in terms of adjustment but internally unsuccessful since it is primarily reactive, the outgrowth of object pressure (usually maternal) and therefore defensive.

The pathology of the self from which my patients suffered resulted from a specific form of identification with the aggressor which occurred at a crucial time in the development of the self. The description of rotten core pathology is an attempt to conceptualize the formation and consequences of a specific split in the self-representation which gave my patients the subjective awareness of a duality of their selves. They described an outer self, the shell or persona which they frequently regarded as "phoney," and a real self, the rotten core. Though the split of the self-representation predominated as the central problem, derivatives of conflicts from various developmental stages were present and combined into different characterological pictures for each patient. However, typical for all these patients was a superego with many primitive sadistic elements experienced by them as a harsh conscience and an ego-ideal containing nonmetabolized grandiose and overidealized elements. A well-developed and wide conflict-free sphere accounted for excellent functioning in many areas of secondary autonomy. Ego functioning was related to a strongly developed conscious wishful self-image (Milrod 1977).

The pathological mother-child interaction affected the nature and quality of the object representation. It partly reinforced the infantile tendency to split the maternal imago and led to a corresponding splitting of the self-representation. The persistence of the splitting process interfered with the consolidating effect of the synthetic function of the ego. As a consequence of these two factors, the achievement of complete self-constancy and libidinal object constancy remained tenuous. Regressive pulls easily eroded this attainment whenever the libidinal object assumed an unconscious, pathogenic maternal significance. When this occurred, like in the instance of a lover's criticism, the ensuing ambivalence triggered splitting with consequent patterns of idealization and devaluation. These patients on the one hand longed to fuse with the idealized object, and on the other acted self-righteously toward the devalued one. Frequently, both these feelings were directed at different times toward the same person. These patients also had a tendency to choose objects onto whom they could project their unconscious devalued self (Lax 1975), as well as objects toward whom they could act out an idealized maternal role.

The patients' pathology, to which there may have been precursors stemming from earlier phases of development, crystallized as a reaction to a specific constellation of internalized object relations (Kernberg 1966, 1976) directly as a response to the consequences of mother's depression. The patients were at that time in the rapprochement subphase. This, as is well-known from the studies of Mahler, is a relatively difficult period in the life of the toddler (Mahler, Pine, and Bergman 1975). The "practicing" subphase (Mahler 1968, 1971, 1974, 1975), characterized by feelings of exuberance and power which found expression in the "love affair with the world," comes to an end. Typically, these developmental sequelae upset the child's emotional equilibrium. Toilet training brings about further tensions which, at least temporarily, may stimulate aggressive impulses. Omnipotent fantasies, related to anal negativism (whether retentive or projective), are sometimes held onto defensively. In more complicated cases, anal submission may lead to various forms of masochism.

"Shadowing" and "darting-away" behavior patterns are indications of the conflict between the wish for reunion with mother and the fear of engulfment by her. This is the time when the child's increasing awareness of growing separateness stimulates an increased need for mother's love and an increased wish to share with her. As is well known, the intensity of the toddler's wooing behavior can be used as an indicator of the magnitude of the rapprochement crisis.

Only mother's loving acceptance of the child with its ambivalence, as well as her encouragement, provides the necessary ambience for further autonomous growth (Mahler 1971) and leads to normal resolutions of the rapprochement crisis.

Analytic work with my patients made it clear that their mothers could not respond to these typical, phase-specific conflicts and longings. Dreams and transference patterns provided evidence indicating that the mother's psychic equilibrium was seriously disrupted as a result of the trauma she experienced. This manifested itself in several ways.

As illustrated by the case of Irene, mother's behavior became inconsistent. This was especially significant for the toddler, to whose spurts towards independence mother responded unpredictably, at times with seemingly angry behavior and at other times with possessive holding-on. It is likely that this "clutching," experienced by the child as an invasion of its body autonomy and an interference with "darting-away" behavior, was an expression of mother's reactivated symbiotic needs. Such maternal behavior, however, seems to have intensified the child's age-specific negativism and led to increased power struggles and outbursts of rage.

Nina's case suggests that the quality of her mother's relating also appears to have changed. The child was now seen much more frequently as either good or bad, possibly indicating a breakdown in mother's libidinal object constancy.

Apparent in every case and of foremost significance, however, was mother's depression, which made her emotionally unavailable to the child. Her withdrawal was interpreted by the toddler as anger. This maternal attitude evoked a "hostile dependency" in the child who eventually developed a "basic depressive mood" (Mahler 1966).

Since a toddler is unable to comprehend the objective origins of mother's depression, he regards his own aggressive as well as libidinal strivings as the causes of her moods. A child may thus come to regard mother's emotional unavailability as a punishment. Such an attitude also interferes with the normal progression of separation and individuation processes. This is especially true if the toddler, due to identification with mother, begins to regard his impulses toward autonomy with the disapproval he ascribes to her.

Margaret Mahler (1971) points out that a stormy separation-individuation process results in the development of:

> an unassimilated foreign body, a "bad" introject in the intrapsychic emotional economy. In the effort to eject this "bad" introject, derivatives of the aggressive drive come into play and there seems to develop an increased proclivity to identify with, or to confuse, the self-representation with the "bad" introject. If this situation prevails during the rapprochement subphase, then aggression may be unleashed in such a way as to inundate or sweep away the "good" object, and with it the "good" self-representation [p. 412, italics mine].

Following such a conflagration, a defensive regression to the stage when object and self are less clearly differentiated and are split into a "good" and "bad" self-object, may occur.

I suggest that the prevalence of such an intrapsychic conflict state may lead to the formation of the rotten core which on the most primitive level represents the fusion of the "bad" (angry-rejecting) maternal introject with the "bad" (rejected) aspects of the self.

Subsequently experienced maternal anger fused with the child's projected anger becomes turned against the self. Under the impact of intensified separation anxiety, a regression may occur, and annihilation anxiety may become reactivated. Such a condition leads to further defensive splitting in an attempt to preserve the "good" object and the corresponding "good" self (Kernberg 1966, Mahler 1971, Giovacchini 1972). As a consequence, not only the object representation but also the self-representation remains (or becomes) divided. The rotten core represents that part of the self which was "hatable" to mother. Continued identification with the aggressor (A. Freud 1936) contributes to the establishment of the rotten core as a permanent substructure. Two aspects of this process can be recognized, each reenforcing the existing split in the self-representation.

First, the identification with the maternal attitude toward the child fosters in the child an *identical* attitude toward his self. Thus, maternal aggression becomes self-aggression, and the self becomes the victimized object. Further, aspects unacceptable to the aggressor-mother also become rejected by the child merging with the primitive rotten core toward which the combined mother-child hatred has been directed.

The second aspect of the process of identification with the aggressor arises from the wish to obtain mother's love and to participate in her power. Identifications so motivated augment early introjections and the fusion with the "good" mother and her beloved aspects. They contribute to the formation of the "good" self and its loved aspects.

The rotten core and "good" self are formed at a developmental stage during which polarization and splitting still prevail (Kernberg 1966, 1971, Mahler 1971). A preponderance of hostility in the vicissitudes of mother-child interaction prevents subsequent merging of these psychic substructures into a consolidated and integrated self-representation.

Internalization of mother's self-destructive tendencies, of her depression, hopelessness and helplessness represents a further aspect of these children's identification with the aggressor. The dynamic continuation of these processes was indicated in the treatment situation by a conviction these patients held that change was not possible. The patients frequently felt desperate.

These patients' adaptive functioning $n their capacity to make use of their resources led me to the assumption that mother-infant-toddler interaction preceding mother's trauma was sufficiently good to result in the formation of a "good" introject. This provided the basis for the unconscious identification with loved, admired and even envied aspects of the maternal imago. In later years, selective identifications consonant with the conscious wishful self-image eventuated in satisfactory autonomous ego functioning in circumscribed areas. Mahler's finding (1966), which indicates that autonomous ego functioning can remain unimpaired in children in spite of intense psychic conflicts, supports my observations and conclusions.

The self to which these patients referred as the "persona" or "outer shell" combined all the "good" identifications. However, an apparent insufficiency of neutralized libido and aggression interfered with the development of an optimal narcissistic cathexis of this self. Thus, adequate self-esteem was lacking. Harmonious interaction between ego, superego, and ego-ideal remained impeded. The self-representation remained split because it contained the non-metabolized rotten core.

I recognized early in my work with this type of patient the cleavage in their self-representation. I remained puzzled, however, by the apparent complete lack of malleability of the rotten core. Its poisonous effect continued in spite of the narcissistically gratifying attainments of the "outer self." Some answers to this enigma were provided by the analyses of the transference and also by the patients' continued and current relationships to their mothers. Thus, in spite of an ungratifying and frustrating interaction, these patients persisted in their tenacious demandingness and holding-on. Likewise, behavior in the transference was demanding, pleading, and provocative.

Analysis of these patterns of relating revealed an unconscious fantasy in which mother was idealized as the good fairy able to gratify the child in every conceivable way, no doubt representing the good symbiotic mother (Mahler 1971). The intensity of longing for this fairy-mother grew depending on the extent of the mother's libidinal unavailability in the child's reality and the painful frustration this evoked. This fantasy persisted into adulthood because the reality of mother's behavior was unconsciously justified by a corresponding unconscious conviction that it was caused by an inability to evoke her goodness. Transgressions in fantasy and reality were used to explain mother's anger, aggression, and hatred. These patients felt mother hated them because they were "rotten." The uncovering and analysis of this fantasy also elucidated the reasons for these patients' openly provocative childhood behavior: it served to change what seemed like mother's incomprehensible anger into an understandable reaction.

Bound up with the rotten core, emanating from the "bad" introject and reinforced by subsequent identifications with the aggressor, the self-turned, hateful anger remained unrelieved in these patients in spite of the gratifications related to the functioning of the "outer self." Their continuous "pain of living" (a patient's phrase) and the identification with the self-destructive elements in the aggressor led to intense suicidal wishes. However, the fantasy belief that sufficient suffering would bring atonement and with it the rescue by the good mother kept these patients in their pervasive self-torture and prevented them from actually committing suicide. Nonetheless, the wish for relief brought by death was great. Expressed in the idiom of the Balinese myth, Rangda, who could not be vanquished, made those fighting her turn their daggers against themselves.

I have observed the rotten core with its related pathological character formation primarily in women. I do not wish to imply, however, that this pathology is prevalent in women only or primarily. Colleagues have reported on similar character constellations in men.

I have not discussed the father since he did not seem to have a direct role in the formation of the rotten core. He was, however, very significant for my patients in their childhood, both in his role as rescuer (Abelin 1971), and as a model for identification (Lax 1977). Frequently the relationship with father was prematurely intense, complicating the subsequent oedipal involvement.

SUMMARY

The formation of a psychic substructure, the *rotten core*, which originates as a reaction to a depressed mother's lack of libidinal availability to the child during the rapprochement subphase, is described as a specific type of self-pathology. The child perceives and experiences such a mother as rejecting. The internalization of the interaction with her results in a specific kind of identification with the aggressor. This identification leads to the formation of a rotten core which on the most primitive level represents the fusion of the "bad" (angry-rejecting) maternal introject with the "bad" (rejected) aspects of the self. In patients with such a pathology, the rotten core and the "good" self do not merge into a consolidated and integrated self-representation. This is due to the preponderance of hostility in the mother/child interaction which accounts for the persistence of defensive splitting.

The description of rotten core pathology is an attempt to conceptualize the formation and consequences of the specific split in the self-representation which gives these patients the subjective awareness of a duality of their selves. Developmental consequences of this pathology are discussed. Three clinical vignettes are presented.

References

Abelin, E. L. (1971). The role of the father in the separation-individuation process. In *Separation-Individuation: Essays in Honor of Margaret S. Mahler*, ed. J. B. McDevitt and C. F. Settlage, pp. 229-253. New York: International Universities Press.

Balint, M. (1968). *The Basic Fault: Therapeutic Aspects of Regression*. London: Tavistock.

Covarrubias, M. (1974). *Island of Bali*. Kuala Lumpur: Oxford University Press.

Freud, A. (1936). *The Ego and the Mechanism of Defense*. New York: International Universities Press.

Giovacchini, P. L. (1972). The symbiotic phase. In *Tactics and Techniques in Psychoanalytic Therapy*, ed. P. L. Giovacchini, pp. 137-169. New York: Jason Aronson.

Grossman, W. I., and Simon, B. (1969). Anthropomorphism: motive, meaning, and causality in psychoanalytic theory. *Psychoanalytic Study of the Child* 24:78-111. New York: International Universities Press.

Hoefer, H. (ed.) (1974). *Guide to Bali*. Singapore: Apa Productions.

Kernberg, O. (1966). Structural derivatives of object relationships. *International Journal of Psycho-Analysis* 47:236-253.

——— (1971). Prognostic considerations regarding borderline personality organization. *Journal of the American Psychoanalytic Association* 19:595-635.

——— (1976). *Object-Relations Theory and Clinical Psychoanalysis*. New York: Jason Aronson.

Lax, R. (1975). Some comments on the narcissistic aspects of self-righteousness: defensive and structural considerations. *International Journal of Psycho-Analysis* 56:283-292.

——— (1977). The role of internalization in the development of certain aspects of female masochism: ego psychological considerations. *International Journal of Psycho-Analysis* 58:289-300.

Mahler, M. S. (1966). Notes on the development of basic moods. In *Psychoanalysis a General Psychology*, ed. R. M. Loewenstein et al., pp. 152-168. New York: International Universities Press. Reprinted in *The Selected Papers of Margaret S. Mahler*, vol. 2, ch. 5. New York: Jason Aronson, 1979.

——— (1968). *On Human Symbiosis and the Vicissitudes of Individuation, volume 1: Infantile Psychosis.* In collaboration with M. Furer. New York: International Universities Press.

——— (1971). A study of the separation-individuation process and its possible application to borderline phenomena in the psychoanalytic situation. *Psychoanalytic Study of the Child* 26:403-424. New York: International Universities Press. Reprinted in *Selected Papers*, op. cit, ch. 11.

——— (1974). Symbiosis and individuation: the psychological birth of the human infant. *Psychoanalytic Study of the Child* 29:89-106. Reprinted in *Selected Papers*, op. cit., ch. 10.

Mahler, M. S., Pine, F., and Bergman, A. (1975). *The Psychological Birth of the Human Infant: Symbiosis and Individuation.* New York: Basic Books.

Milrod, D. (1977). The wished-for self-image. Unpublished manuscript.

Winnicott, D. W. (1954). The depressive position in normal emotional development. In *Collected Papers*, pp. 262-277. New York: Basic Books, 1958.

——— (1956). Primary maternal preoccupation. In *Collected Papers*, op. cit., 300-305.

——— (1960). Ego distortion in terms of true and false self. In *The Maturational Processes and the Facilitating Environment*, pp. 158-165. New York: International Universities Press, 1965.

22

Overindividuation and Underseparation in the Pseudomature Child

Rex W. Speers, M.D. and Dale C. Morter, Ph.D.

Margaret Mahler has suggested that the resolution of the rapprochement crisis in the separation-individuation process may be of the same significance in the organization of preoedipal development as oedipal conflict resolution is in the organization of genital development (Mahler, Pine, and Bergman 1975, p. 230). For a number of years we have attempted (Speers 1974, and Speers et al. 1971) to delineate and describe some of the variations and deviations of the separation-individuation process as studied in 3-year-old children entering nursery school. The methodology of these studies has been detailed in a previous publication (Speers 1974) and will not be repeated here. Of the variations and possible deviations described in 1974 ("prepsychotic," "run and chase," "pseudomature," "little mother," and "immature") the focus in this report is on the pseudomature child. It is our present belief that the "little man" and the "little mother" described in the previous report are best combined under the designation *pseudomature*. They constitute the most frequently observed variation in the separation-individuation process. It is also our belief that this particular variation represents an inadequate resolution of the rapprochement crisis which can result in failures in structuralization and subsequent organizational deviations and personality disorders. In this report we will detail the characteristics of the "pseudomature child" as observed in the nursery school. We will present the typical assessment profile (A. Freud 1965) of the pseudomature child; present the observational studies of two children from entry into nursery school through latency and early preadolescence; and also present relevant material from the analysis of a latency-age child whom we believe to be representative of the pathological development of a pseudomature child.

DESCRIPTIVE CHARACTERISTICS

1. Pseudomature children are exceptionally verbal. By 3 years of age they have an extensive vocabulary with an ability to communicate with adults in a pleasing manner. With other children they are also very verbal but their verbalizations are more of the nature of "bossiness."

2. They verbally inform their mothers, on entering nursery school, that the mother is not needed and can "go home." In the nursery their attitude is distinctly one of "Who needs you? I can do it myself." They thus resist "help" from adults and most certainly from other children. Although they are pleasant and often cooperative with adults, they generally resist "help" as if it were an unwarranted intrusion.

3. All of the children designated as pseudomature were agile, dexterous, and generally quite bright. Because of their verbal abilities, they generally are seen as more intelligent than I.Q. testing reveals (when other than verbally accentuated tests are possible to administer). Nursery school teachers have generally seen these children as the "best" in the class. They give a teacher little or no trouble and are pleasant to have in a classroom.

4. They typically require that they be the center of attention. In the boy, this usually takes the form of "hyper-phallic" behavior which, indeed, captures the attention of all present. The girl, in her "little mother" behavior, is usually a focus for adults in the room and also for other children. However, the "little mother" can also isolate herself and play mothering roles solitarily for hours at a time. We have suggested that such girls avoid separation by "becoming mother" (Jacobson 1964, p. 43).

5. Although these children seem to be able to avoid frustrations

rather well, there are times when frustrations are inevitable. When they do occur, the breakdown of the mature facade is sudden and dramatic. The child becomes enraged to a degree beyond the realities of the situation. Tantrum behavior, screaming, vicious attacks, or uncontrollable sobbing occurs. Although the aggression against other children is usually limited to verbal commands and threats, when severe frustration occurs the aggression becomes annihilative in quality.

6. The need to be seen as the "best," to be in command, and to win in all situations is evident. The rapprochement-like behavior with mother is much more a performance than the usual "look at me" and "watch me" behavior seen in other children when mother is present. The need for applause and admiration is evident.

7. Sociodramatic play (cooperative play with three or more children (Smilansky 1968) is not possible for these children. In all play situations, the pseudomature child is writer, director, producer, and main character. Solitary play, or play with one other child (in which the other child is in the submissive role) may be very much of a drama but does not reach the sophistication of the socio-dramatic play of other children (Speers 1974). Repetitive play is often present.

ASSESSMENT PROFILE CHARACTERISTICS

1. Object constancy, self-constancy and phallic dominance are incomplete, with a preponderance of self-object (Kohut 1971) relationships and interactions. There is an inordinate investment of narcissism in the intellect and in the body-phallus.

2. "Good" and "bad" splits are evident, with repressive and splitting mechanisms maintaining the repression of the "bad self," "bad object," and the "bad self-object." Only the "good self," the "good object," and the "good self-object" are in conscious awareness (Kernberg 1976, p. 49).

3. Separation anxieties and castration-mutilation anxieties are a constant threat and are dealt with by omnipotent fantasies which defend against either threat. Patterns of behavior which invalidate the threats seem readily available to these children.

4. The aggressive fantasies remain annihilative in quality with a failure of movement from annihilative aggression to competitive aggression. The "wish to be" is not replaced by a "wish to be like"

(Greenacre 1964, p. 150). Fantasies of omnipotence relating to the annihilative quality of their rage and the projected rage of the significant other are in constant conflict.

5. Oedipal conflicts are evident precociously and the conflicts are intense. It is as if there is, or should be, no reason why victory cannot be attained in the oedipal situation inasmuch as "specialness" has been their experience in most other situations. Omnipotent fantasies protect them from mutilative or castrative threats and the intellect can arrive at fantasied solutions which assure success.

6. Self-esteem is regulated by their ability to maintain an illusion of the omnipotent dyad; the illusion of total victory in the oedipal struggle; and the illusion of an ability to ward off castrative-mutilative threats.

7. The patterns of behavior which validate omnipotence prevent the experience of ordinary frustration. Therefore, frustration tolerance does not ordinarily appear low, but it is quite low when reality intrudes itself to the point where omnipotence is threatened.

8. The dynamics of these children's behavior is one in which separation and the accompanying overwhelming feelings of helplessness are avoided by maintaining a constant contact with the mother figure through verbal "fascination" or "look at me-watch me" behavior.

9. The progressive and regressive forces are in a constant struggle without resolution.

As we observed these children in the recapitulation of the separation-individuation process on entering nursery school it was our belief that the rapprochement crisis was responded to and dealt with by a mother-child interaction which discouraged regression and insisted that "grown-up" behavior prevail. Words replaced physical contact; thus, an insistence that precociously mature modalities of interaction take precedence over the primitive modalities of touch, smell, taste, and near vision. There was a demand that overt rage be avoided and an insistence that separation and the concomitant anxieties be coped with by words and activities which were pleasing to mother and which did not cause the mother to feel like "bad mother" nor the child to feel like "bad child." The message from the mother was consistently one of: "You are a big boy/girl now." These children were not permitted (nor do they permit themselves) to feel or express the rage of separation, the humiliation of helplessness, nor the loss of omnipotence with an available, empathic mother. The rage and helplessness was denied and omnipotence remained in an illusory dyad. Thus, being pleasing to and being admired by the mother became essential and required a facade of nonangry, competent behavior. The "bad self" and "bad mother" images were repressed and split off with a resultant failure of amalgamation of "good" and "bad" self- and object representations. It seems important to us to recognize that in the split-off and repressed bad self- and bad object representations, the annihilative affect is also repressed and split off, thus not permitting the usual progression from annihilative to competitive aggression. It seems important to note that the gender identity of these children was usually well established yet phallic dominance was not established.

OBSERVATIONAL EXAMPLES

Rita

Rita was a first-born child. A sister was born when Rita was 20 months of age and a brother when she was 38 months of age. Her birth weight was four pounds five ounces and she was in an incubator for two weeks before being released to her mother. Rita walked at 10 months of age. She was weaned and toilet trained at 1 year without difficulty. Rita was seen by Mother as "a great help" when Cathy was born but ignored Matthew when he was born. Mother saw Rita as a "perfect baby and child" in that she was easy to get along with and did most everything that pleased her mother. Mother returned to work when Rita was 6 months of age.

The entry into nursery school at 3 years 8 months was seen as "nearly perfect" by her mother. Rita was eager to attend school and the first to arrive each morning. She said "please" and "thank you" to everyone and was anxious to know the rules and to please. She dutifully recited her ABC's on request. She made no protest when Mother left the room for coffee nor when Mother left the building to return home. When Mother was out of the room Rita was promiscuous in her attachment to adults and attempted to please any and all adults. She ignored the other children and busied herself with each of the activities available to her. When not relating to an adult she was solemn and busy. Whatever she did, she requested excessive praise or wanted it "put on the wall." Her requests to adults for permission to do this or that were in a voice which led the adult to believe she expected refusal (as if she were pleading). She worked hard to find out what was expected of her and she was quick to catch on to routines. She asked innumerable questions, most of which were "What is this?" and "Why?" By the end of the school day she was exhausted, as if she had been through a great ordeal.

Throughout her nursery school years she was seen as an exceptionally "mature" child although each teacher was aware of how Rita was monopolizing the adults. All recognized that Rita had to "know" the rules and to be watched and praised at all times. They were aware of her nearly constant visual attachment to them.

Rita's relationship to peers was one of a demanding, controlling interaction in which she was tolerant of the relationship only if she were "boss." Although she ultimately played "bad, run-away baby" she was most often the "witchy, bossy mother" in dramatic play. She insisted upon exclusiveness with a playmate and would allow no betrayals in this regard. At 4-plus years of age her dramatic themes were of hurt boys and girls, despotic mother, big girl (who incongruously sucked a baby bottle), and blindness. Her drawings at this time were of people in bed.

Psychological testing revealed an I.Q. of 129 at age 4, 123 at 4½, and 120 at 5½. At 9½ her I.Q. was 118. Projective testing each time revealed her dread of abandonment and her great affectional needs: Intellectual control of affect was a constant aspect of each testing.

Throughout the Workshop Club (from age 6 to 11 years) Rita remained much the same. She gained nearly constant attention from female adults and was somewhat flirtatious with male adults. She was demanding of exclusivity with other children, and, even more than in the nursery school, demanded that she be "the boss" in all group endeavors. In competitive activities she quit if she saw she was not going to win. She persisted in denigration of other children's productions and aggrandizement of her own. In arts and crafts she made presents for mother, sister, or brother.

At home Rita was clearly seen as "mother's helper" and the one who took care of the other children in the family. She informed on her sibling's behavior in written reports to her mother. At school she was seen as competent, bright, and a willing student and remained so throughout elementary school. Her grades were nearly always "A's." However, she was not popular with her peer group and spent most of her out of school time at home without a special friend. Although her menarche occurred at age 11, Rita did not participate in the usual preadolescent girl activities.

An assessment profile at age 11 years 8 months revealed self- and object representations to be at a preoedipal level without clear evidence of constancy. The attachment to Mother had not altered significantly. Anal drive influences were pronounced with obsessive-compulsive mechanisms dominating. There was no evidence of a movement into preadolescence or adolescence and oedipal conflicts were deeply repressed. The defense mechanisms were predominantly reaction formation, repression, regression, and passivity. Ego constriction was pronounced. Her self-esteem was regulated by external events, that is, grades in school and pleasing her parents. Her dynamics were those of avoiding separation by being the "good child who pleases Mother." When she was not being the "good child" she was the controlling, dominating mother attempting to make others "good," that is, she became Mother. In these ways Rita avoided psychological separation and the concomitant overwhelming helplessness she had experienced in the past. The regressive forces dominated her personality.

Thus, Rita has remained a pseudomature child with little change in her behavior or psychological structure. The major influences of adolescence are yet to come but the persistence of an underdeveloped psychic structure and organization produces little optimism for a future without personality deviation.

Tommy

The first-born son and first grandson of a rather large, extended family. Father was a highly energetic, hard-working, "self-made man." Mother was strongly in need of being seen as "good mother." She described her pregnancy and delivery as: "The easiest thing I ever did." Every aspect of Tommy's motor and speech development was greeted with effusive praise and pride. These aspects of development were actively encouraged by all the adults so very much focused on him.

Breast feeding was stopped after a few weeks because of a fear the milk was "poisoning" him (colic). He was encouraged to crawl early and walked at 10 months of age. He was seen as a very active child and talked well by 1 year of age. His verbal utterances and motor behavior were applauded enthusiastically by all the adults in his environment. Thus, Father was pleased with his "manliness" and Mother was pleased that she, the "good mother," had produced such a satisfying child. Crying in anger and temper outbursts of any kind were disallowed and treated as an accusation of "bad mothering." Tommy was toilet trained by 2½ but did have occasional daytime accidents until 3½.

Tommy entered nursery school at 3 years 7 months of age and was instantly seen as the "big little man" of the school. He disavowed any need for his mother and made every effort to master nursery school without an outward display of fear or concern. A teacher commented that Tommy completed the daily activities of the nursery school within the first 10 minutes after arrival. "It is as if his feet don't touch the ground because he is in constant motion." He declared himself to be the leader of the group and demanded a near total focus on him. His productions had to be declared "the best." His techniques for maintaining a focus on himself at all times were exceptionally effective because of his superb verbal and motor abilities. Should the focus lag, he would instantly utter an ear-catching remark or turn a cartwheel which everyone was certain to notice. He saw himself as the leader of the group and only his ideas as worthy of group play, with his having the right to include or exclude whomever he wished. He continued to disavow any needs for adults, yet made certain he had their nearly constant attention. The fact of overindividuation and underseparation was evident.

Tommy was a pseudomature child in every respect. He maintained a nearly constant "all good dyad" with "badness" outside the dyad. He entered the nursery school each day with a flourish and announced his arrival for all to take note. He immediately took charge of an activity and pleasantly but forcibly imposed his will on the others. Because of his abilities he was indeed "the leader." His phallic exhibitionism was a delight to the adults and rarely got him into trouble.

At 4 years 7 months of age Tommy presented a depressive affect. He had been intensely oedipal for several months and became openly competitive and derogatory towards his father. His father tolerated a good deal of this behavior for quite some time but finally lost his temper and beat Tommy physically. For several months Tommy played quietly with a selected playmate, constructing elaborate block buildings, but there was a lethargy and quietness heretofore not seen. However, it was noted that he fully expected praise for his constructions and insisted the buildings not be taken down, and when each was completed, that a picture of it be taken and hung on the wall.

Gradually his bombastic behavior returned and he was very much his former self, although perhaps less challenging of adult males.

In the after school Workshop Club (age 6 to 11 years), Tommy continued the phallic aggressive behavior, but now directed it into sports. He knew and enforced the rules of each game; demanded he be seen as the captain and the best. To this end he readily violated any and all rules. If he were challenged, he shouted down the opposition.

At school he was a "good" student, but his grades gradually declined until by the fifth grade he was receiving little more than average grades. He tried out for the team in all sports but was restless at being a benchwarmer in some. He gradually withdrew from the peer group and spent increasingly long periods of time at home watching television.

Psychological testing at age 3 years 7 months revealed an I.Q. in the 99th percentile (Merrill-Palmer) and 125 equivalent (Good-enough). The psychologist summarized her report as follows: "Tommy is an intelligent, highly responsive child who actively reaches out to the world and is exceedingly impressed by what he finds and fantasies there. Psychosexually, he seems to have launched himself into the phallic phase with determination and anxiety. He works over his wishes and anxieties in conversation, play, and fantasy, and when these methods do not bring sufficient relief he turns temporarily to denial and protestations of omnipotence ('I'm Superman')." At age 5½ the I.Q. was measured at 133 (Stanford-Binet) and at 9 years 10 months it was measured at 121 (WISC). In the fifth grade at school an Otis measured his I.Q. at 117. Projective testing over the years has revealed his intense inner turmoil, the oral-phallic fixations, and the use of omnipotent fantasies for the resolution of conflict.

When last seen at age 11, he remained very verbal but with a definitely constricted fantasy life and constricted general activity. His verbalizations readily revealed the persistence of his demands to be seen as special and his disavowal of a need for others; but there were hints of a constant threat of being overwhelmed by forces beyond his control. On Assessment Profile, the libidinal drive was seen as fixed at an oedipal level without evidence of resolution. Castration threats were apparent and anxieties over injury intense. Regressions to phallic and oral levels were evident. Object relationships were seen as both oedipal and preoedipal in nature with an undue fixation on his mother. Separation anxieties were much in evidence. Aggressive fantasies were under rigid control but retained an annihilative quality which threatened to overwhelm him at times. Ego constriction and rigid reaction formations dominated the defense structure. The counterphobic attitudes toward anxieties were less than in earlier childhood. "Dreams of glory" were the dominant resolution fantasies for threatened helplessness, humiliation and injury. The dynamics of Tommy's behavior related to his intense need to avoid helplessness. He continues to behaviorally command a focus of attention on himself which avoids separation and the concomitant overwhelming affect of helplessness and rage.

In all respects Tommy has retained the organization of the pseudomature child and, although adolescence has not exerted its influence on him as yet, one has little to be optimistic about in terms of his avoiding a personality deviation.

DATA FROM PSYCHOANALYSIS

Eddie

Eddie, an 8½-year-old male, was adopted at 5 days of age, six years after Mother had delivered a normal female child but had been unable to conceive a second time. In contrast to her daughter, who had been a passive, quiet, easy to care for child, Eddie was an extremely active baby. At 6 months of age, he got out of his crib alone, crawled, and was walking upright by 8 months of age. From then on, Eddie got into everything and was essentially uncontrollable from Mother's point of view. Severe "tantrums" began at 6 months of age. Although they stopped by 4 years of age, mother felt Eddie to be "seething with rage." Speech came early and by 18 months of age Eddie talked nearly constantly. He could "fascinate" (fasten) an adult audience and hold them for long periods of time. By this time Eddie had verbal and behavioral techniques which forced Mother to be near him and attentive to him most of the time; primarily by persistent questioning and verbalizing his fantasies. She felt pride in his "grown-up" behavior (speech, putting things together, adult questions, etc.) but was aware of her exasperation with his forcing her involvement. By 2 years of age he had set his own sleeping time and toileting patterns. Mother felt a peculiar relationship existed between them in that neither seemed to allow the other any overt expression of anger nor of affection. All interchanges were on a verbal level which Mother felt Eddie controlled. There was very little interaction between Eddie and his sister. It was as if Eddie were convinced he could "move her out" in any situation with Mother. Father was equally a distant figure although gradually Eddie included his father in his omnipotent control. An attempt at nursery school failed at 3, simply because Eddie refused to attend. At 4 he agreed to a play school program one-half day, 4 days a week. Everyone was fascinated with Eddie's verbal ability and they were highly involved with his "great intellect." However, teachers noted his lack of involvement with other children and his difficulty in completing projects unless an adult stayed with him at all times. Eddie could draw representationally by 3 years of age and in perspective by 4 years of age. However, comments were made to the fact he only drew war pictures and explosions.

School was a disaster for Eddie. He had great difficulty attending, fought with every teacher by refusing to do as she wished although he produced elaborate reports on all subjects in which he was interested. He could read easily and did read a fair amount, mostly to collect information with which he could dazzle and amaze others. He had no friends in the class, and, in fact, was actively excluded by the other children. Because of his "great intellect" he was placed in a private school beginning in the second grade but did no better than while in the public school.

By 8 years of age his parents were exasperated with him and worn out by his unalterable demands for a constant focus on him. He asked endless questions and told long, rambling stories. He was evasive in the extreme. Conversations with him were experienced as being "talked at" rather than "talked with." When he began to threaten them with suicide, professional help was sought.

Psychological testing at age 8½ revealed a Wechsler I.Q. of 137 Verbal, 126 Performance, and 135 Full Scale. Scatter between and within subtests was great and interference with intellectual functioning was strongly suggested. Projective testing revealed marked ego constriction with dehumanizations as well as a vigilance against potentially overwhelming affect. In one story he stated that, "All cargo coming in and out of the port had to be carefully and thoroughly inspected to make certain no dangerous explosives were aboard."

In a diagnostic interview Eddie related a dream in which he had been taking down a book from a book shelf and a wave of water struck the wall and knocked it over. The shelf of books and he were both hurled to the floor. He finally stood up but was overwhelmingly embarrassed to discover the wave had pulled off his pants and he was exposed naked. He spent the remainder of the time assuring me that the wave of water was really not very big and certainly not dangerous. When I empathized with his feelings of helplessness around his pants being pulled off and exposing him, he cried and told me it was "just awful." I agreed there was little worse than being caught with your pants down and offered to help try to find a way for him to feel more secure about himself.

As we had seen with both Rita and Tommy, the dynamics of Eddie's behavior relate to his intense needs to avoid the helplessness and rage of separation. He effects avoidance of separation via his verbal "fascination" techniques which, although they had served him well in his earlier years, were now ineffective in controlling the anxiety.

The analysis began, as expected, with Eddie trying to fascinate me with his intellect and controlling the time the sessions started and stopped and all in between. I repeatedly pointed out his fear of being caught with his pants down and finally suggested the waves were his greatest source of anxiety and concern. He fought viciously against this assertion on my part. He insisted he had informed me that the wave was of no consequence: "Not the least bit powerful." However, he brought dreams in the subsequent sessions in which some forces threatened to overwhelm him, but in each instance he won out by devaluating the force (wind, water, fire, explosions). He drew endless pictures of wars with conventional, atomic and interplanetary, futuristic weaponry. I persisted in my attitude of sympathy for the enormous energy he had to devote to fend off the threat of being overwhelmed. Although he periodically became nearly violent in his denial of any such threat, he moved closer to me physically and a feeling of his gradually being able to use me in support of his efforts to cope with the affect appeared. His body often leaned against mine at this time and he would cry, scream, and yell, demanding that I know that the force was not great. I informed him that I believed it felt awfully great to him and perhaps even threatened to destroy him but that I knew it was possible to deal with it in many ways other than belittling it. He would moan and cry that it could not be. However, his body tenseness and rigidity would decrease and a feeling of two people conversing appeared. He would then move away from me and for brief periods of time play on the floor beside me.

After weeks of these kinds of interchanges (which I believed to be corrective experiences around the rapprochement crisis; see discussion below) Eddie moved to game playing. He insisted we play checkers. He moved his men carelessly and without thought. When he saw he was losing badly, he became enraged, cried, and insisted I should allow him to win as his father did. I expressed my puzzlement over this command. He assured me that his winning was essential and I must know it to be true and necessary. When I did not yield to his demands he sulked for weeks, reading the entire hour. However, he made certain he had not lost contact with me by periodically showing me a cartoon and inviting me to join in the laughter. I repeatedly interpreted his anxiety over the checker game and the force dreams. He would again become furious, insist I was lying and that he only read because he liked to read. Near the end of the hour he would put his book down and tell me he would play a game of checkers if I wished. I would assert that we might play because he wanted to try to learn to deal with another person without his control techniques. He would smile, set up the checkers and ultimately ask me to help him play correctly and well. He always cried when he lost but did not become enraged. I often commented, if he lost, that he might feel as if he had been caught with his pants down.

Around a statement he made about an alternative way of setting up the checker game (red on red and black on black) I learned of his recognition of how he alienated potential friends. He was able to tell me that he often made statements which he hoped were true but was not sure if they were. He informed me that he said them as if they were fact and could prove it. If someone "looked it up" and exposed him as wrong, he felt "utterly humiliated." To my question, he assured me it was the same as being caught with his pants down, but not only in such situations was he exposed as naked, he was exposed as being utterly helpless, an incompetent "boob." I suggested "helpless child" rather than "boob." He informed me that "I have felt that way so many times in my life I can't count them." When I informed him I could see how that was a pretty awful feeling and we needed to know what it was all about, he became furious and insisted that I already knew what it was all about. I wondered if he had to believe that "someone knew all the answers even if he did not." For the next several weeks it was as if we were dealing with the idea that someone had to be omnipotent in this relationship and it would pass from him to me and back to him. Each time I would try to get to the anxiety element in these interchanges he demonstrated his "evasiveness" techniques and how he could get issues sidetracked. As I confronted him with the evasiveness he brought numerous memories of his getting his parents involved in irrelevant arguments and gradually was able to tolerate the anxiety of separation without omnipotence residing in either me, or to an increasing degree, in himself. He talked then of his relationship to peers and how all of this did not work with them, informing me that when he got trapped with peers he had to "shout them down."

It was evident that Eddie was becoming increasingly separated but having a difficult time maintaining a sense of self-constancy without omnipotence. It was as if he could not tolerate the humiliation of felt helplessness and was trying to cope with it by fantasies of grandiosity. It was clear at this point that he was better able to deal with the threat of an overwhelming rage affect but that "helplessness" remained a threat to him. The feeling was one of an increasing sense of two separate people conversing, but his anxieties around helplessness and the lack of omnipotence remained high. Eddie called his grandiose verbalizations "fish stories" and try as he might he was unable to stop himself from telling such tales. Invariably in such situations he was called "names" by his peers and peer relationships remained difficult for him. However, it was noted that within the family there was much greater peace and quiet and both mother and father were feeling much more comfortable about Eddie and with him.

Eddie was doing well in a highly structured school I had recommended and his relationship with the teachers had improved markedly. Around fights on the school bus in which Eddie was always the focus, the interactions with the peer group (wherein his imperious attitudes infuriated them to fight him) became clear and Eddie made some changes in himself. His fish stories became less grandiose and he ceased trying to "shout down the opposition." In his hours he talked of how terrible it was to feel "stupid" in relationship to his peers, to his parents, and to me. Together, we had labeled his grandiosity as his wishes to be "first," "best," "king," "emperor," etc., and he was able now to talk about the underlying feelings of "stupid," "boob," and "helpless child." His struggles to bring the grandiose and the devaluated, helpless self into some sort of mid-point were difficult for him but increasingly possible. Humor in his art work appeared and seemed to permit a resolution which was acceptable to himself and to others. In a dream in which he was out on a concrete jetty in the ocean and a storm threatened to cut him off from land, we were able to label the new force as one in which he was rendered helpless (he had insisted it was not the same kind of force as before, i.e., rage). This time he made no effort to belittle the force but talked of his anxiety over being cut off from land and unable to survive. I interpreted his anxiety of separation and related it to his feelings of being helpless in such a situation (and why he had to become grandiose when separated). I suggested he experienced separation as being cut off from mother's power. Although he was momentarily enraged he finally stated: "I cannot do it by myself. The waves will kill me." He angrily accused me of telling him that he had to do it by himself. He insisted I had promised him I would help him and yet I was telling him he had to do it by himself, and he "knows" he cannot do it by himself. When I wondered if he could put the feelings into words, he replied: "Be a big boy." When I said it was hard to be a big boy with waves all around threatening to destroy you, he smiled and said it might pull his pants off and show he was just a stupid little boy. I agreed that would be awfully humiliating.

Eddie and I worked with this in each session. I told him about a boy I had known named Bill who had told me it was like being in the Garden of Eden and suddenly being pushed out and told to be on his own. Eddie said it was just like that, even though he did not believe in the Bible and that it made him so damned mad to be pushed out that way. I reminded him that he had never allowed himself to be pushed out. He laughed and said no, he had held on. I said Bill had sat on the edge and demanded to be let back in. Eddie thought that was funny because he couldn't get all the way back in. I wondered how scary it would be to get all the way back in. He told me: "Too scary." I suggested he then had been just trying to keep from getting pushed out all the way. He emphatically informed me you couldn't let "them" push you all the way out because the waves would get you. This led to a discussion of "them." He angrily talked of Mother. I wondered which one. He denied the first one made any difference at all. He never knew her. He told me he had a calendar from day 5 of his life and that the first five days didn't count.

We had many sessions then around "good" and "bad." Initially Eddie denied "bad" in either mother. He made excuses for the biological mother and insisted the "real mother" (the adopting mother) was all good. He then talked of his own "badness" and related this to the "waves and storms, fires and explosions." He finally informed me that it was because of this "badness" in him that he had been abandoned at 5 days of age and pushed out on his own later. He was surprised when I expressed doubts about the truth of that statement. He accused me then of calling his "mothers" bad. He finally thought it possible his biological mother might have been bad for getting pregnant before marriage. He then allowed that his mother was the "them" who insisted he do it on his own. I wondered if he also was not part of the "them." He talked of his wishes to grow up, not to have to feel like a baby. He then forgave me for not allowing him to win at checkers.

In the analysis there were many times when he cried and spoke of his intense feelings of embarrassment over my telling him that the waves, fires, and explosions had something to do with his feelings about himself. He said he had repeatedly regretted ever having "opened my mouth to you because it always makes me feel so bad and ashamed when you tell me it has meanings about me." However, he began to tell me that it was true and that he was aware that his need to "know it all" and to be a "big shot" (which he decided was best described as a need to impress) got him into a lot of trouble. He felt I would have to hypnotize him to find out why he had this powerful need to impress people because he had no further ideas about it (beyond the defense against "stupid" and "boob" and "helpless child").

In his play he began to make wands, decorated guns (long ones), and finally brought a dream in which a squid or an octopus had a forked tail which was bitten off by another fish. Although there had been periodic allusions to his voyeurism, there had been no sustained focus on sexual matters. There now appeared thoughts about his penis, his envy of his sister (who was Mother's biological child and also preferred by Mother) and his intense curiosity about female genitalia. Over a number of sessions the "forked tail" became clarified in terms of his "forked tongue" (his fish stories) and the female genitals. He was able to admit his wishes to be a girl for he felt then he would not have problems. He had noted his sister was not dating boys, though, and wondered if that meant she might have the same problems around relationships. We were able to agree upon his fantasy that Sister had a very special relationship to Mother which he did not share. He also agreed that he fantasied she was never cut off from Mother as he was. He repeatedly assured me that he truly did want to remain a boy. His feelings about his "inadequate" penis and its relationship to "boob," "stupid," and "helpless child" could then be clarified. One of his recent drawings had shown a man catching a rubber tire, thinking he had caught a fish, and the look on the man's face when he hooked the tire. He now drew a man catching a real fish and the genuine pleasure on the man's face as he reeled in the fish. It became clear to me that over the next few sessions a sense of phallic dominance was realized and in the hours, phallic behavior dominated. His verbalizations centered on discriminations of similarities and differences, primarily between himself and me, Father, Mother, Sister, and peers. I then began to hear about grandmothers, aunts, uncles, and cousins which I would not have believed existed prior to that time.

At that point in the analysis oedipal conflicts appeared which were intense and difficult for Eddie. Although I had seen glimpses of the oedipal complex in the past, it had not been a focus of his until this point in the analysis. I will not detail the events other than to state that the "specialness" and "grandiosity" frequently reappeared and seemed to enhance his difficulties in effecting a resolution (both on the side of his winning and on the side of his deflecting the castration threat).

The analysis of Eddie continues, primarily as a classical oedipal neurosis with classical psychoanalytic techniques possible. The ebb and flow of defensive regression to preoedipal positions and working in the various aspects of the oedipal conflict itself with attendant anxieties and fantasies is as a typical analysis and with expectations of an adequate resolution.

Discussion

The rapprochement crisis seems to be a nodal point in the separation-individuation process in which there is a clustering of events of crisis proportions (Mahler 1975). It is our impression that the "events" are at least three in number: (1) The cognitive-affective awareness of separateness; (2) the cognitive-affective awareness of a lack of omnipotence (with feelings of helplessness); and, (3) an affective awareness of sexual differences. This developmental crisis normally occurs somewhere between 15 and 18 months of age and the concurrent anxiety is behaviorally responded to by a return to the mother in an attempt to regain the relatively anxiety-free state of the omnipotent dyad.

The mother's empathic response to this crisis seems essential for adequate progression toward the attainment of libidinal object constancy and the structuralizations inherent in the completion of the separation-individuation process. The adequate mother seems to recognize the child's needs at the time of the crisis and to respond by accepting the child's return to earlier forms of interaction, giving comfort and body protection, followed by an adequate support of the child's equally strong thrust toward the attainment of a separate, personal identity. The extremes of the inadequate, unavailable mother seem to be of two types: (1) The mother who insists that the child not regress but rather, that the child be a "big boy" or a "big girl" and "do it yourself"; or (2) the mother who acts as if the anxiety were real and the child were unable to survive without mother's constant presence and assistance.

The pseudomature child is a product of the mother-child interaction wherein the child and the mother have difficulties tolerating bodily closeness and dependency, and a strong need for independent mature behavior (the latter need on the part of the mother may be both personal and cultural). It is our belief that, preceeding the rapprochement crisis and possibly beginning early in the symbiosis, the cues from the mother to the child are those of a push towards early maturity and independence. This is not to deny that the strivings of the child may not be unduly powerful in the same direction (some infants seem to resist cuddling and closeness). If the biological capabilities of the child are such as to permit early walking and talking, the mutual gratification of the precocity in these areas initiates a cyclic validation. It thus appears that in order to produce a pseudo-mature child, it is necessary that the child be endowed with high intellectual and neuromotor synthesis potential, as well as a mother whose needs are to produce a child showing early independence and maturity (Tartakoff 1966). It seems as if there is much joy and admiration from these experiences up to the time of the rapprochement crisis, and with the relatively sudden return of infantile behavior there is much dismay and thus the command "Be a big boy." Prior to the time of the rapprochement crisis the omnipotent dyad is present and it appears to be relatively "easy" to be the big boy. But with the anxieties around cognitive-affective awareness of separateness and of helplessness (lack of omnipotence), the child's felt belief in his capacity to remain the big boy is tenuous. Perhaps he can only feel it to be possible in the presence of the mother's admiring gaze. The mechanisms which the child develops for the continuation of the "big boy" behavior and the illusion of an omnipotent dyad (in which the child can cope with the threat of overwhelming affect) become the essence of pseudomature behavior.

The intrapsychic situation seems to be one of a failure to develop a constant self- and object representation, but there are also failures in the structures essential to the progressive development of the aggressive drive. It seems to us that the undifferentiated affect (rage-like aggression) fails to undergo the usual progressive modulations to annihilative aggressive affect and from there to competitive aggression and its attached affect. It seems as if the "bad self-object affective experiences," the "bad self affective experiences," and the "bad object affective experiences" (Kernberg 1976, pp. 61-64) are the essence of this undifferentiated, annihilative affect which must remain split off (perhaps as a felt anxiety over the threat to the "good self-object, the good self and the good object"). It seems as if it is only in the presence of the omnipotent dyad that these can be effectively isolated (leading to the repressive and splitting mechanisms which do not allow amalgamation of "good" and "bad" self- and object representations). The rapprochement crisis is thus experienced as a severe trauma with overwhelming anxiety which must be dealt with by mechanisms which avoid separation, humiliation, and helplessness. These "mechanisms" are of the order of an illusory, omnipotent dyad (without separation), disavowal (repression, split-off) of bad self, bad object, and bad self-object with the accompanying affective experiences related to "bad"; and an investment in those areas of interaction which are praised and admired (the "good"), that is, the intellect, verbal ability, and motor development. The resulting character structure and behavioral patterns is one of pseudomaturity.

It is our belief that the psychic organization of the pseudomature child renders him or her highly vulnerable to oedipal conflicts and may prevent the normal resolution of that complex.

When we are dealing with trauma in the first three years of life (an essentially preverbal period) the question of corrective experience versus interpretation, memory recall, and reconstruction is an issue which cannot be resolved by polemics and dogmatism. In the instance of pseudomature resolution of the rapprochement crisis, the dynamic pattern of avoidance of closeness and distance through creation of an illusory omnipotent dyad is responsive to defense interpretation with release of affect (shame, humiliation, and rage) as well as memories of both the fear of loss of control and experiences of momentary loss of control. Such memories and affects are from the verbal period of life but are relatable to a reconstructed nonverbal period. Thus, the classical technique of defense analysis and reconstruction is possible. When it comes to the essential genetic experiences, however, there is a difference which is noteworthy. Developmental studies speak of the emotional unavailability of the mother during the crisis. Our observations indicate the mother is essentially unavailable for the child's need for affective support at the time of the rapprochement crisis. In fact, we have learned that the mother essentially says, "Do it yourself!" In analysis, regardless of the transference situation, the analyst remains empathically available. It is in this fact of the analyst's empathic availability that a sharp contrast exists between the present experience and the past. For this reason, it seems to us that the term "corrective experience" might well be used to describe that recreation of the rapprochement crisis.

With the increasing cultural pressures for earlier physical separation of mother and child, the problems surrounding the resolution of the rapprochement crisis and the subsequent preoedipal organization seem to us to be of enormous importance. The contributions of Margaret Mahler provide a rational basis for both prevention possibilities and early intervention.

References

Freud, A. (1965). *Normality and Pathology in Childhood: Assessments of Development*. New York: International Universities Press.

Greenacre, P. (1948). Anatomical structure and superego development. In *Trauma, Growth and Personality*. New York: Norton, 1952.

Jacobson, E. (1964). *The Self and the Object World*. New York: International Universities Press.

Kernberg, O. (1976). *Object Relations Theory and Clinical Psychoanalysis*. New York: Jason Aronson.

Kohut, H. (1971). *The Analysis of the Self*. New York: International Universities Press.

Mahler, M., Pine, F., and Bergman, A. (1975). *The Psychological Birth of the Human Infant*. New York: Basic Books.

Smilansky, S. (1968). *The Effects of Socio-Dramatic Play on Disadvantaged Preschool Children*. New York: John Wiley and Sons.

Speers, R. (1974). Variations in separation-individuation and implications for play ability and learning as studied in the 3-year-old group in nursery school. In *The Infant at Risk*. ed. D. Bergsma, pp. 77-100. New York: Intercontinental Medical Book Corporation.

Speers, R., McFarland, M., Arnaud, S., and Curry, N. (1971). Recapitulation of the separation-individuation process when the normal 3 years old enters nursery school. In *Separation-Individuation: Essays in Honor of Margaret S. Mahler*, ed. J. McDevitt, and C. Settlage, pp. 297-324. New York: International Universities Press.

Tartakoff, H. (1966). The normal personality in our culture and the Nobel Prize complex. In *Psychoanalysis: A General Psychology*, ed. R. Loewenstein, L. Newman, M. Schur, and A. Solnit. New York: International Universities Press.

23

Reconstruction of an Accident Experienced During the Rapprochement Subphase: Innovations in Response to Inadequate Phase Progression

MURIEL CHAVES WINESTINE, PH.D.

In normal development, increased perception of one's separateness along with awareness of a diminishing sense of omnipotence, creates the conditions out of which evolve the conflicts and developmental tasks specific to the rapprochement subphase of the separation-individuation process. The child again wishes to share in the benefits of his parents' presumed omnipotence only to be confronted with obstacles from within and without which mitigate the chances for such remerging and, rather, foster progression toward greater self-object differentiation, object constancy, and ego autonomy.

Margaret Mahler (1966) stresses that rapprochement marks the beginning of verbal communication and that if there is an absence of higher level dialogue this circumstance compounds the stress trauma that may have existed during the preverbal mother-child interaction. This deficit tends to result in a diminution of the child's self-esteem and there results a consequent narcissistic vulnerability. She adds that secondary narcissistic investment in a child's own autonomy should take place *gradually*, thereby protecting against sudden

Presented before the New York Psychoanalytic Society, September 25, 1979.

deflation of "omnipotence" and preventing serious injury to self-esteem. Thus, a proposition concerning the rapprochement phase states that if the experience of participating within the orbit of child-parent omnipotence is too abruptly punctured, it constitutes a phase-specific trauma bearing grave consequences for the narcissistic component in character structure. Disturbances in self-regard are then defended with heightened omnipotent strivings accompanied by difficulties in drive integration, object relations, and reality testing.

Psychosexual development and separation-individuation are interrelated developmental processes as stated by Mahler (1968). The maturational spurt, marked by upright locomotion which usually occurs in the second year, puts the normal toddler in a position of relatively advanced physical autonomy and his emotional and developmental growth and independence must catch up and keep pace with the somatic maturational spurt. My clinical report concerns a child patient who displayed excellent but precocious motor development—he walked unaided at 8½ months. As such, he serves to illustrate the two tracks of separation-individuation: maturation versus development; and how an imbalance of these two processes exerts influence on subsequent phase negotiations. When locomotion occurs so early in the first year, the discrepancy between growth of physical autonomy and that of emotional differentiation from the mother is increased and may have deleterious effects upon the negotiation of the accompanying anal phase. Like any out-of-phase emergence, it contributes to brittle and rigid ego formation which may be further enhanced by a mother who capitalizes on the child's independence and fails to respond with warmth and empathy.

Normally, the rapprochement-age toddler undergoes an active struggle during the anal phase characterized by the increased aggression and negativism which contribute to and defend the growing sense of autonomy. The time of the anal phase of *psychosexual* development also brings its problems of sadism, impulse and sphincter control, retention or loss of stool; whereas from an *ego* orientation, rapprochement represents a repertoire of phenomena which continues to be defined: self and object; animate and inanimate; male and female; and heightened separation anxiety and fears of reengulfment.

My patient's continued pattern of precocious motor development, an ability to write and read numbers and letters and words by 3 years of age (although he was never a *verbal* child), proved unavailable for sublimations and learning and was utilized defensively against sadistic drive, to bind anxiety, and to ward off chaos and disorganization. The imbalance between aspects of his ego and drive development reflected deviation not only in the separation-individuation process, but also faulty neutralization of aggression which interfered with differentiation and contributed to a paucity of imaginative play.

Although Mahler herself has avoided overextension of the concept of separation-individuation, neither ignoring psychosexual development nor implying that conflicts from the subphases of the first three years of life persist *unaltered* even in narcissistic or borderline pathology, the powerful explanatory potential of her theory has tempted others to be less cautious. Her theory's uniqueness rests on the specificity with which each subphase accompanies maturational and developmental achievements—perceptual, motoric, cognitive, emotional—landmarks that are never again experienced.

Such specificity seemed demonstrable *during the first two years* of my patient's five years of treatment when it was possible to reconstruct a traumatic experience which had occurred during the rapprochement subphase, that is, its genetic derivatives were represented in a current event as well as in the transference. I have chosen therefore to view this communication describing these early phases of treatment within a framework of Mahler's formulations. I hope that this proves consistent with my own admonition for caution, although, by necessity, this report is selective and limited.

BACKGROUND AND DIAGNOSTIC CONSIDERATIONS

Nathan was referred by his kindergarten when he was 5 years 4 months because of an inability to adapt to his surroundings. Enrolled when he was 4 years 9 months, he was isolated from and complained about the other children, was preoccupied with issues of cleanliness and messiness, unable to rest, refused to participate in any planned or group activities, exerted control even when alone with an adult, drank and urinated with inordinate frequency. He was indifferent to instructions, adamant about doing everything his own way. Although he made overtures to his teachers for physical contact, he was not truly affectionate and sought to control the timing and nature of their responses to him. Parental oblivion to his distress was striking, although once alerted, his parents described symptoms which they attributed to their marital separation: increased physical and emotional constraint, fear of noises, sleeplessness, withdrawal to bed with complaints of belly aches at times when they suspected he felt angry or upset.

Nevertheless, they considered him an active, unusually intelligent, self-sufficient boy and they were admittedly grateful that he spent so much time by himself writing and reading numbers and letters and playing both sides of pretend board games. They emphasized that these traits were consistent with his earlier development when he insisted on doing everything by and for himself. He *always refused to have stories read to him.* Recall of developmental data, although scanty, suggested a physically robust infant who thrived on breast feeding for several months, was a lusty sucker and eater and who possessed adequate drive endowment. The mother was depressed over her deteriorating marriage, and her physical availability and conscientiousness were *not* matched by an emotional availability since she welcomed, perceived, and fostered his precocious maturational growth along lines of specious, premature self-sufficiency and independence.

As already mentioned, Nathan displayed excellent and accelerated motor development. But when he was 21 months, he fell backwards down a steep flight of stairs. His parents found him at the bottom of the stairs, dazed but physically unhurt, and after forty-five minutes he recovered full sensibilities without pathological sequelae. Consistent with their style, they treated this accident too matter-of-factly, fearful that they might create doubts in the child's mind (or in their own) about his independence.

Since the fall involved a function, locomotion, upon which his narcissistic homeostasis depended, it nevertheless constituted a particular blow to his self-esteem combined with the lack of an external object to assist in the maintenance of his psychic equilibrium. Of significance, when he subsequently sustained the falls and bumps that little children routinely experience, he remained aloof from consolation in sharp contrast to what normally characterizes the reaction of rapprochement-age children.

As already stated, while locomotion plays a significant role in the separation-individuation process, on the drive level there is gradual predominance of the anal phase. My patient's too easy compliance during anal training suggests that he separated from his stool with the same physical rapidity that had characterized his earlier physical separation from his mother (occasioned by the early onset of loco-motion). But consistent in both was a lack of emotional differentia-tion and structure, evidenced by his preferred mode of expression, namely, somatization rather than verbalization, fantasy, or play.

Nathan, then, at referral presented many features which placed him among the childhood obsessional disorders with accompanying drive regressions, isolation, negativism, oppositionalism, and intense ambivalence. However, the regression did *not* seem to represent a predominantly defensive move away from a phallic-oedipal organi-zation since he had never relinquished his omnipotence, had weak object ties to peers and adults, and did not evidence the aggressive-ness and competitiveness connected with such development. An emotional aloofness, distancing from objects rather than age-adequate expression of dependencies, perfectionism, humiliation over failure, a startling refusal to learn from anybody, accompanied by an arrogant, superior, and artificial stance, rather suggested that his disturbance rested primarily in the realm of self-esteem regula-tion and narcissistic supplies and appeared as a precursor to a narcissistic borderline personality.

I further suggest that the aforementioned accident served as an organizing trauma during the rapprochement subphase and had reverberations on the interdigitation of the anal sadistic drive and his object relations as well as on his narcissistic character formation—a thesis which will be developed in the rest of this paper.

TREATMENT—PHASE I

Derivatives of the Anal Drive

In the beginning of his four-times-a-week treatment, Nathan greeted me with comments such as, "I guess you know that I'm a boy who likes numbers," with which he then covered reams of papers. An initial gush of charm gave way to insulation, frenetic activities, and an uncommunicativeness regarding the simplest matters. Finally, I ascertained from some of his numerical configurations that they, in part, seemed to refer to his family constellation. This was confirmed when he eventually asked whether I slept in my office (as his father did in his) and I said something to him about his sadness and missing his father.

He obsessively questioned and answered himself, suggesting conflicts which I eventually verbalized to him as referring to his wishes and concerns about being big and strong or little and helpless (I chose only this to tell him although it was already apparent that there were other polarities involved, i.e., good and bad; boy and girl). His mother told me a dream which he had reported to her (before treatment had begun): "Pieces of the wall came out and then they all went back." She offered no ideas of her own concerning this dream. During sessions, Nathan repeatedly encircled numbers as if to contain or reunite his family, adding credence to my own thoughts that a restitutive theme was expressed in the dream. Once, after a long period of silence, he said, "It makes me stupid to be afraid but not stupid when I have dreams." After a rise in disruptive behavior, I verbalized its defensive nature against experiencing fear but that to be bad and out of control also meant to him to feel stupid—a narcissistic blow. I added that he rushed around from one thing to another so that neither of us had a chance to know anything about his feelings—that they all came out in his dreams. He responded, "This whole day seemed like a dream," thereby revealing the degree of splitting off of his affective life, and the detachment from environmental influences that characterized his pathological adaptation.

In addition to writing, he engaged endlessly in stereotyped board games of his own invention in which *he* played both sides. These appeared to represent a narcissistic activity in which he fantasied himself as both subject and object, thus creating a world in which he had total control. One might conclude therefore that it precluded a representation of libidinal or aggressive wishes toward an object and therefore was not subject to conflict. However, rather than being mutually exclusive, it was viewed by me as a defense that proved inapproachable through verbalizations and only later in treatment could be related to conflict.

When his number and letter writing, board games, or frenetic activities subsided, he seemed languid and bored. In response to puppets which I introduced, he responded with disgust. But finally he instructed me to spank the baby's behind while he threw pieces of clay into a basket—some landing on the floor. When I attributed various feelings to the puppet characters—sadness, happiness, anger, disgust—he unexpectedly added, "*meanness.*" Then he went to the bathroom.

In anticipation of a move to a new house located in my neighborhood, he threw piles of paper around the office which he then disregarded. I spoke of the imminent move and the possible disruptions this held for him. He responded by numbering all of the papers in succession and scotch taped them into a streamer the length of my office. He referred to one end as "West" (the old house and neighborhood) and the other as "East" (the new, closer to me) and I verbalized his wishes to connect the two. Later, he referred to his old house and neighborhood as "messy and ugly." My own association to his comments was to an internal explosion which had demolished a house in the vicinity where Nathan lived. I did not mention this to him at this time. But I was astonished to learn, when I later asked his mother, that the day of the explosion, she and Nathan were visiting friends who lived within close sight of it. They had fled onto the street amidst thundering blasts and quakes and once outside, witnessed the conflagration.

This incident occurred when Nathan was approximately 4 years 4 months, shortly *after* the parents' separation. Omitting mention of this event attests not only to the parents' own denial and repression, but also to a lack of attunement with their son, since now some of his symptoms involving fear of loud noises, belly aches, and increasing constraint could be dated to and in part attributed to this event.

When, in conjunction with fears of a thunderstorm, Nathan insisted that his parents' separation would be undone by the move to the new house (expectation that his father would again be sleeping with the family), I introduced the story of the explosion. He blandly assured me that he passed the site of the destroyed house frequently. Over a period of time, I suggested that several things pointed to his wishes to have everything fixed up and whole again, and that perhaps his dream about pieces falling out of the wall and going back in again, could be related to the explosion. I told him, though, that his concerns about his "meanness" (using the affect he had added to my list) combined with the indifference with which he knocked things over in my office suggested a disclaiming of any responsibility, but that nevertheless he might feel badly and responsible for some of the bad things that happened—including Daddy going away. It seemed apparent that "meanness" referred to condensed sadomasochistic impulses which had become concretized through identification with the exploding house. It is likely that he had responded with fear of being overwhelmed from within by accompanying intolerable excitement and fears of exploding and eventual annihilation.

When he responded to my comments by toppling off his chair or rocking until the chair itself toppled over, I considered this confirmation that he equated his body with the exploding, out of control house and I told him so. He tried then to line up dominoes, to play with "pick up sticks," but nothing worked. Once when he announced that he had to make "B.M.," he left open the door to the adjacent bathroom thus enabling both of us to see his reflection in a mirror as he sat on the toilet holding down his penis. Upon finishing, he did not flush the toilet and upon reentering the office said, "Now, I'll make something for you" and reverted to defensive action of covering pages with numbers. After he left, I noted the feces left in the toilet bowl. That the "numbers" and the "pieces of wall" in the dream might represent feces seemed clearer as he left his gifts for me. Derivative of the anal sadistic drive, it indicated how the transference might develop in the service of self-object representations imbued with ambivalence but in which the bad (aggressive), as well as the good (libidinal), could both be entertained and better integrated; that the emotional differentiation and structure building so specific to what had been missed during actual anal training might now be facilitated. A dream produced about this time of his first separation from treatment revealed the trend toward somatization of his anal sadistic aggression, although the channel for verbalization is represented by the question put to him in the dream: "I remember only the middle of the dream—I was holding my teacher around the middle; I knocked over Neil's tower and when he asked why, I was too weak to talk."

Subsequent dreams contained castration and catastrophic themes stimulated by a Charlie Chaplin film in which a house blew up. Any reference to the real house that blew up now evoked great excitement and distractibility. Sessions ended with bursts of random objects thrown high onto shelves. "Fuck" and "shit" now proliferated over papers in lieu of the numbers. When I questioned his mother, I learned that this language was confined to his sessions with me, but had occurred at home when he was younger. At that time, the mother had responded with anger and banned him from her presence whenever he used "foul" words. Although his number and letter writing compulsion had preceded this, it is likely that her aggressive reaction to his language added to the defensive nature of this preoccupation.

During sessions, he now hid in the closet and issued noises. I had to guess the source of the noise. He wanted to look into everything—my desk, files, cabinets, his own folder. He banged his head against my abdomen, kicked me, threw clay at me, collected saliva for a whopping spit at me. But he also enjoyed playing a repetitive game with me where we alternated in hiding and finding small wooden blocks (feces), during which time he often "farted." It became a pleasurable joke when I would inquire, "And what is hiding in there?" A dream about drowning and being rescued established a feces-baby equation and related to his concerns over abandonment due to his mother's recent full-time employment. Increasingly, he ignored boundaries between himself and other objects; walked over my foot, disregarded tables, chairs; squeezed himself between narrow places so that objects had to yield, all of which suggested the equation of body as feces as well as his wishes for merger. I talked with him of his fear of his "hidden explosion" within his body and that he had feared that he too could erupt a blast; that the feces within him had represented the bricks (the pieces of wall) in the house that exploded. Gradually, I continued with the countertheme of his wishes to be saved and cherished (to be contained) like the gifts he had left for me (the feces in the toilet bowl). Finally, instead of throwing blocks, which was accompanied by the feeling that he was bad and should be flushed away, he built haphazardly so that the blocks collapsed and were designated as "messes" for me to clean and pick up. I complied and silently picked up his messes until repetitive play culminated in mounting excitement. Finally, I said that he might end up worrying that the mess damaged not only himself but me as well, that is, it could provoke and excite me so that I too would go out of control and thus become unavailable to him, as his mother had done when she banned him from her when he was younger and used naughty words. After additional work concerning his identification with the aggressor, he eventually converted the blocks to bowling pins which he knocked over with a ball and which I repeatedly set up for him. Thus, some reciprocity found its way into the play which was indicative of better intrapsychic separation and self-boundary—a task that had not been sufficiently achieved, due in part to the imbalance and unrelatedness with which the original anal phase was experienced.

Reconstruction of Trauma Specific to the Rapprochement Subphase

Soon after, his mother reported the following incident: Nathan had refused to obey and follow his nursemaid home from the park but insisted on continuing a game of hide and seek with her. In anger and retaliation, she *refused* to *recognize* him each time he reappeared. She demanded to know who he was and refused to believe him when he insisted that he was Nathan. This crescendoed until he ran away from her and it took many minutes before she could find him. He then followed her home sobbing and screaming and remained inconsolable for the rest of the evening. Albeit, the provocative motivation, Nathan's overwhelmed response was reminiscent of Loewald's statement (1960) that a person comes to recognize himself by his being recognized; or put another way, Nathan experienced confusion during the teasing because of his need to depend on external objects, precisely due to the lack of stability of his self- and object representations.

During his session the following day, Nathan did not mention this incident but he did mount a high table and with his eyes *closed* leaned over backwards, causing me to anticipate his fall. He actually fell and I caught him in my arms. Silently, he repeated this action innumerable times and each time I ran around the table making sure to catch him. Finally I said, "I *know* who you are and can catch you even with your eyes closed." Then I referred to the previous day's event with his nursemaid and correlated it with his behavior with me. Since he repeated this sequence dozens of times during subsequent sessions and without any accompanying verbalizations, I introduced the story of his fall down the stairs when he was 21 months—an event he had heard about from his parents, but of which he probably had no actual recall and which depended on reconstruction for further interpretative and integrative work. I stressed that, not to be recognized and known by his name (as with his nursemaid) at this time of his life must have felt something like it did when he fell down the stairs and there was no one there to catch him. I stressed that his not being able to remember this event resulted in a disconnection between the fall and his fright over not being caught. Now, *not* to be caught or recognized made him feel worthless and not worth knowing or catching, and this also made him angry. As he continued falling and being caught by me, he once murmured, "You *always* catch me."

As he became more accessible, I spoke of the events inside of himself and those outside that had gotten mixed up together and had contributed to his unwillingness to *depend* on or cooperate with adults. I said that he had felt frightened and overwhelmed by the fall down the stairs, then by the loss of Daddy, and finally by the exploding house. But I also stressed his identification with these events, turning passive into active and feeling that bad things inside him could make it all happen. I reminded him of his past efforts to provoke and excite me, as he finally succeeded doing with his nurse-maid by instigating her sadistic teasing and emotional unavailability. I connected this with his equally strong wishes to be caught, found, and recognized and translated how these latter wishes better served building of genuine self-esteem and feelings of cohesiveness.

Shortly thereafter, his mother reported a remarkable improvement: the sleep disturbance subsided, he no longer complained of belly aches, the fears were gone, he was more aggressive and less sticky with her. In school, he no longer wrung his hands in despair, appeared generally less anxious, no longer drank nor urinated excessively, played *impersonally* with the other children and preferred girls. He continued to refuse to listen to stories and despite his excellent ability, refused to read, and derived no pleasure from his few activities.

INNOVATIONS TO FACILITATE UNNEGOTIATED TASKS SPECIFIC TO THE RAPPROCHEMENT SUBPHASE—PHASE II

To the extent that Nathan's initial complaints indicated neurotic conflict as reflected in symbolic displacement that had led to organized symptoms, anxiety had been relatively focused and rendered Nathan amenable to analytic therapy. But having reconstructed a sequence of traumatizing events, interpretation of which had resulted in a dramatic diminution of anxiety, suffering and symptoms, Nathan now appeared for his sessions with apparent eagerness, but then seemed diffuse, listless, unanchored, and isolated. That he demonstrated aberration in the areas of ego functioning and object relations—what binds all children considered borderline (Pine 1974)—emerged most clearly at this time. To sessions he brought himself but no material, and the extent of his boredom, refusal, and inability to talk or play was more fully exposed. By contrast, exhibitionistic components were directly discharged through undisguised, sexualized, effeminate gyrations in conjunction with painful self-consciousness, pointing to his disturbance in self-regard and faulty object cathexis. The picture he presented was one well-described by Weil (1973) of children who experience the phallic-oedipal phase in a distorted way. "Their uncertain identity and their need for identification may create the impression that they have entered oedipal development when actually they are still engaged in yet another dyad. These children merely show 'as if' oedipal tendencies. . . . Hence, the real nucleus for neurotic conflicts of the oedipal phase may be missing or weak" (p. 294-295).

In regard to his self-consciousness, one can speculate that in walking as early as Nathan did, his body schema and spatial orientation at that time were still in some stage of fusion and confusion. Some residual disturbance then in his body image may have robbed him of a solid core of primary identity formation and thus a reliably cathected self-feeling invested with neutralized energy. His original symptoms suggested a depletion of neutralized cathexis of object and self-representations in favor of body organ cathexis; and, as stated by Mahler (1968), his self-consciousness may also have reflected a redistribution of unneutralized energy onto representations of the sexual part of the self-image. Furthermore, the failure of sufficient emotional differentiation that characterized his anal phase and rapprochement experience was reflected in an insufficiently delineated sexual identity which faltered further in response to inevitable castration anxiety which emerged as he came into better contact with his conflicts over loss.

Returning to the boredom that now characterized Nathan's responses, it undoubtedly contained defensive residuals of his unresolved excitement as well as masturbatory equivalents, but any attempt now at further analysis of defenses, affects, or efforts to relate affect to experience came to naught. As such, the model of conflict based on unconscious drive-defense symptom formation did not seem sufficient for the period of treatment that followed.

Efforts at treating preschool age children with faulty structural development have been described by Alpert (1959) as consisting of corrective emotional experiences. Such efforts are viewed as existing outside of the work of child analysis proper and thought of as interventions aimed at inducing sufficient ego growth and object ties so as to make later analysis possible. This work, aimed at correcting developmental faults, was not conceived as serving in lieu of analysis. Weil (1973) also describes a group of young, prelatency children for whom she prescribes preparatory educational therapy which "aims at making up for early interactional failures and at stimulating ego growth and better integration. . . . Subsequently, with their more clearly emerging neurotic symptomatology, these children can be more successfully treated with psychoanalysis" (p. 299). For Weil, the question is not so much *whether* analysis is the treatment of choice, but *when*.

Both Alpert and Weil recommend that such corrective work be done by teachers or therapists trained along such lines. Techniques involving innovations aimed at treatment of faulty structural development within analysis proper, are considered parameters which might prove inimical to the analytic method and process.

However, a problem arises when, like Nathan, youngsters come to our attention at a more advanced age and stage in their development, when structural defects from the preoedipal phases have already intertwined with experiences which produce an overlay of neurotic disturbances giving expression to the type of intense anxiety which characterized Nathan at the outset of his treatment and which prompted an approach which aimed at conflict resolution. Rather than an either/or attitude toward utilizing extra-analytic techniques to facilitate development instead of analysis for such children, a combination might be appropriate using Mahler's separation-individuation process as a model to organize analysis as a *complement* to a model that prescribes interpretation based on drive theory and defense. Brenner (1975) has argued that by the time one has reached maturity, early development has been so reorganized under the aegis of the oedipal complex that the derivatives of the earlier stages are not readily ascertainable in the transference and concludes, "that excellent as the advances in the knowledge of child development during the first two years of life might be, that they carry no substantial implications for psychoanalytic treatment of adults." In my young patient, the specificity with which the derivative of the rapprochement subphase (the accident on the stairs) was evident in the transference (falling into my arms) might be attributed to the uniqueness of treatment with children precisely because the child is still so close to the original stage of development. From this vantage point, analytic treatment of children provides us with just such opportunities to view developmental theory and clinical practice in close tandem.

Settlage and Spielman (1975) have suggested that the psychoanalytic treatment of faulty structure in accordance with the basic precepts of the analytic method would require that the theory of treatment be extended downward to include the psychopathologies of the preoedipal stages of development. In their view, the possibility of developing analytically sound innovations in technique lies in the extension of theory in two areas currently in the forefront of analytic thinking: (1) the nature of therapeutic process, and (2) the nature of transference. They adhere to the basic principle that treatment *differs* from development in the undoing of pathology from the past and the *distinction* between the therapist role and the parent role. In turn, their reasoning rests on the developmentally attuned conceptualization of the therapeutic action of psychoanalysis as stated by Loewald (1960). Noting that the concept of structural change in personality must mean that ego development is resumed in the therapeutic process, Loewald correlated the significance of *object relations* for the development of *psychic structure* with the significance of the *analytic* relationship for *therapeutic* process. Quoting Anna Freud's (1960) conception of the use of the analyst as a new object, it is further reasoned that the analytic process provides such an interaction between child and adult so that the child's psyche becomes structured and lifted to higher levels of organization and function—a process that normally develops out of the differential between the undeveloped psychic apparatus of the maturing child and his interaction with the mature psychic apparatus of a parent.

Since the disruption in the development of Nathan's object relations was so related to the rapprochement subphase (subject to the vicissitudes of earlier and later loss and trauma), it seemed that only if he could pleasurably experience fulfillment of dependent needs within a relationship that also afforded opportunities for greater differentiation of self-object representations could there be a restoration of his self-esteem via correction of the overestimation of his own omnipotence as well as greater attainment of object constancy. Unlike his parents, who welcomed and fostered retreat into specious independent ritualized activities when he seemed bored, I reasoned it would be therapeutic to foster object ties.

Hence, I now repeatedly verbalized aloud to Nathan the contradictory aspects of his behavior and how he made it still impossible to help him with his needs by pushing away, grabbing, in contrast to his wishes to be caught. Now I stressed how he had always been a boy who did so much for himself, but it had prompted him too early and too quickly to give up expressions of help from grown-ups and subsequently deprived him of having fun in connection with his achievements—he became, instead, bored.

I decided to do something which might *engage* him without coercion or undue activity on my part. I began to hum to him across the room and then to sing some folk songs. He began to listen and agreed to hearing some songs selected from a book. He controlled the situation; held the book, turned the pages when he was ready, permitted only the opening phrases of songs and only those with which he had some familiarity. Gradually, he permitted completion of these songs, but designated the order in which they had to be sung. Finally, he permitted me to sing songs which were new to him. Occasionally, he stopped wandering about the office, fetched the song book himself, indicated my place next to him on the couch and bid me to sing. Finally, he relinquished all control and said, "Sing whatever you like—I come here because I like the way you sing." These singing sessions became mutually enjoyed and aimed not merely at providing id satisfaction but steps toward greater ego development. Nathan no longer feigned indifference to my presence while he began to engage in his own activities. For the first time, he chose to play and mess with paints. During this anally regressive behavior he insisted that I sit close by and watch his every move. At such times, in contrast to the previously described gyrations, his body was quiet and calm. The frequency with which he now insisted, "Look, Dr. W., look," produced an atmosphere reminiscent of the rapprochement subphase as he sought my sharing in and exclusive interest in his activities and products. Eventually, this dovetailing of the anal drive with the rapprochement relatedness facilitated self-regulatory mechanisms built more solidly on identifications with the object (the analyst) and contributed to greater internalization as evidenced by diminution of body gyrations.

Mindful of story books as satisfying the need for distancing and for exploring the wider world (by way of symbolization and fantasy) while also serving the purpose of closeness to the person who was reading, I added reading to the repertoire, since this had been thwarted during his development. His initial reaction was, "I can read to myself." Nevertheless, I read aloud a story called "Little Lost Bear," chosen because it was illustrated with Steiff animals, replicas of which were in my office, as well as for its theme of a bear with little self-esteem until he is discovered and loved by a person. It was my intention to provide an experience around which reading could be libidinally cathected; to convert it from an activity which involved a mechanical conformity to one of more genuine autonomy. Nathan loved the story and as is typical of a younger child, asked for repeated readings. He personified the stuffed bear in my office as a self-representation and assigned it to a fixed place so that it remained visible to me between his sessions when he himself was absent. This seemed to be in the service of fostering greater self- and object constancy.

I also read aloud poetry, appealing to his sense of rhythm. Eventually, he repeated the poems *imitating* my intonation. Mindful that authentic insight is a combination of intellectual *and* emotional understanding, accompanied by an urge to change its pathological aspects, I made up limericks about Nathan's experiences, particularly his responses to separation from me. I hoped to further libidinize *content* for him and to encourage growth of his self as a cognitive percept of experience—in this boy who seemed to *think* not at all. I tried to use some of his own expressions, such as punning with the phrase "to dig" something (i.e., to like it). Illustrative is the following:

> The mess he made was very big
> The reason for it we had to dig
> We learned it had a definite meaning
> To keep Dr. Winestine busy cleaning,
> Because she was leaving on vacation
> Which meant there would be a separation
> And when Nathan suffered any loss
> He had to prove that he was boss.

As with the singing and reading, now with the poems, he asked for them repeatedly so that it became an affect-laden means of communication and of rendering interpretations in which Nathan eventually participated in helping to make up limericks.

Now, he invited me to play board games with him rather than engaging in solo play. But he would quit abruptly and announce, "I don't want to play anymore." I agreed to participate in games of his own invention, but insisted upon knowing how we could each anticipate when the game was finished. "When I don't want to play anymore," he said, as though this should be obvious. I introduced my own feelings in order to encourage an empathic reaction: how it felt to be left in the lurch as he either quit or just wandered off. He agreed and adhered to prearranged rules and a score which formally designated the end of the game.

Similarly in connection with his use of the typewriter. Rather than merely accept his mechanical skill, I dictated stories I made up about Nathan and encouraged him to listen and recall full sentences before hitting the keys. In association to this he showed cognizance of his father's fame and expressed pride and identification with him. He looked forward to his father's visit in school and became less frozen in his actual contacts with him. His teacher began reporting that he was writing stories, at first impoverished but gradually longer and more imaginative.

Renewed identification with his father reinforced the primary identification which can be assumed to have taken place during earlier periods of sexual development. It also enforced greater object cathexis, thus facilitating oedipal identifications rather than regressions and faulty object cathexis.

That three subsequent years of analytic treatment (or the third and final phase) could begin to deal with themes of phallic-oedipal organization was evident in his use of the falling accident as a screen memory. He told me, "My father was at the top of the stairs and I wanted to *show off* to him but he wasn't at the bottom to catch me!" Condensed are the regressive wishes and regrets concerning his father's lack of omnipotence (to be both at the top and bottom simultaneously) as well as the role of the superego accommodating to current conflicts over phallic exhibitionism. Transference interpretations could now proceed as though past was subject to conscious recall rather than from genetic reconstruction and reflected aspects of his past and preconscious fantasy.

In summary, Mahler's propositions provided a framework in which to understand the genetic and dynamic aspects of an accident experienced during the rapprochement subphase and reconstruction of its connection with other trauma and loss. This therapeutic work depended essentially on traditional modes of reconstruction and interpretation within the transference, aided by verbalization and clarification and aimed at understanding the patient's conflictual anxiety. The faulty structural development of this boy required subsequent innovations of technique involving interactions and activities related to fixation in his development specific to the rapprochement subphase and aimed at better resolution of the dyadic, independence-dependence conflict epitomized in the rapprochement crisis. These gratifications did not stabilize fixations and primary process but rather fostered integrations and structuralization. It aimed to restore self-esteem and to promote progression toward phallic and oedipal organization.

The rationale for these innovations arises from the linkage between developmental process and therapeutic process especially as it is associated with the separation-individuation phase of the dyadic stage. That faulty structure and structural conflicts of the transference neurosis can coexist was stressed by Anna Freud (1965) and it was in response to this mixed pathology of childhood that she recommended a comprehensive method of child analysis including a whole range of therapeutic possibilities.

References

Alpert, A. (1959). Reversibility of pathological fixations associated with maternal deprivation in infancy. *Psychoanalytic Study of the Child* 14:16-33.
Brenner, C. (1975). Panel: The implications of recent advances in the knowledge of child development for the treatment of adults. Meeting of the International Psycho-Analytic Association, London.
Freud, A. (1965). *Normality and Pathology in Childhood.* New York: International Universities Press.
Loewald, H. (1960). On the therapeutic action of psycho-analysis. *International Journal of Psycho-Analysis* 41:16-33.
Mahler, M. S. (1966). Notes on the development of basic moods: the depressive effect. In *Psychoanalysis: A General Psychology,* ed. R. Loewenstein et al. New York: International Universities Press. Reprinted in *The Selected Papers of Margaret S. Mahler,* vol. 2, ch. 5. New York: Jason Aronson, 1979.
——— (1968). *On Human Symbiosis and the Vicissitudes of Individuation, volume 1: Infantile Psychosis.* In collaboration with M. Furer. New York: International Universities Press.
Mahler, M. S., Pine, F., and Bergman, A. (1975). *The Psychological Birth of the Human Infant.* New York: Basic Books.
Pine, F. (1974). The concept of "borderline children." *Psychoanalytic Study of the Child* 29:341-368.
Settlage, C., and Spielman, P. M. (1975). On the psychogenesis and psychoanalytic treatment of primary faulty structural development. Presented

at the meetings of the Association for Child Psychoanalysis, Bal Harbor, Florida.

Weil, A. (1973). Ego strengthening prior to analysis. *Psychoanalytic Study of the Child* 28:287-301.

Contributors

ERNEST L. ABELIN, M.D. was trained in Switzerland, where he was influenced by Piaget. In his thesis on schizophrenia, he postulated the "early triangulation" model. This led him to join Dr. Mahler's research, and to study the earliest role of the father. Presently, he is practicing psychoanalysis in New York, and preparing a monograph on early triangulation.

SHELDON BACH received his Ph.D. and psychoanalytic training at New York University. He is in full-time analytic practice and is currently on the faculty and board of the New York Freudian Society, Adjunct Associate Professor at the New York University Postdoctoral Program in Psychoanalysis, and Clinical Assistant Professor of Psychiatry at the Albert Einstein College of Medicine.

ANNI BERGMAN is a graduate of the University of California and Bank Street College of Education. Since 1959 she has been a co-worker and Research Associate of Dr. Margaret S. Mahler. She is coauthor of *The Psychological Birth of the Human Infant* and has published several papers on issues related to separation-individuation, as well as childhood psychosis. At present she is on the faculty of the Clinical

Psychology Doctoral Program of the City University of New York and co-directs a day treatment center for psychotic children and their families. She is a member of the Association for Child Analysis and the Society for Freudian Psychologists.

GERTRUDE and RUBIN BLANCK received master's degrees from Columbia University School of Social Work and subsequently took psychoanalytic training. Gertrude Blanck also has a doctorate from New York University, while Rubin Blanck holds two degrees in law from St. Lawrence University. They are cofounders and Directors of the Institute for the Study of Psychotherapy. Gertrude and Rubin Blanck's interest in developmental psychology is reflected in their many publications, including the collaborative studies *Ego Psychology* and *Ego Psychology II*.

HAROLD P. BLUM, M.D. is editor of the *Journal of the American Psychoanalytic Association*, Clinical Professor of Psychiatry, Downstate Medical Center, and Training Analyst, Downstate Psychoanalytic Institute. He serves on the Board of Directors of the American Psychoanalytic Association Research Fund and the Psychoanalytic Research and Development Fund. In addition, he is a member of the Center for Advanced Psychoanalytic Studies, Princeton, New Jersey. Dr. Blum is the recipient of the Inaugural Award, Margaret Mahler Literature Prize, awarded May 21, 1976.

J. ALEXIS BURLAND, M.D. is engaged in the private practice of psychoanalysis with children, adolescents, and adults. He is also Clinical Professor of Psychiatry and Human Behavior at Jefferson Medical College. He is on the faculty of the Philadelphia Psychoanalytic Institute and is current President of the Philadelphia Psychoanalytic Society.

AARON H. ESMAN, M.D. is Clinical Professor of Psychiatry at Cornell University Medical College, Director of Adolescent Services at the Payne Whitney Clinic, New York Hospital, and a member of the faculty, New York Psychoanalytic Institute. He was formerly Chief Psychiatrist, Jewish Board of Family and Children's Services, New York.

LOUISE J. KAPLAN, PH.D. is the author of *Oneness and Separateness:*

From Infant to Individual. She is Director of Child Clinical Services at the Psychological Center of the City University. She was Director of the Mother-Infant Research Nursery at New York University and a research associate of the Separation-Individuation Follow-up Study.

OTTO F. KERNBERG, M.D. is Medical Director of the New York Hospital-Cornell Medical Center, Westchester Division; Professor of Psychiatry at the Cornell University Medical College, and Training and Supervising Analyst at the Columbia University Center for Psychoanalytic Training and Research. Dr. Kernberg is also book editor of the *Journal of the American Psychoanalytic Association.* He was awarded the 1972 Heinz Hartmann Award of the New York Psychoanalytic Institute and Society, and the 1975 Edward A. Strecker Award from the Institute of Pennsylvania Hospital. He is the author of three books: *Psychotherapy and Psychoanalysis: Final Report of the Menninger Foundation's Psychotherapy Research Project* (principal coauthor); *Borderline Conditions and Pathological Narcissism;* and *Object Relations Theory and Clinical Psychoanalysis.*

PAULINA F. KERNBERG, M.D. is Training and Supervising Analyst, Columbia University Center for Psychoanalytic Training and Research in New York. She is also Associate Professor of Psychiatry, Cornell University Medical College.

SELMA KRAMER, M.D. is Professor of Child Psychiatry, Medical College of Pennsylvania; Training and Supervising Analyst, adult and child analysis, Philadelphia Psychoanalytic Institute; and Chairman of the Committee on Child Analysis, American Psychoanalytic Association. In addition, she is an associate editor of the *Journal of the American Psychoanalytic Association.*

RUTH F. LAX received her Ph.D. from New York University. She is Associate Clinical Professor in the Department of Psychiatry, Cornell University Medical College, and serves on the faculties of the Institute for Psychoanalytic Training and Research and the New York Freudian Society, where she is also a member of the board. Dr. Lax is engaged in the practice of psychoanalysis with children, adolescents, and adults. She is a member of the Association for Child Psychoanalysis.

HANS W. LOEWALD received his M.D. from the University of Rome Medical School and his psychoanalytic training at the Washington-Baltimore Psychoanalytic Institute. He has served on the faculties of the University of Maryland and Johns Hopkins Medical Schools and the Baltimore Psychoanalytic Institute. He is currently on the faculties of the Yale University Medical School and the Western New England Institute for Psychoanalysis. Dr. Loewald has been in the private practice of psychoanalysis since 1946.

JOHN B. McDEVITT, M.D. is a member of the faculty of the New York Psychoanalytic Institute and is Chairman of the Professional Advisory Committee of the Margaret S. Mahler Psychiatric Research Foundation.

MARGARET S. MAHLER, M.D. is Clinical Professor of Psychiatry Emeritus, Albert Einstein College of Medicine; Visiting Professor in Child Psychoanalysis at the Medical College of Pennsylvania; and Principal Consultant at the Margaret S. Mahler Psychiatric Research Foundation. She is on the faculties of the New York and Philadelphia Psychoanalytic Institutes and is the author of *On Human Symbiosis and the Vicissitudes of Individuation* and (with Fred Pine and Anni Bergman) *The Psychological Birth of the Human Infant.* In 1979 her seminal articles were brought together in the two-volume *The Selected Papers of Margaret S. Mahler.*

JAMES F. MASTERSON, M.D. is Clinical Professor of Psychiatry, Cornell University Medical College, New York. He has written several books and papers on the treatment of borderline patients and the clinical aspects of character disorders, including "Treatment of the Borderline Adolescent: A Developmental Approach," and "Psychotherapy of the Borderline Adult: A Developmental Approach." He is former head of the Adolescent In-Patient Unit, Payne Whitney Clinic, New York Hospital, and is currently Director of the Masterson Group for the Study and Treatment of the Character Disorders, Adolescent and Adult.

DALE C. MORTER received his Ph.D. in 1966 from the University of North Carolina. After a number of years as Chief Child Psychologist at St. Francis Community Mental Health Center, he entered private practice. He is a member of the faculty by invitation of the

Pittsburgh Psychoanalytic Institute and a consultant to agencies serving preschool children.

BERNARD L. PACELLA, M.D. attended the University of Colorado School of Medicine and did his psychiatric residency at the New York State Psychiatric Institute. He is a graduate, in both adult and child analysis, of the New York Psychoanalytic Institute. Coauthor of *Modern Trends in Child Psychiatry*, he is consultant in psychiatry to the College of Physicians and Surgeons, Columbia University; consultant in child and adolescent psychiatry to St. Luke's-Roosevelt Hospitals Medical Center; and president of the Margaret S. Mahler Psychiatric Research Foundation.

FRED PINE, PH.D. received his training at the Department of Social Relations, Harvard University. He is Professor of Psychiatry, Albert Einstein College of Medicine, and former Research Consultant, Masters Childrens Center.

DONALD B. RINSLEY, M.D. received his training at the Harvard Medical School, Washington University School of Medicine, St. Louis, and the Menninger Foundation. He is Clinical Professor of Psychiatry, University of Kansas School of Medicine, Kansas City; Senior Faculty Member in Adult and Child Psychiatry, Menninger School of Psychiatry; and former Spencer Foundation Fellow in Advanced Studies, Menninger Foundation. In 1968 Dr. Rinsley received the Edward A. Strecker Memorial Award of the Institute of the Pennsylvania Hospital for outstanding contributions in the field of adolescent psychiatry to care and treatment. He is the author of numerous papers on adolescents and adolescence, residential treatment, ego psychology, object relations theory, and borderline and narcissistic personality disorders, as well as two forthcoming books, one on the treatment of the severely disturbed adolescent and another (coauthor) summarizing the results of a twenty-year outcome study of over 400 adolescents in residential treatment.

GILBERT J. ROSE, M.D. attended the Boston University Medical School, and did his psychiatric and psychoanalytic training at the Psychoanalytic Institute of Downstate Medical Center. He is currently engaged in the private practice of psychiatry and psychoanalysis and is Associate Clinical Professor of Psychiatry, Yale

Medical School. He has served as associate editor of *The Psycho-analytic Study of Society* and is a frequent contributor to psycho-analytic journals and author of the forthcoming monograph, *The Power of Form: A Psychoanalytic Approach to Aesthetic Form.*

CALVIN F. SETTLAGE, M.D. is Clinical Professor of Psychiatry, University of California, San Francisco, and Training and Supervising Analyst in adult and child analysis, San Francisco Psychoanalytic Institute.

CHARLES SOCARIDES, M.D. is Clinical Professor of Psychiatry at the State University of New York, Downstate Medical Center. He is a clinical researcher in the pathology and treatment of the sexual deviations and is the author of *The Overt Homosexual, Beyond Sexual Freedom,* and *Homosexuality.* In addition, he is editor of *The World of Emotions: Clinical Studies of Affects and their Expressions* and coeditor of *On Sexuality: Psychoanalytic Observations.*

REX W. SPEERS, M.D. is Training Analyst and Supervising Child Analyst, Pittsburgh Psychoanalytic Institute, and Clinical Professor of Child Development-Child Care, University of Pittsburgh. As Medical Director and later consultant to the Arsenal Family and Children's Center, he has engaged in observational research on normal children.

MURIEL CHAVES WINESTINE, PH.D. is a Clinical Assistant Professor in the Department of Psychiatry of Cornell University School of Medicine, on the faculty of the New York Freudian Society, and a member of the Association for Child Psychoanalysis. She conducts a psychoanalytic practice with children, adolescents, and adults in New York City.

Index